COMPUTER
GRAPHICS

From **Pixels** to **Programmable**
Graphics Hardware

Chapman & Hall/CRC
Computer Graphics, Geometric Modeling, and Animation Series

Series Editor
Brian A. Barsky
Professor of Computer Science and Vision Science
Affiliate Professor of Optometry
University of California, Berkeley

Aims and Scope

The computer graphics, geometric modeling, and animation series aims to cover a wide range of topics from underlying concepts and applications to the latest research advances. The series will comprise a broad spectrum of textbooks, reference books, and handbooks, from gentle introductions for newcomers to the field to advanced books for specialists that present the latest research results. The advanced books will describe the latest discoveries, including new mathematical methods and computational techniques, to facilitate researchers with their quest to advance the field. The scope of the series includes titles in the areas of 2D and 3D computer graphics, computer animation, rendering, geometric modeling, visualization, image processing, computational photography, video games, and more.

Published Titles

Computer Graphics: From Pixels to Programmable Graphics Hardware
Alexey Boreskov and Evgeniy Shikin

An Integrated Introduction to Computer Graphics and Geometric Modeling
Ronald Goldman

Computer Graphics Through OpenGL®: From Theory to Experiments
Sumanta Guha

COMPUTER
GRAPHICS

From **Pixels** to **Programmable** Graphics Hardware

Alexey **Boreskov**
Evgeniy **Shikin**

CRC Press
Taylor & Francis Group
Boca Raton London New York

CRC Press is an imprint of the
Taylor & Francis Group, an **informa** business

A CHAPMAN & HALL BOOK

CRC Press
Taylor & Francis Group
6000 Broken Sound Parkway NW, Suite 300
Boca Raton, FL 33487-2742

Printed on acid-free paper
Version Date: 20130716

International Standard Book Number-13: 978-1-4398-6730-3 (Hardback)

Library of Congress Cataloging-in-Publication Data

Boreskov, Alexey.
   Computer graphics : from pixels to programmable graphics hardware / Alexey Boreskov, Evgeniy Shikin.
      pages cm. -- (Chapman & Hall/CRC computer graphics, geometric modeling, and
      animation series)
   Includes bibliographical references and index.
   ISBN 978-1-4398-6730-3 (hardback : alk. paper)
   1. Computer graphics. 2. Computer graphics--Mathematics. I. Shikin, Evgeniy. II.
Title.

T385.B665 2014
006.6--dc23

                                   2013027680

Visit the Taylor & Francis Web site at
http://www.taylorandfrancis.com

and the CRC Press Web site at
http://www.crcpress.com

Contents

Foreword

The goal of this book was to assemble in one book many subjects that are needed in modern computer graphics. The area of computer graphics evolves very quickly – if this book was written ten years ago it would have been very different. The next ten years will also bring great changes to the area of computer graphics.

The part which remains nearly the same is the mathematics and basic algorithms. But even in this area there are some changes — e.g. spherical harmonics which are widely used now had little use ten years ago. And in the years to follow some new mathematical algorithms and notions may appear and become very useful.

This book starts with basic mathematics and algorithms. It includes a mathematical background not only on vectors and matrices, but also on quaternions, splines, curves and surfaces. This part will be relevant for many years to follow.

Most current games and applications use very big geometrical datasets, which poses the problem of effectively working with such datasets. So material on basic geometrical algorithms in 2D and 3D includes various spatial data structures allowing to work with large datasets.

Chapters on OpenGL are based on OpenGL 3.30 but one feature of OpenGL 4 — tessallation — is also covered; also included is an overview of OpenGL ES 2. A new standard — WebGL allowing use of OpenGL with shaders right in your browser — is also presented. However, these chapters do not cover all commands of OpenGL — it would take a whole book completely devoted to OpenGL.

Modern computer graphics includes various special effects. So many of such effects are covered here. So in this book you will find chapters on procedural modelling and texturing, fractals and non-photorealistic rendering.

A special chapter is devoted to GPGPU (General Programming for GPUs) and covers basics of OpenCL.

On the CRC website (www.crcpress.com/product/isbn/9781439867303) you will find many ready examples of C++ code demonstrating various effects as well as C++ wrappers for basic OpenGL entities such as textures, programs and so on.

List of Figures

List of Tables

Chapter 1

Introduction: Basic concepts

There are some basic mathematical and programming notions and concepts important for understanding the potentials of computer graphics. In this chapter we will just briefly review them and show what we need in order to write OpenGL rendering code. They will be covered in subsequent chapters.

In the beginning of this book we will be writing a program which renders a torus and allows the user to rotate it with the mouse. Initially it be rendered just in one color (see Figure 1.1).

Later we will step-by-step add texture, lighting and bumpmapping (see Figure 1.2). Using this example as our goal we will look at what we need to write corresponding code adding one feature after another.

In Chapter 16 we will cover the creation of various special effects such as bumpmapping, parallax, depth of field and many others.

1.1 Coordinate spaces, transformations

In order to render various objects we need a way to represent these objects and transformations to be applied to them so that they can be directly used by a computer. All the geometric objects are specified by the means of *coordinates*. Coordinates provide a way to represent geometric objects with numbers which can be easily processed on a computer. How many numbers we need to uniquely identify a point defines a *dimension*.

We can uniquely specify a position of any point on a line with a number x in the following way: we have selected two points on the line, point O as

FIGURE 1.1 (See color insert.): Simple torus rendered in one color.

a coordinate origin and another point E (with coordinate $x = 1$) to define direction and scale on it (see Figure 1.3).

A coordinate of any point A is equal to the distance between it and coordinate origin O if the direction from O to A coincides with the chosen direction OE, or the distance multiplied by minus one otherwise. Coordinates of points O and E equal to zero, $x = 0$, and unit, $x = 1$, respectively.

The set of all points of the line together with the origin O and a chosen point E (which defines both a direction on the line and distance scale) form a one-dimensional (or 1D) coordinate space. The space is 1-dimensional because we need only one number to uniquely identify every point of the line. The choice is not unique – we can choose any point O' as a coordinate origin and any other point E' as the unit direction. Hence, on the line there exist many different coordinate systems and the same point A will have different coordinates in different coordinate systems.

A plane is a 2-dimensional space because we need the pair of numbers (x, y) to identify a point on the plane. To make a coordinate space we need two usually perpendicular coordinate axes intersecting in coordinate origin O (see Figure 1.4).

The most common space to us is a three-dimensional or 3D-space; to iden-

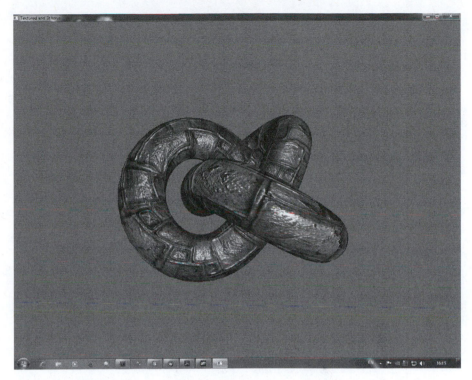

FIGURE 1.2 (See color insert.): Textured and lit torus.

FIGURE 1.3: 1D-coordinate system.

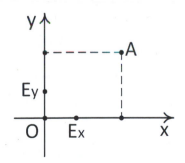

FIGURE 1.4: 2D-coordinate system.

tify a point we need the three numbers (coordinates) x, y and z. As in the previous examples we identify a point relative to some coordinate system. In a 3D-space a coordinate system is formed by tree axes intersecting at one point (a coordinate origin). The axes are usually perpendicular to each other (see Figure 1.5).

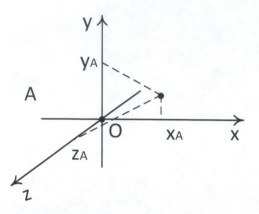

FIGURE 1.5: 3D-coordinate system.

To operate with geometric objects we need to use coordinates, coordinate systems and various transformations. Usually coordinates are represented as vectors; transforms are represented as matrices. So we need vector and matrix algebra to provide a simple and effective mechanism for dealing with them. Chapters 3 and 5 cover 2D- and 3D-coordinate spaces, various transforms and projections.

Also we need some simple geometric algorithms, which will be covered in Chapter 4.

1.2   Graphics pipeline

In order to obtain a rendered image from the source 3-dimensional models, light sources and other parameters, the input data undergoes a series of steps (or stages) called a *graphics pipeline*.

A graphics pipeline determines the steps and order of their execution to get a two-dimensional (2D) image from a given camera model, set of three-dimensional (3D) objects, light sources, textures, lighting equations and many other data.

A camera models the human vision system (or a real digital or analog camera) used to get two-dimensional images. Usually computer graphics uses the simple *pinhole camera* model, corresponding to a single lens with an infinitesimal diameter.

In the following chapters we will describe the OpenGL pipeline in detail. Here we will look at it from a more broader point of view. We can select several major stages:

- application stage;

- geometry stage;

- raster (fragment) stage.

The application stage is a part outside the graphics APIs (Application Programming Interface) such as OpenGL or Direct3D. From game architecture it is what is best described as a *graphics engine*. It can include complex object processing by the CPU (Central Processing Unit), various optimization techniques and algorithms, such as rejecting invisible objects, managing *Level-of-Detail* (LOD), interactions of objects with each other, complex lighting and shadowing algorithms, and many others. This stage may be very complex, as it includes many operations running in parallel on several CPU cores.

The geometry processing is usually done on specialized hardware, *Graphics Processing Unit* (GPU). It consists of many sub-stages working in parallel and processing big amounts of data. Some of these stages are hardcoded into hardware, while others are controlled by special user programs, called *shaders*, which are executed on the GPU.

The fragment stage also runs on the GPU and consists of several sub-stages. In this stage the geometry primitives are scan-converted to the *pixels* (picture elements), and a special shader along with some non-shader parts processes these pixels in to form a 2D-image.

The geometry and fragment stages now run entirely on a GPU and include many different substages.

In order to use graphics hardware for rendering an image we need a special *API* (such as OpenGL or Direct3D) that allows us to write device-independent code. Despite the differences in such APIs the hardware below them is the same and corresponding stages have much in common.

In this book we will be using the third version of OpenGL and for rendering various objects.

1.3 Working with the windowing system

The chosen OpenGL API is a pure rendering API – it does not have code for creating windows for rendering and processing user input (from the mouse and keyboard).

We need some type of library, preferably cross-platform (as OpenGL), which will be doing all window management and user interaction for us.

We will cover one such library **freeglut**. It is open-source and cross-platform and allow to easily write rendering applications using the OpenGL 3 API. Such applications can be easily compiled from the same source in both Microsoft Windows and Linux.

Also we will be using the GLEW (OpenGL Extension Wrangler) library to access OpenGL 3 commands.

1.4   Colors: Color models

The goal of computer graphics is creating two-dimensional still images (or movies composited from still images) by given three-dimensional data. What is the image we want to create ?

From the user's point of view it is just a group of colored points (pixels); the rendering is just choosing an appropriate color for every point of the group. But what is a color? And why in photography are there so many parameters, tools and special tricks to get a slightly different colored image?

We have to understand what the color is and how we can represent the color in the computer to work with it.

Despite the notion of color being so natural it is not quite easy to define. For humans color is just a given property but there are color-blind living beings. Dogs, for example, usually cannot distinguish colors. Also there are humans who cannot distinguish certain colors.

The notion of color is closely tied to a human's visual system and to adequately model the color we need to model some parts of the human vision system. The resulting *color model* represents and processes colors using numbers.

But just as with coordinate systems in space, there are many different color models (or color spaces) – no model fits all purposes. There is an RGB color space, closely related to the human eye, which is often used for rendering. This system is often used in various displays – devices which show colored images by emitting the light.

But color printing is usually based on a different color model – one that works with reflecting and absorbing the incident light. Images, saved as JPEG files, and DVD video are based on the color model which allows for better compression, while producing less noticeable artifacts.

1.5   Raster algorithms

The rendered image is not just any group of colored dots. This group is arranged in a regular rectangular form called a *raster grid*, and every point of this grid is called a *pixel* (see Figure 2.4).

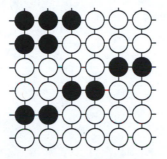

FIGURE 1.6: Raster grid.

When we want to draw or render something it must be converted into pixels on such a grid. The process of converting geometry into pixels on a raster grid is *rasterization*. For basic geometry objects such as lines, arcs, triangles and so on there are several algorithms providing their rasterization. Most of them are implemented in hardware in the GPU, but understanding how it works helps in many areas of computer graphics.

Note that rasterizing is not so simple as it may look. In the Figure 1.7 there are several possible variants of rasterization of a simple line segment, and all of them seem valid.

FIGURE 1.7: Several rasterizations of the same line segment.

1.6   Hidden surface removal

Another important problem in rendering an image from complex geometric data is that while the data are in 3D-space, the rendered image is a 2D-object. That means that we somehow have to map (project) points from a 3D-space on a 2D-plane. In case some objects can be behind the other objects, they may be invisible or hidden (by other objects) in part or in whole.

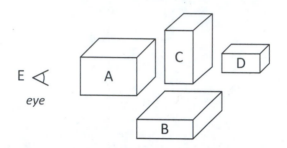

FIGURE 1.8: Occlusion of one object by others.

In Figure 1.8 we have a virtual camera (eye) located at point E and several objects (A, B, C and D) where object D is hidden from the camera by objects A and C.

While the objects are sufficiently simple and their number is not too large, the problem seems very easy. The situation changes drastically when the complexity of the scene grows. Imagine a complex level from a modern 3D-First Person Shooter (FPS) game. It can contain millions of objects, but really only a very small fraction of them can be seen at any given moment of time. So the majority of objects is hidden from the player but the mere fact that the player does not see them will not help us to process all these hidden objects quickly.

So we must not only correctly determine what will be visible at each pixel (which can be solved by common graphics hardware), but quickly determine the majority of hidden objects. This will allow us to skip them early and not waste time and resources on their processing.

The problem is called *Hidden Surface Removal* (HSR). The word *surface* is used because we usually render not-transparent objects and see the boundaries or *surfaces* of 3D-objects.

It can be said that some of the classical FPSs of the past like Wolfenstein3D, Doom or Quake were built around a clever algorithm of hidden surface removal (plus a lot of other algorithms which make up a game).

1.7 Lighting models and shading

The scene to be rendered is not just a set of geometric dull objects. For the image to look real and convincing these objects should be lighted and shaded. The lighting plays a major role in just how real the rendering will look.

But computing realistic lighting (which now includes soft shadows, ambient occlusion and color bleeding) is a very complex and time-consuming task. Besides lighting depends not only on the geometry of the scene, but on the light sources, their types, locations and many other properties.

The lighting depends also on the surface properties of the objects being lit - just how light interacts with them. Usually a set of such properties is called a *material* (from which the object is made). The concept of material applies the same set of properties to many different objects.

There are many models of light interaction with the surface starting with the very simple, from the early days of computer graphics, and up to very complex algorithms used in filmmaking today. Some complex algorithms may require many hours of computations of a big computer cluster for a single frame.

Note that the properties showing how objects interact with the light usually are not constant across the whole object – they vary giving the object a natural and convincing look. Many of these variations are given by special images – *textures* – which are "wrapped" on the object.

There are some mathematical models of such variations. These models create realistically looking objects using just a small set of parameters, for example a whole universe can be created and modeled this way (so-called *procedural texturing* and *procedural modeling*).

Chapter 2

Transforms in 2D

2.1   Vectors and matrices

We start with a 2-dimensional case because 1D is just too simple and 3D is much more complex. We will study some important concepts and notions in a 2-dimensional case. They are easy to explain because in 2D all can be simply drawn on a sheet of paper.

A two-dimensional coordinate space is a plane with an attached coordinate system. The system allows us to use coordinates instead of points. In this case the coordinates are just an ordered pair of numbers which uniquely determine a point on the plane (this presentation depends on the chosen coordinate system)(see Figure 2.1).

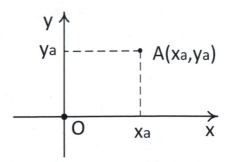

FIGURE 2.1: 2-dimensional coordinate system.

A coordinates system provides bidirectional mapping between points on the plane and a set of pairs of numbers. For a given coordinate system and for every point A there is a unique pair of numbers (x_a, y_a) called its *coordinates*.

Note that on a given plane there exist many different coordinate systems. Because of it, coordinates of the same point in different coordinate systems will be various (see Figure 2.2).

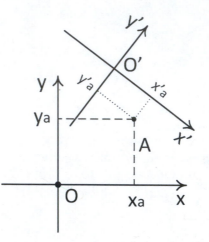

FIGURE 2.2: Two different coordinate systems.

A coordinate system on a plane is defined by a couple of axes intersecting at one point O, called the *coordinate origin*. An *axis* is a line on which we specified a positive direction and a unit length.

Usually we will use only *Cartesian* coordinate systems where axes are perpendicular to each other. However there can be other coordinate systems, not even based on a pair of axes, such as *polar coordinates*.

We can write down a pair of coordinates x_a and y_a of a point either as a row vector (x_a, y_a) or as a column vector $\begin{pmatrix} x_a \\ y_a \end{pmatrix}$. We will stick to the latter notation for the rest of this book.

There is an operation called *transposition* which turns a column vector to row vector and vice versa

$$(x, y)^T = \begin{pmatrix} x \\ y \end{pmatrix}, \tag{2.1}$$

$$\begin{pmatrix} x \\ y \end{pmatrix}^T = (x, y). \tag{2.2}$$

For point A we will write its coordinate as a column vector

$$A = \begin{pmatrix} x_a \\ y_a \end{pmatrix}.$$

With this point we can associate an oriented segment connecting coordinate origin O and point A (usually denoted as $\overrightarrow{OA}$) (see Figure 2.3). The segment is called a *vector* and described by the same two coordinates.

$$\overrightarrow{OA} = \begin{pmatrix} x_a \\ y_a \end{pmatrix}.$$

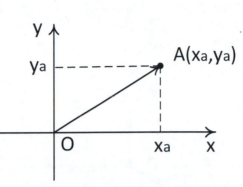

FIGURE 2.3: Vector OA.

For such *geometric vectors* it is easy to introduce two operations – addition of two vectors and multiplication of a vector by a number.

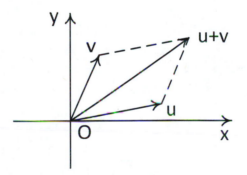

FIGURE 2.4: Sum of two vectors u and v.

If we have vectors $u = \overrightarrow{OA}$ and $v = \overrightarrow{OB}$ then we can construct their sum by building a parallelogram as shown in the figure above (see Figure 2.4).

The multiplication of a vector $u = \overrightarrow{OA}$ by some number α is defined by the following way – we just make our vector shorter or longer $|\alpha|$ times, and revert its direction if α is negative.

All these operations can be written in a coordinate form. If $u = \begin{pmatrix} x_u \\ y_u \end{pmatrix}$ and $v = \begin{pmatrix} x_v \\ y_v \end{pmatrix}$, then addition and multiplication are defined the following way

$$u + v = \begin{pmatrix} x_u + x_v \\ y_u + y_v \end{pmatrix}, \tag{2.3}$$

$$\alpha u = \begin{pmatrix} \alpha x_u \\ \alpha u_y \end{pmatrix}. \tag{2.4}$$

The result of multiplication of some vector by minus one may be received by rotation of our vector by 180°. The resulting vector has the same length and opposite direction (see Figure 2.5).

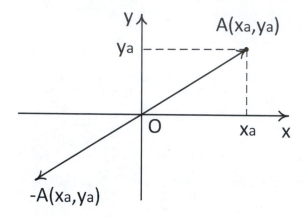

FIGURE 2.5: Vector $-OA$.

Such a vector is called an *inverse* to the original vector and it allows us to introduce the operation of vector subtraction

$$u - v = u + (-1)v. \tag{2.5}$$

Using formulae (2.3) and (2.5) we can write this as

$$u - v = \begin{pmatrix} x_u - x_v \\ y_u - y_v \end{pmatrix}. \tag{2.6}$$

The following properties of vectors operations always hold true

$$u + v = v + u, \tag{2.7}$$

$$(u + v) + w = u + (v + w), \tag{2.8}$$

$$u + (-u) = \begin{pmatrix} 0 \\ 0 \end{pmatrix}, \tag{2.9}$$

$$u + \begin{pmatrix} 0 \\ 0 \end{pmatrix} = u, \tag{2.10}$$

$$1u = u, \tag{2.11}$$

$$\alpha(u + v) = (\alpha u) + (\alpha v), \tag{2.12}$$

$$(\alpha + \beta)u = (\alpha u) + (\beta v). \tag{2.13}$$

We can abstract from the coordinate plane and just work with the 2-dimensional coordinate space (usually denoted by $\mathbb{R}^2$). It consists of all ordered pairs of numbers with operations as defined by formulae (2.3) and (2.4). This space allows us to work with vectors only.

For any couple of vectors u and v we can define the so-called *dot product* written as (u, v), or $u \cdot v$

$$(u, v) = x_u x_v + y_u y_v. \tag{2.14}$$

The dot product satisfies some simple and important properties:

$$(u, v) = (v, u), \tag{2.15}$$

$$(u + v, w) = (u, w) + (v, w), \tag{2.16}$$

$$(\alpha u, v) = \alpha(u, v), \tag{2.17}$$

$$(u, u) \geq 0, \tag{2.18}$$

$$(u, u) = 0 \Leftrightarrow u = \begin{pmatrix} 0 \\ 0 \end{pmatrix}. \tag{2.19}$$

The dot product can be used to define the length (or *norm*) for vectors in $\mathbb{R}^2$

$$\|u\| = \sqrt{(u, u)}. \tag{2.20}$$

The dot product for vectors u and v has a simple geometric meaning – it is a product of the length of the first vector, length of the second vector and cosine of the angle α between them,

$$(u, v) = \|u\| \|v\| cos\alpha. \tag{2.21}$$

It can be easily proved that the norm of the vector introduced by the above equation has the following properties

$$\|\alpha u\| = |\alpha| \|u\|, \tag{2.22}$$

$$\|u + v\| \le \|u\| + \|v\|, \tag{2.23}$$

$$\|u\| = 0 \Leftrightarrow u = \begin{pmatrix} 0 \\ 0 \end{pmatrix}. \tag{2.24}$$

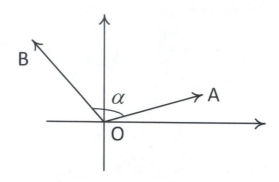

FIGURE 2.6: Angle between two vectors.

The angle α between non-null two vectors u and v may be calculated from their dot product (Figure 2.6)

$$\alpha = \cos^{-1} \frac{(u, v)}{\|u\| \|v\|}. \tag{2.25}$$

Two vectors u and v are called *orthogonal* (or perpendicular) if their dot product is zero, $(u, v) = 0$.

There is another very useful arrangement of numbers – a *matrix*. A matrix is a table with several rows and several columns of numbers. One of the simplest matrices is a matrix with two columns and two rows, 2×2 matrix,

$$A = \begin{pmatrix} a_{11} & a_{12} \\ a_{21} & a_{22} \end{pmatrix}. \tag{2.26}$$

Note that we can treat a column vector as a matrix with one column and several rows (i.e. 2×1 matrix) and a row vector – as a 1×2 matrix.

Elements of the matrices are written as a_{ij}, where the first index i identifies a row in a matrix and the second index j identifies a column. For matrices we can also define an operation of addition and multiplication by a number

$$\begin{pmatrix} a_{11} & a_{12} \\ a_{21} & a_{22} \end{pmatrix} + \begin{pmatrix} b_{11} & b_{12} \\ b_{21} & b_{22} \end{pmatrix} = \begin{pmatrix} a_{11} + b_{11} & a_{12} + b_{12} \\ a_{21} + b_{21} & a_{22} + b_{22} \end{pmatrix}, \tag{2.27}$$

$$\alpha \begin{pmatrix} a_{11} & a_{12} \\ a_{21} & a_{22} \end{pmatrix} = \begin{pmatrix} \alpha a_{11} & \alpha a_{12} \\ \alpha a_{21} & \alpha a_{22} \end{pmatrix}. \tag{2.28}$$

You can see that 2×2 matrices with these operations have the properties analogous to the properties in (2.7)–(2.13) for vectors. With these operation, the set of all such matrices 2×2 form a vector (linear) space denoted as $\mathbb{R}^{2 \times 2}$.

For matrices we can define the multiplication of two matrices using the following rule

$$\begin{pmatrix} a_{11} & a_{12} \\ a_{21} & a_{22} \end{pmatrix} \begin{pmatrix} b_{11} & b_{12} \\ b_{21} & b_{22} \end{pmatrix} = \begin{pmatrix} a_{11}b_{11} + a_{12}b_{21} & a_{11}b_{12} + a_{12}b_{22} \\ a_{21}b_{11} + a_{22}b_{21} & a_{21}b_{12} + a_{22}b_{22} \end{pmatrix}. \quad (2.29)$$

The structure of a matrix product can be written in a more simple way – if we denote an element of the matrix product as c_{ij} then we can write the following formula

$$c_{ij} = \sum_{k=1}^{2} a_{ik}b_{kj}. \quad (2.30)$$

Matrix multiplication satisfies several common properties

$$(AB)C = A(BC), \quad (2.31)$$

$$A(B + C) = (AB) + (AC), \quad (2.32)$$

$$(\alpha A)B = A(\alpha B) = \alpha(AB), \quad (2.33)$$

$$AI = IA = A. \quad (2.34)$$

Here the I is an *identity* matrix

$$I = \begin{pmatrix} 1 & 0 \\ 0 & 1 \end{pmatrix}$$

Note that the matrix multiplication is not commutative, i.e. in the general case $AB \neq BA$.

For matrix A such that $a_{11}a_{22} - a_{12}a_{21} \neq 0$, we can introduce the *inverse matrix* A^{-1} for which the following equation holds true

$$A^{-1}A = AA^{-1} = I. \quad (2.35)$$

Such an inverse matrix can be written as

$$A^{-1} = \frac{1}{a_{11}a_{22} - a_{21}a_{12}} \begin{pmatrix} a_{22} & -a_{12} \\ -a_{21} & a_{11} \end{pmatrix}. \quad (2.36)$$

The expression $a_{11}a_{22} - a_{12}a_{21}$ is a function of a matrix which is called its *determinant* denoted as $\det A$. It satisfies the following properties

$$\det I = 1, \quad (2.37)$$

$$\det(AB) = \det A \det B, \tag{2.38}$$

$$\det(\alpha A) = \alpha \det A. \tag{2.39}$$

There is one more operation which can be introduced for matrices (just as for vectors) – a transposition. The equation reflects a matrix along its main diagonal and is defined by following equality

$$\begin{pmatrix} a_{11} & a_{12} \\ a_{21} & a_{22} \end{pmatrix}^T = \begin{pmatrix} a_{11} & a_{21} \\ a_{12} & a_{22} \end{pmatrix}. \tag{2.40}$$

Transposition satisfies the following properties

$$(AB)^T = (B^T)(A^T), \tag{2.41}$$

$$(A + B)^T = (A^T) + (B^T), \tag{2.42}$$

$$(\alpha \cdot A)^T = \alpha \cdot (A^T), \tag{2.43}$$

$$(A^{-1})^T = (A^T)^{-1}, \tag{2.44}$$

$$\det(A^T) = \det A, \tag{2.45}$$

$$(A^T)^T = A. \tag{2.46}$$

Matrix A is called *symmetric* if $A^T = A$.
We can define a product of a matrix and a vector in the following way

$$\begin{pmatrix} a_{11} & a_{12} \\ a_{21} & a_{22} \end{pmatrix} \begin{pmatrix} x \\ y \end{pmatrix} = \begin{pmatrix} a_{11}x + a_{12}y \\ a_{21}x + a_{22}y \end{pmatrix}. \tag{2.47}$$

The operation satisfies several properties similar to properties of the matrix product

$$(A + B)u = Au + Bu, \tag{2.48}$$

$$A(Bu) = (AB)u, \tag{2.49}$$

$$A(\alpha u) = \alpha(Au), \tag{2.50}$$

$$A(u + v) = Au + Av. \tag{2.51}$$

2.2 Transforms in 2D

A transformation in 2D is a mapping of a plane onto itself. When we work with two-dimensional coordinate space $\mathbb{R}^2$, the transform f can be written as $f : \mathbb{R}^2 \mapsto \mathbb{R}^2$.

The simplest transformation is a translation by a given vector t. To get the result we just add a fixed vector to any vector in $\mathbb{R}^2$

$$f_t(u) = u + t. \tag{2.52}$$

Using a coordinate notation it can be written as

$$f_t(u) = \begin{pmatrix} x_u + x_t \\ y_u + y_t \end{pmatrix}. \tag{2.53}$$

There are many different transforms, including very complex ones. But we start with the very simple transforms which we often encounter – scaling, rotation, reflection and shear. All of these transformations come into the class of *linear transforms*. A transform f is called a *linear* if for any two vectors u and v and any number α the following equalities hold true

$$f(u + v) = f(u) + f(v), \tag{2.54}$$

$$f(\alpha u) = \alpha f(u). \tag{2.55}$$

It can be proved that for any linear transform $f : \mathbb{R}^2 \mapsto \mathbb{R}^2$ there are four numbers a_{11}, a_{12}, a_{21} and a_{22} such that the transformation can be written in the form

$$f(u) = \begin{pmatrix} a_{11}x_u + a_{12}y_u \\ a_{21}x_u + a_{22}y_u \end{pmatrix},$$
$$u = \begin{pmatrix} x_u \\ y_u \end{pmatrix}. \tag{2.56}$$

These four numbers make a 2×2 matrix A. Using this matrix we can write $f(u) = Au$.

2.3 Basic linear transformations

2.3.1 Scale transformation

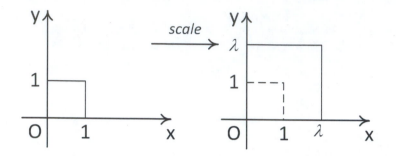

FIGURE 2.7: Uniform scale – magnification.

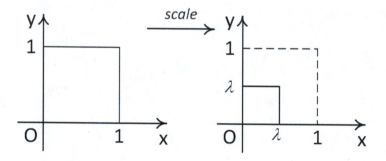

FIGURE 2.8: Uniform scale – minification.

One of the simplest linear transforms is the *uniform scale*. The scale by positive factor λ is defined by the matrix

$$S_\lambda = \begin{pmatrix} \lambda & 0 \\ 0 & \lambda \end{pmatrix}. \tag{2.57}$$

When the scale factor $\lambda > 1$ we have a magnification, otherwise it is minification (see Figures 2.7 and 2.8).

Scale transformation can be *non-uniform* if it applies different scaling factors for coordinates. Non-uniform scale is given by the matrix

$$S_{\lambda\mu} = \begin{pmatrix} \lambda & 0 \\ 0 & \mu \end{pmatrix}. \tag{2.58}$$

Here the λ and μ are positive numbers.

The following figure depicts non-uniform scale (see Figure 2.9).

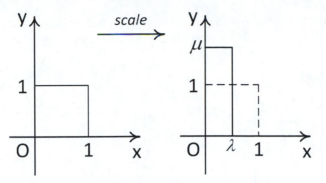

FIGURE 2.9: Non-uniform scale.

Since all scaling factors are strictly positive, then the determinant of a scale matrix is always positive and the scale matrix is invertible. As you can easily guess the inverse of a scale matrix is also a scale matrix

$$S_{\lambda\mu}^{-1} = \begin{pmatrix} \frac{1}{\lambda} & 0 \\ 0 & \frac{1}{\mu} \end{pmatrix}. \tag{2.59}$$

2.3.2 Reflect transformation

Another simple linear transformation is *reflection* with respect to some coordinate axis. Reflection, relative x- and y-axes (see Figure 2.10 and Figure 2.11) are defined by the matrices

$$R_x = \begin{pmatrix} 1 & 0 \\ 0 & -1 \end{pmatrix}, \tag{2.60}$$

$$R_y = \begin{pmatrix} -1 & 0 \\ 0 & 1 \end{pmatrix}. \tag{2.61}$$

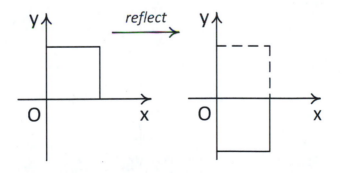

FIGURE 2.10: Reflection relative x-axis.

Note that both the reflection and scale transformations are given by *diagonal* matrices – all elements that are not on the main diagonal of the matrix are zero ($a_{ij} = 0$ if $i \neq j$).

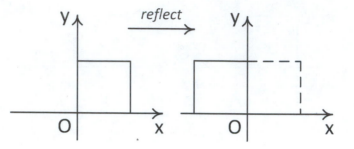

FIGURE 2.11: Reflection relative y-axis.

2.3.3   Rotate transformation

One more classic transformation is rotation around coordinate origin O by a given angle ϕ (see Figure 2.12). We can rotate either clockwise or counterclockwise. The rotations differ by the sign of rotation angle.

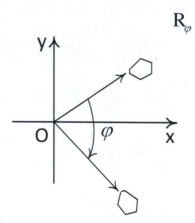

FIGURE 2.12: Rotation around a coordinate origin by angle ϕ.

The matrix R_ϕ, which performs rotation by the angle ϕ clockwise, is given by the formula

$$R_\phi = \begin{pmatrix} \cos\phi & \sin\phi \\ -\sin\phi & \cos\phi \end{pmatrix}. \tag{2.62}$$

A rotation matrix has the following properties

$$\det R_\phi = 1, \tag{2.63}$$

$$R_\phi^{-1} = R_\phi^T = R_{-\phi}. \tag{2.64}$$

Note that for the rest of the book we will be using clockwise rotation matrices.

2.3.4 Shear transformation

The final common linear transformation is *shear*. Simple shear can be along the x-axis or y-axis (see Figure 2.13).

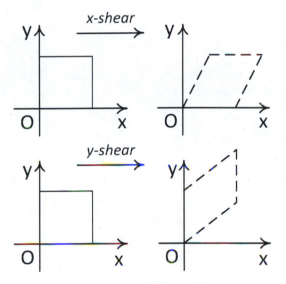

FIGURE 2.13: Shear along the x-axis and y-axis.

For the simple case we can easily write down the corresponding matrices

$$H_x(\lambda) = \begin{pmatrix} 1 & \lambda \\ 0 & 1 \end{pmatrix}, \tag{2.65}$$

$$H_y(\lambda) = \begin{pmatrix} 1 & 0 \\ \lambda & 1 \end{pmatrix}. \tag{2.66}$$

Shear matrices are invertible and their inverse are shear matrices too

$$H_x^{-1}(\lambda) = H_x(-\lambda) = \begin{pmatrix} 1 & -\lambda \\ 0 & 1 \end{pmatrix}, \tag{2.67}$$

$$H_y^{-1}(\lambda) = H_y(-\lambda) = \begin{pmatrix} 1 & 0 \\ -\lambda & 1 \end{pmatrix}. \tag{2.68}$$

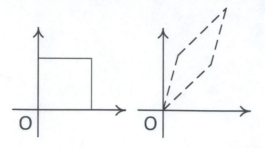

FIGURE 2.14: Generic shear.

A more general form of shear (see Figure 2.14) is given by the matrix

$$H_y(\lambda, \mu) = \begin{pmatrix} 1 & \lambda \\ \mu & 1 \end{pmatrix}. \tag{2.69}$$

Note that we should require $\lambda\mu \neq 1$ for the matrix to be invertible.

A rotation can be represented as three shears one after the other. To see how it can be done, write down the desired representation

$$\begin{pmatrix} \cos\phi & \sin\phi \\ -\sin\phi & \cos\phi \end{pmatrix} = \begin{pmatrix} 1 & \lambda \\ 0 & 1 \end{pmatrix} \begin{pmatrix} 1 & 0 \\ \mu & 1 \end{pmatrix} \begin{pmatrix} 1 & \nu \\ 0 & 1 \end{pmatrix}. \tag{2.70}$$

After performing the matrix product we will get

$$\begin{pmatrix} \cos\phi & \sin\phi \\ -\sin\phi & \cos\phi \end{pmatrix} = \begin{pmatrix} 1+\lambda\mu & \lambda+\nu+\lambda\mu\nu \\ \mu & 1+\mu\nu \end{pmatrix}. \tag{2.71}$$

Hence, we can show how parameters λ, μ and ν depend on the angle ϕ

$$\mu = -\sin\phi,$$
$$\lambda = \nu = \frac{1-\cos\phi}{\sin\phi}. \tag{2.72}$$

The last equation for λ and ν can be rewritten using the half-angle

$$\lambda = \mu = \tan\frac{\phi}{2}.$$

2.3.5 Composite transformations

In the previous sections we have studied the basic linear transformations. Despite their being very simple and intuitive we can build any complex linear transformations by subsequently applying these basic linear transformations. And here the matrix form of linear transformations becomes very handy.

Suppose we have two linear transformations f and g with matrices M_f

and M_g. Then we can build a complex transformation by concatenating these transformations fg. It is defined as $(fg)(u) = f(g(u))$. It can be shown that this complex transformation is a linear transformation and the matrix of this transformation M_{fg} is the product of matrices of transforms f and g

$$M_{fg} = M_f \cdot M_g. \tag{2.73}$$

If the transformation f is invertible (i.e., there is a mapping f^{-1} such that $f(f^{-1}(u) = f^{-1}(f(u)) = u)$ then its inverse transformation has the matrix equal to the inverse matrix of the origin transformation

$$M_{f^{-1}} = M_f^{-1}. \tag{2.74}$$

These two properties allows us to build complex transformations from simple ones just by multiplying matrices in the correct order.

Let's take, as an example, the transformation that performs reflection with respect to an arbitrary line coming through the coordinate origin (see Figure 2.15).

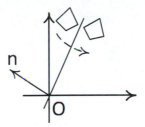

FIGURE 2.15: Reflection with respect to an arbitrary line coming through the coordinate origin.

A line coming through the coordinate origin is a set of points P such that vector $u = \overrightarrow{OP}$ is perpendicular to the some vector n, called the line's *normal*. So we can write an equation for this line as follows

$$(u, n) = 0. \tag{2.75}$$

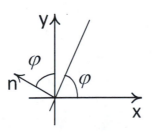

FIGURE 2.16: Line with a normal vector n and angle ϕ with the x-axis.

This line forms some angle ϕ with the x-axis (see Figure 2.16), and we can get sine and cosine of this angle from the normal, assuming that normal has a unit length ($\|n\| = 1$)

$$\cos\phi = n_y, \quad \cos(\phi + \frac{\pi}{2}) = n_x. \tag{2.76}$$

Last equality can be transformed using properties of trigonometric functions into $\sin\phi = -n_x$.

If we rotate the line clockwise by angle ϕ then our line will move onto the x-axis. Since we know how to reflect relative to the x-axis we can do it, but after that we need to rotate back, i.e., by angle $-\phi$. Therefore, our composite transformation becomes the concatenation of three basic transforms – $R_{-\phi}$, R_x and R_ϕ.

Its matrix is a product of three matrices. Since we know the sine and cosine of ϕ we can write rotation matrices in the following form

$$R_\phi = \begin{pmatrix} n_y & -n_x \\ n_x & n_y \end{pmatrix}, \tag{2.77}$$

$$R_{-\phi} = \begin{pmatrix} n_y & n_x \\ -n_x & n_y \end{pmatrix}. \tag{2.78}$$

The resulting matrix R will be given by formula 2.79.

$$R = R_{-\phi}R_xR_\phi = \begin{pmatrix} n_y^2 - n_x^2 & -2n_xn_y \\ -2n_xn_y & n_x^2 - n_y^2 \end{pmatrix} \tag{2.79}$$

2.4   Homogeneous coordinates

Let's consider another composite transformation – rotation by angle ϕ around a given point A. Following the previous example (reflection with respect to a line coming through the coordinate origin) the solution is very easy – translate by minus A, rotate by ϕ and translate back by A (see Figure 2.17).

The translation is not a linear transformation : $f(2u) = (2u+t) \neq 2f(u) = 2(u + t)$ and because of it the transformation cannot be written as a 2×2 matrix. Together with the linear transform it gives a new class of transformations – *affine*. The affine transformation is the transformation that can be written as a combination of a linear transformation and a translation. So if f is affine then

$$f(u) = Mu + t. \tag{2.80}$$

This form of representation affine transforms is clumsy and not nice to deal with. So graphics programmers often use so-called *homogeneous coordinates*.

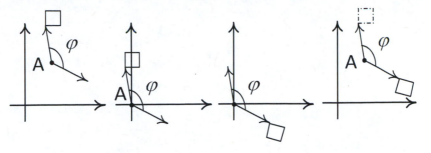

FIGURE 2.17: Rotation around point A as a composite transform: translation by $-A$, rotation and translation back by A.

Here we will only cover part of it sufficient to provide uniform treatment of all affine transformation. More details will be provided in Chapter 5.

For a 2-dimensional vector $u = \begin{pmatrix} x \\ y \end{pmatrix}$ we build a 3-dimensional vector

$h = \begin{pmatrix} x \\ y \\ 1 \end{pmatrix}$ and in doing so establish a one-to-one mapping of all 2D-space

vectors on a plane $z = 1$ in 3D-space.

Coordinates x, y and z of a 3D-vector $h = \begin{pmatrix} x \\ y \\ 1 \end{pmatrix}$ are called *homogeneous*

coordinates of the vector u. And in order to deal with them we should use 3×3 matrices of the following form

$$H = \begin{pmatrix} a_{11} & a_{12} & x_t \\ a_{21} & a_{22} & y_t \\ 0 & 0 & 1 \end{pmatrix}. \tag{2.81}$$

Such a 3×3 matrix H is called a *matrix of homogeneous transformation.*

For the 3-dimensional case we can easily rewrite equations for multiplication of 2×2-matrices 2.29 and 2.47. If $C = AB$ then any element c_{ij} of the matrix will be given by the equality

$$c_{ij} = \sum_{k=1}^{3} a_{ik} \cdot b_{kj}. \tag{2.82}$$

Here

$$A = \begin{pmatrix} a_{11} & a_{12} & a_{13} \\ a_{21} & a_{22} & a_{23} \\ a_{31} & a_{32} & a_{33} \end{pmatrix},$$

$$B = \begin{pmatrix} b_{11} & b_{12} & b_{13} \\ b_{21} & b_{22} & b_{23} \\ b_{31} & b_{32} & b_{33} \end{pmatrix}.$$

The product of a 3×3-matrix and a 3D-vector is given by the formula

$$\begin{pmatrix} a_{11} & a_{12} & a_{13} \\ a_{21} & a_{22} & a_{23} \\ a_{31} & a_{32} & a_{33} \end{pmatrix} \cdot \begin{pmatrix} x \\ y \\ z \end{pmatrix} = \begin{pmatrix} a_{11}x + a_{12}y + a_{13}z \\ a_{21}x + a_{22}y + a_{23}z \\ a_{31}x + a_{32}y + a_{33}z \end{pmatrix} \qquad (2.83)$$

The product of a homogeneous matrix (2.81) and a vector h in homogeneous coordinates may be written in the next form

$$\begin{pmatrix} a_{11} & a_{12} & t_x \\ a_{21} & a_{22} & t_y \\ 0 & 0 & 1 \end{pmatrix} \begin{pmatrix} x \\ y \\ 1 \end{pmatrix} = \begin{pmatrix} a_{11}x + a_{12}y + t_x \\ a_{21}x + a_{22}y + t_y \\ 1 \end{pmatrix}. \qquad (2.84)$$

And coordinates x' and y' of the corresponding vector u' will look like

$$\begin{pmatrix} x' \\ y' \end{pmatrix} = \begin{pmatrix} a_{11}x + a_{12}y + t_x \\ a_{21}x + a_{22}y + t_y \end{pmatrix}. \qquad (2.85)$$

It means that in homogeneous coordinates any affine transformation can be written as a 3×3 matrix of the form (2.81). A simple check shows that the product of any two matrices in the form (2.81) is again a matrix of the same form.

The homogeneous notation for transformations preserves the basic property – the matrix of a composition of two transformations is just a product of matrices of these transformations. It allows us to write complex transformations as a sequence of simple ones and then just multiply matrices to get the result.

But let's continue with the task of rotation around a given point. Translation by A is defined by a homogeneous matrix

$$T_A = \begin{pmatrix} 0 & 0 & x_a \\ 0 & 0 & y_a \\ 0 & 0 & 1 \end{pmatrix}. \qquad (2.86)$$

Rotation is defined by a homogeneous matrix R_ϕ

$$R_\phi = \begin{pmatrix} \cos\phi & \sin\phi & 0 \\ -\sin\phi & \cos\phi & 0 \\ 0 & 0 & 1 \end{pmatrix}. \qquad (2.87)$$

The resulting transformation — rotation by ϕ around A — is given by the following matrix

$$R_{A,\phi} = T_A R_\phi T_{-A} = \qquad (2.88)$$

$$\begin{pmatrix} \cos\phi & \sin\phi & -x_a\cos\phi - y_a\sin\phi + x_a \\ -\sin\phi & \cos\phi & x_a\sin\phi - y_a\cos\phi + y_a \\ 0 & 0 & 1 \end{pmatrix}. \qquad (2.89)$$

Analogously we can describe reflection relative to an arbitrary line (without requiring its coming through the coordinate origin). The generic line equation can be written in one of the next forms

$$(p, n) + d = 0, \qquad (2.90)$$

$$(p - p_0, n) = 0, \qquad (2.91)$$

$$ax + by + c = 0. \qquad (2.92)$$

Here n is a normal to the line, p_0 is some point on the line and $d = -(p_0, n)$. If the normal has a unit length ($\|n\| = 1$) then d is a *signed distance* from the line to the coordinate origin. The last equation is just rewriting of the formula (2.90). It is sufficient to let $a = n_x, b = n_y, c = d$ and use a definition of the dot product.

When the original line is horizontal, we just translate it to coincide with the x-axis, reflect and translate back. Otherwise, we need to find its intersection with the x-axis for $y = 0$ in formula (2.90)

$$x = -\frac{d}{n_x}. \qquad (2.93)$$

Then we translate by the vector $\begin{pmatrix} -\frac{d}{n_x} \\ 0 \end{pmatrix}$ to make the line come through the coordinate origin, reflect with respect to the line (see matrix (2.79)) and translate back by $\begin{pmatrix} \frac{d}{n_x} \\ 0 \end{pmatrix}$.

As a result we get a matrix of homogeneous transformation in the following form

$$R_{n,d} = \begin{pmatrix} n_y^2 - n_x^2 & -2n_x n_y & (n_x^2 - n_y^2)\frac{d}{n_x} \\ -2n_x n_y & n_x^2 - n_y^2 & 2n_x n_y \frac{d}{n_x} \\ 0 & 0 & 1 \end{pmatrix}. \qquad (2.94)$$

We can wrap 2D-vectors in a C++ class **vec2** and 2×2 matrices – in a class **mat2**. Full source code for these classes are not shown here because of its size - it can be found on the CRC website.

Class **vec2** has two public fields x and y, which correspond to x- and y-coordinates of the vector. For this class standard arithmetic operators +, -, * and / are overloaded to provide component-wise operations on these vectors so we can write C++ vector expressions that look very close to mathematical notation.

Also for the **vec2** class some common functions are written which provide some common operations such as the dot product.

The same is true for the **mat2** – it also has overloaded operators and a set of utlity functions.

So if we want to compute vector $a - 2b/(a, b)$ we can use following C++ code:

```
vec3 x = a - 2.0f * b / dot ( a, b );
```

Chapter 3

Geometric algorithms in 2D

This chapter covers many algorithms that we encounter in two-dimensional geometry concerning measuring properties of geometric figures, classification of figures relative to the line and splitting of figures. We will start with simple objects – lines, segments, boxes and finish with polygon algorithms.

The chapter is accompanied with C++ code showing the discussed algorithms. The code uses the **vec2** class for working with 2-dimensional vectors. Full source code for this class, along with all other source code can be found on CRC website.

3.1   Line from two points

It is a well-known geometric fact that two different points a and b define a line (see Figure 3.1). There are several line equations. The simplest equation

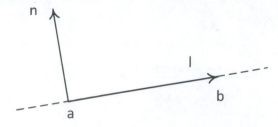

FIGURE 3.1: Line coming through points a and b.

is a parametric one – we establish a mapping between the set of numbers $\mathbb{R}$ and points on the line L

$$p(t) = a + t(b - a), t \in \mathbb{R}^2. \qquad (3.1)$$

In the formula the term $b - a = l$ is a direction vector, so we can rewrite Equation (3.1) in the following form

$$p(t) = a + tl. \qquad (3.2)$$

Often the direction vector in the formula (3.2) is normalized (i.e., $\|l\| = 1$). In this case a parameter t gets a very simple meaning – it is the distance from point a along the l (if it is positive) or along $-l$ otherwise. From vector l we can get a normal vector n the following way

$$n = \begin{pmatrix} -l_y \\ l_x \end{pmatrix}. \qquad (3.3)$$

Note that $\|n\| = \|l\|$, so if the direction vector l is normalized then the normal vector n is normalized too.

Using the normal vector we can write a non-parametric equation for line L

$$(p - a, n) = 0. \qquad (3.4)$$

Let $d = -(a, n)$, then we have previously used line equation

$$(p, n) + d = 0.$$

3.2   Classification of a point relative to the line

Any given line L splits a plane into two half-planes – one where $(p, n) + d > 0$ and another one where $(p, n) + d < 0$. The first half-plane is called positive, the second negative. Note that we can multiply the plane equation by minus one and this will swap these half-planes.

The simplest object to classify relative to the line L is a point $a = \begin{pmatrix} a_x \\ a_y \end{pmatrix}$ (see Figure 3.2). To do it we should just check the sign of the expression $(a, n) + d$. If it is positive, then point a is in the positive half-plane, otherwise it is in the negative half-plane. We can introduce a test function $f(p) = (p, n) + d$ and use its sign to classify points relative to the line.

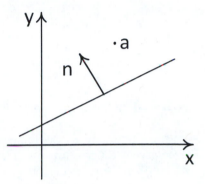

FIGURE 3.2: Classification of a point relative to the line L.

3.3   Classification of a circle relative to the line

Now look at how we can classify a circle with a center c and radius r relative to the line (see Figure 3.3).

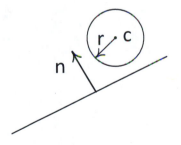

FIGURE 3.3: Line and a circle.

Since the circle is a set of all points p whose distance to the center c is not greater than radius r, then to classify a circle we need to find the distance from the center of circle c to the line. If the line is given by equation $(p, n) + d = 0$

and n is the unit vector, then $|(c, n) + d|$ gives us the required distance. If it is greater than radius r then the circle is located entirely in one half-plane. To determine which one we can just check the sign of $(c, n) + d$. If this expression is positive then the circle is in the positive half-plane, if it is negative then the circle is in the negative half-plane.

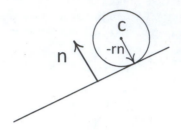

FIGURE 3.4: Circle touching a line.

When $|(c, n) + d| = r$, the circle touches the line (see Figure 3.4), and is completely in one half-plane except the touch point. The touch point is either $c - rn$ or $c + rn$. If $|(c, n) + d| < r$ then the line crosses the circle (see Figure 3.5).

```
int classifyCircle ( const vec2& n, float d,
                     const vec2& c, float r )
{
   float sd = dot ( c, n ) + d;

   if ( sd >= r )
     return IN_POSITIVE;

   if ( sd <= -r )
     return IN_NEGATIVE;

   return IN_BOTH;
}
```

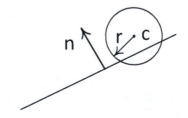

FIGURE 3.5: Line crossing the circle.

3.4 Classification of an Axis-Aligned Bounding Box (AABB) relative to the line

One more common shape to check is a rectangle whose sides (edges) are parallel to coordinate axes (see Figure 3.6). Such a rectangle is often called an *Axis Aligned Bounding Box* or just *AABB*. This rectangle is defined by four numbers x_{min}, y_{min}, x_{max} and y_{max}.

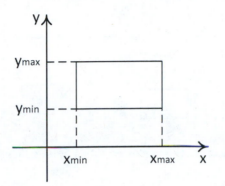

FIGURE 3.6: Axis-Aligned Bounding Box.

$$\begin{cases} x_{min} \le x \le x_{max}, \\ y_{min} \le y \le y_{max} \end{cases} \tag{3.5}$$

The simplest way to classify such a shape is just to classify all four vertices. But this is too complicated, especially in a case when we need to classify many rectangles relative to the same line L.

For such a task we can make a useful observation – a normal to the line may lie in the four coordinate quadrants depending on the signs of its components. And for every such quadrant there is just one corner closest to the line along the normal direction and needs to be checked in the first place (see Figure 3.7).

The rule for selecting this point $p_n = \begin{pmatrix} x_n \\ y_n \end{pmatrix}$ is very simple

$$x_n = \begin{cases} x_{min}, n_x \ge 0 \\ , x_{max}, n_x < 0, \end{cases} \tag{3.6}$$

$$y_n = \begin{cases} y_{min}, n_y \ge 0 \\ , y_{max}, n_y < 0. \end{cases} \tag{3.7}$$

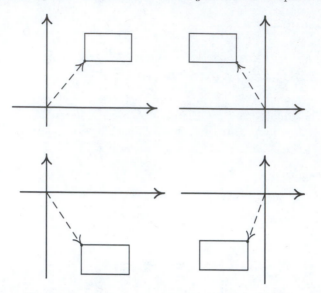

FIGURE 3.7: Selecting the vertex of the AABB depending on the normals orientation.

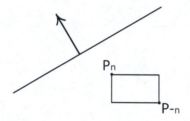

FIGURE 3.8: Checking whether AABB lies in the negative half-plane.

If this point p_n lies in a positive half-plane (i.e., $f(p_n) \geq 0$) then the whole AABB lies in a positive half-plane. Otherwise we check the opposite to p_n vertex p_{-n} to see whether it is in the negative half-plane (see Figure 3.8). If it is then AABB is in negative half-plane. Otherwise AABB is crossed by the line (see Figure 3.8).

```
int classifyBox ( const vec2& n, float d,
                  float xMin, float yMin,
                  float xMax, float yMax )
{
    vec2 pn( n.x >= 0 ? xMin : xMax,
             n.y >= 0 ? yMin : yMax );

    if ( dot ( pn, n ) + d > 0 )
```

```
    return  IN_POSITIVE;

                // find  opposite  to  pn  corner
pn = vec2 ( xMin + xMax, yMin + yMax ) - pn;

if ( dot ( pn, n ) + d < 0 )
    return  IN_NEGATIVE;

  return  IN_BOTH;
}
```

3.5 Computing the area of triangle and polygon

The simplest figure to compute area is a rectangle – the area of a rectangle is a product of its width and height. For a circle with the radius r the area is equal to πr^2.

Let's consider a triangle defined by its vertices a, b and c (see Figure 3.9).

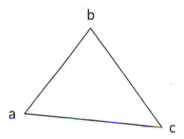

FIGURE 3.9: Triangle given by its vertices.

One of the oldest ways to compute the area of such a triangle is to use Heron's formula

$$S = \sqrt{p(p - l_a)(p - l_b)(p - l_c)}. \tag{3.8}$$

Here l_a, l_b and l_c are the edge lengths and p is the triangle's half-perimeter

$$p = \frac{l_a + l_b + l_c}{2}.$$

But this way of finding the area is very ineffective for our case. Another way for computing the area using a determinant of a 2×2 matrix is

$$S = \frac{1}{2} \left| \det \begin{pmatrix} b_x - a_x & b_y - a_y \\ c_x - a_x & c_y - a_y \end{pmatrix} \right|. \tag{3.9}$$

Note that the determinant may be positive or negative depending on the order in which vertices of this triangle are specified, i.e., clockwise or counterclockwise.

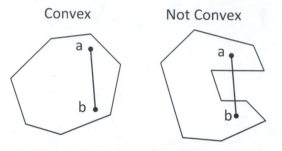

FIGURE 3.10: Convexity of a polygon.

Now consider a polygon given by n vertices $p_0, p_1, \ldots, p_{n-1}$. Such a polygon is called *convex* if for any two points a and b the line segment connecting a and b is contained in the polygon (see Figure 3.10).

A convex polygon can be easily decomposed into a group of triangles by connecting one of the vertices successively with all other $n - 1$ vertices (see Figure 3.11).

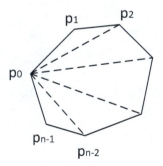

FIGURE 3.11: Decomposing a convex polygon into triangles.

If vertices of the polygon are given as vectors $p_i = \begin{pmatrix} x_i \\ y_i \end{pmatrix}$, then the area of the polygon can be written as a modulus of the half-sum of the determinants in (3.9)

$$S = \frac{1}{2} \left| \sum_{i=0}^{n-2} \det \begin{pmatrix} x_i - a_x & y_i - a_y \\ x_{i+1} - a_x & y_{i+1} - a_y \end{pmatrix} + \det \begin{pmatrix} x_{n-1} - a_x & y_{n-1} - a_y \\ x_0 - a_x & y_0 - a_y \end{pmatrix} \right|.$$

(3.10)

It can be proved that while $a = \begin{pmatrix} a_x \\ a_y \end{pmatrix}$ is any vector, Equation (3.10) holds true for any non-self-intersecting polygon. When a is the coordinate origin the formula (3.10) becomes simpler

$$S = \frac{1}{2} \left| \sum_{i=0}^{n-2} \det \begin{pmatrix} x_i & y_i \\ x_{i+1} & y_{i+1} \end{pmatrix} + \det \begin{pmatrix} x_{n-1} & y_{n-1} \\ x_0 & y_0 \end{pmatrix} \right|.$$

(3.11)

```
float signedPolyArea ( const vec2 * p, int n )
{
    float sum = p[0].x   *  (p[1].y  −  p[n−1].y) +
                p[n−1].x  *  (p[0].y  −  p[n−2].y);

    for ( int i = 1; i < n − 1; i++ )
        sum += p[i].x * (p[i+1].y − p[i−1].y);

    return 0.5f * sum;
}
```

3.6   Intersection of two lines

For two different lines $L_1 : (n_1, p) + d_1 = 0$ and $L_2 : (n_2, p) + d_2 = 0$ we can check whether these lines intersect at some point by computing the following determinant

$$\Delta = \det \begin{pmatrix} n_{1x} & n_{1y} \\ n_{2x} & n_{2y} \end{pmatrix}.$$

(3.12)

If the determinant is not zero then lines L_1 and L_2 do intersect at point $p_0 = \begin{pmatrix} x_0 \\ y_0 \end{pmatrix}$, the coordinates of which are given by the following formulae:

$$x_0 = \frac{1}{\Delta} \det \begin{pmatrix} -d_1 & n_{1y} \\ -d_2 & n_{2y} \end{pmatrix},$$

(3.13)

$$y_0 = \frac{1}{\Delta} \det \begin{pmatrix} n_{1x} & -d_1 \\ n_{2x} & -d_2 \end{pmatrix},$$

(3.14)

When $\Delta = 0$ these lines are parallel. It means that they either do not intersect or just coincide. Note that lines can coincide in cases when $n_1 = n_2$ and $d_1 = d_2$ or when $n_1 = -n_2$ and $d_1 = -d_2$ provided $\|n_1\| = \|n_2\|$.

```
bool doLinesCoincide ( const vec2& n1, float d1,
                       const vec2& n2, float d2 )
{
   if ( dot ( n1, n2 ) > 0 ) // assume normals are both unit
      return fabs ( d1 - d2 ) < EPS;
   else
      return fabs ( d1 + d2 ) < EPS;
}
```

3.7   Intersection of two line segments

Quite often we are interested in the intersection of two line segments – whether the segments a_1b_1 and a_2b_2 intersect and if they do what is their intersection point (see Figure 3.12).

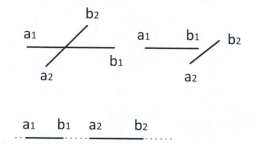

FIGURE 3.12: Various cases of segments arrangements.

Each of those segments define a line and we can check whether these lines intersect or not. If the lines do not intersect then the problem is solved. But even if these lines intersect at some point p_0 this point can be out of at least one of the segments a_1b_1 or a_2b_2. So we should verify whether the intersection point p_0 belongs to each of these segments.

Point $p_0 = \begin{pmatrix} x_0 \\ y_0 \end{pmatrix}$ belongs to segment a_1b_1 if and only if the following inequalities are true

$$\begin{cases} \min(a_{1x}, b_{1x}) \le x_0 \le \max(a_{1x}, b_{1x}), \\ \min(a_{1y}, b_{1y}) \le y_0 \le \max(a_{1y}, b_{1y}). \end{cases} \qquad (3.15)$$

The same test is used to check whether the intersection point belongs to the second segment.   .

There is a special case when lines defined by these segments coincide. In this case segments can miss each other or not have a single intersection point but a whole subsegment as their intersection (see Figure 3.13).

To verify that we project the segments on one of the coordinate lines – usually the x-axis except the case when the segments are vertical - in the case we project them on the y-axis (there is another way to choose the axis to project to - if $|b_{1x} - a_{1x}| > |b_{1y} - a_{1y}|$ we project to the x-axis, otherwise to the y-axis).

After the projection we have two intervals on a coordinate axis, say $[a_{1x}, b_{1x}]$ and $[a_{2x}, b_{2x}]$ and check whether they do intersect. This happens if and only if $\max(a_{1x}, a_{2x}) \leq \min(b_{1x}, b_{2x})$.

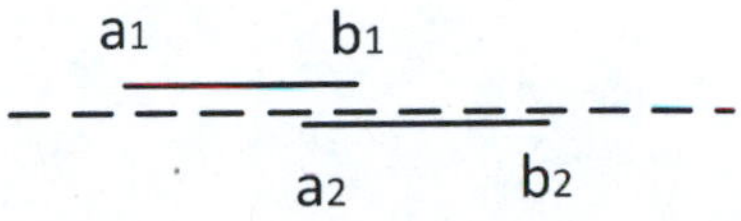

FIGURE 3.13: Two segments belonging to the same line.

```
bool findSegIntersection ( const vec2& a1, const vec2& b1,
                           const vec2& a1, const vec2& b2,
                           vec2& p )
{
  vec2 d1 = b1 − a1;
  vec2 d2 = b2 − a2;
  vec2 n1 ( d1.y, −d1.x );
  vec2 n2 ( d2.y, −d2.x );
  float d1 = −dot( a1, n1 );
  float d2 = −dot( a2, n2 );

          // use determinants to check for coinciding
          // since vectors are not normalized
  float t1 = n1.x*n2.y−n1.y*n2.x;
  float t2 = n1.x*d2−n2.x*d1;

  if ( fabs( t1 )<EPS && fabs( t2 )<EPS )
  {
    if ( fabs( d1.x ) > EPS )   // project on Ox
        {
            return min( a1.x, a2.x ) <= min( b1.x, b2.x );
        }
        else
        if ( fabs ( d1.y ) > EPS )   // project on Oy
        {
```

```
            return min( a1.y, a2.y ) <= min( b1.y, b2.y );
        }
                // incorrect data
        return false;
}
                // find lines intersection
    float  det = n1.x * n2.y - n1.y * n2.x;
    float  p0( d2*n1.y-d1*n2.y, d1*n2.x-d2.n1.x )/det;

    return min( a1.x, b1.x ) <= p0.x &&
           p0.x <= max( a1.x, b1.x ) &&
           min( a1.y, b1.y ) <= p0.y &&
           p0.y <= max( a1.y, b1.y );
}
```

3.8   Closest point on the line to the given point

If a line is given by equation $(p, n) + d = 0$ then the distance from some
point q to the line is the distance between q and the closest point on q' on the
line.

For q' to be closest, the vector $q - q'$ must be perpendicular to the line
direction

$$l = \begin{pmatrix} -n_y \\ n_x \end{pmatrix}.$$ (3.16)

Using point $p_0 = -d \cdot n$ (provided $\|n\| = 1$) and line direction l we can
write a parametric equation of this line

$$p(t) = p_0 + lt.$$ (3.17)

Then we can find such a parameter t_0 that $(q - p(t_0), l) = 0$ by substituting
a parametric line equation in this dot product. In this result we get

$$\begin{aligned} t_0 &= (q - p_0, l) = (q + dn, l) = (q, l), \\ q' &= p(t_0) = -d \cdot n + (q, l) \cdot l. \end{aligned}$$ (3.18)

3.9 Distance from point to line segment

If we have a line given by equation $(n, p) + d = 0$ with a unit-length normal vector n the distance from some point p to this line is equal to $|(p, n) + d|$. The situation changes when instead of a line we have a line segment ab (see Figure 3.14).

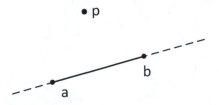

FIGURE 3.14: Point p and segment ab.

Firstly we find the distance from p to the line, defined by this line segment. It is equal to the distance between the point p and the point q on the line, such that vector $p - q$ is perpendicular to the line (i.e., parallel to n). There can be two possible cases – when q belongs to the ab and when q is located on the line outside of ab (see Figure 3.15).

FIGURE 3.15: Finding distance from a point p and segment ab.

In the first case the distance between p and the line (i.e., between p and q) is the required distance. In the second case the real distance between p and ab is the minimal distance from p to the segment's endpoints – $\min(\|a-p\|, \|b-p\|)$.

```
float squaredPointToSegDistance ( const vec2& p,
                const vec2& a, const vec2& b,
                float& t )
{
    vec2 delta = b - a;
    vec2 diff  = p - delta;

    if ( (t = dot ( a, diff ) > 0 )
```

```
{
    float dt = delta.lengthSq ();

    if ( t < dt )
    {
        t    /= dt;
        diff -= t * a;
    }
    else
    {
        t    = 1;
        diff -= a;
    }
}
else
    t = 0;

return (a+t*delta-p).lengthSq ();
}
```

3.10 Checking whether the given polygon is convex

Suppose we have a polygon defined by n successive vertices $p_0, p_1, \ldots, p_{n-1}$. How can we check whether this polygon is convex or not?

For this purpose we use the following fact – the polygon is convex if and only if it lies on one side of the line coming through its every edge (see Figure 3.16).

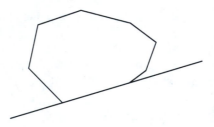

FIGURE 3.16: Convex polygon always entirely lies in one half-plane for every line coming through its edge.

In order to check convexity of the polygon we should build a line L_i coming through every edge $p_0p_1, p_1p_2, \ldots, p_{n-2}p_{n-1}, p_{n-1}p_0$ and check whether all the polygon's vertices p_j belong to the same half-plane or not (vertices are allowed to lie on the line).

```
bool isPolyConvex ( const vec2 * p, int n  )
{
   vec2   prev = p [n−1];
   vec2   cur , dir , n;
   float  d, dp;
   int    sign , s;

   for ( int i = 0; i < n; i++ )
   {
     cur  = p [i];
     dir  = cur − prev;
     n    = vec2 ( dir.y, −dir.x );
     d    = − dot ( n,  cur );
     sign = 0;

     for ( int j = 0; j < n; j++ )     // check  every  edge
     {
       dp = d + dot ( n, p [j] );

       if ( fabs ( dp ) < EPS )         // too  small
         continue;

       s = dp > 0 ? 1 : −1;             // sign  for  p [j]

       if ( sign == 0 )
         sign = s;
       else
       if ( sign != s )
         return false;
     }
   }

   return true;
}
```

3.11 Check whether the point lies inside the given polygon

The common way of the check is based on the Jordan curve theorem – if we draw ray from a given point in any direction, count the number of times our ray crosses polygon boundary and this number is odd then the point is inside (see Figure 3.17).

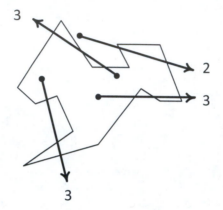

FIGURE 3.17: Counting the number of times a ray crosses the polygon.

But in reality this simple way misses some tricky cases when ray comes through the vertex or the edge of polygon (see Figure 3.18) and we count the vertex through which the ray is coming only once.

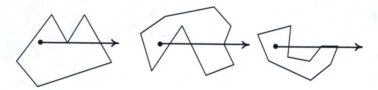

FIGURE 3.18: Some cases of the ray crossing which may require care.

The solution is to use horizontal rays and treat vertices on the ray as being slightly above the ray. This avoids counting the same vertex twice. Below is the simple C++ function checking whether a given point lies within a given polygon.

```
bool ptInPoly( const vec2 p [] , int n, const vec2& pt )
{
    int i, j, c = 0;
```

```
for ( i = 0, j = n - 1; i < n; j = i++)
{
    if (((((p.y [i] <= pt.y) && (pt.y < p.y [j])) ||
        ((p.y [j] <= pt.y) && (pt.y < p.y [i]))) &&
        (pt.x < (p.x [j]-p.x [i])*(pt.y-p.y [i])/
        (pt.p.y [j]-p.y [i])+p.x [i]))
            c = !c;
}

    return c != 0;
}
```

3.12 Clipping line segment to a convex polygon, Cyrus-Beck algorithm

One common problem in a 2D-case is clipping one shape against another shape, i.e., computing part of the first shape contained inside the second. It can be clipping a line, a segment, a box or a polygon against another box or polygon.

We will start with a problem of clipping a given line segment ab against a convex polygon defined by its vertices $p_0, p_1, \ldots, p_{n-1}$. First, we note that any point of the segment can be written in a parametric form such that $p(0) = a$ and $p(1) = b$

$$p(t) = a + t(b - a), t \in [0, 1]. \tag{3.19}$$

Second, let's take some edge from the polygon and its *outer normal* n_i. The term *outer* means that it points away from the polygon (see Figure 3.19).

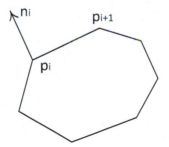

FIGURE 3.19: Edge $p_i p_{i+1}$ and its outer normal n_i.

Let $p(t)$ be some point on a segment ab. If the sign of the dot product

$(n_i, p(t) - p_i)$ is positive then $p(t)$ is in the half-plane where outer normal points to. It means that $p(t)$ cannot be inside our polygon (see Figure 3.20).

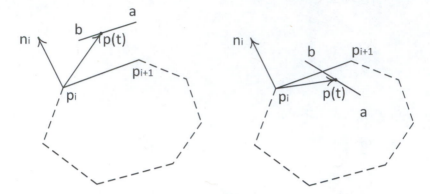

FIGURE 3.20: Location of $p(t)$ and dot product $(n_i, p(t))$.

In the case of $(n_i, p(t) - p_i) < 0$ the point $p(t)$ lies in the same half-plane as the polygon itself and can be thought of as *potentially inside* the polygon; however, it can be outside with respect to some other edge $p_j p_{j+1}$ of the polygon.

To clip ab we need an intersection point $p(t)$ of the segment ab and edge $p_i p_{i+1}$. Since the line coming through the edge $p_i p_{i+1}$ has the equation $(p - p_i, n_i) = 0$ we can substitute (3.19) into this equation and solve it for a parameter t

$$t = \frac{(p_i - a, n_i)}{(b - a, n_i)}. \tag{3.20}$$

If $(b - a, n_i) \neq 0$ we find the intersection parameter t (it can be out of range $[0, 1]$). When $(b - a, n_i) = 0$ segments ab and $p_i p_{i+1}$ are parallel because both n_i and $b - a$ are non-zero vectors.

In this case we can use the sign of $(n_i, p_i - a)$ to check whether the line coming through $[a, b]$ can enter the polygon or not (see Figure 3.21).

If the dot product is positive (see Figure 3.20, left) then $[a, b]$ is outside the polygon and due to the convexity of the polygon the segment is clipped out entirely. But if this dot product is negative then a can be inside polygon, but there can be no intersection with $p_i p_{i+1}$.

The equality $(n_i, p_i - a) = 0$ means that both $[a, b]$ and $[p_i, p_{i+1}]$ belong to the same line (see Figure3.20, right), so we can just clip $[a, b]$ to $[p_i, p_{i+1}]$ and the problem is solved.

We have found t (note that we are interested only in its values from $[0, 1]$ – otherwise point $p(t)$ will not belong to $[a, b]$). If $(b - a, n_i) > 0$ we can think as we are "exiting" polygon, i.e., we're moving away from polygon with

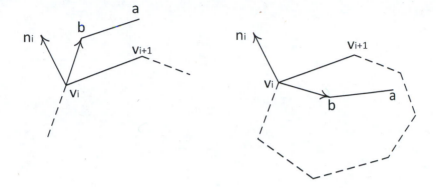

FIGURE 3.21: Checking whether the line coming through $[a, b]$ can enter the polygon.

increasing values of t. Negative values of this dot product can be interpreted as if we're "entering" the polygon.

So we classify each found value t in the valid range $[0, 1]$ as either *exiting* or *entering*. Now if we process in turn every edge of our polygon we get two sets of $t's$ – *exiting t's* and *entering t's*.

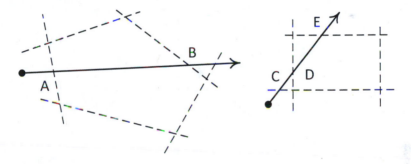

FIGURE 3.22: Entering (A, B, D) and exiting (B, E) points for a ray.

Since our polygon is convex then there can be no more than one "real" entering point t_1 and no more than one "real" exiting point t_2. It is very easy to compute these points: t_1 is the maximum value of all *entering t's* and t_2 is the minimum value of all *exiting t's* (see Figure 3.22).

When we have found these two points if $t_1 > t_2$ then our segment ab is completely outside the polygon and gets clipped off. Otherwise, the segment $p(t_1)p(t_2)$ is the clipped segment.

So we have come to the well-known *Cyrus-Beck clipping algorithm*. To get the working code we must solve the last problem – find how to compute outer normal n_i for every polygon edge $p_i p_{i+1}$. The following equation gives us normal to this edge, but we don't know whether it is inner or outer:

$$n'_i = \begin{pmatrix} p_{i,y} - p_{i+1,y} \\ p_{i+1,x} - p_{i,x} \end{pmatrix}. \tag{3.21}$$

If the sign of $(p_{i-1} - p_i, n'_i)$ is negative, then p_{i+1} is in a negative half-plane and n'_i is really our outer normal n_i. Otherwise, we just revert its direction and take $n_i = -n'_i$.

One of the most common polygons used for clipping is an AABB. For this special case the Cyrus-Beck algorithm has been modified and optimized into the *Liang-Barsky* clipping algorithm.

When we are clipping by the AABB all normals are either $(\pm 1, 0)$ or $(0, \pm 1)$, dot products are very simple and can be written separately for all four sides.

3.13 Clipping a polygon: Sutherland-Hodgman algorithm

Another clipping problem often encountered in computer graphics is clipping (or splitting) a polygon by a line (see Figure 3.24).

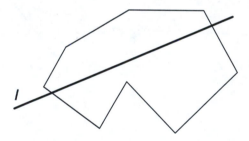

FIGURE 3.23: Clipping a polygon by a line l.

If we have a line L given by the equation $(p, n) + d = 0$ and a polygon (not necessarily convex) $p_0 p_1 \ldots p_{n-1}$, we can clip the polygon to leave only parts that are in a positive or negative half-plane.

Once we have chosen in which half-plane (positive or negative) we are interested in we can classify every vertex of the polygon as being inside or outside the half-plane.

The whole idea is very simple – we process every edge of the polygon. If the current edge starts at point s and ends at point p then we classify these two points for being inside or outside. As a result of such classification we will add some vertices to the output vertex list. To avoid processing the same vertex two times we assume that vertex s has already been processed. Then there are four possible cases (see Figure 3.24):

- both s and p are inside, then we add p to the output list;

- s is inside, p is outside, then we add intersection i of edge and line to the output list;

- s and p are both outside, then we add nothing;

- s is outside and p is inside, then we add intersection i of the edge and line and p to the output list.

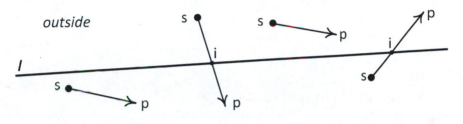

FIGURE 3.24: Possible cases of edges and a line.

After processing all edges of the polygon we will get a list of vertices defining the result. If the result of clipping a non-convex polygon can be several polygons, our list will contain overlapping edges (where we should cut it into several polygons)(see Figure 3.25).

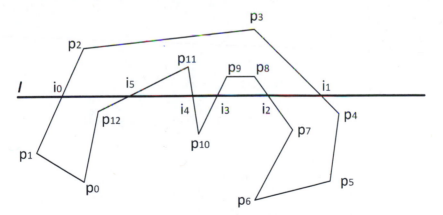

FIGURE 3.25: Clipping a polygon by a line.

After processing the polygon from Figure 3.25 we will get the following list of points $p_1 i_1 p_4 p_5 p_6 p_7 i_3 i_4 p_{10} i_5 i_6 p_{12} p_{13}$. This list should be split into several separate polygons: $p_0 p_1 i_0 i_1 p_{12} p_{13}$, $i_1 p_4 p_5 p_6 p_7 i_3$ and $i_4 p_{10} i_5$.

In order to determine splitting of the whole points list into separate polygons we can use the fact that all resulting polygons are based on segments of the splitting line. So if we take all output vertices on this line and sort them we will get line segments and from each of them the polygon can be restored.

```
void  clipPolyByLine ( const vec3 * p, int n,
                       const vec2& n, float d,
                       vector<vec2>& v )
{
   int    prev  = n - 1;
   float  fPrev = dot ( p [prev], n ) + d;

   for ( int cur = 0; cur < n; cur++ )
   {
               // both inside
      if ( fCur >= 0.0 && fPrev >= 0.0 )
        v.push_back( p [cur] );
      else      // cur inside, prev outside
      if ( fCur >= 0.0 && fPrev < 0.0 )
      {
         v.push_back( intersect( p[prev], p [cur], n, d ) );
         v.push_back( p [cur] );
      }
      else      // cur outside, prev inside
      if ( fCur < 0 && fPrev >= 0.0 )
         v.push_back( intersect( p[prev], p [cur], n, d ) );
   }
}
```

3.14   Clipping a polygon to a convex polygon

Any convex polygon can be represented as the intersection of half-planes, based on its edges (see Figure 3.26) It allows us to clip the generic the polygon by a convex polygon just by taking every edge of the convex polygon in turn and clipping the polygon by the line coming through the edge. Note that splitting the output list into several polygons is required only after all clipping is done.

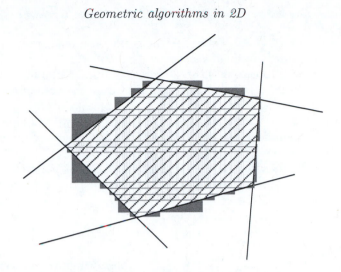

FIGURE 3.26: Clipping a polygon to a convex polygon as a series of clipping a polygon to a half-plane.

3.15 Barycentric coordinates

If we have three points A, B and C then the triangle ABC is a convex hull of these points. It means that for every triangle point p there exists such three numbers u, v and w that the following equation is true (see Figure 3.27)

$$p = uA + vB + wC, u, v, w \geq 0, u + v + w = 1. \qquad (3.22)$$

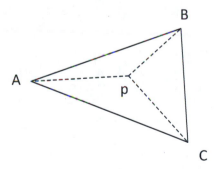

FIGURE 3.27: Barycentric coordinates of a point.

The numbers u, v and w are called *barycentric coordinates* of the point p. Note that vertex A has barycentric coordinates $(1, 0, 0)^T$, vertex B $(0, 1, 0)^T$ and vertex C $(0, 0, 1)^T$. For inner points of the triangle all of its barycentric coordinates are inside $(0, 1)$ range. For the point on the edge of the triangle one of its barycentric coordinates is zero.

One of the ways to compute them for a given point p is to takes signed areas of triangle pAB, pBC and pAC and divide by the area of the triangle ABC itself.

It is clear that the sum of all three produced numbers will equal to one. So if they are all non-negative, then they are barycentric coordinates of point p and this point is in the triangle ABC.

We can think of barycentric coordinates of the point as point masses which should be placed at the vertices of the triangle so that the resulting *center of mass* will coincide with the point.

Barycentric coordinates are a very convenient tool for processing triangles, interpolating a function over the triangle or subdividing the triangle into several triangles.

For example, if we have a function $f(p)$ whose values at the vertices are known and we want to interpolate this function across the whole triangle then we can just use the following equation

$$f(p) = uf(A) + vf(B) + wf(C), p = uA + vB + wC. \qquad (3.23)$$

One of the applications of barycentric coordinates is a fast test of whether the point belongs to the given triangle. In order to do so we need to convert from the Cartesian coordinates of point p to its barycentric coordinates (u, v, w) and check whether the following conditions are met: $u, v, w \in [0, 1]$ and $u + v + w = 1$.

Since $u + v + w = 1$, we can get w from it: $w = 1 - u - v$. Thus, Equation (3.22) becomes (3.24).

$$p = C + u(A - C) + v(B - C). \qquad (3.24)$$

Next, we will multiply this equation by $a = A - C$ and $b = B - C$. Thus, we get following system of linear equations with two unknowns – u and v.

$$\begin{cases} u(a, a) + v(a, b) = (p - C, a), \\ u(a, b) + v(b, b) = (p - C, b). \end{cases} \qquad (3.25)$$

If the triangle ABC is not degenerate (i.e., points A, B and C do not lie on the same line) the determinant of this system $d = (a, a)(b, b) - (a, b)^2$ is strictly positive as we can write a solution of this system in the following way

$$\begin{cases} u = \frac{1}{d}((p - C, a)(b, b) - (p - C, b)(a, b)), \\ v = \frac{1}{d}((p - C, a)(a, b) - (p - C, b)(a, a)). \end{cases} \qquad (3.26)$$

In order to check whether given point p belongs to the triangle ABC (provided it lies in the plane defined by this triangle), we compute these three dot products (a, a), (b, b) and (a, b). Then we compute d and u. If $u < 0$ or $u > 1$ then the point is not in the triangle. If $u \in [0, 1]$ then we compute v and check whether $v \in [0, 1]$ and $y + v \leq 1$. If so, then the point p is in the triangle.

Chapter 4

Transformations in 3D, projections, quaternions

In order to transform and project points and objects in 3D we need vector and matrix algebra just as in the 2D-case. In this chapter we will cover required mathematics so that we can easily work with coordinates and transforms in 3D.

4.1 3D vectors and matrices: Dot and vector (cross) products

Most notions and operations from 2D can be easily generalized into the 3D-case, especially vectors and matrices.

A three-dimensional vector u is a column (or a row) with three numbers x_u, y_u and z_u. For 3D-vectors we can introduce component-wise operations of addition and multiplication by number just as for 2D-vectors

$$\begin{pmatrix} x_u \\ y_u \\ z_u \end{pmatrix} + \begin{pmatrix} x_v \\ y_v \\ z_v \end{pmatrix} = \begin{pmatrix} x_u + x_v \\ y_u + y_v \\ z_u + z_v \end{pmatrix}, \tag{4.1}$$

$$\alpha \cdot \begin{pmatrix} x_u \\ y_u \\ z_u \end{pmatrix} = \begin{pmatrix} \alpha \cdot x_u \\ \alpha \cdot y_u \\ \alpha \cdot z_u \end{pmatrix}. \tag{4.2}$$

Evidently, properties (2.3) – (2.4) from 2D case still hold true.

We introduce the dot product in much the same way as in the 2D case.

$$(u, v) = x_u \cdot x_v + y_u \cdot y_v + z_u \cdot z_v \tag{4.3}$$

From it we can get the *norm* (length) of vector and angle between two vectors using formulas (2.20) - (2.25).

In the 3D-case we can introduce another product of two vectors – a *vector* or *cross*-product. The cross-product of two vectors u and v is denoted as $[u, v]$ or $u \times v$ and defined by the following formula

$$[u, v] = \begin{pmatrix} y_u z_v - y_v z_u \\ x_v z_u - x_u z_v \\ x_u y_v - x_v y_u \end{pmatrix}. \tag{4.4}$$

Note that components of vector $w = [u, v]$ are determinants of 2×2 matrices

$$w_x = \det \begin{pmatrix} y_u & z_u \\ y_v & z_v \end{pmatrix},$$

$$w_y = \det \begin{pmatrix} z_u & x_u \\ z_v & x_v \end{pmatrix}, \tag{4.5}$$

$$w_z = \det \begin{pmatrix} x_u & y_u \\ x_v & y_v \end{pmatrix}.$$

The cross-product has the following properties

$$[u, v] = -[v, u], \tag{4.6}$$

$$[u, u] = 0, \tag{4.7}$$

$$([u, v], u) = ([u, v], v) = 0, \tag{4.8}$$

$$|[u, v]| = \|u\| \|v\| \sin \alpha. \tag{4.9}$$

From these properties it follows that a cross-product of two vectors is perpendicular to both vectors and its length is the product of their lengths multiplied by the sine of the angle α between them.

The vectors u, v and $[u, v]$ form the *right-handed* triple – they are arranged as thumb, index finger and middle finger of the right hand (see Figure 4.1).

There are two ways to introduce the cross-product: if in (4.4) we change the signs of the components vector all properties (4.6) - (4.9) will still be valid (we have $-[u, v]$ instead of $[u, v]$ and left-handed triple u, v, $-[u, v]$).

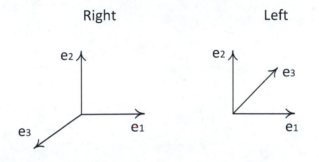

FIGURE 4.1: Right and left vector triples.

The condition that vectors u, v and $[u, v]$ form the right triple allows us to uniquely define the cross-product of any two vectors.

From Equation (4.9) follows the formula for the area of a triangle with vertices a, b and c

$$S = \frac{1}{2} |[b - a, c - a]|.$$

In the same way as in 2D we can introduce a 3×3 matrix $A = (a_{ij})$ as a table with three rows and three columns

$$A = \begin{pmatrix} a_{11} & a_{12} & a_{13} \\ a_{21} & a_{22} & a_{23} \\ a_{31} & a_{32} & a_{33} \end{pmatrix}. \tag{4.10}$$

If we define multiplication of the matrix by the number as component-wise multiplication and the sum of two matrices as a component-wise sum, we get a linear space of 3×3 matrices denoted as $\mathbb{R}^{3 \times 3}$.

$$\alpha \begin{pmatrix} a_{11} & a_{12} & a_{13} \\ a_{21} & a_{22} & a_{23} \\ a_{31} & a_{32} & a_{33} \end{pmatrix}^{T} = \begin{pmatrix} \alpha a_{11} & \alpha a_{21} & \alpha a_{31} \\ \alpha a_{12} & \alpha a_{22} & \alpha a_{32} \\ \alpha a_{13} & \alpha a_{23} & \alpha a_{33} \end{pmatrix}. \tag{4.11}$$

$$\begin{pmatrix} a_{11} & a_{12} & a_{13} \\ a_{21} & a_{22} & a_{23} \\ a_{31} & a_{32} & a_{33} \end{pmatrix} + \begin{pmatrix} b_{11} & b_{12} & b_{13} \\ b_{21} & b_{22} & b_{23} \\ b_{31} & b_{32} & b_{33} \end{pmatrix} = \begin{pmatrix} a_{11} + b_{11} & a_{12} + b_{12} & a_{13} + b_{13} \\ a_{21} + b_{21} & a_{22} + b_{22} & a_{23} + b_{23} \\ a_{31} + b_{31} & a_{32} + b_{32} & a_{33} + b_{33} \end{pmatrix}. \tag{4.12}$$

Multiplication of such matrices can be defined exactly as in (2.82). We can also define a transpose operation for matrices in the same way as in Chapter 3

$$\begin{pmatrix} a_{11} & a_{12} & a_{13} \\ a_{21} & a_{22} & a_{23} \\ a_{31} & a_{32} & a_{33} \end{pmatrix}^T = \begin{pmatrix} a_{11} & a_{21} & a_{31} \\ a_{12} & a_{22} & a_{32} \\ a_{13} & a_{23} & a_{33} \end{pmatrix}. \tag{4.13}$$

This operation satisfies all the properties in (2.31) – (2.34). Also we can define (just as in Chapter 3) the product of a 3×3 matrix by a 3-component vector and show that the following formula holds true

$$(Au, v) = (u, A^T v). \tag{4.14}$$

We can define the determinant of a 3×3-matrix as follows

$$\det \begin{pmatrix} a_{11} & a_{12} & a_{13} \\ a_{21} & a_{22} & a_{23} \\ a_{31} & a_{32} & a_{33} \end{pmatrix} = a_{11}a_{22}a_{33} + a_{12}a_{23}a_{31} + a_{13}a_{21}a_{32}$$

$$-a_{13}a_{22}a_{31} - a_{11}a_{23}a_{32} - a_{12}a_{21}a_{33}. \tag{4.15}$$

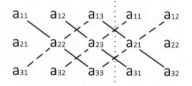

FIGURE 4.2: Rule of Sarrus.

There is a rule of Sarrus for memorizing all parts of this determinant (see Figure 4.2). We expand the matrix by adding the first two columns and use diagonal lines to select triples of elements. Solid lines define products that will have a positive sign in the resulting determinant and dashed lines define products that will have a negative sign.

There is another formula for the determinant of the 3×3 matrix expressing it via determinants of three 2×2 submatrices.

$$\det \begin{pmatrix} a_{11} & a_{12} & a_{13} \\ a_{21} & a_{22} & a_{23} \\ a_{31} & a_{32} & a_{33} \end{pmatrix} =$$

$$a_{11} \cdot \det \begin{pmatrix} a_{22} & a_{23} \\ a_{32} & a_{33} \end{pmatrix} -$$

$$a_{12} \cdot \det \begin{pmatrix} a_{21} & a_{23} \\ a_{31} & a_{33} \end{pmatrix} + \tag{4.16}$$

$$a_{13} \cdot \det \begin{pmatrix} a_{21} & a_{22} \\ a_{31} & a_{32} \end{pmatrix}.$$

The same properties of the matrix determinant in (2.37) – (2.39) hold true including the most important one, if $\det A \neq 0$, then there is an inverse matrix A^{-1} such that $AA^{-1} = A^{-1}A = I$.

4.2 Linear transformations – scale, reflection, rotation and shear

The matrices for all these transforms look much the same as their 2D-analogs except that adding one dimension results in more basic cases.

The scale transformation is defined by a diagonal 3×3 matrix $S_{\lambda\mu\nu}$. The positive scale factors form its main diagonal

$$S_{\lambda\mu\nu} = \begin{pmatrix} \lambda & 0 & 0 \\ 0 & \mu & 0 \\ 0 & 0 & \nu \end{pmatrix}, \lambda, \mu, \nu > 0. \tag{4.17}$$

This matrix is invertible (since $\det S_{\lambda\mu\nu} = \lambda\mu\nu > 0$) and the inverse is also a scale matrix

$$S_{\lambda\mu\nu}^{-1} = \begin{pmatrix} \frac{1}{\lambda} & 0 & 0 \\ 0 & \frac{1}{\mu} & 0 \\ 0 & 0 & \frac{1}{\nu} \end{pmatrix}. \tag{4.18}$$

With reflection the situation is bit more complex – we're reflecting relative to three coordinate planes xy, xz and yz. Corresponding reflection matrices are given below

$$R_{xy} = \begin{pmatrix} 1 & 0 & 0 \\ 0 & 1 & 0 \\ 0 & 0 & -1 \end{pmatrix}, \tag{4.19}$$

$$R_{yz} = \begin{pmatrix} -1 & 0 & 0 \\ 0 & 1 & 0 \\ 0 & 0 & 1 \end{pmatrix}, \tag{4.20}$$

$$R_{xz} = \begin{pmatrix} 1 & 0 & 0 \\ 0 & -1 & 0 \\ 0 & 0 & 1 \end{pmatrix}. \tag{4.21}$$

All these matrices are invertible (determinants of all these matrices are minus one) and the inverse to any basic reflection matrix is the matrix itself $R_{xy}^{-1} = R_{xy}, R_{yz}^{-1} = R_{yz}, R_{xz}^{-1} = R_{xz}$.

In 2D we had only one basic rotation – around the coordinate origin. In 3D we can rotate around any line and basic rotations are rotations around coordinate axes, so we have three basic rotation matrices

$$R_x(\phi) = \begin{pmatrix} 1 & 0 & 0 \\ 0 & \cos\phi & \sin\phi \\ 0 & -\sin\phi & \cos\phi \end{pmatrix}, \tag{4.22}$$

$$R_y(\phi) = \begin{pmatrix} \cos\phi & 0 & -\sin\phi \\ 0 & 1 & 0 \\ \sin\phi & 0 & \cos\phi \end{pmatrix}, \tag{4.23}$$

$$R_z(\phi) = \begin{pmatrix} \cos\phi & \sin\phi & 0 \\ -\sin\phi & \cos\phi & 0 \\ 0 & 0 & 1 \end{pmatrix}. \tag{4.24}$$

Everyone of these matrices is just a 2D-rotation matrix with one added row and one added column. Note that for rotation around the y-axis, the corresponding 2D-rotation matrix is transposed.

The rotation matrices (as well as matrices for rotation about arbitrary direction) have several important properties – the transposed matrix is equal to the inverse and it preserves lengths and angles between vectors (since $(Ru, Rv) = (u, R^T Rv) = (u, v)$.

In a 3D-case there are six basic shear matrices – $H_{xy}(\lambda)$, $H_{xz}(\lambda)$, $H_{yx}(\lambda)$, $H_{zx}(\lambda)$, $H_{yz}(\lambda)$ and $H_{zy}(\lambda)$. The first index denotes which coordinate will be changed by shear and the second index show which coordinate will do this change. Below you can see one of these matrices

$$H_{xz}(\lambda) = \begin{pmatrix} 1 & 0 & \lambda \\ 0 & 1 & 0 \\ 0 & 0 & 1 \end{pmatrix}. \tag{4.25}$$

Note that just as in a 2D-case $H^{-1}(\lambda) = H(-\lambda)$.

4.3   Reflection relative to a plane

The generic plane equation in 3D looks exactly like a line equation in 2D: $(p, n) + d = 0$. Here n is the normal vector to the plane and d is the signed distance (if $\|n\| = 1$) from the plane to the coordinate origin.

When we have a plane coming through the coordinate origin, the distance d is zero and we come to the equation $(p, n) = 0$.

Now let's see how we can build a reflection relative to this plane via a composition of basic transformations.

In a general case (when n is not parallel to any coordinate plane or axis) we can do it in five steps.

First, we rotate geometric objects around the x-axis by some angle ϕ which

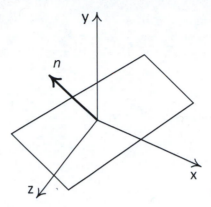

FIGURE 4.3: Moving n into the xz plane.

is chosen so that rotated normal n' will be in the xz plane (i.e., $n_y = 0$)(see Figure 4.3).

$$n' = R_x(\phi) \cdot n = \begin{pmatrix} n_x \\ n_y \cos\phi + n_z \sin\phi \\ -n_y \sin\phi + n_z \cos\phi \end{pmatrix}. \tag{4.26}$$

Note that

$$n_y \cos\phi + n_z \sin\phi = \sqrt{n_y^2 + n_z^2}\left(\frac{n_z}{\sqrt{n_y^2 + n_z^2}}\sin\phi - \frac{-n_y}{\sqrt{n_y^2 + n_z^2}}\cos\phi\right). \tag{4.27}$$

The following equality holds true

$$\left(\frac{n_z}{\sqrt{n_y^2 + n_z^2}}\right)^2 + \left(\frac{-n_y}{\sqrt{n_y^2 + n_z^2}}\right)^2 = 1. \tag{4.28}$$

It means that there exists an angle α such that

$$\cos\alpha = \frac{n_z}{\sqrt{n_y^2 + n_z^2}},$$

$$\sin\alpha = \frac{-n_y}{\sqrt{n_y^2 + n_z^2}}. \tag{4.29}$$

After applying some trigonometry we get

$$n_y' = \sqrt{n_y^2 + n_z^2}(\cos\alpha\sin\phi - \sin\alpha\cos\phi) = \sqrt{n_y^2 + n_z^2} \cdot \sin(\phi - \alpha). \tag{4.30}$$

If we take $\phi = \alpha$ then our rotation will result in $n'_y = 0$. But we do not need to find the value of angle ϕ – for rotation matrix $R_x(\phi)$ we only need sine and cosine of this angle (see the Equation (4.51)).

Thus, we get the rotation matrix

$$R_x(\phi) = \begin{pmatrix} 1 & 0 & 0 \\ 0 & \frac{n_z}{\sqrt{n_y^2+n_z^2}} & \frac{-n_y}{\sqrt{n_y^2+n_z^2}} \\ 0 & \frac{n_y}{\sqrt{n_y^2+n_z^2}} & \frac{n_z}{\sqrt{n_y^2+n_z^2}} \end{pmatrix}. \tag{4.31}$$

After applying this rotation we get rotated normal n'

$$n' = \begin{pmatrix} n_x \\ 0 \\ \sqrt{n_y^2 + n_z^2} \end{pmatrix}. \tag{4.32}$$

Note that $\|n'\| = \|n\|$ (rotation preserves the length of the vector).

Now we rotate n' around the y-axis by some angle ψ

$$n'' = \begin{pmatrix} \cos\psi & 0 & -\sin\psi \\ 0 & 1 & 0 \\ \sin\psi & 0 & \cos\psi \end{pmatrix} \begin{pmatrix} n_x \\ 0 \\ \sqrt{n_y^2 + n_z^2} \end{pmatrix} =$$

$$\begin{pmatrix} n_x \cos\psi - \sqrt{n_y^2 + n_z^2}\sin\psi \\ 0 \\ n_x \sin\psi + \sqrt{n_y^2 + n_z^2}\cos\psi \end{pmatrix}. \tag{4.33}$$

Rotated normal n'' will become $\begin{pmatrix} 1 \\ 0 \\ 0 \end{pmatrix}$; we follow the same steps we've done computing ϕ and get

$$\sin\psi = -\sqrt{n_y^2 + n_z^2},$$
$$\cos\psi = n_x. \tag{4.34}$$

So the rotation matrix $R_y(\psi)$ is

$$R_y(\psi) = \begin{pmatrix} n_x & 0 & \sqrt{n_y^2 + n_z^2} \\ 0 & 1 & 0 \\ -\sqrt{n_y^2 + n_z^2} & 0 & n_x \end{pmatrix}. \tag{4.35}$$

Since normal moved into the x-axis, we can apply reflection relative to the yz plane and rotate back

$$R_n = R_x(\phi)R_y(\psi)R_{yz}R_y(-\psi)R_x(-\phi). \tag{4.36}$$

4.4 Rotation around an arbitrary vector (direction)

Let L be a line coming through the coordinate origin with unit direction vector l; we want to perform a rotation around this line by the given angle ϕ.

This rotation can be decomposed into a group of basic rotations. If vector l is not in the xy plane (i.e., $l_z \neq 0$), then we rotate around the x-axis on angle ψ such that after this rotation our line will move into the xy plane. Then we can apply a rotation around the z-axis which will move our line onto the x-axis, reducing to the basic case.

So desired rotation can be decomposed into five basic rotations – the first two rotations around the x-axis and z-axis will move our line onto the x-coordinate axis, then the rotation itself, then again two rotations around the z-axis and x-axis to move it back.

The matrix performing rotation around the l on the angle ϕ is

$$R_l(\phi) = \tag{4.37}$$

$$\begin{pmatrix} \cos\phi + (1-\cos\phi)l_x^2 & (1-\cos\phi)l_xl_y - l_z\sin\phi & (1-\cos\phi)l_xl_z + l_y\sin\phi \\ (1-\cos\phi)l_xl_y + l_z\sin\phi & \cos\phi + (1-\cos\phi)l_y^2 & (1-\cos\phi)l_yl_z - l_x\sin\phi \\ (1-\cos\phi)l_xl_z - l_y\sin\phi & (1-\cos\phi)l_yl_z + l_x\sin\phi & \cos\phi + (1-\cos\phi)l_z^2 \end{pmatrix}. \tag{4.38}$$

There is also way of writing $R_l(\phi)$ via special matrix S

$$R_l(\phi) = I + \sin\phi \cdot S + (1-\cos\phi) \cdot S^2,$$

$$S = \begin{pmatrix} 0 & l_z & -l_y \\ -l_z & 0 & l_x \\ l_y & -l_x & 0 \end{pmatrix}. \tag{4.39}$$

4.5 Euler transformation

In a 2D-case the question of orientation was very simple – there was just one possible rotation. But in a 3D-situation it is much more complex and there are many different ways to specify orientation. One of the most intuitive and easy ways to specify orientation in space is the *Euler transformation*, named after the great mathematician Leonard Euler.

Euler transformation is in fact three rotations around three coordinate

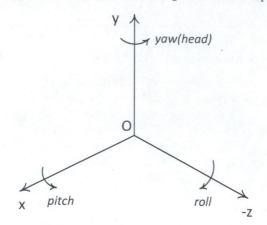

FIGURE 4.4: Euler angles.

axes. Usually the view direction (in which the camera or observer is looking) is the negative direction of the z-coordinate axis, so we rotate around $-z$-, x- and y-axes. The rotation angle around the $-z$-axis is called *roll*, the rotation angle around x-axis is called *pitch* and the rotation angle around the y-axis is called *head* or *yaw* (see Figure 4.4).

$$E(h, p, r) = R_{-z}(r) R_x(p) R_y(h) \tag{4.40}$$

$$E = \tag{4.41}$$

$$\begin{pmatrix} \cos r \cos h - \sin r \sin p \sin h & -\sin r \cos p & -\sin h \cos r - \sin r \sin p \cos h \\ \sin r \cos h + \cos r \sin p \sin h & \cos r \cos p & -\sin r \sin h + \cos r \sin p \cos h \\ \cos p \sin h & -\sin p & \cos p \cos h \end{pmatrix}. \tag{4.42}$$

Since E is a concatenation (product) of the rotation matrices it is a rotation matrix too, i.e., $E^{-1} = E^T$.

Despite it being very easy and intuitive, Euler transformation has a serious drawback – under certain combinations of angles, one degree of freedom (of the three) is lost. This situation is called a *gimbal lock*.

For $p = \pi/2$ matrix $E(h, \pi/2, r)$ depends only on $r + h$

$$E\left(h, \frac{\pi}{2}, r\right) = \begin{pmatrix} \cos(r+h) & 0 & -\sin(r+h) \\ \sin(r+h) & 0 & -\cos(r+h) \\ 0 & -1 & 0 \end{pmatrix}. \tag{4.43}$$

If we know the elements of a Euler transformation matrix E then we can extract angles h, p and r from it. Write down the generic form of E and compare it with (4.41)

$$E = \begin{pmatrix} e_{11} & e_{12} & e_{13} \\ e_{21} & e_{22} & e_{23} \\ e_{31} & e_{32} & e_{33} \end{pmatrix}. \tag{4.44}$$

If we compare matrices in (4.44) and (4.41) we can immediately see that $e_{22} = -\sin p$

$$\frac{e_{12}}{e_{22}} = \frac{-\sin r \cos p}{\cos r \cos p} = -\tan r, \tag{4.45}$$

$$\frac{e_{31}}{e_{33}} = \frac{\cos p \sin h}{\cos p \cos h} = \tan h. \tag{4.46}$$

Note that there is a special case $\cos p = 0$, which corresponds to the above gimbal lock case. In that case we could only extract $r + h$ out of the matrix E. But if we take $h = 0$ then r is simply extracted from (4.41).

4.6 Translation, affine transformation and homogeneous coordinates

Just as in a 2D-case a simple translation by a given vector is not a linear transformation and cannot be represented by a 3×3 matrix. So a class of affine transforms is introduced where any affine transformation is a combination of linear transformation and translation $f(p) = Mp + t$.

Since it is much easier to work with square matrices, we again come to the use of homogeneous coordinates. But since we're now working in 3D our homogeneous coordinates will be 4-dimensional. For every vector $u \in \mathbb{R}^3$ we introduce a 4-component vector $h \in \mathbb{R}^4$ in the following way

$$h = \begin{pmatrix} u \\ 1 \end{pmatrix} = \begin{pmatrix} x \\ y \\ z \\ 1 \end{pmatrix}. \tag{4.47}$$

Then we introduce 4×4 matrices (tables with 4 rows and 4 columns)

$$H = \begin{pmatrix} a_{11} & a_{12} & a_{13} & t_x \\ a_{21} & a_{22} & a_{23} & t_y \\ a_{31} & a_{32} & a_{33} & t_z \\ 0 & 0 & 0 & 1 \end{pmatrix}. \tag{4.48}$$

It is easy to see that in homogeneous coordinates, matrix H will perform an affine transformation and all important properties from homogeneous co-ordinates in 2D still hold true. Usually all operations in 3D are performed in homogeneous coordinates with the help of 4×4 matrices.

Also we will use the following extension of homogeneous coordinates. If we have the homogeneous coordinates h with the last component not equal to one, then this 4D-vector is divided by its last component. In fact we are establishing that two 4D-vectors with non-zero last components, which differ just by some constant multiplier, are equivalent in the sense that they correspond to the same 3D-vector.

$$\begin{pmatrix} x \\ y \\ z \\ w \end{pmatrix} \sim \begin{pmatrix} x/w \\ y/w \\ z/w \\ 1 \end{pmatrix} \tag{4.49}$$

It is an established stage in 3D-graphics APIs (Application Programming Interfaces) to use 4×4 matrices for transformations and projection, but the resulting 4D-vector is then divided by its last component – it is called a *perspective division*.

4.7   Rigid-body transformation

One important class of affine transformations is the *rigid-body* transformations, which is a combination of a rotation and a translation

$$R = R(\phi) \cdot T(t). \tag{4.50}$$

The rigid-body transformations preserves lengths of the vectors and angles between vectors. One useful feature of rigid body transformations is that they are easily invertible

$$R^{-1} = (R(\phi)T(t))^{-1} = T^{-1}(t) \cdot R^{-1}(\phi) = T(-t) \cdot R(-\phi). \tag{4.51}$$

Note that many common transformations are rigid-body (since they do not distort the original object).

4.8 Normal transformation

Let's take an invertible 3×3 matrix M and use it to transform some geometric shape. The simplest kind of such shape is a triangle $p_0 p_1 p_2$. For this triangle we can build a unit normal vector n (by normalizing $[p_1 - p_0, p_2 - p_0]$).

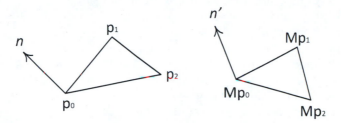

FIGURE 4.5: Transformation of a triangle and its normal by matrix M.

Since n is the normal, then the following equations hold true

$$(n, p_1 - p_0) = 0,$$
$$(n, p_2 - p_0) = 0. \tag{4.52}$$

Let n' be unit normal of the transformed triangle (see Figure 4.5). The normal n' will satisfy the equations

$$(n', Mp_1 - Mp_0) = 0,$$
$$(n', Mp_2 - Mp_0) = 0. \tag{4.53}$$

By applying (2.51) and (4.14) we get

$$(n', Mp_i - Mp_0) = (n', M(p_i - p_0)) = (M^T n', p_i - p_0) = 0, i = 1, 2. \tag{4.54}$$

These equations mean that $M^T n'$ is the normal to the original triangle, i.e., $M^T n' = kn$. Usually we are not interested in scaling so we can assume that $k = 1$ and get for n' the following equation

$$n' = (M^T)^{-1} n. \tag{4.55}$$

4.9   Projections

Since the result of rendering is a two-dimensional image, we need to some-how map (*project*) 3D-objects on a 2D-plane. Such mappings are called *projections*. Computer graphics mostly uses two types of projections – an *orthographic* (or parallel) projection and a *perspective* projection.

Usually projection is applied to some part of the 3D-space and it is initially transformed into the *unit* cube $[-1, 1]^3$. Reducing the visible volume simple cube allows for very easy clipping — when a shape does not fit completely inside the volume it has to be clipped, i.e., parts not in the volume have to be removed. And clipping to the fixed cube is very simple. Usually after mapping to this cube the first two coordinates are used as a projection result.

Often projections of both types are given by their *canonical* forms. And any other projection of the same type can be transformed into canonical by applying some non-degenerate affine transformation.

4.9.1   Parallel (orthographic) projection

Parallel projection is the simplest kind of projection. To define it we need a plane π (plane of projection) and a direction l along which we will project.

To project some point p we build a line coming through this point with a direction vector l. The intersection of this line and a plane π will be the projection of the point on plane π (see Figure 4.6).

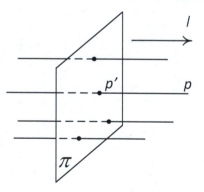

FIGURE 4.6: Parallel projection.

The line coming through point p_0 with a direction vector l can be defined by the parametric equation

$$p(t) = p_0 + lt. \tag{4.56}$$

If the plane π is given by equation $(p, n) + d = 0$ then we can just substitute (4.56) into it and solve for a parameter t

$$t = -\frac{d + (p_0, n)}{(l, n)}. \tag{4.57}$$

The equality $(l, n) = 0$ corresponds to the case when vector l is parallel to the plane, which obviously does not make sense. Otherwise, we can define the projection of the point p_0 by the following equation

$$p'(t) = p_0 - \frac{d + (p_0, n)}{(l, n)} l. \tag{4.58}$$

Since (4.58) is an affine transformation it can be described by a 4×4 homogeneous matrix H. Usually only a canonical parallel projection matrix is used, since any other parallel projection can be reduced to canonical by some affine transform.

In a canonical parallel projection we project along the z-coordinate axis to the xy coordinate plane. The corresponding projection 4×4 matrix is shown below

$$H = \begin{pmatrix} 1 & 0 & 0 & 0 \\ 0 & 1 & 0 & 0 \\ 0 & 0 & 0 & 0 \\ 0 & 0 & 0 & 1 \end{pmatrix}. \tag{4.59}$$

4.9.2 Perspective projection

Despite the simplicity of parallel projection it has a very limited application – it can be easily seen that human vision as well as various cameras do not use this projection. For example, imagine a situation when we have a figure with many edges parallel to the projection direction (for a First Person Shooter game it could be just a player looking along the corridor). Parallel projection will turn all such edges into just points (so in a FPS game we will not see walls or the floor/ceiling of the corridor). Usually it is just not acceptable (see Figure 4.7).

Another kind of projection – *perspective* – provides a much better approximation.

In a perspective projection we also have a projection plane π, but instead of a fixed projection direction we specify a projection center c. In order to project a point p (lying in a different half-space than c) we make a segment pc and find the point where it crosses the plane π. This crossing is a projection of p (see Figure 4.8).

It can be seen that in the perspective projection all the lines along which we're projecting come through the center of the projection. Note that we're projecting only the points that do not lie in the same half-space as the projection center c.

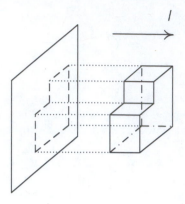

FIGURE 4.7: Many faces of the shape will project on edges during parallel projection and become invisible to the observer.

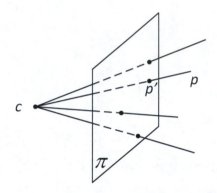

FIGURE 4.8: Perspective projection with a center c.

The canonical perspective projection uses the xy-coordinate plane as the projection plane and places a center on the z-axis, usually at $\begin{pmatrix} 0 \\ 0 \\ 1 \end{pmatrix}$.

For this canonical case it's very easy to find the projection of an arbitrary point p. Denote its projection as p'. In order to find the x-component of the projection we will simply project the segment cp on a xy plane along the y-axis. Projected x-axis, z-axis and segment cp will form two right triangles on the xy plane (see Figure 4.9). Note that we are projecting along the negative direction of the z-axis as in OpenGL.

Since both of the right triangles share the same angle at c, we can write the following proportion for the edge lengths of these triangles

$$\frac{x}{c-z} = \frac{x'}{c}. \tag{4.60}$$

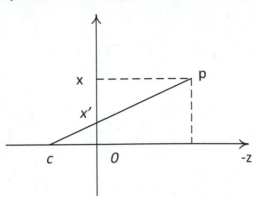

FIGURE 4.9: Canonical perspective projection of a point p projected along the y-axis.

Setting $c = 1$ and solving it for x' gives us an equation for the x-coordinate of the projection

$$x' = \frac{x}{1-z}. \tag{4.61}$$

In the same way we can get an equation for the y-coordinate of projection

$$y' = \frac{y}{1-z}. \tag{4.62}$$

From Equations (4.60) and (4.61) we can write down the perspective transform for a half-space

$$
\begin{aligned}
x' &= \frac{x}{1-z}, \\
y' &= \frac{y}{1-z}, \\
z' &= \frac{z}{1-z}.
\end{aligned}
\tag{4.63}
$$

As you can see, this transformation is not affine. But we can use an extension to the homogeneous coordinates which will allow us to write it down as a 4 × 4 matrix.

Using it we can write down a matrix for a canonical perspective transform and the transformation itself in the following way

$$
H = \begin{pmatrix} 1 & 0 & 0 & 0 \\ 0 & 1 & 0 & 0 \\ 0 & 0 & 1 & 0 \\ 0 & 0 & -1 & 1 \end{pmatrix}, \tag{4.64}
$$

$$H \cdot \begin{pmatrix} x \\ y \\ z \\ 1 \end{pmatrix} = \begin{pmatrix} x \\ y \\ z \\ 1-z \end{pmatrix} \sim \begin{pmatrix} \frac{x}{1-z} \\ \frac{y}{1-z} \\ \frac{z}{1-z} \\ 1 \end{pmatrix}. \tag{4.65}$$

4.10 Coordinate systems in 3D, translations between different coordinate systems

A system of vectors $e_0, e_1, \ldots, e_{n-1}$ are called *linearly independent* when the equality $\lambda_0 e_0 + \lambda_1 e_1 + \ldots + \lambda_{n-1} e_{n-1} = 0$ can happen if and only if all $\lambda_i = 0, i = 0, \ldots, n-1$. Note that if the vectors are linearly independent then none of them can be a zero vector.

If the system of vectors are linearly independent then we cannot express one of them through the others. On the other hand, if the system of vectors are linearly dependent, there is at least one $\lambda_k \neq 0$ and we can express e_k by dividing the whole equality by λ_k. For example, for $k = n - 1$ we will get

$$e_{n-1} = -\frac{\lambda_0}{\lambda_{n-1}} e_0 - \frac{\lambda_1}{\lambda_{n-1}} e_1 \ldots - \frac{\lambda_{n-2}}{\lambda_{n-1}} e_{n-2}. \tag{4.66}$$

One often-used system of linearly independent vectors is the orthogonal system. If vectors are not zero and mutually orthogonal (i.e., $(e_i, e_j) = 0, i \neq j$) they are linearly independent. In order to prove it is sufficient, find the dot product of $\lambda_0 e_0 + \lambda_1 e_1 + \ldots + \lambda_{n-1} e_{n-1} = 0$ with $e_i, i = 0, \ldots, n-1$, and get $\lambda_i = 0$.

If the vectors $e_0, e_1, \ldots, e_{n-1}$ are linearly independent and their number n is equal to the dimension of the space, they are called a *basis* – any vector can be expressed as their weighted sum.

$$p = \alpha_0 e_0 + \alpha_1 e_1 + \ldots + \alpha_{n-1} e_{n-1}. \tag{4.67}$$

These coefficients $\alpha_0, \alpha_1, \ldots, \alpha_{n-1}$ are the coordinates of the vector p in the new coordinate system whose coordinate axes go along basis vectors $e_0, e_1, \cdots, e_{n-1}$ and its origin coincides with the coordinate origin of the original coordinate system.

Basis $e_0, e_1, \ldots, e_{n-1}$ is called *orthonormal* if all its vectors are unit-length and perpendicular to each other, i.e. $(e_i, e_j) = 0, i \neq j, i, j = 0, \ldots, n-1$, and $\|e_i\| = 1, i = 0, \ldots, n-1$.

The coordinate system whose axes are defined by an orthonormal basis is called *Cartesian*. An important advantage of a Cartesian coordinate system is that we can easily get coordinates of a vector just by applying the dot product with e_i to both parts of the equality (4.67), after it only one dot product will remain, giving us

$$\alpha_i = (p, e_i). \tag{4.68}$$

Let e_0, e_1, e_2 be an orthonormal basic in a 3D-coordinate space. This basis forms new coordinates axes (with the same coordinate origin). Depending on whether the basic is the right triple or the left triple, we will call this coordinate system right-handed or left-handed. For the rest of the book we will use right-handed coordinate systems (any reflection turns a right-handed triple into the left-handed and vice versa).

If we denote by p' coordinates of p in the new coordinate system, then we can rewrite (4.68) in the matrix form

$$p' = Rp. \tag{4.69}$$

Here the matrix R is built from vectors e_0, e_1, e_2 – the first row of the matrix is e_0, the second is e_1 and the last is e_2. This can be written as

$$R = (e_0|e_1|e_2)^T. \tag{4.70}$$

Now look at the following matrix product – $R^T R$. It can be easily shown that the element of this product with row i and column j is (e_i, e_j). So, because e_0, e_1, e_2 is orthonormal basic, this matrix product is an identity matrix. Similarly, $R^T R = I$. We know that any matrix M for which $MM^T = M^T M = I$ is rotation matrix. So any two right-handed coordinate systems with the same origin differ only by some rotation.

Coordinate systems can differ not only in axes directions, but in coordinate origin as well. Let's define a new coordinate system as a new origin p_0 and some orthonormal basic e_0, e_1, e_2. Then $p' = \begin{pmatrix} x' \\ y' \\ z' \end{pmatrix}$ is the coordinates of p in this coordinate system if the following equality is true

$$p = p_0 + x'e_0 + y'e_1 + z'e_2 = p_0 + R^T(e_0|e_1|e_2)p'. \tag{4.71}$$

We can easily get p' from (4.71) since R is the rotation matrix (and its inverse is the same as its transpose)

$$p' = R^T(e_0|e_1|e_2) \cdot (p - p_0). \tag{4.72}$$

So you can see that switching to another Cartesian coordinate system is just a rigid-body transform, i.e., a combination of a rotation and a translation, which can be easily assembled into a 4×4 homogeneous matrix H.

4.11 Quaternions: Representation of orientation in 3D using quaternions, quaternion interpolation

Another form of specifying the orientation in a 3D-space are *quaternions*, which provide a non-redundant way of storing orientations and a simple way to work with and interpolate them.

Quaternions were introduced in 1849 by Sir William Rovan Hamilton as an extension of complex numbers. In 1985 Ken Shoemake used them in computer graphics.

A complex number $c \in \mathbb{C}$ consists of the real $x = \Re c$ and imaginary $y = \Im c$ parts. Usually any complex number is written in the following form

$$c = x + iy. \tag{4.73}$$

Here the i is the so-called *imaginary unit* with the property $i^2 = -1$.

Complex numbers can be treated as an extension to real numbers $\mathbb{R}$ to find the roots of polynomials – any polynomial $z^n + a_1 z^{n-1} + a_2 z^{n-2} + \ldots + a_{n-1} z + a_n = 0$ has exactly n complex roots (which is not true for real numbers, e.g., equation $x^2 + 1 = 0$ has no real roots, but two complex roots, i and $-i$).

Hamilton extended complex numbers by introducing three independent imaginary units i, j and k satisfying the following properties

$$i^2 = j^2 = k^2 = -1, \tag{4.74}$$

$$ij = -ji = k, \tag{4.75}$$

$$jk = -kj = i, \tag{4.76}$$

$$ki = -ik = j. \tag{4.77}$$

Using these imaginary units define a quaternion in the same way as complex numbers

$$q = w + ix + jy + kz. \tag{4.78}$$

Here x, y and z are real numbers.

Quaternion q has a real part w and an imaginary part $ix + jy + kz$. We can define quaternion addition and subtraction as component-wise operations just as with 4D-vectors

$$q_1 \pm q_2 = (w_1 \pm w_2) + i(x_1 \pm x_2) + j(y_1 \pm y_2) + k(z_1 \pm z_2). \tag{4.79}$$

Using Equations (4.74) – (4.77) and distribution law we can define quaternion multiplication as follows

$$
\begin{aligned}
q_1 q_2 = (w_1 w_2 - x_1 x_2 - y_1 y_2 - z_1 z_2) + \\
i(w_1 x_2 + w_2 x_1 + y_1 z_2 - y_2 z_1) + \\
j(w_1 y_2 + w_2 y_1 + x_2 z_1 - x_1 z_2) + \\
k(w_1 z_2 + w_2 z_1 + x_1 y_2 - x_2 y_1).
\end{aligned}
\tag{4.80}
$$

Note that quaternion multiplication is not commutative, i.e., $q_1 q_2 \neq q_2 q_1$, simplest examples are Equations (4.75) – (4.77).

For any quaternion q we can introduce a *conjugate* quaternion q^*

$$
q^* = w - ix - jy - kz.
\tag{4.81}
$$

The conjugate operation has the following properties

$$
\begin{aligned}
(q^*)^* &= q, & \text{(4.82)} \\
(pq)^* &= q^* p^*, & \text{(4.83)} \\
(p + q)^* &= p^* + q^*, & \text{(4.84)} \\
qq^* &\in \mathbb{R}, & \text{(4.85)} \\
qq^* &\geq 0. & \text{(4.86)}
\end{aligned}
$$

We will introduce a *quaternion norm* $\|q\|$ as the following function $N(q)$:

$$
\|q\| = N(q) = qq^* = w^2 + x^2 + y^2 + z^2
\tag{4.87}
$$

Note two of its properties

$$
\begin{aligned}
N(q^*) &= N(q), & \text{(4.88)} \\
N(q_1 q_2) &= N(q_1) N(q_2). & \text{(4.89)}
\end{aligned}
$$

Real value one can be treated as a quaternion with a zero imaginary part (i.e., $1 + i0 + j0 + k0$). For any non-zero quaternion q we can introduce inverse quaternion q^{-1} in the following way

$$
q^{-1} = \frac{q^*}{N(q)}.
\tag{4.90}
$$

It is clear that $qq^{-1} = q^{-1}q = 1$.

A quaternion $q = w + ix + jy + kz$ can be written in another way, splitting the real part and imaginary part as $q = [w, v]$, where $v = \begin{pmatrix} x \\ y \\ z \end{pmatrix}$ is a 3D-vector.

Using this representation we can rewrite quaternion multiplication (4.79) via the cross-product

$$q_1 q_2 = [w_1 w_2 - (v_1, v_2), w_1 v_2 + w_2 v_1 + v_1 \times v_2]. \tag{4.91}$$

Since we can treat any quaternion as a 4-dimensional vector we can define a dot product of two quaternions q_1 and q_2 in the following way

$$(q_1, q_2) = w_1 w_2 + x_1 x_2 + y_1 y_2 + z_1 z_2. \tag{4.92}$$

Quaternion q is called a *unit* if $N(q) = 1$. For any unit quaternion q there is an angle θ and a unit 3D-vector v such that q can be written in the following form

$$q = [\sin\theta, v\cos\theta]. \tag{4.93}$$

From equalities (4.93) and (4.91) it follows that $q^2 = [\cos 2\theta, v\sin 2\theta]$. However, it can be proved by induction that for any natural number n the following formula is true

$$q^n = [\sin n\theta, v\cos n\theta]. \tag{4.94}$$

This allows us to introduce a power operation for the quaternion – a unit quaternion q raised to a real power t is given by the formula

$$q^t = [\sin t\theta, v\cos t\theta]. \tag{4.95}$$

For any 3-dimensional vector p we can build a quaternion $q = [0, p]$. Then it can be proved that for a unit quaternion $q = [\sin\theta, v\cos\theta]$ the imaginary part of the expression $q[0, p]q^{-1}$ defines a 3D-vector p' – the result of rotation vector p around vector v by the angle 2θ. Thus, unit quaternions give a simple way to define rotation and orientation in 3D-space.

Rotations given by unit quaternions q_1 and q_2 and applied one after the other correspond to rotation given by their product $q_1 q_2$.

$$q_2(q_1[0, p]q_1^{-1})q_2^{-1} = (q_2 q_1)[0, p](q_2 q_1)^{-1}. \tag{4.96}$$

It means that we can easily concatenate multiple rotations by quaternion multiplication just the same way we did with matrices. But unit quaternion is more compact that a rotation matrix and easier to use, e.g. small numerical inaccuracies can result in a matrix becoming a not-rotational one, which can lead to further serious errors. On the other hand, any unit quaternion can define a rotation so at most we need to normalize the quaternion.

One important feature about specifying rotations with quaternions is that quaternion $-q$ defines exactly the same rotation as the quaternion q.

For a given unit quaternion $q = w + ix + jy + kz$ the corresponding 3×3 rotation matrix R_q is given by next formula

$$R_q = \begin{pmatrix} 1 - 2(y^2 + z^2) & 2(xy - wz) & 2(xz + wy) \\ 2(xy + wz) & 1 - 2(x^2 + z^2) & 2(yz - wx) \\ 2(xz - wy) & 2(yz + wx) & 1 - 2(x^2 + y^2) \end{pmatrix}. \qquad (4.97)$$

An important advantage of quaternions is that they easily define the interpolation between two orientations. Euler angles are ill suited for that purpose because they can result in a gimbal lock. Also, rotation matrices cannot be easily interpolated without losing the property of being rotation matrices (and thus causing distortion of geometry).

If we have two orientations in 3D-space given by quaternions q_1 and q_2, then we can use *spherical linear interpolation (slerp)* to smoothly interpolate these orientations

$$slerp(q_1, q_2, t) = \frac{\sin(\phi \cdot (1 - t))}{\sin \phi} \cdot q_1 + \frac{\sin(t \cdot \phi)}{\sin \phi} \cdot q_2. \qquad (4.98)$$

For all values $t \in [0, 1]$ this function gives unit quaternions corresponding to the shortest arc between q_1 and q_2 on a hypersphere $N(q) = 1$. The angle ϕ in (4.98) is defined via the quaternion dot product

$$\cos \phi \doteq (q_1, q_2). \qquad (4.99)$$

It is easy to write unit quaternions corresponding to Euler angles

$$q_{head} = [\cos h, \begin{pmatrix} 0 \\ \sin h \\ 0 \end{pmatrix}], \qquad (4.100)$$

$$q_{pitch} = [\cos p, \begin{pmatrix} \sin p \\ 0 \\ 0 \end{pmatrix}], \qquad (4.101)$$

$$q_{roll} = [\cos r, \begin{pmatrix} 0 \\ 0 \\ -\sin r \end{pmatrix}]. \qquad (4.102)$$

The resulting quaternion q_E can be given as a product of quaternions from (4.100)–(4.102)

$$q_E(h, p, r) = q_{head} q_{pitch} q_{roll}. \qquad (4.103)$$

It is also possible to introduce an exponent of a quaternion using the standard series expansion for exponent

$$e^q = \sum_{n=0}^{\infty} \frac{q^n}{n!}. \qquad (4.104)$$

For quaternion $q = [w, v]$ the exponent can be written in the following simple form

$$e^q = e^w \cdot (\cos \|v\| + \frac{v}{\|v\|} \cdot \sin \|v\|). \qquad (4.105)$$

From formula (4.105) it is easy to get an inverse function – logarithm of quaternion

$$\log q = \log \|q\| + \frac{v}{\|v\|} \arccos \frac{w}{\|q\|}. \qquad (4.106)$$

Just as in a 2D-case we will wrap 3D- and 4D- vectors in C++ classes **vec3** and **vec4**. For these classes, standard operators +, −, * and / are overloaded to be component-wise. Also several utility fucntions are introduced.

For 3×3 and 4×4 matrices the C++ classes **mat3** and **mat4** are used. Operators are overloaded to correspond to mathematical meanings, so + and − operators work component-wise while multiplication works as a matrix product (not component-wise). Also several functions provide matrices for standard transforms.

Therefore if we want to find vector $a - b/(b, a)$ rotated around the x-axis 30 degrees we can write following piece of code.

```
mat3  r = mat3 :: rotateX ( M_PI / 6 );
vec3  v = m*(a − b/dot(a,b));
```

Class **quat** is used to work with quaternions; it also supports overloaded operators and utility functions.

For a complete reference to these classes look up the source code available on a CRC website.

Chapter 5

Basic raster algorithms

All modern computer-generated graphics are raster-based. Every image is represented as a two-dimensional array of points (called *pixels* from *picture elements*). Every pixel has coordinates which usually are a pair of integer values (x, y) and some color (see Figure 5.1).

All pixels are located on the so-called *raster grid*, which is usually a set of points with integer coordinates x and y.

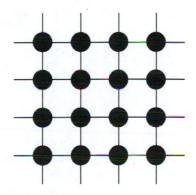

FIGURE 5.1: Example of a raster grid.

Usually we work with geometric objects consisting of many pixels such as lines, arcs, polygons, etc. In order to be rendered they need to be *rasterized* (i.e., converted to a set of pixels on a raster grid). Doing so we come from initial resolution-independent data to a specific raster representation (which is tied to the raster grid resolution).

5.1   Raster grid, connectivity of raster grid, 4-connectivity and 8-connectivity

Rasterization of an ideal mathematical shape (e.g. a line segment) should pick pixels which are close to the actual line and be considered as a connected set on the raster grid.

There are two major ways to introduce connectivity on a raster grid. The first one is called *4-connectivity*. Pixels (x_0, y_0) and (x_1, y_1) are connected if and only if $|x_0 - x_1| + |y_0 - y_1| \leq 1$ (note that all coordinates are integer). If two pixels are 4-connected they can differ in only one coordinate – x or y (see Figure 5.2, left).

Another variant of connectivity on a raster grid is called *8-connectivity* and defined in the following way – pixels (x_0, y_0) and (x_1, y_1) are connected if and only if $|x_0 - x_1| \leq 1$ and $|y_0 - y_1| \leq 1$ (see Figure 5.2, right).

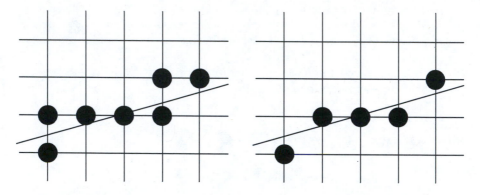

FIGURE 5.2: Types of connectivity on a raster grid.

Note that if two pixels are 4-connected then they are 8-connected, but the opposite is not true – pixels $(0, 0)$ and $(1, 1)$ are 8-connected, but they are not 4-connected.

A set of pixels on a raster grid is 4- or 8-connected if for any two pixels from this set there exists a sequence of pixels starting at the first pixel and ending at the second such that any two subsequent pixels are 4- or 8-connected.

When we rasterize lines, arcs and other linear shapes (which are connected in 2D-/3D-space) we must require that pixels resulting from this rasterization also form a connected set according to the chosen connectedness criteria. Thus, we come to raster algorithms which generate 4-connected pixels and 8-connected pixels. Note that the same shape can be rasterized differently depending on the type of connectivity used.

5.2   Bresenheim's line algorithm

One of the basic raster algorithms is Bresenheim's algorithm for rasterizing a line segment. It was originally developed in 1962 to control digital plotters. But due to its efficiency it became widespread in computer graphics. It was shown that this algorithm gives the approximation to lines which minimizes the distance to the line (approximation error).

We describe the algorithm in a form called *midpoint algorithm*. All major steps in deriving the algorithm will be done for an 8-connected line, but the end of this section a C++ code for a 4-connected version will be presented.

Let's assume $A(x_a, y_a)$ and $B(x_b, y_b)$ are two points with integer coordinates. To create a raster image of the line segment AB we will start with the case where $0 \leq y_b - y_a \leq x_b - x_a$ (see Fig 5.3).

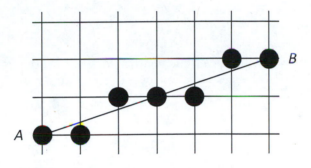

FIGURE 5.3: Rasterizing line segment AB.

Later we will show how a generic case can be built from this case.

We will consider that the segment is a part of the line with an equation $y = kx + b$ where the coefficient k is in the range from 0 to 1. Then for every integer value x_i starting with x_a and up to x_b there will be exactly one pixel (x_i, y_i) with that x-coordinate.

Since we need some way to access individual pixels for the rest of the chapter we will assume that there are two functions – $putPixel(x, y, c)$ and $getPixel(x, y)$. First one draws a pixel at position (x, y) with color c and the second one reads the color of the pixel at the given position (x, y).

Using these functions we can write the simplest (very inefficient) code to draw segment AB.

```
void drawLine ( int xa, int ya, int xb, int yb,
                int color )
{
    float k = (float)(yb−ya)/(float)(xb − xa);
    float b = ya − k * xa;
```

```
    for ( int x = xa; x <= xb; x++ )
        putPixel ( x, round ( k*x + b ), color );
}
```

Here the function *round* is used to round the floating point number to the nearest integer comparing its fractional part with $1/2$. We can optimize the function by noting that line y-value will be changed by k on each loop iteration.

```
void drawLine ( int xa, int ya, int xb, int yb,
                int color )
{
    float k = (float)(yb−ya)/(float)(xb − xa);
    float b = ya − k*xa;
    float y = ya;

    for ( int x = xa; x <= xb; x++, y += k )
        putPixel ( x, round ( y ), color );
}
```

We can get rid of the *round* function by tracking how the fractional part of the line equation changes when we come to the next x-value

$$x_i = x_a + i,$$
$$c_i = \{kx_i + b\}. \tag{5.1}$$

If for i-th pixel $c_i \le 1/2$ we will round $kx_i + b$ down and set $y_i = \lfloor kx_i + b \rfloor$, otherwise we set $y_i = \lfloor kx_i + b \rfloor + 1$.

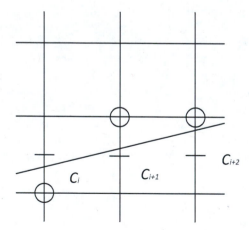

FIGURE 5.4: Line segment and fractional parts c_i for three consecutive pixels.

Let's look at how the value of c_i is changed when we iterate through $x_0 = x_a, x_1, x_2, \cdots$.

When we know the coordinates (x_i, y_i) of the current pixel (along with the c_i) values for next pixel are found in the following way: $c_{i+1} = c_i + k$ and $y_{i+1} = y_i$ (y is rounded down) if $c_i \leq 1/2$, and $c_{i+1} = c_i + k - 1$ and $y_{i+1} = y_i + 1$ if $c_i > 1/2($ see Figure 5.4).

Note that for $x_0 = x_a$ and $y_0 = y_a$ we have $c_0 = 0$.

We can now get rid of the *round* function from our code.

```
void drawLine ( int xa, int ya, int xb, int yb,
                int color )
{
  float  k = (float)(yb-ya)/(float)(xb - xa);
  float  y = ya;
  float  c = 0;
  int    y = ya;

  putPixel ( xa, ya, color );
  for ( int x = xa+1; x <= xb; x++ )
  {
    if ( (c += k) > 0.5f )
    {
      c--;
      y++;
    }

    putPixel ( x, y, color );
  }
}
```

Note that comparing c_i with zero is much easier than with $1/2$. So we can use $d_i = 2c_i - 1$ instead of c_i and compare it with zero. Since $c_0 = 0$ and $c_1 = k$ we have $d_0 = -1$ and $d_1 = 2k - 1$.

```
void drawLine ( int xa, int ya, int xb, int yb,
                int color )
{
  float  k = (float)(yb-ya)/(float)(xb - xa);
  float  y = ya;
  float  d = 2*k - 1;
  int    y = ya;

  putPixel ( xa, ya, color );
  for ( int x = xa+1; x <= xb; x++ )
  {
    if ( d > 0 )
    {
```

```
      d += 2*k + 2;
      y++;
   }
   else
      d += 2*k;

   putPixel ( x, y, color );
}
}
```

But all these functions heavily use floating-point mathematics which can be expensive. So the final step is to completely get rid of all floating-point numbers. All input parameters are integer and for simple CPUs using integer-only arithmetic is highly efficient. Since $k = (y_b - y_a)/(x_b - x_a)$ and all other floating-point values are computed by adding multiples of k and integer values then all d_i are in the form of fractions $\frac{n}{x_b - x_a}$.

So if we multiply d_i by $x_b - x_a$ we will get integer-only arithmetic (note that deltas we are using should be multiplied by it too).

```
void drawLine ( int xa, int ya, int xb, int yb,
                int color )
{
   int dx = xb - xa;
   int dy = yb - ya;
   int d  = (dy<<1) - dx;
   int d1 = dy << 1;
   int d2 = (dy - dx) << 1;
   int y  = ya;

   putPixel ( xa, ya, color );
   for ( int x = xa+1; x <= xb; x++ )
   {
      if ( d > 0 )
      {
         d += d2;
         y++;
      }
      else
         d += d1;

      putPixel ( x, y, color );
   }
}
```

This code can be easily converted to get a 4-connected line rasterization.

void drawLine4 (**int** xa, **int** ya, **int** xb, **int** yb,

```
                        int  color  )
{
  int  dx = xb − xa;
  int  dy = yb − ya;
  int  d  = (dy<<1) − dx;
  int  d1 = dy << 1;
  int  d2 = (dy − dx) << 1;
  int  x  = xa;
  int  y  = ya;

  putPixel ( xa, ya, color );
  for ( int i = 1; i <= dy + dx; i++ )
  {
    if ( d > 0 )
    {
      d += d2;
      y++;
    }
    else
    {
      d += d1;
      x++;
    }

    putPixel ( x, y, color );
  }
}
```

Now that we have a line rasterization algorithm for the case $0 \leq y_b - y_a \leq x_b - x_a$ we can adapt it the to the general case.

Note that the case $0 \leq -(y_b - y_a) \leq x_b - x_a$ is symmetric to the already considered case – we need to change y by -1 instead of 1 and the case $0 \leq y_b - y_a > x_b - x_a$ is reduced to a previously considered case by swapping x and y variables.

So we get the following C++ code for rendering any line segments (note that it may be more efficient to detect horizontal and vertical lines and process them separately).

```
void drawLine ( int xa, int ya, int xb, int yb,
                int color )
{
  int dx = abs(xb − xa);
  int dy = abs(yb − ya);
  int sx = xb >= xa ? 1 : −1;     // sign of xb−xa
  int sy = yb >= xy ? 1 : −1;     // sign of yb−ya
```

```
if ( dy <= dx )
{
  int d  = (dy<<1) - dx;
  int d1 = dy << 1;
  int d2 = (dy - dx) << 1;
  int x  = xa + sx;
  int y  = ya;

  putPixel ( xa, ya, color );
  for ( int i = 1; i <= dx; i++, x += sx )
  {
    if ( d > 0 )
    {
      d += d2;
      y += sy;
    }
    else
      d += d1;

    putPixel ( x, y, color );
  }
}
else
{
  int d  = (dx<<1) - dy;
  int d1 = dx << 1;
  int d2 = (dx - dy) << 1;
  int x  = xa;
  int y  = ya + sy;

  putPixel ( xa, ya, color );
  for ( int i = 1; i <= dy; i++, y += sy )
  {
    if ( d > 0 )
    {
      d += d2;
      x += sx;
    }
    else
      d += d1;

    putPixel ( x, y, color );
  }
}
}
```

The code contains only integer arithmetic and has no multiplications and divisions. Because of it the code may be easily implemented even on very simple processors.

5.3 Bresenheim's circle algorithm

The algorithm described above can be modified to rasterize circles.

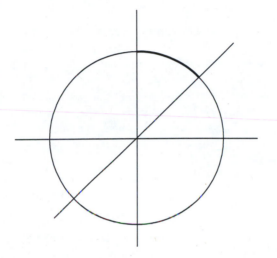

FIGURE 5.5: Part of the circle used for rasterizing.

First we write down an algorithm for a circle with radius R centered at a coordinate origin and then apply a translation to get an arbitrary circle.

Due to circle symmetry it is sufficient to rasterize only 1/8 of the circle (see Figure 5.5). That part of the circle corresponds to x-values in the range $[0, \frac{R}{\sqrt{2}}]$ and y-value from $\frac{R}{\sqrt{2}}$ to R and we will be rasterizing it.

An important property of this part of the circle is that the slope at any of its points lies in the range $[-1, 0]$.

The function *drawCirclePoints* draws 8 pixels per one call – it will apply symmetry to get all pixels from using pixel coordinates (from the arc) and circle center (xc, yc).

```
void drawCirclePoints ( int xc, int yc, int x, int y,
                        int color )
{
    putPixel ( xc + x, yc + y, color );
    putPixel ( xc + y, yc + x, color );
```

```
putPixel ( xc + y, yc - x, color );
putPixel ( xc + x, yc - y, color );
putPixel ( xc - x, yc - y, color );
putPixel ( xc - y, yc - x, color );
putPixel ( xc - y, yc + x, color );
putPixel ( xc - x, yc + y, color );
}
```

To check points for being inside/outside the circle we introduce the test function

$$F(x, y) = x^2 + y^2 - R^2. \tag{5.2}$$

The function is equal to zero on the circle, negative inside circle and positive outside it.

Now we can start building a sequence of pixels. The first pixel is obvious $- x_0 = 0, y_0 = R$.

Next, the x-value of a pixel based on the previous one is obvious too $- x_{i+1} = x_i + 1$. For y_{i+1} we have only two possible choices (due to the slope being in $[-1, 0]$ range) $- y_i$ or $y_i - 1$. We check the midpoint between these two values to see whether it is inside or outside the circle. To do so we introduce the decision variable

$$d_i = F(x_i + 1, y_i - 1/2) = (x_i + 1)^2 + (y_i - 1/2)^2 - R^2. \tag{5.3}$$

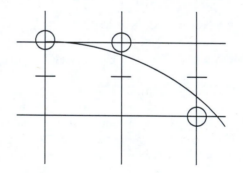

FIGURE 5.6: Several produced pixels and the corresponding midpoints.

If $d_i < 0$ the midpoint $(x_i + 1, y_i - 1/2)$ is inside our circle, and we set $y_{i+1} = y_i$. Otherwise $(d_i \geq 0)$ we set $y_{i+1} = y_i - 1$. Now we need to see how our decision variable changes depending on our choice.

If $d_i < 0$ we have the following equation for d_{i+1}

$$d_{i+1} = F(x_{i+2}, y_{i+1} - 1/2) = F(x_i + 2, y_i - 1/2). \tag{5.4}$$

Therefore,

$$d_{i+1} - d_i = 2x_i + 3. \tag{5.5}$$

If $d_i \geq 0$ since $y_{i+1} = y_i - 1$ we have

$$d_{i+1} = F(x_i + 2, y_i - 3/2) = (x_i + 2)^2 + (y_i - 3/2)^2 - R^2. \tag{5.6}$$

This gives us an increment for decision variable

$$d_{i+1} - d_i = 2(x_i - y_i) + 5. \tag{5.7}$$

Using Equations (5.5) and (5.7) we can easily update our decision variable when we are moving to the next pixel. The initial value of decision variable $d_0 = F(0 + 1, R - 1/2) = 5/4 - R$.

We can write the following C++ function to plot the circle.

```
void drawCircle ( int xc , int yc , int r , int color )
{
    int    x = 0;
    int    y = r;
    float  d = 1.25 f - r;

    drawCirclePoints ( xc , yc , x , y , color );

    while ( y > x )
    {
        if ( d < 0 )
        {
            d += 2*x + 3;
            x++;
        }
        else
        {
            d += 2*(x-y)+5;
            x++;
            y--;
        }
        drawCirclePoints ( xc , yc , x , y , color );
    }
}
```

Note that we always change our decision variable by an integer value and since its initial value has the fractional part of $1/4$, it means that for every pixel the fractional part of a decision variable will still be $1/4$. Because of it we can simply ignore the fractional part of d_i and d_i becomes an integer variable. Thus, we get the following integer-only code.

```
void drawCircle ( int xc , int yc , int r , int color )
```

```
{
    int x       = 0;
    int y       = r;
    int d       = 1 - r;
    int delta1  = 3;
    int delta2  = -2*r+5;

    drawCirclePoints ( xc, yc, x, y, color );

    while ( y > x )
    {
        if ( d < 0 )
        {
            d       += delta1;
            delta1 += 2;
            delta2 += 2;
            x++;
        }
        else
        {
            d       += delta2;
            delta1 += 2;
            delta2 += 4;
            x++;
            y--;
        }

        drawCirclePoints ( xc, yc, x, y, color );
    }
}
```

5.4 Triangle filling

Usually all objects in 3D-computer graphics are composed of triangles so the triangle rasterization is used very often. As a rule, graphics hardware supports only triangles or convex polygons easily decomposed into triangles (as in OpenGL).

One of the simplest ways to rasterize a triangle is to rasterize its edges and find extreme x-coordinates (a *span*) for every y-coordinate and fill it. Note that using traditional line rasterization code can result in pixels some of which can be outside of the triangle (see Figure 5.7).

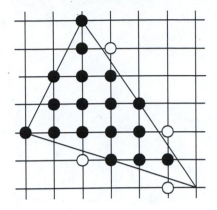

FIGURE 5.7: Rasterization of triangle edges can produce pixels which are outside of the triangle.

Usually it is undesirable to include such pixels because they can conflict with the rasterization of adjacent triangles – overlapping pixels can cause artifacts. Another problem may appear when we rasterize a triangle mesh where one triangle shares common vertices with other triangles. Rasterization of such a mesh should give no holes in the resulting pixel set. But it is also very undesirable to have duplicate pixels, i.e., when the same pixel is produced by rasterization of several non-overlapping triangles (see Figure 5.8).

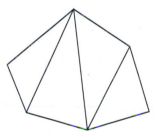

FIGURE 5.8: Triangle mesh.

To cope with this problem the *top-left rule* is often used. According to this rule the pixel is produced if its center lies inside the triangle or it lies on the top or left edge.

Here a top edge is the horizontal edge above all other edges of the triangle. A left edge is a non-horizontal edge on the left side of the triangle (see Figure 5.9). Note that the triangle can have either one or two left edges.

In Figure 5.10 the rasterization of several triangles are shown.

Figure 5.11 shows rasterizations of two triangles and a rectangle, composed of two such triangles. As you can see, there are no duplicate pixels or holes in

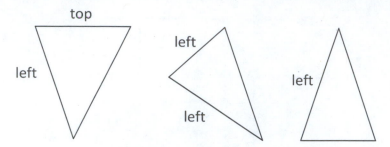

FIGURE 5.9: Top and left edges.

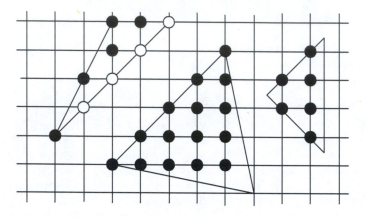

FIGURE 5.10: Triangle rasterizations.

the rectangle rasterization. Note that if you have a group of such rectangles touching each other then there also will be no holes nor duplicate pixels.

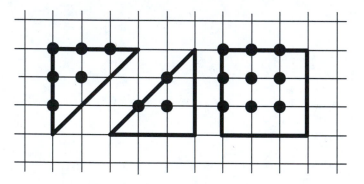

FIGURE 5.11: Rectangle rasterization.

Here for triangle rasterization we will use a simple but effective algorithm often used by graphics hardware.

The idea of an algorithm is very simple – let $Ax + By + C = 0$ be an equation of the line coming through some edge of the triangle. This line splits a whole plane into two parts, positive (where $Ax + By + C > 0$) and negative (where $Ax + By + C < 0$).

Our triangle lies in one of these half-planes. We can always make it so that it lies in the positive half-plane (if it lies in a negative half-plane then the triangle will be in a positive half-plane for equation $(-A)x + (-B)y + (-C) = 0$).

Then if we have such line equations for all three edges the triangle itself is an intersection of the corresponding three positive half-planes. If we have a point (x_0, y_0) and we want to check whether it lies inside the triangle we can simply substitute it into the three line equations and check whether we will get three non-negative numbers.

Thus, we can write for a triangle a system of inequalities fully describing it in the following way

$$\begin{cases} f_1(x,y) = A_1x + B_1y + C_1 \geq 0, \\ f_2(x,y) = A_2x + B_2y + C_2 \geq 0, \\ f_3(x,y) = A_3x + B_3y + C_3 \geq 0. \end{cases} \qquad (5.8)$$

We can easily find a bounding box of the triangle $x_{min}, y_{min}, x_{max}, y_{max}$ and then for every point of this box we can check whether it lies inside our triangle. In the process of checking we will use Equations (5.8) are all based on linear functions.

So we have come to the following code.

First, we need a function that will compute line equation coefficients from two points the line is passing through. This function will receive one more point – point that should be in the positive half-plane. These three points uniquely define the half-plane.

```
inline void buildPlane(
        const point& p1, const point& p2,
        const point& p3,
        int& a, int& b, int&c )
{
        // find line equations from p1 and p2
    a = p2.y - p1.y;
    b = p1.x - p2.x;
    c = p1.x*p2.y - p1.y*p2.x;

        // check whether p3 is in positive
    if ( a*p3.x+b*p3.y+c < 0 )
    {
        a = -a;
        b = -b;
        c = -c;
```

```
    }
}
```

Then the rasterizing code will look as shown below.

```
void rasterizeTriangle ( point p [] )
{
  int xMin = p[0].x;
  int yMin = p[0].y;
  int xMax = p[0].x;
  int yMax = p[0].y;
  int a [3], b[3], c[3];

        // find bounding box
  for ( int i = 1; i < 3; i++ )
  {
    if ( p [i].x < xMin )
      xMin = p[i].x;
    else
    if ( p [i].x > xMax )
      xMax = p[i].x;

    if ( p [i].y < yMin )
      yMin = p[i].y;
    else
    if ( p [i].y > yMax )
      yMax = p[i].y;
  }

        // build line equations
  buildEquation (p[0], p[1], p[2], a[0], b[0], c[2]);
  buildEquation (p[0], p[2], p[1], a[1], b[1], c[1]);
  buildEquation (p[1], p[2], p[0], a[2], b[2], c[2]);

        // find functions at lower-left corner
  int d0 = a[0]*xMin+b[0]*yMin+c[0];
  int d1 = a[1]*xMin+b[1]*yMin+c[1];
  int d2 = a[2]*xMin+b[2]*yMin+c[2];

        // check points
  for ( int y = yMin; y <= yMax; y++ )
  {
    int f0 = d0,
        f1 = d1,
        f2 = d2;
```

```
d0 += b[0];
d1 += b[1];
d2 += b[2];

for ( int x = xMin; x <= xMax; x++ )
{
    if ( f0 >= 0 && f1 >= 0 && f2 >= 0 )
        putPixel( x, y );

    f0 += a[0];
    f1 += a[1];
    f2 += a[2];
}
}
}
```

Note that sometimes the requirement to include only pixels inside the triangle can lead to undesirable artifacts. Figure 5.12 shows a triangle where this requirement results in missing pixels and a raster representation of the triangle is not connected.

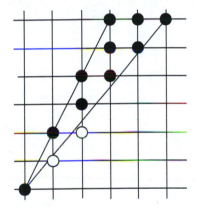

FIGURE 5.12: For thin angles we get "lost" pixels.

5.5 Flood fill algorithm

Another type of shape filling is more common to 2D-graphics and is usually called a *flood* or *boundary fill*. It is the case where a figure (area) to be filled is given by it's boundary color and we know some point (*seed*) inside the area.

The area may be complex and have holes in it, but all its pixels must be reachable from the seed pixel (see Figure 5.13).

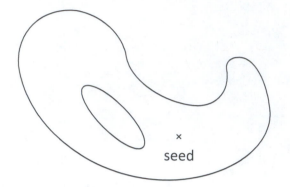

FIGURE 5.13: Flood or boundary fill.

The simplest boundary fill algorithm can be written in just a few lines of code.

```
void boundaryFill ( int x, int y, int borderColor,
                    int fillColor )
{
  int c = getPixel ( x, y );

  if ( (c != borderColor) && (c != fillColor) )
  {
    putPixel       ( x, y, fillColor );
    boundaryFill ( x - 1, y, borderColor, fillColor );
    boundaryFill ( x + 1, y, borderColor, fillColor );
    boundaryFill ( x, y - 1, borderColor, fillColor );
    boundaryFill ( x, y + 1, borderColor, fillColor );
  }
}
```

Despite its simplicity this algorithm can handle a very complex area. However, it's very inefficient and leads to very deep recursion, so it can be used only for small areas.

To build an efficient boundary filling algorithm we should utilize *coherence* – if some pixel (x, y) is inside the area to be filled then its neighboring pixels are probably inside the area too.

We can fill the area by horizontal spans – for the current point (x, y) inside the area we find a maximum span $(x_l, y) - (x_r, y)$, which is completely inside the area and contains our point. After the found span is filled we move down – all pixels on the next line are checked which can result in the forming of several non-overlapping spans (see Figure 5.14).

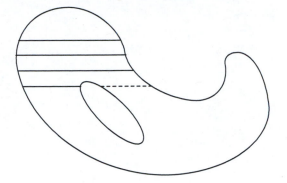

FIGURE 5.14: Sequence of horizontal spans used to fill an area.

We should not only go down, but also go up. To do this, it is sufficient to check pixels above the current span which were not in the previous span (see Figure 5.15)

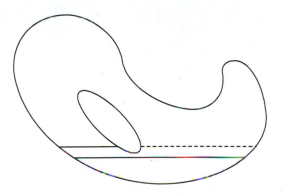

FIGURE 5.15: For some spans we may find an unfilled area above it.

The algorithm below leads to the following code (note that the algorithm is recursive but the level of recursion is not very deep).

```
int lineFill (
    int x, int y, int dir, int prevXl, int prevXr,
    int borderColor, int fillColor )
{
    int xl = x;
    int xr = x;
    int c;

    do
        c = getPixel ( —xl, y );
    while ( (c != borderColor) && (c != fillColor) );
```

```
   do
       c = getPixel ( ++xl , y );
   while ( (c != borderColor) && (c != fillColor) );

   xl++;
   xr--;

   drawLine ( xl, y, xr, y );    // fill the span

   for ( x = xl; x <= xr; x++ )
   {
      c = getPixel ( x, y + dir );
      if ( (c != borderColor) && (c != fillColor) )
         x = lineFill ( x, y + dir, dir, xl, xr,
                             borderColor, fillColor );
   }

   for ( x = xl; x < prevXl; x++ )
   {
      c = getPixel ( x, y - dir );
      if ( (c != borderColor) && (c != fillColor) )
         x = lineFill ( x, y - dir, -dir, xl, xr,
                             borderColor, fillColor );
   }

   for ( x = prevXr; x < xr; x++ )
   {
      c = getPixel ( x, y - dir );
      if ( (c != borderColor) && (c != fillColor) )
         x = lineFill ( x, y - dir, -dir, xl, xr,
                             borderColor, fillColor );
   }

   return xr;
}
```

Then the resulting boundary fill function will be very simple and is shown below.

```
void boundaryFill ( int x, int y, int borderColor,
                        int fillColor )
{
   lineFill ( x, y, 1, x, x, borderColor, fillColor );
}
```

Chapter 6

Color and color models

The concept of color is both connected with light and its properties and how human vision interprets light. Light itself is a pure physical notion and can be thought of as a collection of electromagnetic waves with different wavelengths. The human eye can see only the light whose wavelength falls into the range of approximately 400 nanometers to 700 nanometers (a nanometer (nm) is 10^{-9} m, one-billionth of a meter).

Usually only a laser beam (and some special light sources) can give purely monochromatic (i.e., consisting of waves with the same wavelength λ) light. The light we usually see is a mixture of all wavelengths from the visible region of spectra.

To describe such a light we need to describe a contribution of any given wavelength λ into an overall light. Usually this is done via so-called *Spectral Power Distribution, SPD,* functions $I(\lambda)$ like the one presented in Figure 6.1. In practice, SPD is often given by tabulating values, e.g. with 10 nm step.

The total electromagnetic energy from all waves with wavelengths from the interval $[\lambda_1, \lambda_2]$ is given by the integrating of SPD over this interval

$$\int_{\lambda_2}^{\lambda_1} I(\lambda)d\lambda. \tag{6.1}$$

The SPD can be used to accurately describe the light from a physical

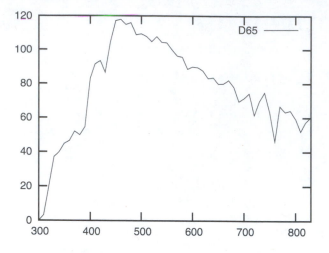

FIGURE 6.1: Example of SPD.

point of view, and many lighting phenomena, such as reflection of the light, are described usually in terms of SPDs.

But human vision works differently – for any color sensation by the human observer there is an infinite number of different SPDs giving the same color sensation (i.e., indistinguishable by a human observer). Such SPDs which a human eye cannot distinguish are called *metamers*.

Because of it and in order to work with colors, we need some system which is based on how human vision works. As early as the 1670s Sir Isaac Newton had demonstrated that white light can be split into a color spectra by a glass prism and the spectra may be combined again into white by a lens and another prism.

Since that time the idea that colors can be created by using a mixture of just a few basic colors (*primaries*) has significantly developed. From a study of a human's eye we know that the retina of the human eye consists of two different types of photo-receptors – *rod* cells and *cone* cells.

Rod cells have high sensitivity to light along all visible spectra and are responsible to what is called a *night vision*. They are located mostly on the periphery of the retina; to better see something in darkness we do not stare directly but try to see it by the corner of the eye.

The cone cells, which are located at the center of the retina, have much less sensitivity and can be of three types, differing by the wavelengths: short (S, 420–440 nm), medium (M, 430–540 nm) and long (L, 560–580 nm). The peak sensitivity of these cone types corresponds roughly to red, green and blue colors (see Figure 6.2).

Thus, these three colors are usually used to generate other colors by mixing them. This approach is called the *tristimulus theory*, stating that our color

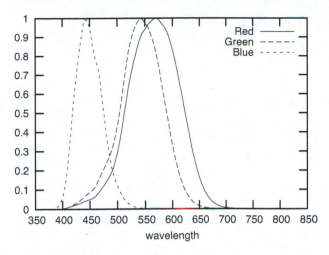

FIGURE 6.2: Normalized sensitivities of cones.

vision is based on three basic components (signals) which allows us to distinguish different colors.

Detailed study of tristimulus theory was conducted independently in the late 1920s by W. David Wright and John Guild. In their experiments a group of observers were shown two colored dots. One dot was some chosen color and the other was a mixture of pure red, green and blue colors. The proportions of red, green and blue colors were adjustable. Observers were asked to adjust these proportions so that both dots appeared to be of the same color. One of the limitations of those experiments was that the field of view was very narrow (2°).

It was found that for the most pure spectral colors it was impossible to select a mixture of red, green and blue which was indistinguishable from the original. But if one of the primaries was added to the color then there existed an indistinguishable mixture of other primaries. Such cases were treated as if a negative amount of one primary was used. So it was found that for several colors (including pure spectral colors) amounts of red, green and blue contained negative values.

As a result of all these experiments the exact proportions of red, green and blue were obtained for pure spectral colors and for other colors. In Figure 6.3 you can see the weight for every pure spectral color from visible range using the following primaries – red (700 nm), green (546.1 nm) and blue (435.8 nm).

In Fig. 6.2 the normalized sensitivities of basic cones to various wavelengths are shown (they are scaled to the [0, 1] range).

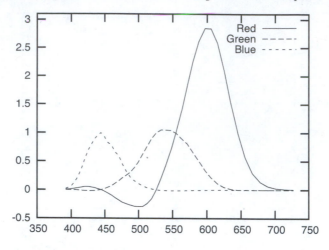

FIGURE 6.3: RGB weights for pure spectral colors.

6.1 $CIEXYZ$ color space

Since using negative weights made a color model based on mixing red, green and blue (RGB) inconvenient the Comision Internationale de L'Eclairage (CIE) in 1931 developed a new color model, called $CIE1931XYZ$. This model was based on the investigations of W. David Wright and John Guild. To ensure that any visible color can be described by three non-negative coefficients they used a linear transform.

The $CIE1931XYZ$ model has standardized the X, Y and Z standard observer color-matching functions $\bar{x}(\lambda)$, $\bar{y}(\lambda)$ and $\bar{z}(\lambda)$ (see Figure 6.4) converting SPD of any visible light into three non-negative coefficients X, Y and Z

$$X = \int I(\lambda)\bar{x}(\lambda)d\lambda,$$

$$Y = \int I(\lambda)\bar{y}(\lambda)d\lambda, \qquad (6.2)$$

$$Z = \int I(\lambda)\bar{z}(\lambda)d\lambda.$$

Every two colors which are observed as the same will have the same X-, Y- and Z-coordinates, so the $CIEXYZ$ color system provides a universal and device-independent (since primaries are given as tabulated color-matching functions $\bar{x}(\lambda)$, $\bar{y}(\lambda)$ and $\bar{z}(\lambda)$) way of measuring colors.

The color-matching function for the Y-component was intentionally chosen to coincide with the human's eye sensitivity – it shows how bright light with a given SPD is considered by an average observer.

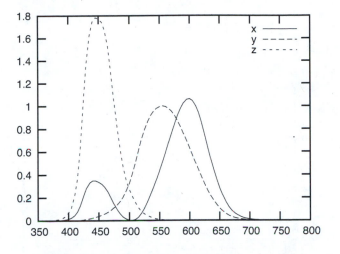

FIGURE 6.4: Standard CIE XYZ curves.

The $CIE1931XYZ$ color model is *additive* – we can add color coordinates X, Y and Z just as we add spectra. Additiveness of the $CIEXYZ$ model follows from Equations 6.2 — adding spectra means adding color coordinates.

Besides the $CIE1931XYZ$ color system based on observations using a 2° field of view, later a corrected color space $CIE1964XYZ$ was introduced which was based on a 10° field of view.

Using this color model we can just use 3D-vectors to represent various colors.

The three color coordinates X, Y and Z contain information about both the brightness of the color and its *chromaticity*. Usually it is convenient to separate brightness from chromaticity, which can be done by introducing x and y *chromaticity coordinates* by

$$x = \frac{X}{X + Y + Z},$$
$$y = \frac{Y}{X + Y + Z}. \tag{6.3}$$

Using chromaticity coordinates xy and brightness Y leads to the $CIE\,xyY$ color space. Equations (6.4) show how to convert it to the standard $CIEXYZ$ color space

$$X = \frac{Y}{y}x,$$

$$Z = \frac{Y}{y}(1 - x - y). \tag{6.4}$$

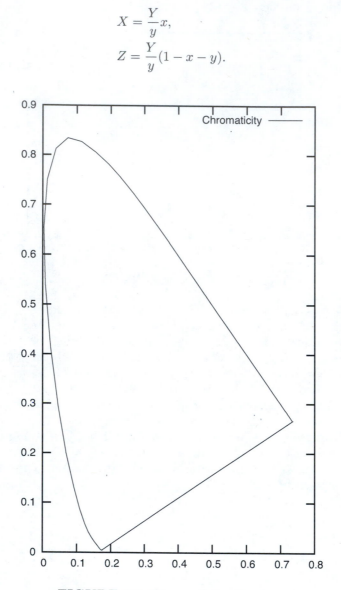

FIGURE 6.5: Chromaticity diagram.

Light with a flat power spectrum (SPD is constant over a visible spectrum) corresponds to chromaticity coordinates $x = \frac{1}{3}, y = \frac{1}{3}$.

We can plot chromaticities for all visible colors on an xy-coordinate plane. Thus, we get a shape called a *chromaticity diagram* (see Figure 6.5). Its upper bound (called a *spectral locus*) corresponds to pure spectral (monochromatic) colors. Lower bound (*line of purples*) corresponds to all colors which result in mixing together red and blue colors.

A line segment, connecting any two points A and B on the chromaticity diagram corresponds to all colors which can be obtained by mixing colors, corresponding to these points.

If we choose three points A, B and C on the chromaticity diagram then all colors, which can be obtained by mixing A, B and C in various proportions form a triangle ABC on the chromaticity diagram. From this fact it follows that no three selected colors can be used to generate all visible colors (the *gamut* of human vision is not a triangle).

On the other hand, a triangle formed by primaries red, green and blue as primaries covers most parts of the gamut and the colors are widely used in television and various monitors.

Besides $CIEXYZ$ and $CIExyY$ there are other color spaces, often derived from $CIEXYZ$ and more suitable for specific contexts and purposes. Below we will give a brief description of some color models most often used.

6.2   RGB color space

The color model, most often used in rendering as well as required in various monitors is an RGB color model. In this model to get colors three basic colors, Red, Green and Blue, are mixed in various proportions.

Every color in this model is described by proportions of red, green and blue in which they should be mixed to get this color. These proportions (r, g, b) are called *coordinates* of the color. Usually all coordinates are in the range $[0, 1]$, however sometimes they are assumed to be in the $[0, 255]$ range when 8-bit unsigned integers are used to keep these coordinates.

So for this model too (just as for the $CIEXYZ$ model) we can use 3D-vectors to represent colors in the RGB color space.

Despite RGB being used in many devices, it is not a *device-independent* model. Every device can have its own set of primaries which may look like red, green and blue, but be slightly different from primaries used elsewhere. So in order to be able to work with all these different variants, the devices have their primaries described by means of the $CIEXYZ$ color model, which allows easy conversion to and from the $CIEXYZ$ color space.

The NTSC (National Television System Committee) television in 1953 specified a set of primaries corresponding to the phosphors used in CRTs (Cathode Ray Tube) of that time. But since the characteristics of monitors have changed, now it is more correct to use the primaries from international agreement on primaries for HDTV (High-Definition television).

To convert colors between Rec. 709 RGB (ITU-R (ITU Radiocommuni-cation Sector) Recommendation BT.709, usually known by the abbreviation

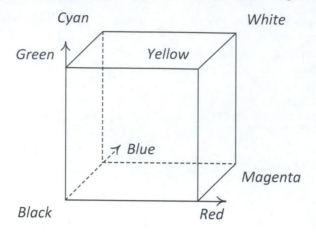

FIGURE 6.6: RGB color space.

Rec. 709 standardizes the format of high-definition television) and $CIEXYZ$ the following formulae should be used

$$\begin{pmatrix} R_{709} \\ G_{709} \\ B_{709} \end{pmatrix} = \begin{pmatrix} 3.240479 & -1.537150 & -0.498535 \\ -0.969256 & 1.875992 & 0.041556 \\ 0.055648 & -0.204043 & 1.057311 \end{pmatrix} \begin{pmatrix} X \\ Y \\ Z \end{pmatrix}, \qquad (6.5)$$

$$\begin{pmatrix} X \\ Y \\ Z \end{pmatrix} = \begin{pmatrix} 0.412453 & 0.357580 & 0.180423 \\ 0.212671 & 0.715160 & 0.072169 \\ 0.019334 & 0.119193 & 0.950227 \end{pmatrix} \begin{pmatrix} R_{709} \\ G_{709} \\ B_{709} \end{pmatrix}. \qquad (6.6)$$

The RGB color space is a unit cube $[0,1]^3$. Just as the $CIEXYZ$ color model, the RGB color model is also additive and colors can be simply added just as ordinary 3D-vectors.

For the purpose of rendering, the RGB color space is used to specify various colors and to perform various color calculations. However, there are tasks for which other color spaces are more adequate.

6.3 CMY and CMYK color spaces

The RGB color model is simple, intuitive and works well with light-emitting devices (such as monitors) and digital cameras. But when we come to color printing the situation changes. In color printing we deposit colored pigments (dyes) on the sheet of white paper. These pigments absorb some part of the incoming light spectra; the absorbed amount depends on the pigment properties and amount of pigment. The color we see on the paper when it is illuminated with white will contain all wavelengths from incoming spectra which were not absorbed by pigments.

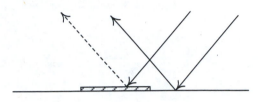

FIGURE 6.7: Reflected light from paper.

In some sense the pigment subtracts some color from the white color on the paper (see Figure 6.7). When we deposit several pigments on a paper they subtract corresponding colors from white (to be more precise, their absorption curves do multiply, but usually the absorption is measured by logarithmic densities of pigments and when spectras multiply densities add).

To achieve a wide range of reproducible colors three basic colors, cyan (C), magenta (M) and yellow (Y), should be used. If we look at the RGB color cube (see Figure 6.6) we will see that these colors correspond to corners of the RGB cube which are opposite to corners of red, green and blue colors.

The color model which describes the colors by the amount of cyan, magenta and yellow pigments applied to the paper is called the textitCMY color model. By its nature it is a *subtractive* color model – we subtract cyan, magenta and yellow from white. Note that the CMY color model is also device dependent – it depends on the absorption curves for the used pigments as well as properties of the paper on which they are deposited. The simplified equations (6.7) – (6.8) usually used to connect RGB and CMY color models are based on an assumption that absorption curves of pigments do not overlap, which is usually not true

$$\begin{pmatrix} c \\ m \\ y \end{pmatrix} = \begin{pmatrix} 1 - r \\ 1 - g \\ 1 - b \end{pmatrix}, \qquad (6.7)$$

$$\begin{pmatrix} r \\ g \\ b \end{pmatrix} = \begin{pmatrix} 1 - c \\ 1 - m \\ 1 - y \end{pmatrix}. \qquad (6.8)$$

Since in reality absorption curves of used pigments do overlap and their interaction with paper is not trivial, the high quality color printing is a complex task out of the scope of this book.

One of the drawbacks of the CMY color model is that printing gray colors requires equal amounts of all three pigments. It is bad since gray colors are used quite often and because used pigments are usually expensive; the printed paper gets wet due to the amount of deposited pigments and it can cause visible artifacts.

When we need to print a black (or gray) dot we need to print three colored dots located exactly on each other. But usually there are small inaccuracies which result in these three dots being slightly misplaced (see Figure 6.8). And due to these inaccuracies we see a black dot with "colored" border.

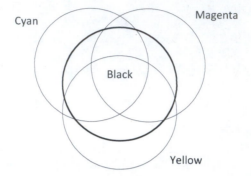

FIGURE 6.8: Dots misalignment resulting in a color border around black dots.

Often in order to cope with these problems a fourth pigment, black (K), is added to cyan, magenta and yellow. It replaces equal amounts of all colored pigments with the black pigment. This model is called a $CMYK$ and to translate from CMY to $CMYK$ color space the following equations (6.9) are used

$$
\begin{aligned}
k_{CMYK} &= \min(c, m, y), \\
c_{CMYK} &= c - k_{CMYK}, \\
m_{CMYK} &= m - k_{CMYK}, \\
y_{CMYK} &= y - k_{CMYK}.
\end{aligned}
\tag{6.9}
$$

6.4 HSV and HSL color spaces

All color models ($CIEXYZ$, $CIExyY$, RGB, CMY and $CMYK$) considered above, despite being very simple to work with, share one common drawback – they do not fit into the way artists usually think of colors. Artists tend to think of colors in terms of *brightness* (or *lightness*), *hue* and *saturation*.

Hue defines the pure color, *saturation* defines the purity of the color – how much it differs from the gray color of the same brightness. So hue and saturation together define the chromaticity of the color but in a more intuitive way.

There are two basic color spaces based on these parameters – HSV (Hue, Saturation, Value) and HSL (Hue, Saturation, Lightness), which are good for specifying colors.

6.4.1 HSV color model

The *HSV* color model was created by Alvy Ray Smith in 1978. Its color space is a top-down hex-cone whose top corresponds to bright colors ($V = 1$) and bottom – to black (see Figure 6.9).

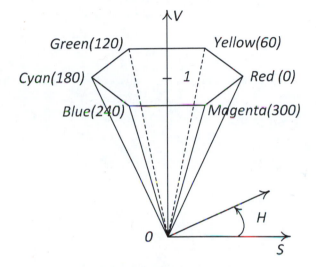

FIGURE 6.9: HSV color space.

In this model value roughly corresponds to brightness (so sometimes the model is called *HSB*) and is kept in the range $[0, 1]$. It is computed as a maximum of RGB components.

Note that this is not correct – the brightness of the color as perceived by an observer is really a mix of red, green and blue components with weights depending of the chosen primaries, but they are far from being equal.

Hue is measured as an angle and takes values from 0°(red) through yellow (60°), green (120°) and so on up to 360°. Saturation takes values from 0 to 1.

The following equations show conversion rules from the *RGB* to *HSV* color model (note that for zero value the hue is undefined)

$$V = M,$$

$$S = \frac{d}{M}, M > 0,$$

$$H = 60 \times \begin{cases} \frac{g-b}{d}, M = r, \\ \frac{b-r}{d} + 2, M = g, \\ \frac{r-g}{d} + 4, M = b. \end{cases} \tag{6.10}$$

Here

$$M = \max(r, g, b),$$
$$m = \min(r, g, b), \tag{6.11}$$
$$d = M - m$$

The following C++ code shows how to invert color between the HSV and RGB color spaces.

```cpp
vec3 rgbToHsv ( const vec3& rgb )
{
    int iMax = 0;        // index of maximum value
    int iMin = 0;        // index of minimum value

    for ( int i = 0; i < 3; i++ )
        if ( rgb [i] > rgb [iMax] )
            iMax = i;
        else
        if ( rgb [i] < rgb [iMin] )
            iMin = i;

    float mx = rgb [iMax];
    float mn = rgb [iMin];
    float d  = mx - mn;

    if ( mx < 0.001 )           // Hue undefined
        return vec3 ( 0 );

    float v = mx;
    float s = d / mx;
    float h;

    if ( iMax == 0 )
        h = 60 * (g - b) / d;
    else
    if ( iMax == 1 )
```

```
    h = 60 * (b - r) / d + 120;
  else
    h = 60 * (r - g) + 240;

  return vec3 ( h, s, v );
}

vec3 hsvToRgb ( const vec3& hsv )
{
  if ( hsv.y < 0.001 )
    return vec3 ( v );

  float h  = hsv.x * 6.0;
  float fi = floor ( h );
  int   i  = int ( fi );
  float f = h - fi;
  float p = hsv.z * (1.0 - hsv.y);
  float q = hsv.z * (1.0 - hsv.y * f);
  float t = hsv.z * (1.0 - hsv.y * (1.0 - f));

  if ( i == 0 )
    return vec3 ( v, t, p );
  else
  if ( i == 1 )
    return vec3 ( q, v, p );
  else
  if ( i == 2 )
    return vec3 ( p, v, t );
  else
  if ( i == 3 )
    return vec3 ( p, q, v );
  else
  if ( i == 4 )
    return vec3 ( t, p, v );
  else
    return vec3 ( v, p, q );
}
```

6.4.2   HSL color model

The *HSL* color space (sometimes called *HLS*) is very close to *HSV*, but uses slightly different component to measure brightness. Its color space is a bi-hexcone – the bottom point corresponds to black (where hue has no sense) and a top point to white color where hue is also undefined (see Figure 6.10).

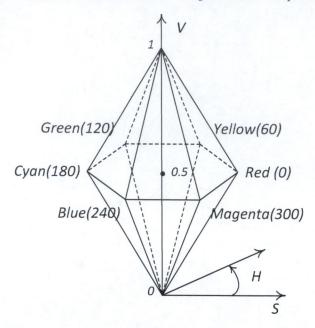

FIGURE 6.10: HSL color space.

To convert color from the RGB color space to HSL color space the following equations are used.

$$L = \frac{1}{2}(M + m),$$

$$S = \begin{cases} 0, d = 0, \\ \frac{d}{1 - |2L - 1|}, d > 0, \end{cases}$$

$$H = 60 \times \begin{cases} \frac{g-b}{d}, M = r, \\ \frac{b-r}{d} + 2, M = g, \\ \frac{r-g}{d} + 4, M = b. \end{cases}$$

(6.12)

Here M, m and d are defined as follows

$$M = \max(r, g, b),$$
$$m = \min(r, g, b),$$
$$d = M - m.$$

(6.13)

The following C++ code can be used to convert color from RGB to HSL and vice versa.

```
vec3 rgbToHsl ( const vec3& rgb )
```

```
{
    int iMax = 0;        // index of maximum value
    int iMin = 0;        // index of minimum value

    for ( int i = 0; i < 3; i++ )
        if ( rgb [i] > rgb [iMax] )
            iMax = i;
        else
        if ( rgb [i] < rgb [iMin] )
            iMin = i;

    float mx = rgb [iMax];
    float mn = rgb [iMin];
    float d  = mx - mn;

    if ( mx < 0.001 )            // Hue undefined
        return vec3 ( 0 );

    float l = (mx + mn) * 0.5;
    float s = d / (1 - fabs(2*l - 1));
    float h;

    if ( iMax == 0 )
        h = 60 * (g - b) / d;
    else
    if ( iMax == 1 )
        h = 60 * (b - r) / d + 120;
    else
        h = 60 * (r - g) + 240;

    return vec3 ( h, s, l );
}

vec3 hslToRgb ( const vec3& hsl )
{
    if ( hsl.y < EPS )           // S is zero
        return vec3 ( hsl.z );

    float v2  = (hsl.z <= 0.5) ? hsl.z * (1.0 + hsl.y) :
                (hsl.z + hsl.y - hsl.y * hsl.z);
    float v1 = 2 * hsl.z - v1;

    float h = hsv.x / 360.0;
    vec3   t ( h + 1.0/3.0, h, h - 1.0/3.0 );
```

```
if ( 6 * t.x < 1 )
    t.x = v1 + (v2-v1)*6.0*t.x;
else
if ( 2 * t.x < 1 )
    t.x = v2;
else
if ( 3 * t.x < 2 )
    t.x = v1 + (v2-v1)*((2.0/3.0)-t.x)*6.0;
else
    t.x = v1;

if ( 6 * t.y < 1 )
    t.y = v1 + (v2-v1)*6.0*t.y;
else
if ( 2 * t.x < 1 )
    t.y = v2;
else
if ( 3 * t.y < 2 )
    t.y = v1 + (v2-v1)*((2.0/3.0)-t.y)*6.0;
else
    t.y = v1;

if ( 6 * t.z < 1 )
    t.z = v1 + (v2-v1)*6.0*t.z;
else
if ( 2 * t.z < 1 )
    t.z = v2;
else
if ( 3 * t.z < 2 )
    t.z = v1 + (v2-v1)*((2.0/3.0)-t.z)*6.0;
else
    t.z = v1;

return t;
}
```

Another usage of these color models is that both of these models quickly locate pixels which are just shades of a specific color, e.g. if we want to locate green then the condition $|h - 120| < \epsilon$ will locate all green pixels regardless of their saturation and brightness. Also both spaces allow easy saturation changes, but it can lead to small changes of overall brightness due to the inaccurate definition of V and L.

6.5 Gamma correction

There is one more interesting fact about human vision – it has a non-linear response to light energy (*luminance*). Both $CIEXYZ$ and RGB color models use sensitivity curves to measure light energy (per unit area). So $CIEXYZ$ coordinates are a measure of energy and not a response to energy.

But human *perceptive response* to luminance is a non-linear function of luminance. The CIE defines the perceptive response to luminance as *lightness* and uses for it the following formula

$$L^* = \begin{cases} 116(\frac{Y}{Y_n})^{\frac{1}{3}} - 16, \frac{Y}{Y_n} > 0.008856, \\ 903.3\frac{Y}{Y_n}, \frac{Y}{Y_n} \leq 0.008856. \end{cases} \qquad (6.14)$$

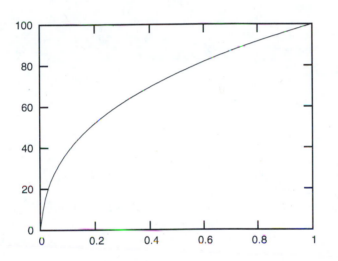

FIGURE 6.11: L^* as a function of Y.

Here Y_n denotes the reference luminance which is usually the luminance of white. As you can see from (6.14) L^* is a modified cube root function of luminance with a small linear segment near zero. Lightness defined by this formula takes values from 0 to 100. The linear segment is used to avoid singularity near zero (see Figure 6.11).

We can say that human vision has a non-linear transfer function which takes input luminance and produces a perceptual response to it as lightness.

The same can be said about most digital and analog devices, including monitors and digital cameras. For example, the Cathode Ray Tube (CRT) resulting luminance depends on the input voltage, so transfer function maps input voltage to output luminance. But in all of these cases the transfer function mapping an input signal to output takes a form of power function

$$f(x) = x^{\gamma}. \tag{6.15}$$

The transform (6.15) can be applied to video signals. In this case it is called *gamma correction*. Rec. 709 proposes a non-linear transfer function consisting of a small linear segment and a power function (see Figure 6.12)

$$E'_{709} = \begin{cases} 4.5E, E \leq 0.018, \\ 1.099E^{0.45} - 0.099, E > 0.018. \end{cases} \tag{6.16}$$

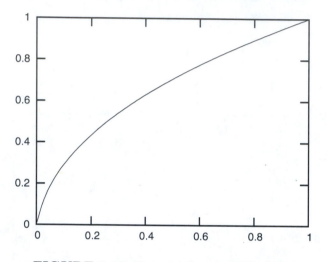

FIGURE 6.12: Transfer function $E'_{709}(E)$.

This transfer function is applied to all RGB components (which are called *linear*) and transforms them into non-linear components denoted as $R'G'B'$. A typical monitor inverts this transformation and given non-linear $R'G'B'$ input produces linear RGB output luminance

$$E = \begin{cases} \frac{E'_{709}}{4.5}, E'_{709} \leq 0.081, \\ (\frac{E'_{709}+0.099}{1.099})^{\frac{1}{0.45}}, E'_{709} > 0.081. \end{cases} \tag{6.17}$$

6.6 Yuv and YC_BC_R color spaces

The introduction of color television had posed a problem – how to encode a color signal so that old black-and-white TVs will be able to show it (as a black-and-white image). The obvious solution was to use some color model separating color luminance Y from chromaticity. So that brightness can be encoded just as for black-and-white TVs and chromaticity information will be sent in such a form that old TVs will ignore it.

6.6.1 $Y'uv$ color space

To the luminance Y color television had added two new chromaticity coordinates u and v. The resulting Yuv color space is used in major component video standards – PAL (*Phase Alternation Law*), NTSC (*National Television System Committee*) and SECAM (*Se'quentiel Couleur Avec Me'moire* or *Sequention Color with Memory*).

This color model is based on $R'G'B'$ components

$$
\begin{aligned}
Y' &= 0.299R' + 0.587G' + 0.114B', \\
u &= 0.492(B' - Y'), \\
v &= 0.877(R' - Y').
\end{aligned}
\tag{6.18}
$$

We can get $R'G'B'$ components back

$$
\begin{aligned}
R' &= Y' + 1.140v, \\
G' &= Y' - 0.395u - 0.581v, \\
B' &= Y' + 2.032u.
\end{aligned}
\tag{6.19}
$$

6.6.2 $Y'C_bC_r$ color space

The $Y'C_bC_r$ color space is defined as a part of ITU-R B5.609. It is a scaled and biased version of $Y'uv$ color space defined by the following equations

$$
\begin{aligned}
Y'_{609} &= 0.299R' + 0.587G' + 0.114B', \\
C_b &= -0.172R' - 0.339G' + 0.511B' + 128, \\
C_r &= 0.511R' - 0.428G' - 0.083B' + 128.
\end{aligned}
\tag{6.20}
$$

The inverse transformation is given by the formulae

$$
\begin{aligned}
R' &= Y'_{609} + 1.371(C_r - 128), \\
G' &= Y'_{609} - 0.698(C_r - 128) - 0.336(C_b - 128), \\
B' &= Y'_{609} + 1.732(C_b - 128).
\end{aligned}
\tag{6.21}
$$

In these equations it is assumed that $R'G'B'$ components take values from the 16 to 235 for reserving some place for signal processing and noise.

According to Rec. 709 for HDTV the $Y'_{709}C_bC_r$ is defined with slightly different coefficients

$$Y'_{709} = 0.213R' + 0.715G' + 0.007B',$$
$$C_b = -0.117R' - 0.394G' + 0.511B' + 128, \qquad (6.22)$$
$$C_r = 0.511R' - 0.464G' - 0.047B' + 128.$$

6.7 Perceptually uniform color spaces, $L^*u^*v^*$ and $L^*a^*b^*$ color spaces

All previous color spaces have one common drawback – they are not *perceptually uniform*. It means that if we change slightly color coordinates then the difference between original color and a modified one perceived by an observer will be strongly dependent on the color itself. So the same change of color coordinates will be perceived as a small change for some colors and as a big change for other colors.

The perceptual uniformity is a desirable property for many cases – it can help in selecting colors, allow for more accurate locating of specific colors and ensures that errors introduced by compression of color images do not vary wildly depending on the color.

There are two well-known perceptually uniform color models, both are based on the $CIEXYZ$ color space – $CIEL^*u^*v^*$ and $CIEL^*a^*b^*$.

To convert color from the $CIEXYZ$ color space to both of these color spaces we need to compute lightness by Equation (6.14) and use some color which is our *reference white color* - X_n, Y_n and Z_n.

For $CIEL^*u^*v^*$ we compute u' and v'

$$u' = \frac{4X}{X + 15Y + 3Z},$$
$$v' = \frac{9Y}{X + 15Y + 3Z}. \qquad (6.23)$$

Having computed these values we can get u^* and v^* using the equations

$$u^* = 13L^*(u' - u'_n),$$
$$v^* = 13L^*(v' - v'_n). \qquad (6.24)$$

And then for $CIEL^*a^*b^*$ we compute a^* and b^*

$$a^* = 500\left[(\frac{X}{X_n})^{1/3} - (\frac{Y}{Y_n})^{1/3}\right],$$
$$b^* = 200\left[(\frac{Y}{Y_n})^{1/3} - (\frac{Z}{Z_n})^{1/3}\right]. \qquad (6.25)$$

6.8 *sRGB* color space

Widely used in various devices such as LCD monitors, digital cameras, scanners and many others is the sRGB color space, created by HP and Microsoft. Now it is endorsed by W3C, Exif, Intel, Pantone, Corel and many others. It has hardware support in modern GPUs, which allows reading textures specified in *sRGB* and rendering a result in *sRGB*.

This color space is based on the same primaries which are used in HDTV. Designed to match typical home and office viewing conditions, it includes its own transfer function.

To convert color from $CIEXYZ$ to $sRGB$ we first need to compute linear components R_l, G_l and B_l using the equation

$$\begin{pmatrix} R_l \\ G_l \\ B_l \end{pmatrix} = \begin{pmatrix} 3.2406 & -1.5372 & -0.4986 \\ -0.9689 & 1.8758 & 0.0415 \\ 0.0557 & -0.2040 & 1.0570 \end{pmatrix} \cdot \begin{pmatrix} X \\ Y \\ Z \end{pmatrix} \quad (6.26)$$

Then each of these linear components (all of them are in the range $[0, 1]$ is converted to resulting *sRGB* values by using the transfer function $c_s(x)$ defined by the formula (6.27)

$$c_s(x) = \begin{cases} 12.92x, x \leq 0.0031308, \\ (1.055)x^{1/2.4}, x > 0.0031308. \end{cases} \quad (6.27)$$

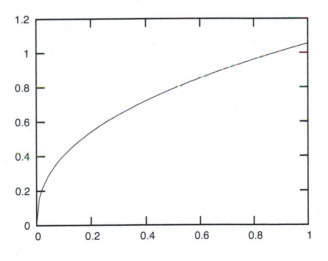

FIGURE 6.13: Transfer function $c_s(x)$.

To convert from *sRGB* non-linear components to linear ones we use the inverted transfer function $c_l(x)$

$$c_l(x) = \begin{cases} \frac{x}{12.92}, x \le 0.04045, \\ (\frac{x+0.055}{1.055})^{2.4}, x > 0.04045. \end{cases} \tag{6.28}$$

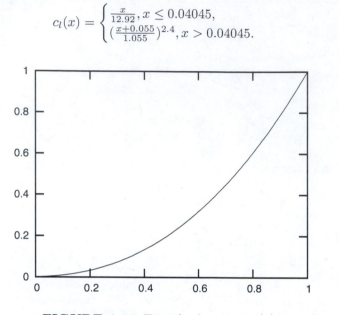

FIGURE 6.14: Transfer function $c_l(x)$.

Chapter 7

Basics freeglut and GLEW for OpenGL rendering

One of the simplest libraries proving window creation and user interaction is a GLUT library. It is the cross-platform library written for OpenGL and in OpenGL style. This library contains a small number of functions allowing the user to create one or more windows for OpenGL rendering and process events from the mouse and keyboard.

The GLUT library supports only basic window events – the window has been resized, the window needs to draw its contents, a key on the keyboard has been pressed or released, a mouse has moved or a mouse button was pressed or released. All such events processing is based on *callbacks* – you write functions to process specific events and set them as callbacks for a specific window. When the event happens, a corresponding callback function is called.

Various OpenGL demos and examples have been written using GLUT – it is very small and easy to use. However, GLUT is not open-source.

Using OpenGL 3 and higher requires creation of a special context for it and original GLUT cannot create such a context. Fortunately, there is an open-source (and cross-platform) library **freeglut** which supports all the functionality of GLUT and adds a functionality of its own.

One part of such added functionality is the creation of an OpenGL 3 context in an easy way. We will be using freeglut throught this book for OpenGL examples.

All the code using freeglut and OpenGL is cross-platform – you can compile and execute it on both Microsoft Windows and Linux.

7.1 freeglut initialization

Just as with the original GLUT library, freeglut needs to be properly initalized before any windows can be created. Below you can see how GLUT is initialized.

```
int main ( int argc, char * argv [] )
{
  glutInit( &argc, argv );
  glutInitDisplayMode( GLUT_DOUBLE | GLUT_RGB |
                       GLUT_DEPTH );
```

Here the **glutInit** command initializes the library itself and the **glutInit-DisplayMode** command is used to specify various display properties for the windows that will be later created.

Using this command we specify that we want *double buffering* for smooth and flicker-free animation (GLUT_DOUBLE), RGB color buffer (GLUT_RGB or GLUT_RGBA) and a depth buffer (GLUT_DEPTH). The following command will set the creation of color, depth and stencil buffers.

```
glutInitDisplayMode( GLUT_DOUBLE | GLUT_RGB |
                     GLUT_DEPTH | GLUT_STENCIL );
```

Double buffering means that we have two color buffers – contents of one of these buffers is shown in the window and another one is used for rendering into. When rendering into the buffer is complete, freeglut swaps these two buffers so that in the window we only see the complete result of the rendering. A *single buffering* (using the same buffer for showing its contents in the window and rendering into) can result in seeing parts of the image which should not be seen due to being obscured later from our view in the rendering – the so-called *flicker*.

Our next step in freeglut initialization (which differs from what we have in GLUT) is specifying just what OpenGL context we want. The following example shows creations of OpenGL 3.3 forward-compatible context (i.e., with all deprecated functionality removed) and debug context with a core profile.

```
glutInitContextVersion ( 3, 3 );
glutInitContextFlags ( GLUT_FORWARD_COMPATIBLE |
                                    GLUT_DEBUG );
glutInitContextProfile ( GLUT_CORE_PROFILE );
```

7.2 Window creation

After we have specified what context we want, we can create one or more windows. For some reason we specify window size and position in additional commands before window creation. Commands shown below create a window labeled "Text window" with the upper-left corner at a pixel with position (100,200) and with the width and height of client area equal to 500 pixels.

```
glutInitWindowPos( 100, 200 );
glutInitWindowSize( 500, 500 );
glutCreateWindow( "Test_window" );
```

Actually **glutCreateWindow** returns an integer window id which can be later used if we want to work with more than one window. Also this command makes the created window the active window so that the following commands setting various callbacks set them for this window only.

Please note that **glutCreateWindow** also creates the OpenGL context. So you can call various OpenGL commands only after the first call to **glutCreateWindow**.

7.3 Processing events

One of the first callbacks we should set (one that really will be called first) is a *resize* (or *reshape*) handler. This callback will be called after the window creation and every time the window is resized.

Resize callback receives the new size of the window in its parameters and in the simplest case just calls **glViewport** to set up a rendering area to coincide with the client area of the window.

```
void reshape ( int newWidth, int newHeight )
{
    glViewport ( 0, 0, newWidth, newHeight );
}
```

Function **glutReshapeFunc** sets the resize callback for the active window. The following example will set reshape callback to the function *reshape* we have shown above.

```
glutReshapeFunc ( reshape );
```

Another callback which should be set is a *display* callback. This callback is called every time a window needs to draw its contents. It renders an image using OpenGL commands and then calls **glutSwapBuffers** when rendering is complete. Note that it is safe to call **glutSwapBuffers** even if no double buffering is used. Shown below is the simplest variant of a display callback which just clears the window.

```
void display ()
{
  glClear ( GL_COLOR_BUFFER_BIT | GL_DEPTH_BUFFER_BIT );
  glutSwapBuffers ();
}
```

Function **glutDisplayFunc** sets the display callback for the active window.

```
glutDisplayFunc ( display );
```

Also we can specify callbacks for various keyboard and mouse events. The simplest keyboard event which can be processed is when a key is pressed generating a character. The callback receives the generated character and mouse coordinates in pixels (relative to the top-left window corner).

Below is shown simple keyboard handler which just quits the application when the Escape or 'Q' key is pressed.

```
void keyPressed ( unsigned char ch, int x, int y )
{
  if ( ch == 27 || ch == 'q' || ch == 'Q' )
    exit ( 0 );
}
```

To set this keyboard handler, the **glutKeyboardFunc** command is used.

```
glutKeyboardFunc ( keyPressed );
```

Freeglut also provides another keyboard callback which is called when the key generating a character is released. It is similar to the above callback and can be set by calling the **glutKeyboardUpFunc** command.

There are keys which do not generate characters when pressed such as functional keys, shift, control, arrows keys, etc. For such keys you can also set a *keypress* callback which receives a value identifying the key being pressed and mouse coordinates at the time of the key being pressed.

```
void specialKey ( int key, int x, int y )
{
  if ( key == GLUT_SHIFT )
    printf ( "Shift_is_pressed\n" );

  if ( key == GLUT_KEY_F1 )
    printf ( "F1_is_pressed\n" );
}
```

Such a callback is set up by the following function call.

```
glutSpecialFunc ( specialKey );
```

It is possible to set up callback not only for a special key press, but also for a special key release. It also receives a key code and mouse coordinates at the moment of key release.

```
void specialKeyUp ( int key, int x, int y )
{
  if ( key == GLUT_SHIFT )
    printf ( "Shift_is_released\n" );
}
```

To set this callback, the **glutSpecialUpFunc** command is used.

GLUT (and freeglut) also allow to set up various mouse handlers. The simplest mouse handler is called when a mouse button is either pressed or released.

```
void mouse ( int button, int state, int x, int y )
{
  if ( button == GLUT_LEFT_BUTTON )
    if ( state == GLUT_DOWN )
      printf ( "Left_button_pressed_at_(%d,%d)\n", x, y );
    else
      printf ( "Left_button_released_at_(%d,%d)\n", x, y );
}
```

This callback is set for an active window by calling the **glutMouseFunc** command.

Also it is possible to set callback, which will be called when the mouse is moved. GLUT (and freeglut) differentiate mouse movements when some mouse is pressed (active) and when no mouse button is pressed (passive).

```
void mouseMove ( int x, int y )
{
  printf ( "x_=_%4d_y_=_%4d\r", x, y );
}
```

To set up callback for active mouse movements **glutMotionFunc** is called and to set callback for passive mouse movement **glutPassiveMition** is called.

```
glutMotion        ( mouseMove );
glutPassiveMotion ( mouseMove );
```

Another type of callback, which may be very useful for animations, is an *idle* callback – it is called whenever there are no events, which means very often.

```
void idle ()
{              // get time in seconds since program start
  float time = 0.001f*glutGet( GLUT_ELAPSED_TIME );
```

```
        // perform some animation
  . . .
        // request window be redrawn .
  glutPostRedisplay ();
}
```

The function shown above demonstrates how animation should be done. We set an idle handler and at the beginning it computes time in seconds since program start (by calling **glutGet**). Next it uses computed time to animate various properties, such as positions, angles, etc. Then we request that the window should be redrawn by calling **glutPostRedisplay**.

You should never directly call display function (or any other callback). Instead use **glutPostRedisplay**, which marks the window as needing a redraw so that it will be redrawn soon (by indireclty calling the display function).

In order to install idle callback use the **glutIdleFunc** command.

After the window is created and corresponding callbacks are set we should call the **glutMainLoop** function to start an event loop.

In this loop events for all set callbacks are processed by calling corresponding callbacks. Note that **glutMainLoop** never returns – it is an endless loop. So if you want to close the application you should directly call **exit** (as did our keyboard handler shown earlier).

7.4 Using the GLEW library

If you have a Microsoft Windows computer then by default you have either OpenGL 1.1 (Windows XP) or OpenGL 1.5 (Windows Vista and later). So how do we get access to OpenGL 3?

In order to access OpenGL 3 functions we use the same way we work with OpenGL extensions. In fact, the development of OpenGL is just the process of moving some functionality from an extension into the core OpenGL.

When we work with OpenGL extensions we get pointers to the functions we want (and which are absent in what OpenGL we have). On any major platform we can get OpenGL functions (from various extensions and OpenGL 3 and later) just by name. We use functions like **wglGetProcAddress** (for Microsoft Windows) which takes the name of the command and returns the pointer to it.

Then we can define a variable whose name coincides with the function whose address we get and set it to point to this command. After this we can just use this variable as if it was a function.

But manually creating such variables and initializing them in such a way is very tedious so we will use a library which will do it for us. The GLEW library is an open-source cross-platform library allowing access to nearly all OpenGL extensions and also OpenGL 3 and OpenGL 4 commands.

All you need in order to use GLEW is to include corresponding headers in your source files, include GLEW library for linking and perform GLEW initialization before using it at runtime.

Below is shown a correct way to include GLEW headers. It not only includes headers common to all platforms but will also include headers specific for the platform you are compiling.

```
#include <GL/glew.h>
#ifdef _WIN32
    #include <GL/wglew.h>
#else
    #include <GL/glxew.h>
#endif
```

In order to initialize GLEW you need to set global variable **glewExperimental** to GL_TRUE and call **glewInit**. After that call **glGetError** as GLEW often creates an OpenGL error.

```
glewExperimental = GL_TRUE;
glewInit ();
glGetError ();
```

GLEW comes with predefined macros, which can be used for checking whether the specific OpenGL extension or OpenGL with a given version is supported.

```
if ( !GLEW_VERSION_3_3 )
    printf ( "OpenGL 3.3 not supported\n" );
```

```
if ( GLEW_ARB_tessellation_shader )
    printf ( "Extension GL_ARB_tessellation_shader is supported\n" );
```

7.5   Wrapping freeglut in a C++ class

We will wrap freeglut functionality in a simple class *GlutWindow*. It will automatically call all required initializers for freeglut and GLEW. Here handlers correspond to virtual methods of this class.

The simplest application using this class is shown below.

```
#include "GlutWindow.h"

class MyWindow : public GlutWindow
{
```

```
public :
  MyWindow () :
    GlutWindow  ( 200, 200, 500, 500, "GL_3.3_demo" )
  {
    if ( !GLEW_VERSION_3_3 )
    {
      printf ( "OpenGL_3.3_not_supported.\n" );

      exit ( 1 );
    }
  }

  virtual        void      redisplay ()
  {
    glClear ( GL_COLOR_BUFFER_BIT | GL_DEPTH_BUFFER_BIT );
  }
};

int main ( int argc, char * argv [] )
{
  GlutWindow :: init ( argc, argv );

  MyWindow        win ;

  GlutWindow :: run ();

  return 0;
}
```

Chapter 8

Hidden surface removal

When we need to render a group of 3D-polygons/objects usually some of them are obscured (at least partially) from the observer by others. For a large number of objects the number of really visible objects constitutes usually only a small fraction of all objects – it is easily observed for architectural scenes.

And so we have to determine what is visible for a given observer location (and orientation in space) and what is not. For the simplest cases we can use graphics hardware (i.e., the *z-buffer*) for this purpose. But when we have complex scenes we need special optimizations for our code to work fast.

When we have selected a projection (we will assume a perspective projection with center c for the rest of the chapter) we obtain an image plane onto which we are projecting and a set of projectors – lines along which projection occurs.

All points on a projector are projected into the same point in the image plane. For points P_1 and P_2 lying on the same projector the point which is closer to the image plane will be considered as visible and the other point hidden (see Figure 8.1).

The task of *Hidden Surface Removal* (HSR, or as it is also called *visible surface determination*) is to determine what point will be visible for every pixel of the image plane (for every projector).

There are cases when only edges of polygons are rendered and we want to remove edges hidden by polygons if polygons were to be drawn. It leads to

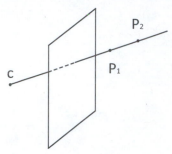

FIGURE 8.1: A projector coming through two points.

the task of hidden edges removal (see Figure 8.2 – in the left figure no edges are removed; in the right, the hidden edges are removed).

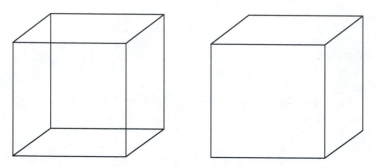

FIGURE 8.2: Removing hidden edges.

In modern computer graphics we usually need to display whole polygons and objects, determining for every pixel what object will be visible.

This task looks easy for a few simple objects but it can become very complex and time-consuming when the complexity of the scene increases and we are dealing with millions of objects. For such scenes only a small percentage of all the objects are really visible and therefore checking every object (as well as checking every object against every other object) becomes prohibitively expensive for real-time applications.

We will start with some basic notions, review various algorithms used for hidden surface removal and then proceed to several complex algorithms which can be used for rendering complex scenes.

It was shown that all HSR algorithms are based on sorting and really differ in the type of sorting used. We don't care about hidden objects but want to locate the visible ones. For classical algorithms this sorting is pretty evident. The modern algorithms are usually a combination of several simpler ones including various optimizations and spatial indices to handle complex scenes in realtime. Note however that for complex scenes we do not need complete sorting.

To determine visibility we need to compare objects with each other to find which parts are obscured. This analysis can be performed in 3D-space (called *object space*), usually comparing objects with each other or in *image space*, comparing objects' projections for every pixel of the image plane.

Usually *object-space* algorithms are more complex and have complexity $O(N^2)$, where N is the total number of objects. Image-space algorithms tend to be simpler and have complexity $O(NP)$, where P is the total number of pixels.

8.1 Basic notions

8.1.1 Front-facing and back-facing polygons

If we have a closed polyhedron then we can specify for each of its faces the normal that points outside of the polyhedron, the normal is called *outer normal*.

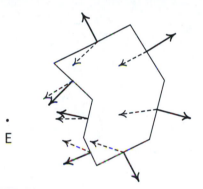

FIGURE 8.3: Front-facing and back-facing faces of the polygon.

The closed polyhedron has no holes through which we can see its interior. Because of it the only faces we can see are the faces whose outer normals point in the direction of the observer (see Figure 8.3).

Such faces are called *front-facing* and faces for which outer normals point from the observer are called *back-facing*. The observer cannot see any of the back-facing faces – they will always be hidden by front-facing ones.

For a convex polyhedron all of its front faces will be completely visible (no front face will hide another front face due to convexity), so for this case the visibility task is easily solved. But for a non-convex polyhedron or for a set of convex polyhedrons some front-facing polygons can hide other front-facing polygons from the observer (see Figure 8.4).

When we trace a ray from the observer (just as for the 2D-test of points

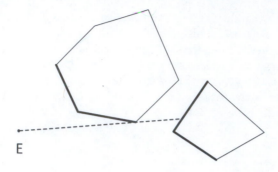

FIGURE 8.4: For non-convex scenes some front-facing faces can occlude other front-facing faces.

inside the polygon) the number of times the ray pierces front-facing polygons is equal to the number of times it pierces back-facing polygons (see Figure 3.17).

In general, the number of back-facing polygons is about half of all the polygons, so by rejecting them (as they are always hidden from the observer) we can reduce the number of processed polygons by a factor of two.

8.1.2 Depth complexity

For a projector coming through some pixel of the image plane, we can count the number of its intersections with front-facing polygons. This number is called the *depth complexity* for the pixel. Depth complexity of one or zero corresponds to a simple case – no more than one object covers this pixel; determining visibility for it becomes very easy.

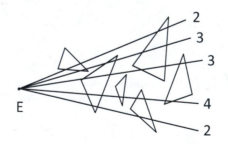

FIGURE 8.5: Depth complexity for several rays.

But when the depth complexity grows the problem becomes more difficult. If the depth complexity is equal to 10 we have 10 objects projecting onto this pixel and only one of them is really visible, the other 9 are a waste of resources.

Taking all pixels of the image to be rendered we can define average depth complexity for the scene. It depends on the scene and also on the position and orientation of the observer. An example of scenes with very high depth complexity is any architectural scene.

When we are dealing with scenes with high depth complexity the more important task is not to find what objects are visible but to reject as quickly as possible most of the objects which are not visible. Remaining objects can be handled by some traditional algorithms (provided we can quickly find a small set of visible objects).

8.1.3   Coherence

A very important notion that we have first encountered in filling shapes is *coherence*. Utilizing coherence is a key to building efficient HSR algorithms.

There are several types of coherence which we can utilize:

- object coherence

- face coherence

- edge coherence

- area (pixel) coherence

- frame (time) coherence.

Object coherence means that two nearby objects tend to be visible (or hidden) simultaneously. *Face coherence* implies that if one face of an object is visible (hidden) then adjacent faces are visible (hidden) too. *Edge coherence* means that nearby edges usually belong to the same face or faces that are close to each other and usually have the same visibility. *Area coherence* means that if some pixel corresponds to a specific face/object then pixels nearby usually also correspond to the same face/object. *Frame* (or *time*) *coherence* means that a set of visible faces/objects usually changes very little from frame to frame.

Note that all these types of coherence are not strict rules – there are exceptions; they just reflect a common tendency or behavior which can be used to obtain a performance gain.

8.1.4   Occluders

Another important notion is an *occluder*. It is any object occluding some other objects. If we have an object or a polygon and an observer location then we can build an area in 3D-space which is occluded from the observer by this object/polygon (see Figure 8.6). Any object which lies completely within this area can be discarded as hidden.

If we have several occluders then we can utilize *occluder fusion* – testing against several occluders combined tend to get better results than testing

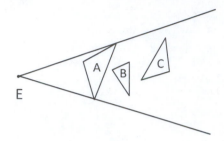

FIGURE 8.6: Polygon A as the occluder hides other polygons (B and C).

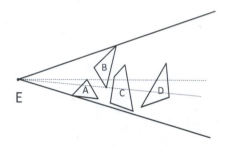

FIGURE 8.7: Occluder fusion.

each occluder in turn. In Figure 8.7 neither of the occluders A and B can hide object C but taken together they hide it.

It is a common technique in modern games to pick a set of occluders (making them as simplifications of real geometry) and use these occluders to cull hidden geometry. Creating such occluders we need to use simple polygons (the checks against them are easy), which give a *conservative estimate* to visibility. The given occluded area must always be inside a real occluded area so we cannot cull a visible object.

8.2 Ray casting

One of the simplest algorithms to determine what exactly is visible at every pixel of the image plane is just to build a ray from the position of the observer through the pixel. Then all objects are checked for intersecting this ray and the closest intersection to the observer gives a visible point for the pixel (see Figure 8.8).

This algorithm is called *ray casting*. It can be generalized to *ray tracing* – an algorithm for creating a photo-realistic images which not only determines

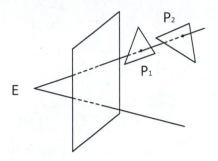

FIGURE 8.8: Ray casting.

visibility, but also computes shadows, reflections, refractions and many other effects.

The ray casting algorithm can be shown using the following pseudo-code.

```
for all pixels:
  for all objects:
    compare distance
```

The complexity of this algorithm is $O(NP)$ for the naive implementation checking every object for every ray. There exist many of its optimizations (usually based on various spatial index structures) which have the complexity of $O(P \log N)$.

One additional benefit of ray casting is its ability to work with non-polygonal data – any object for which we can compute an intersection with a ray can be processed.

In real-time tasks ray casting is sufficiently rarely used for visibility determination, however it is often used in other tasks, e.g., tracing a bullet through the scene to find a hit spot is usually done via ray casting.

8.3 z-buffer

Another classical HSR algorithm is called the *z-buffer* or *depth buffer* (we will use both terms interchangeably). This algorithm requires an additional buffer, where for each pixel the z-value of the projected point is kept. Usually depth values are kept as 16/24/32 bit unsigned integer values.

The choice of z is based on the fact that for canonical perspective projection z-value of the point correlates with the distance to the observer (center of projection). To find for two points P_1 and P_2 on the same projector which of them is closer to the observe,r we can just compare their z-coordinates, point with a smaller z-coordinate is closer to the observer (see Figure 8.9).

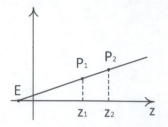

FIGURE 8.9: Comparing depths of two points P_1 and P_2 is the same as comparing z_1 and z_2.

The z-coordinate can be treated as the *depth* of the point.

A depth buffer algorithm keeps depth values for all pixels in a special buffer (2-dimensional array), called the *z-buffer* or *depth buffer*. At the start the depth for every pixel is set to the maximal value which can be represented with available bits (e.g., if we use 32-bit unsigned integers to keep depth then maximal value will be $2^{32} - 1$). Modern GPUs support using floating-point values for the z-buffer.

So each polygon is rasterized and for every resulting pixel its z-coordinate is computed using bilinear interpolation. Note that when we are rasterizing a polygon for every two pixels (x, y) and $(x + 1, y)$ their depths differ by the same amount Δz_1 and for every two pixels (x, y) and $(x, y + 1)$ their depths differ by amount Δz_2. These two deltas depend on the polygon so they are computed at the start of polygon rasterization and getting depth for the next pixel requires just one addition.

A computed z-value for the pixel is compared with the z-value for this pixel from the z-buffer. If the z-value for the produced pixel is smaller than the value in the buffer the pixel is closer to the observer and its z-value is written to the z-buffer and its color written to the frame buffer. If the z-value of the pixel is bigger or equal to the value in the buffer then the pixel is simply rejected.

The depth buffer algorithm can be described as the following pseudo-code.

```
for all objects:
  for all covered pixels:
    compare z
```

The depth buffer algorithm works in image space (just as the ray casting) and processes each polygon in turn. The algorithm utilizes coherence by using an incremental scheme for computing depth values. It produces correct results independently of the order in which polygons are processed.

From a sorting point of view it can be said that the depth buffer algorithm performs *radix sort* by x- and y-coordinates and then does z-sorting using only one comparison per pixel per polygon.

If we compare the depth buffer algorithm with the ray casting algorithm we note that they both use a loop for polygons and a loop for pixels, but these two loops are swapped. The ray casting outer loop is over pixels and the depth buffer outer loop is over polygons.

Both algorithms are easily parallelized but for the depth buffer an operation to be performed in parallel (comparing a depth) is much simpler than for ray casting (checking all objects for intersection with a ray). So right now the depth buffer algorithm is a defacto standard – it is implemented in hardware in all GPUs for many years.

There are hardware implementations of ray casting but they are not so widespread and cheap and usually used for specialized tasks such as volume rendering.

Hardware depth buffer is very fast and efficient but it still requires the processing all of the polygons; so for very large scenes it can become slow unless some other optimizations are performed.

8.4   Hierarchical z-buffer

A major improvement of the z-buffer algorithm utilizing all major types of coherence (in object space, in image space and frame coherence) was proposed by Ned Green, Michael Kass and Gavin Muller in 1993 and called the *hierarchical z-buffer*.

An important trick used in this algorithm is testing a polygon against the depth buffer. The polygon is rasterized and for every produced pixel its depth is compared with the corresponding value in the z-buffer (without modifying the buffer). If for every produced pixel its depth is greater or equal to the value in the depth buffer then the polygon is called *hidden* with respect to this z-buffer (see Figure 8.10). Note that rendering a polygon which is hidden with respect to the depth buffer does not change anything – all its pixels are rejected.

For a bounding box we can check its front-facing polygons against the depth buffer. If all of them are hidden then the box itself is called hidden with respect to the depth buffer (see Figure 8.11) and if the bounding box is hidden then all objects it contains are also hidden. It means we can use checking the bounding box of a polygon for being hidden to quickly reject whole groups of objects. To effectively use this possibility we need to organize all objects into some spatial tree.

A hierarchical z-buffer algorithm organizes all objects into an oct-tree. All rendering is done recursively, starting with a root of the tree and ending when leaves are reached.

If the node is a leaf then all objects contained in it are rendered by using a conventional z-buffer (and they are marked as already rendered for this frame so we do not attempt to render them again).

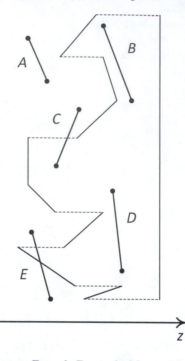

FIGURE 8.10: Polygons B and D are hidden with respect to the depth buffer. Polygons A, C and E are not hidden.

If the node is not a leaf then all of its child nodes starting with the closest to the observer are processed. Processing of the child node checks its bounding box for visibility against the z-buffer. If the node's bounding box is hidden the node is skipped. Otherwise we recursively process this node.

We utilize object space coherence by using an oct-tree and checking nodes for visibility. By processing child nodes in front-to-back order we process objects being closer to the observer (and therefore can hide other objects) first (see Figure 8.12).

It is evident that the sooner visible object will be processed the more hidden objects can be culled away. We don't know exactly what objects will be visible in the current frame, but we can utilize frame coherence by assuming that a set of visible objects for the current frame has only a small difference with a set of visible objects from the previous frame. So we keep a list of objects we rendered in the previous frame and start rendering a new frame by processing all these objects (and marking them as already rendered).

Then the hierarchical processing of the oct-tree starts. If visibility has not changed much from the previous frame then the majority of invisible objects will be quickly rejected by checking a bounding box of the node for visibility.

In this method we are constantly checking visibility of various bounding boxes. So making these checks faster can result in significant speed-up. In

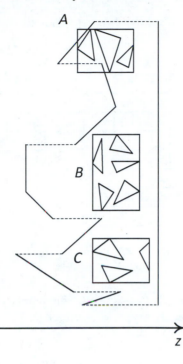

FIGURE 8.11: Testing a bounding box against the depth buffer – boxes B and C are hidden.

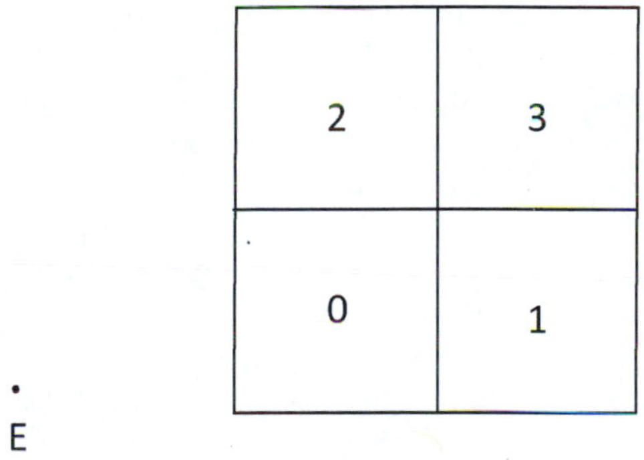

2	3
0	1

E

FIGURE 8.12: Order of processing child nodes for a given observer location E.

order to make it more efficient we can utilize coherence in image space. To do so we build from the z-buffer (after all objects visible in last frame are rendered) so-called *z-pyramid*.

The last level (base) of this pyramid is the z-buffer itself. To build the next level we group pixels from the previous level into 2×2 blocks and for every block select the maximal z-value from the four values of the block. Thus, we get a z-buffer whose size in each dimension is only one-half of the previous level.

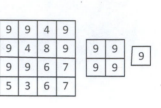

8	9	9	9	4	3	9	9
9	8	8	9	4	4	9	9
9	2	3	3	4	8	8	9
2	3	3	4	4	7	7	8
3	9	9	9	6	6	7	7
5	6	6	3	3	1	5	5
1	1	2	3	3	2	6	6
3	5	2	2	6	5	7	7

FIGURE 8.13: Levels of the z-pyramid.

This way we build a set of depth buffers, each one is 2×2 times smaller than the previous one. The last depth buffer is just one value – maximum z from the initial z-buffer. If we put one buffer on top of the previous one we get a pyramid (see Figure 8.13).

A depth pyramid can be used to quickly reject hidden polygons. The value at the top of depth pyramid corresponds to furthest point from the observer. If for all vertices of the polygon (or a bounding box) their depths are bigger than this value, then this polygon (or a box) cannot be visible and is hidden.

If we are not that lucky and checking vertices (it is sufficient to choose only one vertex - the one with minimal depth) against the value at the top of depth pyramid brings no success, then we go down one level using other levels of the pyramid going from the top (the most crude one but at the same time the cheapest of all) to the bottom (the most detailed but also the most expensive to check).

Thus, the algorithm of checking visibility of the polygon starts at the top of the pyramid – if value at the top is bigger than minimal depth of a polygon's vertices, then the polygon is hidden.

Otherwise we go one level down, trying to compare parts of the polygon against four depth values. If we're lucky we will be able to prove that the polygon is hidden or that some parts of it are hidden.

For parts that we are unable to prove are hidden we go down. As we go down we may simply use low-resolution rasterization of the polygon to check against levels of a pyramid. If all fails we come to the last level, i.e., the initial z-buffer, and perform pixel-by-pixel tests at initial resolution.

Using a depth pyramid helps us to prove that the polygon is hidden, making it sometimes very quick and easy. But it comes with a price – every time the initial z-buffer is modified we must update the pyramid, propagating changes up to the top. So it is not efficient to update the z-buffer every time the change is made and is usually done after a group of polygons have been rendered.

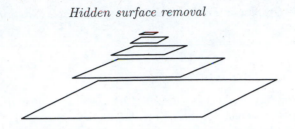

FIGURE 8.14: Levels arranged as a pyramid.

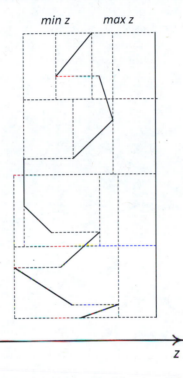

FIGURE 8.15: Depth pyramid.

Modern GPUs usually adopt some form of z-pyramid to accelerate rejecting of invisible parts of polygons and also support *Hardware Occlusion Queries (HOQs)*, sending test geometry to the GPU and getting visibility results for the sent geometry. But current architecture makes sending the query results back from the GPU to the CPU slow.

8.5 Priority algorithms

Since sorting lies at the heart of all HSR algorithms, naturally there is a group of algorithms which are based on the explicit sorting of polygons.

These methods sort the objects (usually polygons) so that if we simply rasterize and draw them in the sorted order the correct image will be obtained. Usually it means that we render distant polygons first and close to observer polygons last (*back-to-front order*).

For some datasets this approach works perfectly well, for example plotting a surface $z = f(x, y)$. Other cases require that polygons should be split, otherwise such ordering is impossible (see Figure 8.16).

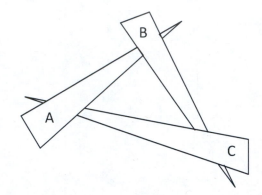

FIGURE 8.16: Triangles A, B and C cannot be sorted by occlusion.

8.5.1 Painter's algorithm

The simplest variant of a priority algorithm is a method that sorts all polygons according to either a minimal z-coordinate of its vertices or by a z-coordinate of the average of its vertices (see Figure 8.17).

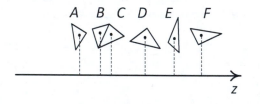

FIGURE 8.17: Sorting polygons by their center.

This algorithm is usually called a *painter's algorithm* – by analogy how a painter starts drawing with the farthest objects and then draws the nearest objects on top of the farther ones.

For the polygonal approximation of torus and other mathematical surfaces this algorithm works perfectly well, but there are cases when it fails producing an incorrect image.

The painter's algorithm does explicit sorting in object space and then performs comparison in the images space. For every frame of animation it requires explicit sorting, however it's possible to benefit from frame coherence – the order of sorted objects usually changes very little from frame to frame, so it's possible to use sorting methods which can benefit from this. No polygon splitting is performed, so not all cases can be handled correctly.

8.5.2 Using BSP-trees for HSR

The binary space partitioning trees (will be described in Chapter 10) can provide the correct ordering for any set of polygons and any observer location. Instead of sorting polygons, it organizes them into a binary tree using the simple property – if polygons A and B are located in different half-spaces relative to a given plane π, then a polygon located in the same half-space as the observer in no way can be hidden by the polygon located in another half-space (see Figure 8.18).

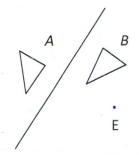

FIGURE 8.18: Ordering polygons A and B for a given observer location E.

In the process of building a BSP-tree, all necessary polygon splits are performed so for every tree node we have two subtrees located in different half-spaces. To get a correct back-to-front ordering for a given observer location, we need only to traverse the tree so that in each node we are choosing the order of traversal of both children so that we first traverse the child node corresponding to a half-space not containing the observer.

One of the most well-known applications of BSP-trees for hidden-surface removal is their usage in legendary First Person Shooter (FPS) Doom by idSoftware. The game is not pure 3D, but rather what is called *2.5D* – a flat 2D-map extruded into the third dimension.

All levels of the game were drawn as 2D-maps and their heights and material were assigned to edges (which became walls) and polygons (which became floors and ceilings). All edges comprising the level were compiled at the preprocessing stage into a 2D-BSP-tree.

The procedure for building a BSP-tree is just recursive processing of the set of edges which stops as soon as the edges form a part of a convex polygon boundary (a more detailed overview of BSP-trees will be given in Chapter 10). It is done because if edges are a part of the convex polygon boundary then no further ordering is required; we just have to remove back-facing ones. For the room in Figure 8.19 we need only one splitting plane (root of the tree) which forms two leaf nodes A_+ and A_-.

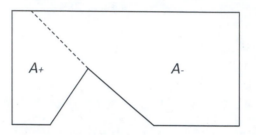

FIGURE 8.19: Splitting a non-convex room into two convex A_- and A_+.

The procedure decreases the height of the resulting BSP-tree and allows faster traversing. Also a game engine uses another property of the BSP-tree – a tree partitions space (plane for the 2D-case) into a set of convex polyhedrons (polygons for 2D case). In the Doom engine they are called *sectors*.

The BSP-tree is performing several tasks – using a bounding box for every node of the tree it quickly rejects all sectors which are out of a player's *field of view* and sorts remaining sectors.

However, the engine uses a *front-to-back* ordering of sectors – for this variant we start drawing polygons with the closest polygons. But then we have to track which pixels are already drawn and protect them from overwriting, which in Doom engine was performed using two *horizon lines* – all drawn pixels are either below the lower horizon line or above the upper horizon line. As polygons are drawn, the horizon lines are updated.

Another usage of the BSP-tree in the game engine is for collision detection.

8.6 Portals

Another simple and elegant algorithm used in many games is based on *portals*. Initially it was used for architectural geometry. It requires adding additional polygons (called *portals*) which split the geometry into a set of convex polyhedrons (see Figure 8.20).

The resulting geometry can be represented as a graph where nodes correspond to these convex polyhedrons (called *rooms*) and portal links (edges) between the nodes.

Once this graph is built, the rendering becomes very easy. We start with determining the room the observer is in. Then since it is convex all front-facing polygons of this room are drawn. Any other rooms are seen only through portals. So we check every portal connecting the room with others and build a frustum for every portal, determining the area of space which can be seen through this portal. This frustum is clipped by the portal itself since we are not interested in the current room itself, only in adjacent rooms (see Figure 8.22).

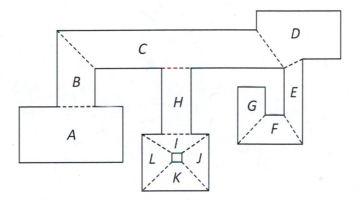

FIGURE 8.20: Portals splitting the scene into convex polygons.

Figure 8.21 shows the graph of nodes corresponding to Figure 8.20.

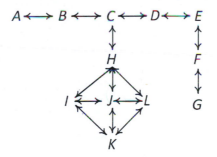

FIGURE 8.21: Graph of nodes for Fig. 8.20.

Then for every portal an adjacent room is clipped to the corresponding frustum and clipped polygons are drawn. All of its portals are clipped too and after clipping they are used to build new frustums, which are used to render rooms adjacent to it (see Figure 8.24). The process recursively renders rooms following chains of portals, tracking only the rooms which are seen by the observer.

Convexity of the rooms and the fact that we always clip geometry by the frustum ensures that the resulting image will be correct. Note that in fact we are doing portal-based front-to-back ordering of the rooms.

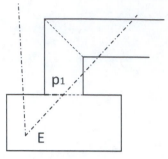

FIGURE 8.22: Viewing frustum for an observer located at E and the portal (p_1) it overlaps.

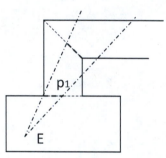

FIGURE 8.23: Frustum for the clipped portal p_1.

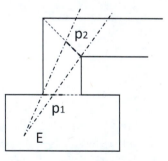

FIGURE 8.24: Frustum for the clipped portal p_2.

The rendering algorithm can be described by the following python-style pseudo-code.

```
def renderScene ( viewFrustum , room ):
  for poly in room.polygons:
    if not poly.isFrontFacing:
      continue

    clippedPoly = viewFrustum.clip ( poly )
    if not clippedPoly.isEmpty ():
      draw ( clippedPoly )

  for portals in room.portals:
    if not poly.isFrontFacing:
      continue

    clippedPortal = viewFrustum.clip ( portal )
    if not clippedPortal.isEmpty ()
      newFrustum = buildFrustum ( viewFrustum.origin ,
                                  clippedPortal )
      newFrustum.addClipPlane ( portal.plane )
      renderScene ( newFrustum ,
                    portal.adjacentRoom ( room ) )
```

This algorithm can be combined with the z-buffer algorithm removing the requirement that resulting rooms must be convex. The clipping of geometry by frustum for polygons can also be done in hardware (portals are usually clipped in software since they require more complex processing).

This allows the use of moderate number of portals even for complex scenes preserving the main advantage of the algorithm – it traverses only the rooms which are visible. The rooms which the observer cannot see will never be even touched. So the complexity of this algorithm depends only on the really visible geometry. Such algorithms are called *output-sensitive*.

The portals can be used to create various special effects, such as mirrors and what is called portals in fantasy and games – a hole into some other place.

8.7 Potentially-Visible Sets (PVS), computing PVS via portals

For determining visibility for static architecture there is another approach: the scene is split into parts and for every part a set of other parts which can be seen from it is precomputed and used later for rendering. The set of all parts which can be seen from one part (for all possible locations of observer inside this part and all possible observer orientations) is called a *Potentially Visible Set (PVS)* and was extensively used in all Quake games by idSoftware.

For all Quake games the 3D-BSP-tree is used to partition the game level into a set of convex polyhedrons – every leaf of the tree corresponds to one such polyhedron. The set of polygons associated with a leaf of the tree forms a part of the polyhedron's boundary. The missing part of its boundary are portals connecting adjacent polyhedrons (see Figure 8.25).

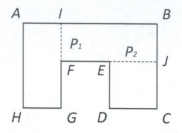

FIGURE 8.25: Using portals to split the scene into convex polygons.

In this figure the initial polygon $ABCDEFGH$ is split into three convex polygons $AIFGH$, $IBJEF$ and $EJCD$. The introduced portals are IF and EJ.

From node $AIFGH$ we can see only node $IBJEF$, from node $EJCD$ we can see only $IBGF$ and from $IBJEF$ we can see both of the other nodes. So we have just found PVS for every node of this scene. In reality computing PVS is a complex and time-consuming task and it is usually performed by portals (which is a reason why they are here).

One of the algorithms that creates such sets of potentially visible nodes is based on so-called *anti-penumbrae*.

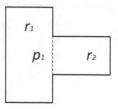

FIGURE 8.26: Room r_2 is always visible from r_1 through portal p_1 (there is at least one observer position and orientation allowing the observer to see part of room r_2).

If we have two nodes (rooms) r_1 and r_2 which are connected by a portal p_1, then obviously the PVS of room r_1 contains r_2 and vice versa (see Figure 8.26).

Having established that r_2 can be seen from r_1 through portal p_1 we check every portal p_i of the room r_2 – whether an observer can see rooms that are connected to r_1 through both portals p_1 and p_i.

If we have a portal p_2 which connects rooms r_2 and r_3, then we can build anti-penumbrae using these two portals (see Figure 8.27). We can describe of anti-penumbrae as follows. Imagine that room r_1 is filled with light. Then all areas which are directly lit by this light form anti-penumbrae.

To actually build anti-penumbrae we need to build a set of planes which bounds it. Each of this planes passes through the vertex of one portal and the edge of the other portal so that these portals are in different half-spaces relative to this plane (see Figure 8.27).

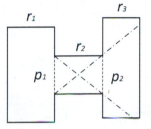

FIGURE 8.27: Planes forming anti-penumbrae for portals p_1 and p_2.

The resulting anti-penumbrae is an intersection of all half-spaces defined by these planes which do contain portal p_2 in them. Anti-penumbrae defines the area of space which can be seen through both portals.

If anti-penumbrae for portals p_1 and p_2 is not empty then room r_3 is added to the PVS of r_1. Then every portal of r_3 is clipped by this anti-penumbrae. Some of the portals will not be intersected by anti-penumbrae – it means that they lead to the rooms which cannot be seen through p_1 and p_2.

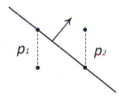

FIGURE 8.28: Planes bounding an anti-penumbrae come through the vertex of one portal and edge of other portal so that both portals are in different half-spaces relative to this plane.

Portals that have a not-empty intersection with anti-penumbrae connect r_3 to other rooms which can be seen. Each of them is clipped and from p_1 and each of the clipped portals we build new anti-penumbras (see Figures 8.29–8.30).

Using this procedure we track all rooms which can be seen from r_1 through portal p_1. At runtime it is sufficient to locate the node (room) the observer is in (which can be easily done using a BSP-tree) and take an already computed list of visible nodes. Then the list can be sorted using a BSP-tree and rendered using the order. So in runtime we process only nodes which can be seen, not even touching all other nodes however much they are.

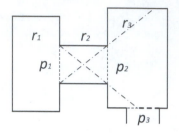

FIGURE 8.29: Anti-penumbrae built from portal p_1 and p_2 clips portal p_3.

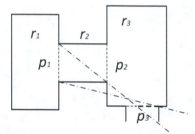

FIGURE 8.30: New anti-penumbrae is built from p_1 and p_3.

8.8 Hardware occlusion queries and their usage

As it was already mentioned in the section on the hierarchical z-buffer, the modern GPUs support *Hardware Occlusion Queries* (HOQs) – we can send test geometry objects to the GPU. These test objects will be rasterized and for every produced fragment a z-test will be performed. The resulting amount of fragments which pass this test (i.e., which should modify the contents of a z-buffer) we can get back from the GPU.

The main problems with these queries are that they impose some additional overhead (on processing and rasterizing test geometry) and high latency. The latency of such queries is due to the fact that requests for GPU are sent through a special queue. At one end the CPU is adding commands to this queue, at the other – the GPU is taking and executing them. It means that when we send a request to the GPU (e.g., to render test geometry) it will be rendered somewhere in the future. And if we want to get a feedback from it we have to wait. During it the CPU is waiting (*stalling*) and therefore puts nothing to the queue.

Since the CPU is waiting the command queue does not receive new requests, so when the GPU is done with our request it has nothing to do – it *starves*. So the resources of both the CPU and GPU are simply wasted because the whole architecture is mostly targeted and optimized at sending requests in one direction.

It means that we cannot just take the hierarchical z-buffer and simply rewrite it to use hardware occlusion queries. We should not process the tree depth-first as does hierarchical z-buffer algorithm, but rather process it breadth-first, trying to process many nodes simultaneously.

We send queries for many nodes interleaving them with some actual rendering, so we do not wait for results (because GPUs support asynchronous tests for HOQ results being ready) but do some work. As some of the results becomes ready we pick them and perform what can be done. But in many cases it will be cheaper not to wait, but to assume that the node in question is visible and proceed with it (we may get the actual result for this node on the next frame).

There are several algorithms targeted at effective usage of HOQ and we will describe one of them in detail – CHC++, the improved version of CHC (Coherent Hierarchical Culling) algorithm.

This algorithm is based on several important ideas:

- Organize all geometry into a hierarchy (BVH, kD-tree or oct-tree).

- In many cases it is more efficient (cheaper) to render geometry (or some parts of geometry) immediately without checking its visibility.

- If some object or node of the hierarchy is visible it's likely that it will remain visible for some time (several frames of animation).

- The CPU should not wait for the query results – after the query is sent it can render geometry immediately (using the query result in the next frame) or just continue to process other nodes in the hierarchy.

- It is more efficient to send queries by groups minimizing the number of GPU state changes.

The processing of geometry starts with the root of the tree and traverses the tree in the front-to-back order. Note that when processing nodes this way the CPU always has some more nodes to check (until tree processing is complete).

Traversing the tree is done via the priority queue – when we want to process a node we add its children to this queue. Nodes in it are prioritized by their distance to the observer.

Not all of the hierarchy nodes should be checked. It makes sense to check visibility of visible leaves of the tree (after they were rendered). Also it makes sense to check nodes in the tree where the visibility boundary lies (see Figure 8.31).

Not all inner nodes of the tree should be checked for visibility – we skip checking of the previously invisible node if its parent node was invisible on the previous frame too.

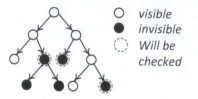

FIGURE 8.31: Tree whose nodes are marked with their status.

Testing previously visible and invisible nodes differs, so the algorithm groups all the visibility requests into two queues – the *v-queue*, containing the requests for previously visible nodes, and the *i-queue*, containing the queries for previously invisible nodes.

Since the results from the *v*-queue will be used only in the next frame they are issued all at once only when the CPU has no more work to do. The *i*-queue accumulates requests and when its size comes above some threshold (usually about 20-80 queries) they are send to the GPU as one group (batch).

One more optimization was used in CHC++ – combining several queries from the *i*-queue into one query (*multiquery*). If such multiquery returns no visible pixels, then all elementary queries from it are not required and corresponding nodes remain invisible.

Otherwise, the multi-query is split into original queries, so we get a gain from using it only when we're combining nodes with the high probability of being invisible. The basic criteria of such combining is a statistical one. To estimate the chance that the invisible node will remain invisible, we can use the number of consecutive frames the node was invisible. The bigger this number is the higher the probability that this node will remain invisible.

The whole algorithm can be represented with the following python-style pseudo-code.

```
def renderScene ( root ):
  distanceQueue.push ( root ) # start with root
                              # while we have more nodes
                              # or there are queries
    while (not distanceQueue.empty ()) or
        (not queryQueue.empty ()):
      while not queryQueue.empty ():
        if queryQueue.firstResultReady ():
          q = queryQueue.deque ()  # get query with result
```

```
          handleQuery ( q )    # process  result
      else:                    # send  next  query
        issueQuery ( vQueue.pop () )
                               # there  are  unprocessed  nodes
    if not distanceQueue.empty ():
      node = distanceQueue.deque ()
      if viewFrustum.overlap ( node ):
        if not node.wasVisible ():
          queryPreviouslyInvisible ( node )
        else:
          if node.isLeaf () and
             queryReasonable ( node ):
            vQueue.push ( node )

        traverse ( node )

    if distanceQueue.empty ():
      issueMultiQueries ()

  while not vQueue.empty ():
    issueQuery ( vQueue.pop () )

def traverse ( node ):
  if node.isLeaf ():
    render ( node )
  else:
    distanceQueue.pushChildren ( node )
    node.isVisihle = False

def pullUpVisibility ( node )
  while (node != None) and (not node.isVisible ):
    node.isVisible = True
    node = node.parent

def handleQuery ( query ):
                             # assume  node  visible
  if query.visiblePixels >= threshold:
    if query.isMultiquery ():
      queryIndividualNodes ( query )
    else:                    # node  has  become
      if not node.wasVisible (): # visible
        traverse ( node )
      pullUpVisibility ( node )  # update  tree  status
  else:
    node.isVisible = False
```

```
def queryPreviouslyInvisible ( node ):
  iQueue.push ( node )
  if iQueue.size >= maxBatchSize:
    issueMultiQueries ()

def issueMultiQueries ():
  while not iQueue.empty ():
    mq = iQueue.getNextMultiQuery ()
    issueQuery ( mq )
    iQueue.popNodes ( mq )
```

One important note about checking previously visible nodes – when a leaf node becomes visible we can assume that it will remain visible for at least n_{av} frames and skip checking for this number of frames.

So for such a node we should check it on the $n_{av} + 1$ frame after it was checked last time. But this fixed delay can result in bad behavior – imagine a situation when a camera moves or rotates so that many leaf nodes become visible. Then we will be sending queries from these nodes every $n_{av} + 1$ frame, possibly resulting in an uneven distribution of queries across the frames.

CHC++ uses a randomized approach – after the check that establishes the node is visible, for this node the random number r, such that $0 < r \leq n_{av}$ is chosen and its visibility will be checked at the $r + 1$ frame.

Chapter 9

Modern OpenGL: The beginning

Right now OpenGL is a mature cross-platform and cross-vendor Application Programming Interface (API) for both 2D- and 3D-graphics. It has been successfully used in many serious applications and games (including such titles as Doom III, Quake IV and Rage). There are OpenGL bindings for many languages including Java, C#, Python and many others. There is OpenGL ES (OpenGL for Embedded Systems) targeted at mobile systems like iOS- and Android-based phones and tablets. Also there is WebGL – binding for the java-script allowing use of OpenGL-accelerated graphics right in your browser.

9.1   History of OpenGL

OpenGL was based on a proprietary library IRIS GL by SGI Inc. but OpenGL is open and exists on a variety of platforms. The first version (1.0) of OpenGL appeared in 1992.

TABLE 9.1: Versions of OpenGL

Version	Released
1.0	January 1992
1.1	July 1992
1.2	March 1998
1.2.1	October 1998
1.3	August 2001
1.4	July 2002
1.5	July 2003
2.0	September 2004
2.1	July 2006
3.0	August 2008
3.1	March 2009
3.2	August 2009
3.3	March 2010
4.0	March 2010
4.1	July 2010
4.2	August 2011
4.3	August 2012

Initially the development of OpenGL was governed by the OpenGL Architectural Review Board (ARB) which at the beginning consisted of SGI, Microsoft, IBM, DEC and Intel. In 2006 control of the OpenGL specification passed to the Khronos group.

One of the important features of OpenGL is that vendors can add their own extensions to OpenGL, each such extension is identified by a string. There are many such extensions from various vendors (e.g., GL_NV_fence or GL_ATI_texture_mirror_once).

The whole development of OpenGL mostly consists of moving some functionality from extensions to the core OpenGL. Table 9.1 lists major versions of OpenGL with the release year.

In this book we work with OpenGL 3.0, but in Chapter 14 we will cover tessellation which is a feature of OpenGL 4.

9.2   Main concepts of OpenGL

OpenGL itself is based on several very simple principles and ideas and it is important to understand them in order to write correct and efficient code.

First of all, OpenGL is based on a *client-server model* (see Figure 9.1). Here the application is a client and the OpenGL driver/hardware is the server. Now it is commonplace that both client and server are on the same computer, but it does not need to be so. It implies that all commands to OpenGL are queued and executed strictly in the order in which they are sent (but usually not immediately since they are usually buffered in the queue).

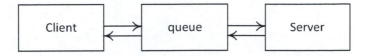

FIGURE 9.1: Client-server model.

OpenGL has its state. And this state comes in two parts – the *client-side state* and *server-side state.* The state of OpenGL is changed only by explicit commands from the application. From the state point of view OpenGL can be considered as a *Finite State Machine* (FSM).

An application working with OpenGL usually creates a window with a framebuffer to render to it. The application should create a context, only after creation of the context OpenGL commands can be used. The server-side state is kept with the context.

Creating context as well as creating a window is out of the OpenGL scope and is provided by the window system API.

OpenGL was developed to be portable and cross-platform. So it is completely dedicated to the rendering. All operations with windows and interacting with a user are out of the OpenGL scope – they should be provided by the window system. However, there are several cross-platform libraries which do provide such functionality.

When describing the depth buffer algorithm in Chapter 8 we have seen that it can be useful to associate with each pixel not only its color but also its depth value. OpenGL goes further and introduces the concept of buffers. Buffer is a 2D-array which stores some value for every pixel. OpenGL supports up to four color buffers, depth buffer, stencil buffer and accumulation buffer (see Figure 9.2). Also it can render into user-created framebuffers – so-called *render to texture.*

All rendering by OpenGL is performed into a framebuffer consisting of several buffers such as color buffers, depth buffer, stencil buffer and so on. Color buffer(s) contain RGBA color values – every color is represented by a 4D-vector containing values for red, green, blue and alpha components. Alpha component values are treated as *opacity* values. But the alpha value in a color buffer is not used to control transparency - it will not allow you to see through an OpenGL window.

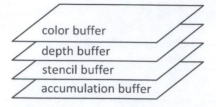

FIGURE 9.2: OpenGL buffers.

9.3   Programmable pipeline

From an architectural point of view OpenGL consists of several stages – data comes from one stage to the next. How the data is processed at each stage depends on the OpenGL state but these stages are fixed and the order of passing data between them is fixed too.

So the way OpenGL processes input data can be described as a pipeline consisting of various stages. Here we will cover the *programmable pipeline* it which several stages correspond to special programs executed on the GPU (*shaders*).

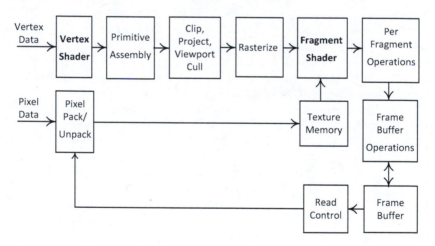

FIGURE 9.3: Programmable pipeline.

As you can see in Figure 9.3 vertex processing has been replaced by the *vertex shader* and most of fragment processing (excluding tests and blending) – by the *fragment shader*.

The vertex shader generates several per-vertex values which are interpolated during rasterization, and the fragment shader receives corresponding interpolated values for every fragment.

Initially the programmable pipeline appeared as a group of extensions and later (since OpenGL 2) became part of OpenGL. Below are shown the simplest vertex and fragment shaders.

The programmable pipeline was added to the OpenGL core since version 2.0. OpenGL 2.0 and OpenGL 2.1 support both fixed and programmable pipelines making it easy to migrate from a fixed pipeline to a programmable one.

OpenGL 3.0 (released in August, 2008) marked a serious change in OpenGL. It introduced a *deprecation* model – certain functions were marked as deprecated. These deprecated functions were planned to remove in future OpenGL versions.

All Fixed Function Pipeline (FFP) was marked as deprecated. Also such commands as **glBegin**, **glEnd** along with *immediate* mode and standard attributes were marked as deprecated too.

In *OpenGL Shading Language* (GLSL) all uniforms connected with the FFP (such as *gl_ModelViewMatrix*) were marked as deprecated. The alpha test as a part of FFP was marked as deprecated because such functionality can be easily implemented using shaders. All matrix operations (such as **glLoad-Identity**, **glPushMatrix** and others) were marked as deprecated. Primitive types GL_QUAD, GL_QUAD_STRIP and GL_POLYGON also were marked as deprecated.

Most of deprecated functions were removed in OpenGL 3.1 (released in March 2009). With a deprecation model came two possible contexts – *full context* which contains all deprecated functionality (it was moved into a GL_ARB_compatibility extension) and a *forward-compatible* context from which all deprecated functionality were removed.

Writing code for forward compatible context ensures full compatibility with later OpenGL versions.

OpenGL 3.2 (August 2009) introduced *profiles*. Profile defines some subset of OpenGL functionality. In OpenGL 3.2 two profiles – *core* and *compatibility* – were defined.

The API for creation context also was changed – context creation extensions was added for major platforms (*WGL_create_context* and *GLX_create_context*). Both these extensions create a specified context implementing a chosen profile (note that context can support only one profile).

But this creation API contains a catch – in order to create context with required properties we need a function exported by *WGL_create_context* or *GLX_create_context* OpenGL extensions. And in order to access extensions we need a valid OpenGL context!

So the common way for creating a new OpenGL context is the following – create a normal OpenGL context using standard means. Then this context is used to get a pointer to the function from the correct extension and to create a new context with required properties. After this old context is destroyed, only the new one is used.

All vertices specifying the primitives undergo transformations by the vertex shader in the *Vertex Shader* stage. The vertex shader must compute homogeneous coordinates for every vertex. Also it can process other vertex attributes and output several values for every vertex.

Transformed vertices together with connectivity information (telling how to build primitives from the vertices) go to the *Primitive Assembly* stage where the primitives are assembled from vertices.

The next stage clips these primitives against several planes (*Clipping*) and perspective division is performed (*Project*).

Then projected vertices are mapped into a viewport (a window, a part of the window or the whole screen). On this stage it is possible to perform culling of primitives based on whether they are front-face or back-face.

After this stage the projected 2D-primitives go to the *Rasterization* stage where they are converted into *fragments*. The term *fragment* means result of rasterization which may become a pixel (but may be rejected on some stage). The fragment has many additional attributes that the resulting pixel lacks (such as interpolated texture coordinates, interpolated normal and so on).

All produced fragments undergo a *Fragment Processing* stage. At this stage the fragment shader is executed for every fragment in order to produce an output value(or several output values). Usually this output value is a color.

The next stage, *Per-Fragment Operations*, performs various tests, rejecting fragments (depth, stencil and scissors tests). It also performs alpha-blending and logic operations with the contents of a framebuffer.

OpenGL can perform various image transfers – a block of data can be packed/unpacked either to the OpenGL internal format or from it and drawn on the screen or copied into the GPUs memory. The term *packing* corresponds to reading data from GPU memory to CPU memory and *unpacking* – copying from CPU memory to GPU memory.

9.3.1 Vertex processing

It is convenient to follow the approach from the fixed pipeline where every incoming vertex is processed in several steps. At the first step it is multiplied by a *model-view matrix*. This operation converts coordinates from the *object* (or *model*) *space* into the *eye-space* (*camera space*).

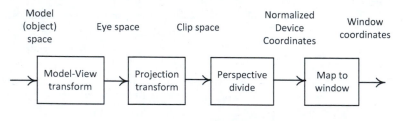

FIGURE 9.4: Vertex processing.

After that, the vector is multiplied by a *projection* matrix which transforms it into the *clip space*. Then a perspective divide follows resulting in *Normalized Device Coordinates (NDC)*. And the final step in vertex transformation is mapping from normalized device coordinates to the window coordinates (see Figure 9.4).

9.3.2 Rasterization

Rasterization of primitives produces so-called *fragments*. Each fragment corresponds to some pixel in a window (i.e., has its own window coordinates). But a fragment also contains additional information such as depth, interpolated color, texture coordinates and other attributes.

During rasterization all output of the vertex shader (except position) are interpolated over the primitive.

9.3.3 Fragment processing

At the fragment processing stage the color of the fragment is computed (but it is possible for a fragment shader to generate more than one value for each incoming fragment).

The fragment shader is executed on the GPU for every fragment generated during rasterization. It receives interpolated values of vertex shader outputs. The fragment shader also can simply reject the fragment instead of computing the output value.

9.3.4 Per-fragment operations

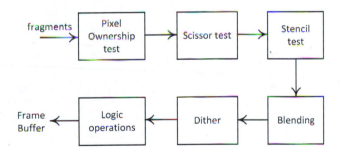

FIGURE 9.5: Per-fragment operations.

Per-fragment operations (see Figure 9.5) consist of several steps performed one after another in a predefined sequence. The first such step is a *pixel ownership* test. It checks whether the corresponding pixel on the screen belongs to OpenGL or is obscured by other windows. If the pixel does not belong to OpenGL then the window system is used to decide what to do with this fragment. Usually it is simply dropped (discarded).

If the fragment survives this test then a *scissor test* checks whether the corresponding pixel belongs to a given rectangular area, specified by programmer in the window coordinates. It may result in a fragment being dropped too. Note that this step can be disabled using OpenGL commands.

The *stencil test* fetches a corresponding value from a stencil buffer and based on it rejects the fragment. If no stencil buffer is present this test is simply skipped (the step may be disabled too).

And the last test for the fragment to pass is the *depth test* – interpolated depth value of the fragment is compared with the corresponding value from the depth buffer. This comparison may result in a fragment being dropped.

Then *blending* combines the color of the fragment with the corresponding color value stored in the color buffer. This step may be configured to choose one of several blending functions or just be disabled.

The computations of the color may be done with higher precision than we have in the framebuffer. In this case we have to round the computed color (losing some precision by doing so). If the *dithering* step is enabled then we will be choosing between two color values (corresponding to rounding up and down). This selection can depend only on the color value of the fragment and x- and y-window coordinates of the fragment. It is performed so that taking nearby pixels and averaging their colors will get a closer color to the original computed color than both variants of rounding (up and down).

In fact, dithering is the same technique which allows printing grayscale images in newspapers that are black-and-white only.

The last step executes a bitwise logic operation (such as *AND*) between the contents of the color buffer and resulting color of the fragment.

9.4   Our first OpenGL program

Now it is time for our first OpenGL program which renders something. It will simply draw a red triangle in a window, providing the variables in which we will keep identifiers of various OpenGL objects – vertex buffer object with vertices, vertex array objects, vertex and fragment shaders and program object.

In the beginning we need to subclass class GlutWindow.

```
class    MyWindow : public GlutWindow
{
    GLuint  program;
    GLuint  vertexShader, fragmentShader;
    GLuint  vao;
    GLuint  vbo;
    int     status;
```

```
public:
  MyWindow () : GlutWindow  ( 200, 200, 400, 400,
                             "First_GL_3.3_demo" )
  {
    createProgram ();
    glUseProgram   ( program );
    createBuffers ();
    setAttrPtr     ( "position", 3, VERTEX_SIZE,
                     (void *) 0 );
  }
```

The first thing that we need to do is to create a *vertex buffer object* (VBO) containing a triangle's vertices and corresponding *vertex array object* (VAO) that will contain all buffer bindings for us. Using standard OpenGL commands the corresponding code for method *createBuffers* will look as shown below.

```
void  MyWindow :: createBuffers ()
{
  glGenVertexArrays ( 1, &vao );
  glBindVertexArray ( vao );
  glGenBuffers      ( 1, &vbo );
  glBindBuffer      ( GL_ARRAY_BUFFER, vbo );
  glBufferData      ( GL_ARRAY_BUFFER,
                      NUM_VERTICES * VERTEX_SIZE,
                      vertices, GL_STATIC_DRAW );
}
```

As you can see in this method we create a vertex array object and vertex buffer object and fill the vertex buffer object with vertex data. A vertex array object contains buffer bindings.

The global variable *vertices* and macros are defined in the following way.

```
#define NUM_VERTICES   3
#define VERTEX_SIZE    (3*sizeof(float))

static const float vertices [] =
{
  -1.0f, -1.0f,  0.0f,
   0.0f,  1.0f,  0.0f,
   1.0f, -1.0f,  0.0f
};
```

The next part is the *createProgram* method which loads vertex and fragment shaders, creates a corresponding OpenGL program object and stores its identifier in the *program* member variable.

```
void   MyWindow :: createProgram ()
{          // load shaders
  vertexShader    = loadShaderFromFile (
            "simple.vsh", GL_VERTEX_SHADER );
  fragmentShader = loadShaderFromFile (
            "simple.fsh", GL_FRAGMENT_SHADER );

  if ( !vertexShader || !fragmentShader )
    exit ( 1 );
            // create program object
  program = glCreateProgram ();
            // attach shaders and link it
  glAttachShader ( program, vertexShader   );
  glAttachShader ( program, fragmentShader );
  glLinkProgram   ( program );
  glGetProgramiv ( program, GL_LINK_STATUS,
                &status );
            // check for result
  if ( status != GL_TRUE )
  {
    int length ;
            // get error message
    glGetProgramiv ( program, GL_INFO_LOG_LENGTH,
                    &length );

    char * buf = (char *) malloc ( length );

    glGetProgramInfoLog ( program, length, NULL, buf );
            // print error log
    printf ( "Link_failure.\n%s\n", buf );
    free    ( buf );
    exit    ( 1 );
  }
}
```

This method uses the *loadShaderFromFile* method to load vertex and fragment shaders for our program. After the shaders are loaded we create our OpenGL program object, attach our shaders to it and link the program. In case of error we get and print an error log.

```
GLuint   MyWindow :: loadShaderFromFile (
            const char * fileName, GLenum type )
{
  FILE * file = fopen ( fileName, "rb" );

  if ( file == NULL )
```

```
{
    printf ( "Error opening %s\n", fileName );

    return 0;
}

printf ( "Loading %s\n", fileName );
fseek  ( file, 0, SEEK_END );

GLint size = ftell ( file );

if ( size < 1 )
{
    fclose ( file );
    printf ( "Error loading file %s\n", fileName );

    return 0;
}

char * buf = (char *) malloc ( size + 1 );

fseek ( file, 0, SEEK_SET );

if ( fread ( buf, 1, size, file ) != size )
{
    fclose ( file );
    free   ( buf );
    printf ( "Error loading file %s\n", fileName );

    return 0;
}

fclose ( file );
                    // append zero terminator
buf [size] = '\0';

GLuint shader = loadShader ( buf, type );

free ( buf );

return shader;
}
```

This method tries to open a corresponding file, checks for its length being greater then zero, then loads, appends a zero byte to the loaded shader text and uses *loadShader* to compile a corresponding shader.

```
GLuint MyWindow :: loadShader ( const char * source ,
                                GLenum type )
{
    GLuint shader = glCreateShader ( type );
    GLint status , length ;

    if ( shader == 0 )
        return 0;
                    // pass all source as one string
    glShaderSource  ( shader , 1, &source , NULL );
    glCompileShader ( shader );
    glGetShaderiv   ( shader , GL_COMPILE_STATUS, &status );

    if ( status != GL_TRUE )
    {
        glGetShaderiv ( shader , GL_INFO_LOG_LENGTH, &length );

        char * buf = (char *) malloc ( length );

        glGetShaderInfoLog ( shader , length , NULL, buf );

        printf          ( "Compile_failure.\n%s\n" , buf );
        free            ( buf );
        glDeleteShader  ( shader );

        return 0;
    }

    return shader ;
}
```

This method creates a corresponding shader object, sets its source to the given parameter and tries to compile it. In case of error, a corresponding error message is printed.

For the initialization we have only one method left – *setAttrPtr*. The task of this method is to set a pointer for the given vertex attribute (the position in our case) inside the VBO and enable the corresponding vertex attribute array.

```
void   MyWindow :: setAttrPtr (
    const char * name, int numComponents , GLsizei stride ,
    void * ptr , GLenum type = GL_FLOAT,
    bool normalized = false )
{
    int loc = glGetAttribLocation ( program , name );
```

```
if ( loc < 0 )
    exit ( 1 );   // cannot find this attribute

glVertexAttribPointer ( loc, numComponents, type,
                        normalized ? GL_TRUE : GL_FALSE,
                        stride, (const GLvoid*) ptr );
glEnableVertexAttribArray ( loc );
}
```

Now we are left with implementing the *reshape* and *redisplay* methods. The first of these methods is very simple – we just need to call inherited methods and **glViewport**.

```
void  MyWindow :: reshape ( int w, int h )
{
    GlutWindow :: reshape ( w, h );

    glViewport ( 0, 0, (GLsizei)w, (GLsizei)h );
}
```

The second method – *redisplay* – just clears the window, binds our vertex array object (our program object is already bound) and calls the **glDrawArrays** command to render our triangle (and binds out of our VAO at the end).

```
void  MyWindow :: redisplay ()
{
    glClear ( GL_COLOR_BUFFER_BIT | GL_DEPTH_BUFFER_BIT );

    glBindVertexArray ( vao );
    glDrawArrays      ( GL_TRIANGLES, 0, NUM_VERTICES );
    glBindVertexArray ( 0 );
}
```

The only remaining CPU part is the *main* function which is very simple too.

```
int main ( int argc, char * argv [] )
{
    GlutWindow :: init ( argc, argv );

    MyWindow        win;

    GlutWindow :: run ();

    return 0;
}
```

Now we have to write our shaders – vertex and fragment. Since our triangle is already inside $t[-1, 1]^3$, our vertex shader just passes coordinates further converting them to homogeneous.

```
#version 330 core

in vec3 position;

void main(void)
{
        gl_Position    = vec4(position, 1.0);
}
```

Our fragment shader is very simple too – it just outputs red color for all fragments.

```
#version 330 core

out vec4 color;

void main(void)
{
        color = vec4(1.0, 0.0, 0.0, 1.0);
}
```

9.5   First OpenGL program using C++ classes

As can be seen from our first example, we have a lot of code used for working with buffers and shaders. All of this can be encapsulated in C++ classes – **VertexBuffer**, **VertexArray** and **Program**. This will make our program much shorter and simpler.

Usually it is much easier to keep vertex and fragment shaders together in one file. The used class **Program** supports it – it loads all shaders from a specified text file, where strings *–vertex* and *–fragment* mark the start of each shader. So our simple shaders from the example above will be kept in a single GLSL file in the following form.

```
--vertex
#version 330 core

in vec3 position;

void main(void)
{
  gl_Position = vec4(position, 1.0);
```

```
}

—fragment
#version 330 core

out vec4 color;

void main(void)
{
  color = vec4(1.0, 0.0, 0.0, 1.0);
}
```

Then our class **MyProgram** will look as shown below.

```
class   MyWindow : public GlutWindow
{
  Program        program;
  VertexArray  vao;
  VertexBuffer  buf;

public:
  MyWindow () : GlutWindow  ( 200, 200, 400, 400,
                             "First _GL_ 3.3 _demo"  )
  {
    if ( !program.loadProgram ( "simple.glsl" ) )
    {
      printf ( "Error_building _program: _%s\n",
               program.getLog ().c_str () );

      exit ( 2 );
    }

    program.bind  ();
    vao.create    ();
    vao.bind      ();
    buf.create    ();
    buf.bind      ( GL_ARRAY_BUFFER );
    buf.setData   ( NUM_VERTICES * VERTEX_SIZE, vertices,
                    GL_STATIC_DRAW );
    program.setAttrPtr ( "position", 3, VERTEX_SIZE,
                         (void *) 0 );
    buf.unbind  ();
    vao.unbind  ();
  }
```

Method *reshape* will not change and method *redisplay* will look as shown below.

```
void   MyWindow :: redisplay ()
{
   glClear ( GL_COLOR_BUFFER_BIT | GL_DEPTH_BUFFER_BIT );

   vao.bind ();
   glDrawArrays ( GL_TRIANGLES, 0, NUM_VERTICES );
   vao.unbind ();
}
```

As you can see, code has become more compact and easier to both write and understand with all key OpenGL objects encapsulated inside C++ classes.

9.6   Parameter interpolation

All outputs of the vertex shaders (i.e., variables having the **out** qualifier) are interpolated during rasterization and the fragment shader receives interpolated value for each fragment.

To illustrate how it works we will modify our previous example so that we specify for every vertex not only its position but also its color (which will be interpolated across the whole triangle).

```
---vertex
#version 330 core

in   vec3 position;
in   vec3 color;
out vec3 clr;

void main(void)
{
   gl_Position = vec4(position, 1.0);
   clr         = color;
}

---fragment
#version 330 core

in   vec3 clr;
out vec4 color;

void main(void)
{
   color = vec4(clr, 1.0);
}
```

As you can see, the vertex shader receives two attributes (both as 3D-vectors) – position and color. The received color is output to the fragment shader via the *clr* output variable. The fragment shader receives this value (already interpolated across a triangle) and makes the resulting RGBA color from it.

We must also modify the C++ source in order to provide a color attribute for rendering. There are two ways how we can pass this attribute – *interleaved* and *separate.*

In the interleaved way we keep all our attributes inside one vertex buffer proving different offsets inside the buffer for each attribute. In this way we need only to modify a *vertices* array, macros and **MyWindow** constructor. All other methods remain intact.

```
#define NUM_VERTICES    3
#define VERTEX_SIZE            (6*sizeof(float))

static const float vertices [] =
{       /* Coords: */  /* Color: */
  -1.0f, -1.0f, 0.0f, 1.0f, 0.0f, 0.0f,
   0.0f,  1.0f, 0.0f, 0.0f, 1.0f, 0.0f,
   1.0f, -1.0f, 0.0f, 0.0f, 0.0f, 1.0f
};

class    MyWindow : public GlutWindow
{
  Program        program;
  VertexArray    vao;
  VertexBuffer   buf;

public:
  MyWindow () : GlutWindow  ( 200, 200, 500, 500,
                             "GL_3.3_demo" )
  {
    if ( !program.loadProgram ( "simple-2.glsl" ) )
    {
      printf ( "Error_building_program:_%s\n",
               program.getLog ().c_str () );

      exit ( 2 );
    }

    program.bind  ();
    vao.create    ();
    vao.bind      ();
    buf.create    ();
    buf.bind      ( GL_ARRAY_BUFFER );
```

```
    buf.setData   ( NUM_VERTICES * VERTEX_SIZE, vertices,
                        GL_STATIC_DRAW );
    program.setAttrPtr ( "position", 3, VERTEX_SIZE,
                             (void *) 0 );
    program.setAttrPtr ( "color",     3, VERTEX_SIZE,
                             (void *)(3 * sizeof ( float ) ) );
    buf.unbind ();
    vao.unbind ();
}
```

Another approach is to use a separate vertex buffer for each attribute. We still use the same vertex array object to keep all our vertex buffers binding for us.

```
#define NUM_VERTICES   3
#define VERTEX_SIZE    (3*sizeof(float))

static const float vertices [] =
{
   -1.0f, -1.0f, 0.0f,
    0.0f,  1.0f, 0.0f,
    1.0f, -1.0f, 0.0f
};

static const float colors [] =
{
    1.0f, 0.0f, 0.0f,
    0.0f, 1.0f, 0.0f,
    0.0f, 0.0f, 1.0f
};

class   MyWindow : public GlutWindow
{
    Program        program;
    VertexArray    vao;
    VertexBuffer   buf1, buf2;

public:
    MyWindow () : GlutWindow ( 200, 200, 500, 500,
                                  "Separate_attrs" )
    {
        if ( !program.loadProgram ( "simple-2.glsl" ) )
        {
            printf ( "Error_building _program:_%s\n",
                        program.getLog ().c_str () );
```

```
      exit ( 2 );
   }

   program.bind  ();
   vao.create    ();
   vao.bind      ();
   buf1.create   ();
   buf1.bind     ( GL_ARRAY_BUFFER );
   buf1.setData  ( NUM_VERTICES * VERTEX_SIZE, vertices ,
                   GL_STATIC_DRAW );

   program.setAttrPtr ( "position", 3, VERTEX_SIZE,
                              (void *) 0 );

   buf1.unbind   ();
   buf2.create   ();
   buf2.bind     ( GL_ARRAY_BUFFER );
   buf2.setData  ( NUM_VERTICES * VERTEX_SIZE, colors ,
                   GL_STATIC_DRAW );
   program.setAttrPtr ( "color",   3, VERTEX_SIZE,
                              (void *) 0 );
   buf2.unbind   ();
   vao.unbind    ();
 }
```

In both above examples we have used attribute names in the shader and then queried for their locations using these names. But there is another way – we can specify the locations of attributes right in the shader source using a **layout** qualifier. Then we can use these locations in the code instead of attribute names.

```
---vertex
#version 330 core

layout(location = 0) in vec3 position;
layout(location = 1) in vec3 color;

out vec3 clr;

void main(void)
{
   gl_Position = vec4(position , 1.0);
   clr         = color;
}

---fragment
```

```glsl
#version 330 core

in   vec3 clr;
out vec4 color;

void main(void)
{
   color = vec4(clr , 1.0);
}
```

Then the constructor of our window class will be shown as below.

```cpp
MyWindow () : GlutWindow ( 200, 200, 500, 500,
                    "Interleaved_attrs_with_location" )
{
   if ( !program.loadProgram ( "simple-3.glsl" ) )
   {
      printf ( "Error_building_program:_%s\n",
                     program.getLog ().c_str () );

      exit ( 2 );
   }

   program.bind   ();
   vao.create     ();
   vao.bind       ();
   buf.create     ();
   buf.bind       ( GL_ARRAY_BUFFER );
   buf.setData    ( NUM_VERTICES * VERTEX_SIZE, vertices ,
                    GL_STATIC_DRAW );

   program.setAttrPtr ( 0, 3, VERTEX_SIZE,
                     (void *) 0 );
   program.setAttrPtr ( 1, 3, VERTEX_SIZE,
                     (void *)(3 * sizeof ( float ) ) );

   buf.unbind ();
   vao.unbind ();
}
```

9.7 Matrix operations

Classical OpenGL 1 (or OpenGL 2) contains many commands for various matrix operations including commands for setting up various projections. Since in OpenGL 3 all these commands are deprecated we need to provide something to replace them. For this purpose we will use the **mat4** class introduced earlier in Chapter 4 to represent 4×4 matrices.

One of the simplest commands to set a projection in OpenGL 1 was **glOrtho**. It received six numbers defining a rectangular area in 3D-space – *left, right, bottom, top, near* and *far* (see Fig 9.6).

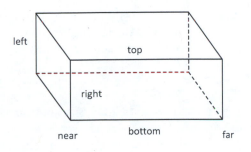

FIGURE 9.6: Parameters for **glOrtho**.

This command created the following matrix

$$P = \begin{pmatrix} \frac{2}{right-left} & 0 & 0 & tx \\ 0 & \frac{2}{top-bottom} & 0 & ty \\ 0 & 0 & \frac{-2}{far-near} & tz \\ 0 & 0 & 0 & 1 \end{pmatrix}. \tag{9.1}$$

In this equation parameters tx, ty and tz are given by the following equations

$$\begin{cases} tx = -\frac{right+left}{right-left}, \\ ty = -\frac{top+bottom}{top-bottom}, \\ tz = -\frac{far+near}{far-near}. \end{cases} \tag{9.2}$$

Now we can easily create this matrix using our **mat4** class.

```
mat4 ortho (
          float left , float right , float bottom ,
          float top , float zNear , float zFar )
{
```

```
float m00 = 2.0 f/(right  − left );
float m11 = 2.0 f/(top  − bottom);
float m22 = 2.0 f/(zNear − zFar);
float tx  = (left + right )/(left  − right );
float ty  = (bottom + top)/(bottom − top);
float tz  = (zNear + zFar)/(zNear − zFar);

return mat4 ( m00, 0,   0,   tx ,
              0,  m11, 0,   ty ,
              0,   0,  m22, tz ,
              0,   0,   0,   1 );
}
```

A common command to set up a perspective projection was **gluPerspective** provided by the GLU (OpenGL Utilities) library. It received four parameters – *fovy, aspect, near* and *far*. Parameter *fovy* specified the *field of view* in the *y* direction, parameter *aspect* specified the ratio of window width to the window height. And parameters *near* and *far* defined the near and far clipping plane.

Note that it is quite common to define near and far clipping planes. It happens because usually graphics hardware uses unsigned integer values in the depth buffer, so that floating-point values can be rescaled to these integer values. And in order to make such a rescaling it is vital to have minimal and maximal depth values known beforehand.

The **gluPerspective** command forms the following matrix

$$P = \begin{pmatrix} \frac{f}{aspect} & 0 & 0 & 0 \\ 0 & f & 0 & 0 \\ 0 & 0 & \frac{far+near}{near-far} & \frac{2\,far\,near}{near-far} \\ 0 & 0 & -1 & 0 \end{pmatrix}. \tag{9.3}$$

Here $f = cotan(fovy/2)$.

For this we will use the following function.

```
mat4 perspective ( float fov , float aspect ,
                   float zNear , float zFar )
{
    float f   = 1.0/tanf ( 0.5 f * toRadians ( fov ) );
    float m22 = (zNear + zFar)/(zNear − zFar);
    float m23 = (2.0 f*zFar*zNear)/(zNear − zFar);

    return mat4 ( f / aspect , 0, 0,   0,
                  0,           f, 0,   0,
                  0,           0, m22, m23,
                  0,           0, −1,  0 );
}
```

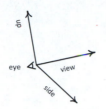

FIGURE 9.7: Orientation for **gluLookAt**.

Another often-used command allowing for easy camera positioning was the **gluLookAt** command, which formed the matrix which changed the coordinate system to the one with a given origin, given look-at point and up vector (see Figure 9.7). This matrix was defined by the following equation.

$$M = \begin{pmatrix} s_x & s_y & s_y & 0 \\ u_x & u_y & u_z & 0 \\ -f_x & -f_y & -f_z & 0 \\ 0 & 0 & 0 & 1 \end{pmatrix}.$$ (9.4)

Vectors s, u and f are defined by the equations

$$\begin{cases} s = \frac{[f',u']}{\|f'\| \cdot \|u'\|}, \\ u = \frac{[s,f']}{\|f'\|}, \\ f = \frac{f'}{\|f'\|}. \end{cases}$$ (9.5)

Here the coefficients f' and u' are given by Equation (9.6)

$$\begin{cases} f' = \begin{pmatrix} toX - eyeX \\ toY - eyeY \\ toZ - eyeZ \end{pmatrix}, \\ u' = \begin{pmatrix} eyeX \\ eyeY \\ eyeZ \end{pmatrix}. \end{cases}$$ (9.6)

The following function builds the same matrix.

```
mat4 lookAt ( const vec3& eye ,
              const vec3& center , const vec3& up )
{
    vec3 f = normalize ( eye − center );
    vec3 s = cross     ( normalize ( up ), f );
    vec3 u = cross     ( f, s );
    mat4  m ( s.x,   s.y,   s.z, −dot(s, eye),
             u.x,   u.y,   u.z, −dot(u, eye),
```

```
    f.x,    f.y,    f.z,  -dot(f, eye),
     0,      0,      0,    1 );

  return m;
}
```

9.8   Rotating the object by mouse

Now we can modify our example with a triangle to support placed some-where in the space triangle which we will be rotating with the mouse. For this we will use two matrices – the *model-view matrix* which will keep our rotation and *projection matrix* which will be responsible for setting up our perspective projection.

Corresponding shaders are shown below and from the vertex shader you can see how these matrices are applied. In order to support rotation we will add two uniform variables to our vertex shader – *mv* and *proj* – which will contain model-view and projection matrices. Note that in order to apply these matrices we need to convert an input position from 3D-vector to homogeneous coordinates.

```
--vertex
#version 330 core

in   vec3 position;
in   vec3 color;
out vec3 clr;

uniform mat4 proj;
uniform mat4 mv;

void main(void)
{
    gl_Position = proj * mv * vec4(position, 1.0);
    clr         = color;
}

--fragment
#version 330 core

in   vec3 clr;
out vec4 color;
```

```
void main ( void )
{
        color = vec4 ( clr , 1.0 );
}
```

The C++ code is also not difficult – it uses mouse moves (with any mouse button pressed) to change two angles used to rotate our triangle.

We won't show the text of window constructor because its difference with earlier examples is only in the name of GLSL file with a shader source. Below is shown the declaration of corresponding class which shows the instance variables we will be using.

```
class    MyWindow : public GlutWindow
{
    int          mouseOldX;
    int          mouseOldY;
    vec3         rot;
    Program      program;
    VertexArray  vao;
    VertexBuffer buf;
```

Variables *mouseOldX* and *mouseOldY* will contain the mouse cursor position in the window in pixels for the last time we processed the mouse input. The variable *rot* will contain rotation angles (in degrees) for all coordinate axes.

The *reshape* method computes a projection matrix using the new window's size and sets this matrix as uniform for our shader program.

```
void MyWindow :: reshape ( int w, int h )
{
    vec3  eye ( 3, 3, 3 );      // camera position

    GlutWindow :: reshape ( w, h );

    glViewport ( 0, 0, (GLsizei)w, (GLsizei)h );

    mat4 proj = perspective( 60.0f, (float)w/(float)h,
                    0.5f, 15.0f )*
                lookAt( eye, vec3 :: zero, vec3 ( 0, 0, 1 ) );

    program . bind ();
    program . setUniformMatrix ( "proj", proj );
    program . unbind ();
}
```

The *redisplay* method computes a new rotation matrix, passes it to the shader and renders our triangle just as we did before.

```
void MyWindow :: redisplay ()
{
   glClear ( GL_COLOR_BUFFER_BIT | GL_DEPTH_BUFFER_BIT );

   mat4 mv = mat4 :: rotateZ (toRadians(−rot.z)) *
             mat4 :: rotateY (toRadians( rot.y)) *
             mat4 :: rotateX (toRadians( rot.x ));

   program.bind ();
   program.setUniformMatrix ( "mv", mv );
   vao.bind ();
   glDrawArrays ( GL_TRIANGLES, 0, NUM_VERTICES );
   vao.unbind ();
   program.unbind ();
}
```

The only methods left were our methods handling mouse presses and active mouse movements. These methods will track mouse movements when the mouse button is pressed and use these movements to adjust rotation angles.

```
void MyWindow :: mouseMotion ( int x, int y )
{
   rot.x −= ((mouseOldY − y) * 180.0f) / 200.0f;
   rot.z −= ((mouseOldX − x) * 180.0f) / 200.0f;
   rot.y = 0;

   if ( rot.z > 360 )
     rot.z −= 360;

   if ( rot.z < −360 )
     rot.z += 360;

   if ( rot.y > 360 )
     rot.y −= 360;

   if ( rot.y < −360 )
     rot.y += 360;

   mouseOldX = x;
   mouseOldY = y;

   glutPostRedisplay ();
}

void MyWindow :: mouseClick ( int button, int state,
               int modifiers, int x, int y )
```

```
{
  if ( state == GLUT_DOWN )
  {
    mouseOldX = x;
    mouseOldY = y;
  }
}
```

To simplify following examples we will be using the **GlutRotateWindow** class, which inherits from **GlutWindow** but adds to the mouse ability to rotate object with the mouse. This class redefines the mouse handling methods and adds the new method *getRotation* to return the rotation matrix corresponding to current rotation angles.

9.9 Working with meshes

A single triangle is not a very interesting figure to be working with. So in our later examples we will be using various *triangle meshes*. A triangle mesh is a set of triangles which we will be rendering using one **glDrawElements** command.

The meshes we will be using contain a set of vertex attributes, such as position, texture coordinates, normals, tangents and binormals. All these attributes will come in handy when we will be creating some advanced effects such as bumpmapping. The structure **BasicVertex** used to contain all vertex data is shown below.

```
struct    BasicVertex
{
  vec3  pos;
  vec2  tex;
  vec3  n;
  vec3  t, b;
};
```

The **BasicMesh** class will contain a vertex array buffer containing vertex data (in an interleaved form), vertex array buffer with index data and vertex array object to keep all buffer bindings.

The index data are used to build triangles from the vertices data. Usually the same vertex is shared by several triangles so it is convenient to use separate array for all vertices and separate array for indices which shows how to form triangles from these vertices.

```
class  BasicMesh
{
```

```
    int              numVertices;
    int              numTriangles;
    VertexArray   vao;      // array with all bindings
    VertexBuffer  vertBuf;  // vertex data
    VertexBuffer  indBuf;   // index buffer
    std :: string    name;

public:
    BasicMesh ( BasicVertex * vertices , const int * indices ,
                int nvertices , int ntriangles );

    void render ();

    const std :: string& getName () const
    {
       return name;
    }

    int getNumVertices () const
    {
       return numVertices;
    }

    int getNumTriangles () const
    {
       return numTriangles;
    }

    void setName ( const string& theName )
    {
       name = theName;
    }
};
```

In the constructor of this class corresponding arrays are created and filled with vertex data, if source normals have zero length then normals for vertices are computed.

In order to compute a normal at the given vertex we find all triangles sharing this vertex, find their normals and use the normalized average of these normals as the normal at the vertex.

The **glVertexAttribPointer** command is used to bind vertex attributes to data in the buffer by the indices (which should be defined in the *layout* qualifier in the shader). Index 0 corresponds to position, index 1 corresponds to texture coordinates and indices 2–4 correspond to normal, tangent and binormal vectors.

Using such buffers the *render* method of this class becomes very simple.

```
void       BasicMesh :: render ()
{
  vao.bind ();

  glDrawElements ( GL_TRIANGLES,  3*numTriangles,
                   GL_UNSIGNED_INT, NULL );

  vao.unbind ();
}
```

Also we will be using several utility functions which can create mesh for the quad, box, sphere, torus and knot. Our example, which renders a knot that can be rotated using mouse drags, is simple. Below you can see the definition of our window class and its constructor.

```
class MeshWindow : public GlutRotateWindow
{
  Program      program;
  BasicMesh * mesh;
  vec3         eye;    // position of camera

public:
  MeshWindow () : GlutRotateWindow ( 200, 200, 400, 400,
                                     "Rotating_mesh" )
  {
    if ( !program.loadProgram ( "rotate -2.glsl" ) )
    {
      printf ( "Error_building_program:_%s\n",
               program.getLog ().c_str () );
      exit ( 2 );
    }

    program.bind ();

    mesh = createKnot ( 1, 4, 120, 30 );
    eye = vec3 ( 5, 5, 5 );
  }
```

Its *reshape* method prepares the matrix for the perspective projection for a given camera position, field of view and near and far depth values.

```
void MeshWindow :: reshape ( int w, int h )
{
  GlutWindow :: reshape ( w, h );

  glViewport ( 0, 0, (GLsizei)w, (GLsizei)h );
```

```
mat4 proj = perspective( 60.0f, (float)w/(float)h,
                         0.5f, 20.0f )*
              lookAt( eye, vec3::zero, vec3( 0, 0, 1 ) );

    program.bind ();
    program.setUniformMatrix ( "proj", proj );
    program.unbind ();
}
```

The *redisplay* method is also very simple – it sets the rotation matrix as a model-view matrix and calls the method *render* of the mesh.

```
void MeshWindow::redisplay ()
{
    glClear ( GL_COLOR_BUFFER_BIT | GL_DEPTH_BUFFER_BIT );

    program.bind ();
    program.setUniformMatrix ( "mv", getRotation () );

    mesh -> render ();

    program.unbind ();
}
```

One small addition to this example is the ability to move the camera position using a mouse wheel. For this we have to override the *mouseWheel* method of the class **GlutWindow**. Note that when we move the camera position (*eye*) we have to recompute the projection matrix which we do by calling the *reshape* method.

```
void MeshWindow::mouseWheel ( int wheel, int dir, int x, int y )
{
    eye += 0.5 * vec3 ( dir, dir, dir );

        // since eye value has changed
    reshape ( getWidth(), getHeight() );
        // request that window should be redrawn
    glutPostRedisplay ();
}
```

9.10   Working with textures

Mesh rendered by our previous example looks completely flat – it is rendered with one color. It is difficult to determine from the image in the window what is closer to the camera and what is further from the camera. One of the simplest ways to improve our image is to use textures. Our next several examples will be rendering textured meshes.

A texture is an array of values (called *texels* from texture element) which can be read from the shader. Usually this array is 2D but it is possible to have 1D- and 3D- texture. Also there is *cubemap* texture, which we will cover a little bit later.

But in order to access texture values (which can have 1, 2, 3 or 4 components) instead of array indices we use *normalized texture coordinates*. They do not depend on the size of the original texture and are vectors of the corresponding dimension. The unit cube of this dimension corresponds to the whole texture.

Usually when we access texture using such texture coordinates the graphics hardware performs some additional steps – texture coordinates are clamped to the $[0, 1]$ – it is possible to use any values for texture coordinates and before accessing the texture these coordinates will be reduced to the unit cube. Common ways of such reducing are *clamping* and *repeating*. In the first case if some texture coordinate is less than zero it is replaced with zero and if it is greater than one it is replaced with one. Repeating (usually used) just takes a fractional part of texture coordinates.

Also texture hardware performs *texture filtering*. It takes several closest texels to the texture coordinate specified and uses them to provide a new value which is returned. A mipmapping is also supported by hardware and provides a simple and effective mechanism to cope with texture aliasing.

Usually data for textures are provided in image files such as *JPEG* images. But OpenGL has no built-in support for loading images from files. Also there are many different file formats which can contain texture image.

So we will wrap all work with the texture in the **Texture** class. This class will have the support of loading images from files and providing other convenient methods for working with textures. Our next example will be of the textured knot. Below you can see the window class with its constructor we are using for rendering our knot.

```
class MeshWindow : public GlutRotateWindow
{
    Program      program;
    BasicMesh  * mesh;
    Texture      tex;
    vec3         eye;

public:
    MeshWindow () : GlutRotateWindow ( 200, 200, 400, 400,
                                        "Textured _mesh" )
    {
        string texName = "../../Textures/Fieldstone.dds";
```

```
if ( !tex.load2D ( texName.c_str () ) )
{
    printf ( "Error loading texture %s\n",
             texName.c_str () );
    exit ( 1 );
}

if ( !program.loadProgram ( "rotate-3.glsl" ) )
{
    printf ( "Error building program: %s\n",
             program.getLog ().c_str () );
    exit ( 2 );
}

program.bind ();
program.setTexture ( "image", 0 );

mesh = createKnot ( 1, 4, 120, 30 );
eye = vec3 ( 5, 5, 5 );
}
```

The *redisplay* method of this class differs from our previous example – we have to bind our texture to same texture unit as was used in the *setTexture* method (in our **Texture** class by default the *bind* method binds texture to texture unit 0).

```
void MeshWindow::redisplay ()
{
    glClear ( GL_COLOR_BUFFER_BIT | GL_DEPTH_BUFFER_BIT );

    tex.bind ();
    program.bind ();
    program.setUniformMatrix ( "mv", getRotation () );

    mesh -> render ();

    program.unbind ();
    tex.unbind ();
}
```

In our fragment shader we define a uniform variable of type **sampler2D** with the name *image*, which is used to get the values from the texture using the *texture* function. Note that texture coordinates which are passed in the vertex shader as a vertex attribute vertex shader must output to the fragment shader.

```
---vertex
```

```
#version 330 core

layout ( location = 0 ) in vec3 pos;
layout ( location = 1 ) in vec2 tex;
out vec2   tx;

uniform mat4 proj;
uniform mat4 mv;

void main(void)
{
  gl_Position = proj * mv * vec4(pos,  1.0);
  tx          = tex;
}

---fragment
#version 330 core

uniform sampler2D image;
in   vec2 tx;
out vec4 color;

void main(void)
{
   color = texture ( image,  tx*vec2(1,4)  );
}
```

Another type of texture used is a 3D-texture. A 3D-texture is just a 3D-array of texel values. Usually 3D-textures are specified as *.dds* files. Class **Texture** can load them just as easily as a 2D-texture – the only difference is that we call the *load3D* method to load texture data from the file.

In the shader we specify **sampler3D** as our texture. Since texture coordinates are often 2D, for our example we will use source 3D-vertex coordinates as our texture coordinates for accessing 3D-texture. These coordinates are passed unprocessed from the vertex shader to the fragment shader as shown below.

```
---vertex
#version 330 core

layout ( location = 0 ) in vec3 pos;
layout ( location = 1 ) in vec2 tex;
out vec3   p;

uniform mat4 proj;
uniform mat4 mv;
```

```
void main(void)
{
    gl_Position = proj * mv * vec4(pos, 1.0);
    p           = pos;
}

—fragment
#version 330 core

uniform sampler3D image;
in   vec3 p;
out vec4 color;

void main(void)
{
    color = texture ( image, p );
}
```

The last type of texture we will be using is a *cubemap* texture. While all previous textures can be thought of as a function defined in a 2D- or 3D-unit cube, the texture cubemap can be thought of as a function defined on the surface of a unit sphere (or a unit cube) – it uses a 3D-vector as its texture coordinates.

Cubemap texture consists of six 2D-textures (with the same size and width equal to the height) which are interpreted as images glued on the sides of the unit cube. If we have a 3D-vector v then we can build a ray going from the center of this cube in the direction v. This ray will pierce one side of this cube at some point. The color value for this coordinate v is the value from the corresponding 2D-texture at the intersection point (see Figure 9.8).

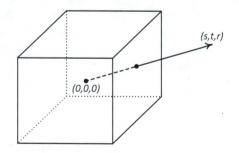

FIGURE 9.8: Cubemap texture.

Our first cubemap example will just render the interior of the texture mapped cube. We will use the simplest shaders for this case. As with 3D-texture we use original vertex coordinates (after they are interpolated) as texture coordinates for accessing the cubemap texture.

```
—vertex
#version 330 core

layout ( location = 0 ) in vec3 pos;
out vec3   p;

uniform mat4 proj;
uniform mat4 mv;

void main(void)
{
  gl_Position = proj * mv * vec4(pos, 1.0);
  p           = pos;
}

—fragment
#version 330 core

uniform samplerCube      image;
in   vec3 p;
out vec4 color;

void main(void)
{
  color = texture ( image, p );
}
```

The only difference for loading textures using our **Texture** class is that we call *loadCubemap* to load the texture image into our OpenGL texture – we will use a *.dds* file which can contain cubemap textures just as 2D- and 3D-textures.

Note that the cubemap can be loaded not from one *.dds* file but from six separate 2D-texture images.

One of the very common usages of cubemaps is simulating the reflection from some surface. For this we need for every fragment the following two vectors – vector to the camera v and normal vector n. Then we can use the built-in function *reflect* to obtain the reflected vector and use it as our texture coordinates for accessing cubemap texture.

Since normals are transformed by an inverted transpose of the upper-left 3×3 matrix of our model-view matrix, we will need to pass this matrix (we will call it nm) into the vertex shader for the normals to be correctly transformed.

In the result we obtain following shaders:

```glsl
--vertex
#version 330 core

layout ( location = 0 ) in vec3 pos;
layout ( location = 2 ) in vec3 normal;

out vec3 n;      // normal
out vec3 v;      // vector to the eye

uniform mat4 proj;  // projection matrix
uniform mat4 mv;    // model-view matrix
uniform mat3 nm;    // normal transform matrix
uniform vec3 eye;

void main(void)
{
  vec4 p = mv * vec4 ( pos, 1.0 );

  gl_Position  = proj * p;
  n            = normalize ( nm * normal );
  v            = normalize ( eye - p.xyz );
}

--fragment
#version 330 core

uniform samplerCube       image;

in   vec3 n;
in   vec3 v;
out vec4 color;

void main(void)
{
  color = texture ( image,
          reflect ( normalize(v), normalize(n) ) );
}
```

Below code for the *redisplay* function of our window is shown. The *normal-Matrix* helper function is used to build the matrix for transforming normals from our model-view matrix.

```cpp
void MeshWindow :: redisplay ()
{
  glClear ( GL_COLOR_BUFFER_BIT | GL_DEPTH_BUFFER_BIT );
```

```
mat4 mv = getRotation    ();
mat3 nm = normalMatrix ( mv );

tex.bind ();
program.bind ();
program.setUniformMatrix ( "mv",   mv );
program.setUniformMatrix ( "nm",   nm );
program.setUniformVector ( "eye", eye );

mesh -> render ();

program.unbind ();
tex.unbind ();
}
```

9.11   Instancing

OpenGL provides an ability to render a group of primitives many times with just one draw call. For this, two OpenGL commands **glDrawArraysInstanced** and **glDrawElementsInstanced** are used. Each of these commands will render specified primitives the number of times specified in the last argument. The vertex shader can distinguish these instances by using the *gl_InstanceID* built-in variable.

We can easily modify functionality of the BasicMesh class to add support of instancing. All we need to do is just call **glDrawElementsInstanced** instead of calling **glDrawElements**.

```
void    BasicMesh :: renderInstanced ( int primCount )
{
  vao.bind ();

  glDrawElementsInstanced ( GL_TRIANGLES, 3*numTriangles,
                    GL_UNSIGNED_INT, NULL, primCount );

  vao.unbind ();
}
```

We need just a small modification to our C++ code in order to render many instanced toruses.

Now we will modify the *redisplay* method to render a group of 100 toruses with a single draw call.

```
void MeshWindow :: redisplay ()
```

```
{
   glClear ( GL_COLOR_BUFFER_BIT | GL_DEPTH_BUFFER_BIT );

   mat4 mv = getRotation ();
   mat3 nm = normalMatrix ( mv );

   tex.bind ();
   program.bind ();
   program.setUniformMatrix ( "mv", mv );
   program.setUniformMatrix ( "nm", nm );
   program.setUniformVector ( "eye", eye );

   mesh -> renderInstanced ( 100 );

   program.unbind ();
   tex.unbind ();
}
```

Most of the changes will be in the vertex shader. In it we must use an instanced number of the primitive to place it on a 10×10 grid and scale correspondingly.

```
#version 330 core

layout ( location = 0 ) in vec3 pos;
layout ( location = 2 ) in vec3 normal;

out vec3 n;      // normal
out vec3 v;      // vector to the eye

uniform mat4 proj;
uniform mat4 mv;
uniform mat3 nm;
uniform vec3 eye;

void main(void)
{
   vec3 offs = vec3 ( gl_InstanceID % 10 - 5,
                      gl_InstanceID / 10 - 5, 0.0 );
   vec4 p    = mv * vec4 ( 0.3*pos + 5.0*offs, 1.0 );

   gl_Position  = proj * p;
   n            = normalize ( nm * normal );
   v            = normalize ( eye - p.xyz );
}
```

9.12   Framebuffer object and rendering into a texture

OpenGL supports creation of custom framebuffers which can be used for rendering into. It is possible to attach a 2D-texture (or a slice of 3D-texture or a side of cubemap) as a color buffer of such a framebuffer to get the resulting rendered image as a texture (so-called *render-to-texture*).

Here we will be using the **FrameBuffer** class to represent such framebuffers and make working with them nice and easy. Our next example will render a rotating textured torus to such a framebuffer. Then a cube will be rendered and the resulting texture image with a torus will be used to texture this cube.

So in our window class we need two **BasicMesh** objects (torus and cube) and a **FrameBuffer** object. Below you can see declaration of window class and its constructor.

```
class     MeshWindow : public GlutRotateWindow
{
   Program       program;
   BasicMesh * mesh;
   Texture       tex;
   BasicMesh * cube;
   Texture     * tex2;
   FrameBuffer  fb;
   vec3          eye;

public:
   MeshWindow () : GlutRotateWindow (
            200, 200, 400, 400, "Render-to-texture" ),
            fb ( 512, 512, FrameBuffer :: depth24 )
   {
      string texName = "../../Textures/Fieldstone.dds";

      if ( !tex.load2D ( texName.c_str () ) )
      {
         printf ( "Error_loading_texture_%s\n",
                  texName.c_str () );
         exit    ( 1 );
      }

      if ( !program.loadProgram ( "rotate-8.glsl" ) )
      {
         printf ( "Error_building_program:_%s\n",
                  program.getLog ().c_str () );
         exit    ( 2 );
```

```
      }

      program.bind ();
      program.setTexture ( "image", 0 );

      fb.create ();
      fb.bind ();
            // create and attach 2D texture to framebuffer
      fb.attachColorTexture ( fb.createColorTexture () );
      fb.unbind ();

      if ( !fb.isOk () )
      {
         printf ( "Error with Framebuffer object\n" );
         exit    ( 3 );
      }

      mesh = createKnot ( 1, 4, 120, 30 );
      cube = createBox   ( vec3 ( -1, -1, -1 ),
                           vec3 (  2,  2,  2 ) );
      eye  = vec3 ( 2.5, 2.5, 2.5 );
}
```

In this class we will put rendering of the torus into a separate method *displayBox* as shown below. This method will bind our framebuffer object (so that we render into it instead of the default framebuffer) and perform rendering. Later we can obtain the resulting image as a texture from our framebuffer.

```
void MeshWindow :: displayBoxes ()
{
   fb.bind ();

   glClearColor( 0, 0, 0, 1 );
   glClear       ( GL_COLOR_BUFFER_BIT | GL_DEPTH_BUFFER_BIT );
   glViewport   ( 0, 0, fb.getWidth (), fb.getHeight () );

   tex.bind  ( 0 );
   program.bind ();
   program.setUniformMatrix( "mv", mat4::rotateX (getTime ()) );
   program.setUniformVector( "eye", vec3 ( 7, 7, 7 ) );

   mesh->render ();

   tex.unbind ();
   fb.unbind ();
```

```
  program.unbind ();
}
```

Then our rendering code – *redisplay* method – will consist of a call to *displayBox* and using texture from the framebuffer object.

```
void MeshWindow :: redisplay ()
{
  displayBoxes ();

  glClearColor ( 0.5, 0.5, 0.5, 1 );
  glClear        ( GL_COLOR_BUFFER_BIT | GL_DEPTH_BUFFER_BIT );

  fb.getColorBuffer () -> bind ();
  program.bind ();
  program.setUniformMatrix ( "mv", getRotation () );

  cube -> render ();

  program.unbind ();
  fb.getColorBuffer () -> unbind ();
}
```

9.13   Point sprite in OpenGL

One of the features OpenGL supports is rendering of points (GL_POINTS) as sprites, i.e., squares with a texure applied to it. For this, in our vertex shader we not only specify the **gl_Position** variable, but also specify the **gl_PointSize** variable. And this veriable specifies the size of a square which will be rendered instead of our point. In the example below we set our sprite to be a square with the size of 15 pixels.

```
#version 330 core

layout ( location = 0 ) in vec3 pos;


uniform mat4 proj;
uniform mat4 mv;

void main(void)
{
  gl_Position  = proj * mv * vec4 ( pos, 1.0 );
```

```
gl_PointSize = 15;
}
```

In our fragment shader we can access texture coordinates for the current fragment being rendered via the **gl_PointCoord** built-in variable.

```
#version 330 core

uniform sampler2D          image;

out vec4 color;

void main(void)
{
    color = vec4 ( texture ( image, gl_PointCoord.xy ).r );
}
```

The corresponding C++ code for the window class and its constructor is shown below.

```
#define NUM_VERTICES 1000
#define VERTEX_SIZE          3*sizeof(float)

class MeshWindow : public GlutRotateWindow
{
    Program          program;
    VertexArray      vao;
    VertexBuffer     buf;
    vec3             vertices [NUM_VERTICES];
    Texture          tex;
    vec3             eye;

public:
    MeshWindow() : GlutRotateWindow( 200, 200, 400, 400,
                                     "Point_sprites" )
    {
        string texName = "../../Textures/Fire.bmp";

        if ( !tex.load2D ( texName.c_str () ) )
        {
            printf ( "Error_loading_texture_%s\n",
                     texName.c_str () );
            exit    ( 1 );
        }

        if ( !program.loadProgram ( "sprite.glsl" ) )
        {
```

```
    printf ( "Error_building_program:_%s\n",
                program.getLog ().c_str () );
    exit    ( 2 );
  }

  program.bind ();
  program.setTexture ( "image", 0 );

  eye = vec3 ( 7, 7, 7 );

  for ( int i = 0; i < NUM_VERTICES; i++ )
    vertices [i] = vec3 ( randUniform (),
                          randUniform (),
                          randUniform () )*10.0-vec3 ( 5.0 );

  vao.create  ();
  vao.bind    ();
  buf.create  ();
  buf.bind    ( GL_ARRAY_BUFFER );
  buf.setData ( NUM_VERTICES * VERTEX_SIZE, vertices,
                GL_STATIC_DRAW );

  program.setAttrPtr ( 0, 3, VERTEX_SIZE, (void *) 0 );

  buf.unbind  ();
  vao.unbind  ();
}
```

Such point sprites are usually alpha-blended (and therefore should be sorted by the distance from the camera, but for our example we will render them unsorted).

```
void MeshWindow :: redisplay ()
{
  glClear ( GL_COLOR_BUFFER_BIT | GL_DEPTH_BUFFER_BIT );

  mat4 mv = getRotation ();

  tex.bind ();
  program.bind ();
  program.setUniformMatrix ( "mv", mv );
  vao.bind ();

  glEnable    ( GL_BLEND );
  glDisable   ( GL_DEPTH_TEST );
  glBlendFunc ( GL_SRC_ALPHA, GL_ONE_MINUS_SRC_ALPHA );
```

```
   glDrawArrays ( GL_POINTS, 0, NUM_VERTICES );
   glDisable     ( GL_BLEND );
   vao.unbind ();

   program.unbind ();
   tex.unbind ();
}
```

Chapter 10

Working with large 2D/3D data sets

Working with large sets of objects, whether in 2D or in 3D, often requires performing various *spatial queries* to locate objects satisfying certain spatial conditions.

An example of a spatial query may be to find all objects in the given area or near the given object or to find the first object intersected by a given ray and so on.

Despite the query itself being usually very simple for large amounts of objects (we will use N to denote total number of objects), the brute-force approaches usually requiring $O(N)$ or $O(N^2)$ operations are simply unacceptable for performance reasons.

This situation is very close to that of finding records in a large relational database. Almost every database employs so-called *indices* to speed up such queries. An *index* is some special data structure that locates a record or object in a sublinear time (usually the number of required operations varies from $O(1)$ to $O(\log^k N), k = 1, 2$).

For geometric tasks such indices, called *spatial indices*, also exist and in this chapter we will cover most of the widely used ones. Note that almost every such index can work with 2D-data as well as with 3D-data, so we will be giving mostly 3D-examples but using 2D-pictures to explain the applied algorithm.

10.1   Bounding volumes

One of the simplest tricks used in working with complex objects or groups of objects is to use *Bounding Volumes*(BVs). The bounding volume is just a sufficiently simple shape (usually convex) containing a complex shape (or a group of shapes) inside (see Figure 10.1).

Ideally a bounding volume should be a minimal convex set containing the given object(s). But in practice, building such a set can be expensive, so simpler approaches are used instead.

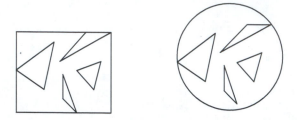

FIGURE 10.1: Examples of bounding volumes – AABB and sphere.

Now suppose we want to test whether some complex object A intersects another object B.

FIGURE 10.2: Using bounding volumes of shapes A and B to check for their intersection.

For a complex object A, a direct test on the intersection can be expensive, so it makes sense to start first with some cheap test. Such a test can clear up whether A's bounding volume A' intersects object B (or bounding volume of B if B is a complex object too) (Figure 10.2).

Since a bounding volume is a very simple object this check will be quick and inexpensive to perform. And if bounding volume A' does not intersect B then object A cannot intersect B (because B cannot intersect A without intersecting bounding volume A' containing A). So checking bounding volumes give us a chance to reject quickly many cases when there is no intersection.

But even if bounding volume A' and object B do intersect it does not

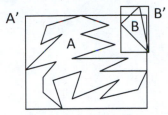

FIGURE 10.3: Even if bounding volumes do intersect, objects they contain may not intersect each other.

necessarily means that object *B* intersects object *A* itself (see Figure 10.3), so in this case we need to run the full intersection check.

Using bounding volumes does not completely replace the need for a detailed check but quickly rejects many cases and thus helps to avoid detailed and expensive tests.

10.1.1 Axis-Aligned Bounding Box (AABB)

A simple and most often-used bounding volume is a rectangle with sides parallel to coordinate axes (*AABB*). It is very simple to build such a volume and checks with it also tend to be very simple and fast (see Chapter 3).

FIGURE 10.4: Axis-Aligned Bounding Box for a group of objects.

To build an AABB from a set of polygons we just have to find the minimum and maximum of a coordinate's components of all vertices (see Figure 10.4).

```
void buildBoundingBox ( const vec3 * p, int n,
                        vec3& pMin, vec3& pMax )
{
    pMin = p [0];
    pMax = p [1];

    for ( int i = 1; i < n; i++ )
    {
        if ( p [i].x < pMin.x )
            pMin.x = p [i].x;
```

```
    if ( p [i].y < pMin.y )
        pMin.y = p [i].y;

    if ( p [i].z < pMin.z )
        pMin.z = p [i].z;

    if ( p [i].x > pMax.x )
        pMax.x = p [i].x;

    if ( p [i].y > pMax.y )
        pMax.y = p [i].y;

    if ( p [i].z > Max.z )
        pMax.z = p [i].z;
    }
}
```

Classifying AABB relative to a plane in 3D is pretty much the same as in the 2D-case which was covered in Chapter 3.

10.1.2 Sphere

Another simple bounding volume is a sphere. A simple procedure to build a bounding sphere for a set of vertices is to take the per-component average of all vertices as its center c and then compute the radius as a maximal distance from the center to these vertices

$$c = \frac{1}{n} \sum_{i=0}^{n-1} v_i, \tag{10.1}$$

$$r = \sqrt{\max \|c - v_i\|}. \tag{10.2}$$

Spheres are simple shapes to check for intersection. If we have a sphere with the center at c_1 and radius r_1 and another sphere with the center at c_2 and radius r_2, then they intersect if and only if $\|c_1 - c_2\| < r_1 + r_2$ (see Figure 10.5).

```
void buildBoundingSphere ( const vec3 * p, int n,
                           vec3& c, float& r )
{
    vec3 c vec3 :: ave ( p, n );

    float r2 = c.distanceToSq ( v [0] );

    for ( int i = 1; i < n; i++ )
```

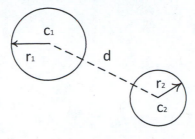

FIGURE 10.5: Checking two spheres for intersection.

```
{
    float rt = c.distanceToSq ( v [i] );

    if ( rt > r2 )
        r2 = rt;
}

r = sqrtf ( r2 );
}
```

10.1.3   k-DOP

Sometimes an AABB or a sphere are not good enough – they can include a lot of extra space being not tight enough for a given object (see Figure 10.6).

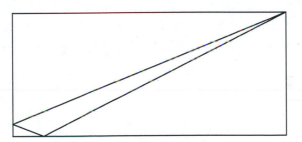

FIGURE 10.6: Using AABB in this case gives a very bad approximation of the object inside.

One of such bounding volumes which often provides a better approximation than AABB (and whose approximation can be easily improved) is so-called *k-DOP* (*Discrete Oriented Polytop*). Let's select $k/2$ unit vectors n_i, where k should be bigger than the dimension of the space and it should be possible to pick up a basis from chosen unit vectors (see Figure 10.7). We use these vectors n_i to build a set of planes $(p, n_i) + d = 0$.

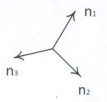

FIGURE 10.7: Example of picking normals for the 2D-case.

For a given set of objects (vertices) in each such set of planes we find just pair of planes (corresponding to values d_0 and d_1) that all objects will be contained in part of the space between these two planes – a *slab* with minimal thickness (see Figure 10.8).

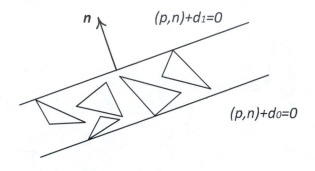

FIGURE 10.8: Slab for a group of objects.

The k-DOP is defined as an intersection of such slabs constructed for every vector n_i. By increasing the number of slabs we get a more tight bounding volume. But since we're fixing the set of vectors n_i, then all operations with these k-DOPs are quick and efficient.

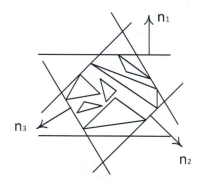

FIGURE 10.9: k-DOP for a group of triangles using normals from Figure 10.7.

10.1.4 Oriented Bounding Box (OBB)

Another type of bounding volume is a rectangle (box) with an orientation which can be chosen arbitrarily. The ability to pick any orientation (instead of a predefined one like in k-DOP and AABB) builds tighter bounding volumes accommodating to specific geometry (see Figure 10.10).

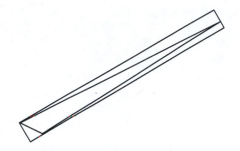

FIGURE 10.10: Oriented Bounding Box (OBB) in this case gives a much better approximation than the AABB or sphere.

An *oriented bounding box* may be described as follows

$$p = c + (e_0|e_1|e_2)y, |y_i| \leq s_i, i = 0, 1, 2. \tag{10.3}$$

Here the c is the center of an OBB, e_0, e_1 and e_2 are unit edge directions (they are mutually perpendicular and have unit lengths) and values s_0, s_1 and s_2 define the half-size of the box along its edges (see Figure 10.11).

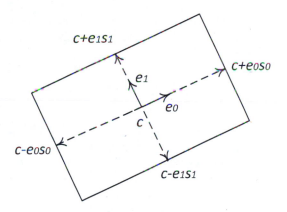

FIGURE 10.11: Oriented Bounding Box for 2D.

The most important part of building an OBB is choosing its center and orientation. The procedure for selecting the center of an OBB is the same as for the bounding sphere – we just select an average of all vertices v_i

$$c = \frac{1}{n} \sum_{i=0}^{n-1} v_i. \tag{10.4}$$

But finding optimal directions e_0, e_1 and e_2 is more complicated. Usually vertices v_i are used to build a *covariance matrix* M

$$M = \frac{1}{n} \sum_{i=0}^{n-1} (v_i - c)(v_i - c)^T. \tag{10.5}$$

Then we need to find *eigenvectors* of the covariance matrix M and normalize them. Note that since $M^T = M$ it always has three mutually orthogonal eigenvectors e_0, e_1 and e_2.

When they are found (we do not go into details of doing this, the corresponding matrix class *mat3* on the CRC website contains corresponding method) half-sizes can be found by the following formula

$$s_i = \max |(e_i, v_k - c)| \tag{10.6}$$

Below is C++ code used to build an OBB for an array of 3D-points.

```
void buildOBB ( const vec3 * v, int n, vec3& c,
                vec3& e1, vec3& e2, vec3& e3, vec& s )
{
            // compute an average for vertices
   c = vec3 :: ave ( v, n ) / n;
   s = vec3 ( 0, 0, 0 );

            // now build a covariance matrix M
   mat3 m ( 0 );

   for ( int i = 0; i < n; i++ )
   {
      vec3 p = v [i] - c;

      m += mat3 ( p.x*p.x, p.x*p.y, p.x*p.z,
                  p.y*p.x, p.y*p.y, p.y*.p.z,
                  p.z*p.x, p.z*p.x, p.z*p.z );
   }

   m /= n;
            // get m's eigenvectors and normalize them
   float lambda [3];    // eigenvalues
```

```
vec3   e [3];              // eigenvectors

m. mat3GetEigen ( lambda , e );

e1 = normalize ( e [0] );
e2 = normalize ( e [1] );
e3 = normalize ( e [2] );

for ( int i = 0; i < n; i++ )
{
    float s1 = dot ( e1 , v [i] − c );
    float s2 = dot ( e2 , v [i] − c );
    float s3 = dot ( e3 , v [i] − c );

    if ( s1 > s.x )
        s.x = s1;

    if ( s2 > s.y )
        s.y = s2;

    if ( s3 > s.z )
        s.z = s3;
}
}
```

The problem of location of an OBB relative to some plane $(n, p) + d = 0$ is slightly more complex that for other bounding volumes.

We need to project our bounding volume on the line given by the n direction (see Figure 10.12). This projection is usually defined by projection of the center c and extent r, which is given by the following formula

$$r = \sum_{i=0}^{2} |s_i^2| \cdot |(e_i^1, n)|. \tag{10.7}$$

If $r < |(c, n) + d|$ then the whole OBB does not intersect the plane and therefore lies in the same half-plane as its center c.

Checking two OBBs on an intersection is much more complex that checking previously discussed bounding volumes because orientations of OBBs to be checked usually differ.

A standard intersection check for OBBs is based on the *separating axis theorem*, stating that two convex objects (such as OBB) do not intersect if and only if there is an axis such that projections of these objects on it do not overlap.

For two OBBs it is sufficient to check only fifteen possible axes – three are given by orientation of OBB_1, three are given by orientations of OBB_2 and

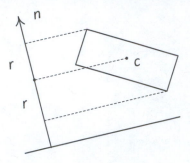

FIGURE 10.12: Checking OBB for intersection with a line.

nine come from cross-products of orientations from OBB_1 and orientations from OBB_2.

Since we need to check projections on the axis we are interested only in axis direction l. If we know some axis direction l we can easily find the distance between projections of OBB centers – c_1 and c_2 and their projected extents r_1 and r_2 (see Figure 10.13)

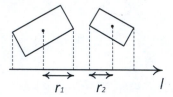

FIGURE 10.13: Checking for overlap of two OBBs.

$$r_1 = \sum_{i=0}^{2} |s_i^1| \cdot |(e_i^1, l)|, \tag{10.8}$$

$$r_2 = \sum_{i=0}^{2} |s_i^2| \cdot |(e_i^2, l)|. \tag{10.9}$$

Projections of these OBBs on an axis with direction l overlap if and only if $|(c_1 - c_2, l)| > r_1 + r_2$.

Usually checks are started with edge directions of OBBs because for this case we get simpler equations. If we are checking direction $l = e_i^1$ then we get for the r_1 and r_2 following equations

$$r_1 = |s_i^1|, \tag{10.10}$$

$$r_2 = \sum_{j=0}^{2} |s_j^2| \cdot |(e_j^2, e_i^1)|. \tag{10.11}$$

Using the 3×3 matrix R such that $r_{ij} = |(e_i^1, e_j^2)|$, we can rewrite the equation for r_2 in the following way

$$r_2 = \sum_{j=0}^{2} |s_j^2| r_{ij}. \tag{10.12}$$

So once matrix R is computed, the first six checks can be easily performed using simplified Equations (10.10) and (10.12).

If however these checks have not given an answer to our main question – an absence of intersection then we have to check the remaining nine directions of the form $l = [e_i^1, e_j^2]$. Here again we can make simplifications using the fact that in this case l will be perpendicular to both e_i^1 and e_j^2 so that the corresponding dot products are zero. Note the product $|(l, e_k^1)| = |([e_i^1, e_j^2], e_k^1)|$ can be rewritten in the following form

$$|(l, e_k^1)| = |([e_i^1, e_j^2], e_k^1)| = |([e_i^1, e_k^1], e_j^2)|. \tag{10.13}$$

But $[e_i^1, e_k^1], i \neq k$ being the cross-product of two edge directions of one OBB should give third edge direction (maybe with a negative sign, but since we want absolute values we don't care), so it is equal to e_m^1, where the m is an integer from 0 to 2 not equal to i and k and we can express it as $3 - i - k$. Therefore, we have

$$|(l, e_k^1)| = |([e_{3-i-k}^1, e_j^2])| = r_{3-i-k,j}. \tag{10.14}$$

This way we can simplify all terms for r_1 and r_2 and perform the last 9 checks.

10.2 Regular grids

Bounding volumes can simplify checks between objects, but to effectively process large amounts of data we need special data structures.

One of the simplest ways to organize a search among a lot of objects (usually when sizes of objects do not vary much) is to organize this data into a so-called *regular grid*.

To create a regular grid we build an AABB for the whole data and split it into many equal-sized boxes (*grid cells*)(see Figure 10.14). For every such cell we build a list of all objects which, at least partially, overlap the cell. Usually the cell size is chosen close to the typical size of the object.

The following C++ code shows how regular grids can be defined.

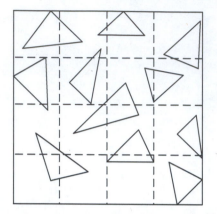

FIGURE 10.14: Regular grid for a set of triangles.

```
template<class Shape>
struct GridCell
{
    bbox          box;
    list <Shape *> objects;
};

template<class Shape>
class RegularGrid
{
    bbox               box;        // bounds of all shapes
    int                n1, n2, n3; // number of splits
                                   // for each axis
    float              h1, h2, h3;
    GridCell<Shape> * cells;
public:
    RegularGrid ( int c1, int c2, int c3, const bbox& theBox );
    ~RegularGrid ();

    void addShape ( Shape * shape )
    {
        bbox b = shape -> getBox ();

        int i1 = (int)(b.getMinPoint().x - box.getMinPoint().x) / h1;
        int i2 = (int)(b.getMinPoint().y - box.getMinPoint().y) / h2;
```

```
int i3 = (int)(b.getMinPoint().z − box.getMinPoint().z) / h3;

i1 = clamp( i1, 0, n1−1 );
i2 = clamp( i2, 0, n2−1 );
i3 = clamp( i3, 0, n3−1 );

for(i=i1;box.getMinPoint().x+i*h1<=b.getMaxPoint().x;i++)
    for(j=i2;box.getMinPoint().y+j*h2<=b.getMaxPoint().y;i++)
        for(k=i3;box.getMinPoint().z+k*h3<=b.getMaxPoint().z;i++)
            getCell( i, j, k )−> objects.push_back ( shape );
    }
};
```

Once such a structure is built we can use it to quickly find all objects, located in the given area. If we have bounding box B and want to find all the objects inside it, we just find all grid cells intersecting B, then merge object lists from these cells (to avoid processing the same object twice) and check every object from the merged list for being inside B. For many cases it requires $O(1)$ operations (checks) to locate objects within the given area (provided the area is not too big).

A more complex example is locating all object pairs (a, b) which are within some distance d from each other. Such a problem often arises in collision detection.

The brute-force approach requires $O(N^2)$ operations which is unacceptable for large datasets. Using the regular grid we can find all such pairs for $O(N)$ operations – for every object we need to check only the objects from the same cell and from the cells withing the required distance d (see Figure 10.15).

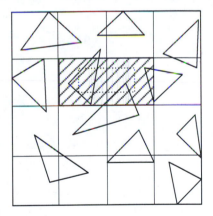

FIGURE 10.15: Locating objects overlapping a given area.

A uniform grid is not the "ideal" spatial index – there are many cases when it works really bad. The main problem with regular grids is best illustrated with the so-called "teapot on the stadium" example.

Imagine a big stadium with a small highly-detailed teapot in the center of the field (see Figure 10.16). If in this situation we choose a small cell size to capture details of the teapot then we will get a huge number of grid cells, most of which will be empty, and many cells with identical object lists. Traversing such a huge grid can be very expensive.

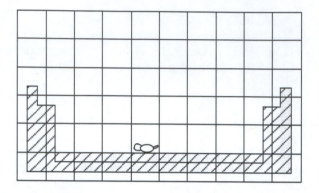

FIGURE 10.16: Teapot on the stadium case.

Choosing a big cell size will decrease the amount of empty cells but the whole teapot will be in one or two cells, because of that the grid will not help us in locating teapot details.

Uniform grid cells work very well when we have a nearly uniform distribution in space of objects of nearly the same size. The "teapot in the stadium" example clearly violates both assumptions – it has small and big objects and a lot of empty space, i.e., non-uniform distribution of shapes.

To handle such cases, the spatial index must be flexible enough. It is usually achieved through various hierarchies.

10.3   Nested (hierarchical) grids

We can add flexibility to regular grid structures by making them multilevel (nested). First, we perform a coarse gridding of the data. Then the cells whose object lists contain many objects (above the given threshold) are gridded again into subgrids. If there are resulting sub-cells which still contain too many objects we can again build grids inside such cells and so on (see Figure 10.17).

This approach solves the "teapot in the stadium" problem, using coarse partitioning in most of the areas with fine gridding near the teapot.

With this approach it is possible to create multilevel grids, choosing detalization depending on the object's density. The scheme of building such a

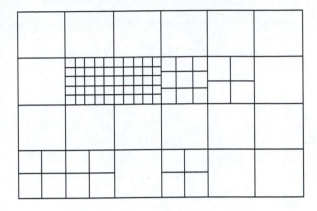

FIGURE 10.17: Example of a nested grid.

nested grid from a set of objects remains pretty simple, but the objects located in it can be complex and require traversing several levels of hierarchy.

Class declarations below show how nested grids can be implemented in C++.

```
template <class Shape>
class Grid;

template<class Shape>
class GridNode // node of nested grid, leaf or internal node
{
  bbox box;
  bool isLeaf;
  union
  {
    list<Shape *> objects;     // for leaf node
    Grid<Shape> * subgrid;     // for internal node
  };
};

template <class Shape>
class Grid
{
  bbox               box;
  int                n1, n2, n3;
  GridNode<Shape> * cells;
};
```

Usually it is sufficient to create no more than 2 or 3 levels of such grids – making more levels incurs overhead for traversing them.

10.4 Quad-trees and Oct-trees

Another example of an adaptive hierarchical spatial index are *quad-trees* or *oct-trees*. They have very much in common; the only difference is the dimension of the data they are built on. Quad-trees are usually built for 2D-data or data which is mostly 2D (e.g., terrains). Oct-trees are usually built for 3D-data.

Let's look at what a quad-tree is and how it is built. The first step is computing an AABB of the dataset. Then this AABB is split into four equal boxes (for oct-trees an AABB is split into eight equal boxes) – we perform one split along each coordinate axis. For each child box we compute a list of all objects intersecting the box.

If for some child box this list is big, this box is subdivided again into four (eight) equal boxes and the list of objects is created for each of them. This process of subdivision can be performed many times resulting in a tree, whose root corresponds to the whole dataset and its AABB. Each node either contains exactly four (eight) child nodes or is a leaf node, which has no child nodes – only the objects list (see Figure 10.18).

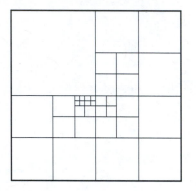

FIGURE 10.18: Example of a quad-tree subdivision.

The listing below shows a class which can be used to represent oct-trees and work with them.

```
template<class Shape>
class OctTreeNode
{
public:
   typedef list <Shape *> ShapeList;

protected:
   list <Shape *> objects;   // list of all objects for this node
   bbox           box;       // bounding box for the node
```

```
  OctTreeNode * child [8];
public:
  OctTreeNode ();
  ~OctTreeNode ();

  void addShape ( Shape * shape );
  void setChiid ( int no, OctTreeNode * subnode );

  const list <Shape *> getObjects () const
  {
    return objects;
  }

  OctTreeNode * getChild ( int no ) const
  {
    return no >= 0 && no < 8 ? child [no] : NULL;
  }

  const bbox& getBox () const
  {
    return box;
  }

  void setBox ( const bbox& theBox )
  {
    box = theBox;
  }
};
```

For such a simplified node class we can use the following function to build an oct-tree from a list of shapes (here the shape is just any object which can provide its bounding box).

```
template<class Shape>
OctTreeNode<Shape> * buildOctTree
                          ( const list <Shape *>& lst )
{
  OctTreeNode<Shape> * root = new OctTreeNode<Shape>;
  bbox                    box ( lst.begin () -> getBox () );

                // compute total AABB of all objects
  for ( list <Shape *>::const_iterator it = lst.begin ();
        it != lst.end (); ++it )
    box.merge ( it -> getBox () );

  root -> setBox ( box );
```

```
                    // too small list , make a leaf
if ( lst.size () < THRESHOLD )
{
  root -> setList ( lst );

  return;
}

bbox   cb [8];      // boxes for child nodes
vec3   center (. box.getCenter () );

for ( int i = 0; i < 8; i++ )
{
  cb [i] = box;

  if ( i & 1 )    // x-split
    cb [i].minPoint.x = center.x;
  else
    cb [i].maxPoint.x = center.x;

  if ( i & 2 )    // y-split
    cb [i].minPoint.y = center.y;
  else
    cb [i].maxPoint.y = center.y;

  if ( i & 4 )    // z-split
    cb [i].minPoint.z = center.z;
  else
    cb [i].maxPoint.z = center.z;
}

for ( int i = 0; i < 8; i++ )
{
  list <Shape *> tempList;

  for ( list <Shape *>::const_iterator it = lst.begin ();
            it != lst.end (); ++it )
    if ( cb [i].intersects ( it -> getBox () ) )
      tempList.push_back ( *it );

  root -> setChild ( i, buildOctTreeNode ( tempList ) );
}

return root;
```

}

An oct-/quad-tree provides an adaptive hierarchical spatial index, allowing easy spatial location of objects – we just recursively check the child nodes.

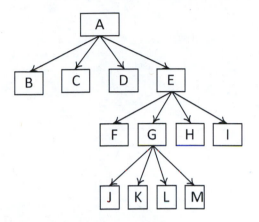

FIGURE 10.19: Quad-tree nodes.

```
template<class Shape>
void findShapes ( OctTreeNode<Shape> * root,
        const bbox& box, list <Shape *>& result )
{
  if ( !box.intersects ( root -> getBox () ) )
    return;

  const list <Shape *>& lst ( root -> getObjects () );

  if ( lst.size () > 0 )  // a leaf
  {
    for ( list <Shape *>::const_iterator it = lst.begin ();
            it != lst.end (); ++it )
      if ( box.intersects ( it -> getBox () ) )
        result.push_back ( *it );

    return;
  }

  for ( int i = 0; i < 8; i++ )
  {
    OctTreeNode<Shape> * child = root -> getChild ( i );

    if ( child == NULL )
      continue;
```

```
    if ( box.intersects ( child -> getBox () )
        findShapes ( child, box, result );
    }
}
```

For some tasks, such as tracing a ray through a set of objects, we can use the fact that child nodes are ordered and we can traverse them along the ray starting with the first node entered by the ray and ending with the last node the ray enters. This allows to skip processing other nodes if we want to find the closest ray intersection (see Figure 10.20).

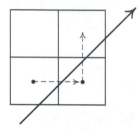

FIGURE 10.20: Order of traversing nodes for tracing along the ray.

But choosing the correct ordering for a quad-tree or oct-tree is not self-evident. In the case when an initial bounding box is much longer in one or two dimensions and much shorter than in others, both a quad-tree and oct-tree may result in very bad splitting (see Figure 10.21).

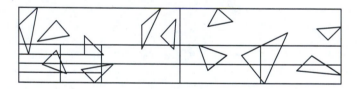

FIGURE 10.21: Improportional child nodes with nearly identical object lists resulting from improportional initial data bounds.

10.5 kD-tree

A simple solution to possible improportional boxes is to split the box in two parts every time along only one axis, choosing the axis for every split. The usual scheme is to select an axis along which the bounding box has the biggest size and split the box into two equal-sized halves (see Figure 10.22). This approach leads us to the binary tree called a *kD-tree*.

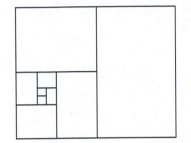

FIGURE 10.22: kD-tree subdivisions.

It is very close to quad-/oct-trees and has all their benefits, but it is simpler to work with and provides a solution for too long or too thin bounding boxes.

kD-trees have one more advantage – it is much easier to build balanced (or optimized in some sense) trees. Usually on each step instead of using a middle point for splitting we can select several (possibly random) candidates (usually from 2 to 10) and select the one which gives the best score for the chosen criteria.

One of the simplest criteria to optimize for is to make the numbers of shapes in both child nodes to be as close as possible. As a result we have a more balanced tree (see Figure 10.23).

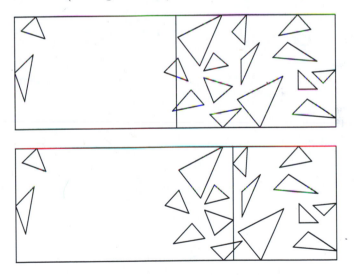
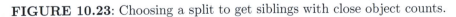

FIGURE 10.23: Choosing a split to get siblings with close object counts.

Working with kD-trees is simple – we have only two child nodes and can easily select which one to process first.

Below is the C++ definition of class which can be used to represent a kD-tree node.

```
template<class Shape>
class kDTreeNode
{
public:
  typedef list<Shape *> ShapeList;

protected:
  list <Shape *>      objects; // list of all objects for this node
  bbox                box;     // bounding box for the node
  int                 axis;    // axis used for splitting
  float               pos;     // splitting position along axis
  kDTreeNode<Shape> * child [2];
public:
  kDTreeNode ();
  ~kDTreeNode ();

  void setChiid ( int no, kDTreeNode * subnode );

  kDTreeNode * getChild ( int no ) const
  {
    return no >= 0 && no < 2 ? child [no] : NULL;
  }

  const list <Shape *> getObjects () const
  {
    return objects;
  }

  const bbox& getBox () const
  {
    return box;
  }

  void setBox ( const bbox& theBox )
  {
    box = theBox;
  }
};
```

10.6 Binary Space Partitioning (BSP) tree

In all previous tree structures the same shape can be in several tree nodes, so when we are processing the tree, we should keep track of which shapes have already been processed. Note that while these trees do provide some kind of ordering of the shapes, this ordering is only partial (it is due to the fact that different tree nodes may share some shapes between them).

Another kind of spatial index tree – the *Binary Space Partitioning (BSP) tree* – avoids these drawbacks and can get shapes ordered by possible occlusion to a given camera position. Although the algorithm was described as early as 1980, its first real success was in a Doom first-person shooter by idSoftware. The ability of game engine to do quick hidden surface removal even on a 386-based PCs was due to a combination of several algorithms, BSP-trees being the most important one. Many of the idSoftware games (such as the Quake series and Doom III) still used some variants of BSP-trees.

The key difference of the BSP-trees from other trees is that they do split shape in parts if the shape is crossed by the partitioning plane. Because of it, every shape can be in only one child node. The tree is usually built for polygons so for every polygon we have a plane which can be used to partition other polygons.

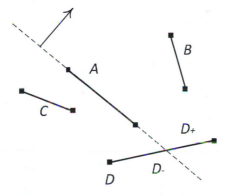

FIGURE 10.24: First step of building a BSP-tree.

Let's see how it works. If we have a group of polygons A, B, C and D then we can choose one of them (we choose polygon A (see Figure 10.24)). Then we use a plane, containing this polygon, to classify all other polygons. For any other polygon there are only four possibilities

- the polygon entirely lies in a positive half-space relative to the plane (as polygon B);

- the polygon entirely lies in a negative half-space relative to the plane (as polygon C);

- a polygon lies in the plane itself;

- a polygon is crossed by the plane (as polygon D).

The first two cases give us two sets (lists) of polygons – the first list contains all of the polygons from the positive half-space and the second – all polygons from the negative half-space. The last case (the polygon is crossed by the plane), requires splitting the polygon by the plane and after splitting all of its parts it can be classified as either lying in a positive or negative half-space and thus put the parts into the corresponding lists. Polygons that lie in the plane itself can be added to any of these two lists, it does not matter to which one.

After application of this procedure we get two polygon lists (B, D_+) and (C, D_-) and a splitting plane (or polygon A which was used to get the plane) instead of the initial list (A, B, C, D). We can take polygon A (its plane) as a root of the binary tree and obtained polygon lists will correspond to its children.

Then we apply the same procedure to both lists (each list is processed independently from the other) and get two more nodes and four polygon lists. Repeating this procedure until the resulting lists will contain no more than one polygon will end in a binary tree.

For our polygons A, B, C and D we can end up with a tree shown in Figure 10.25 (note that there can be other BSP-trees for this set of polygons).

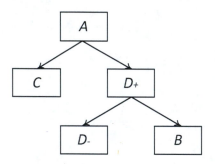

FIGURE 10.25: BSP-tree from the previous figure.

Each step of selecting a polygon (and a plane) forms a node in the BSP-tree. The node itself is completely defined by a chosen polygon. There are many ways to choose a polygon for a node. Usually one polygon is selected from several randomly chosen polygons according to some criteria.

Any node of the BSP-tree is useful to associate with a bounding box (AABB) for all polygons in its child subtrees – it can make processing the tree faster. The node of a typical BSP-tree can be represented with the following C++ class.

```cpp
class BspNode
{
  Polygon * poly;
  plane      p;
  bbox       box;
  BspNode * positive;
  BspNode * negative;
public:
  BspNode ( Polygon * );

  const bbox& getBox () const
  {
    return box;
  }

  Polygon * getPoly ()
  {
    return poly;
  }

  BspNode * getPositive ()
  {
    return positive;
  }

  BspNode * getNegative ()
  {
    return negative;
  }

  const plane& getPlane () const
  {
    return plane;
  }

  void setBox ( const bbox& b )
  {
    box = b;
  }

  void setPositive ( BspNode * node )
  {
    positive = node;
  }
```

```
void setNegative ( BspNode * node )
{
    negative = node;
}

void setPlane ( const plane& pl )
{
    plane = pl;
}
}
```

The function building of a BSP-tree from a list of polygons can be as simple as shown below.

```
BspNode * buildBspTree ( list <Polygon *>& lst )
{
    if ( lst.size () < 1 )
        return NULL;

    if ( lst.size () == 1 )
    {
        Polygon * splitter = *lst.begin;
        BspNode * root      = new BspNode ( splitter );

        root -> setBox        ( splitter -> getBox () );
        root -> setSplitter ( splitter -> getPlane () );
        root -> setPositive ( NULL );
        root -> setNegative ( NULL );

        return root;
    }

    Polygon * splitter = chooseBestSplitter ( lst );
    BspNode * root      = new BspNode ( splitter );
    Polygon * p1, * p2;
    list <Polygon *> pos, neg;
    bbox        box ( lst.begin () -> getBox () );

    for ( list <Polygon *>::iterator it = lst.begin ();
            it != lst.end (); ++it )
    {
        box.merge ( it -> getBox () );

        if ( *it != splitter )
        {
            switch ( classify ( *it, splitter -> getPlane () )
```

```
        {
            case IN_POSITIVE:
                pos.push_back ( *it );
                break;

            case IN_NEGATIVE:
                neg.push_back ( *it );
                break;

            case IN_PLANE:
                pos.push_back ( *it );
                break;

            case IN_BOTH:
                it -> split ( splitter -> getPlane (), p1, p2 );
                pos.push_back ( p1 );
                neg.push_back ( p2 );
                break;

            default:
                break;
        }
    }
}

root -> setBox        ( box );
root -> setSplitter ( splitter -> getPlane () );
root -> setPositive ( buildBspTree ( pos ) );
root -> setNegative ( buildBspTree ( neg ) );

return root;
}
```

Here the function *chooseBestSplitter* selects a polygon to define a splitting plane (and to form a new node of the tree). Such a simple function will return the first polygon in the list. There exist other ways to select a polygon using various criteria. Two of the most common of them are:

- creating a more balanced tree (make the sizes of positive and negative lists to be as close as possible);

- minimizing the number of splits (since it increases the total number of polygons).

Usually both of these criteria are combined with some weights. Then one polygon giving the best score is selected from several randomly chosen candidates (making a full optimization requires too much computation and is impractical).

One of the unique features of the BSP-tree is its ability to provide a list of sorted polygons for any given location of observer (camera) such that direct rendering in this order will result in the correct image (without the aid of any hidden surface removal algorithms). This feature is based on this simple fact – if an observer E is located in one half-space and a polygon is located in another half-space, then this polygon cannot occlude any polygon in the observer's half-space (see Figure 10.26).

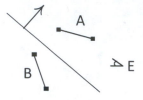

FIGURE 10.26: Polygon B cannot occlude polygon A from observer E.

To get polygons with such an ordering we should traverse the tree at each node visiting the child, corresponding to the half-space without the observer before visiting the child, corresponding to the same half-space the observer is in.

The code below shows how to traverse a BSP-tree in a back-to-front approach using the Visitor Pattern.

```
void travserseBspTree ( BspNode * root,
                const vec3& observer, Visitor& vis )
{
    if ( root->getPlane().classify( observer ) == IN_POSITIVE )
    {
        traverseBspTree ( root -> getNegative () );
        vis.process     ( root -> getPoly    () );
        traverseBspTree ( root -> getPositive () );
    }
    else
    {
        traverseBspTree ( root -> getPositive () );
        vis.process     ( root -> getPoly    () );
        traverseBspTree ( root -> getNegative () );
    }
}
```

10.7 Bounding Volume Hierarchy (BVH)

Another way to create a hierarchy is based on the bounding volumes. When we have a bounding volume for a group of objects we can skip checking every object of the group if the check for this bounding volume fails. For example, if we are looking for all objects inside a given area and the bounding volume of the group of objects does not intersect this area, then none of the objects contained in it can be inside the area and the whole group can be trivially rejected.

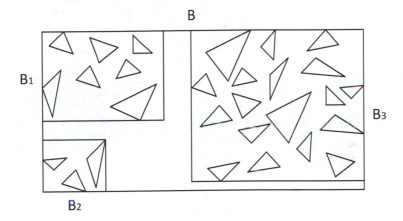

FIGURE 10.27: Grouping objects into bounding volumes.

But what if our bounding volume does intersect the area in question? In this case instead of individually checking every object (which can be very expensive for big object groups) we can split this group into several subgroups and build bounding volumes for each of these subgroups (see Figure 10.25). The checking of these bounding volumes gives us a chance to quickly reject some of the subgroups.

For subgroups which we cannot quickly discard we proceed with this subdivision scheme resulting in a tree of bounding volumes (see Fig. 10.28). Every node of this tree corresponds to some group of objects and contains a bounding volume for the group. If the group is big enough then it is split into several subgroups creating child nodes. Leaf nodes of the tree contain small lists of objects.

The resulting tree is called a *Bounding Volume Hierarchy (BVH)*. Usually this tree is built (just as all other spatial indices) at a preprocessing stage, so when we're rendering we have a ready tree to process. Note that bounding volumes for the child nodes can overlap, but usually locating all objects inside some area requires $O(\log N)$ checks.

The BVH-tree is close to other hierarchical structures such as quad-/oct-

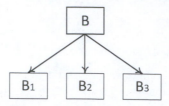

FIGURE 10.28: Tree for Figure 10.27.

trees and kD-trees, but provide more flexibility in splitting an object's list into subgroups. Note that any internal node can have any number of child nodes.

There are many ways to build a BVH-tree. Usually they are classified into *top-down* and *bottom-up* approaches.

All top-down algorithms recursively divide the current set of objects into two or more subsets and build bounding volumes for them. The same procedure is applied to resulting subgroups and so on (see Figure 10.29).

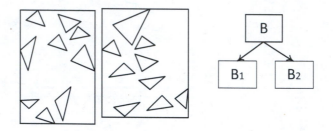

FIGURE 10.29: Splitting the root node into child nodes for a top-down approach.

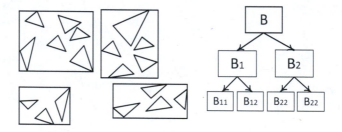

FIGURE 10.30: Next step of splitting for Figure 10.29.

For bottom-up algorithms, instead of splitting a large set of objects, start with gathering individual objects into many small groups (2–3 objects). Then for each such group a bounding volume is built. Resulting groups are gathered into bigger groups and so on. In this approach a hierarchy starts from leaves of the tree and goes up to the root (see Figures 10.32–10.34).

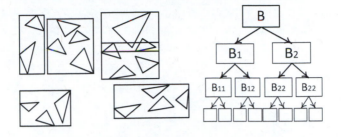

FIGURE 10.31: Last step for Figure 10.29.

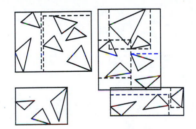

FIGURE 10.32: First step of grouping for a bottom-up approach.

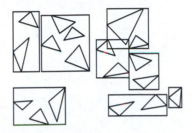

FIGURE 10.33: Next step of grouping for Figure 10.32.

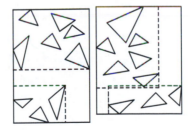

FIGURE 10.34: One more step of grouping for Figure 10.32.

One of the simplest algorithms for building a BVH-tree from a set of objects uses a top-down approach. On each step one axis is selected and all objects are sorted along this axis. Then the set of sorted objects is split into two parts which form subnodes. The usual heuristic is to choose an axis which minimizes the sum of resulting bounding volumes (see Figure 10.35).

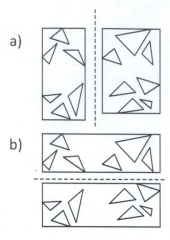

FIGURE 10.35: Choosing an axis for the split.

10.8   R-trees

Another example of a hierarchical spatial index is an *R-tree*, modeled after B-trees widely used in various databases.

An R-tree of order (m, M) (typically $m = M/2$) has the following properties:

- every leaf node of the tree contains between m and M records, each record consists of pointers to the object and its bounding box (AABB);

- every non-leaf node (except the root) contains between m and M child nodes with their bounding boxes;

- a root node has at least two child nodes;

- all leaves are on the same level (from the root);

- for every node, its bounding box contains all objects in the corresponding subtree (from all leaf nodes descending this node).

The process of locating data in an R-tree is very simple – we recursively process the tree starting from the root, check every node's bounding box, and descend on a node whose bounding box overlaps the area of interest.

```cpp
template<class Shape>
class RTreeNode
{
  struct Record
  {
    union
    {
      RTReeNode * child;
      Shape      * object;
    };
    bbox   box;
  };

  int            count;      // number of child records
  Record     * recs;        // child records
  bbox          box;         // bounding box for the node
  bool          leaf;        // true if node is a leaf
  RTreeNode * parent;        // link to the parent node
};

template<class Shape>
void RTreeNode::locate ( list <Shape*>& result, const bbox& b )
{
  for ( int i = 0; i < count; i++ )
    if ( b.intersects ( recs [i].box () ) )
    {
        if ( leaf )
            result.push_front ( recs [i].object );
      else
        recs [i].child -> locate ( result, b );
    }
}
```

The R-tree is built by insertion of objects one by one. Insertion starts at the root and proceeds down the tree to the leaves.

At every non-leaf node we should select an appropriate child node based on its bounding box and the bounding box of an object being inserted. When we add an object to the node, its bounding box may become bigger and its volume may increase. So we select a child node whose bounding box increases by adding an object which will be minimal. Then we proceed to the child node and so on until we reach the leaf node. Then we simply insert an object and its bounding box into that leaf.

Adding a new object to the node may overflow it (the number of objects will become bigger than M). In this case the node is split into two nodes which results in adding a record to the parent node. The parent node itself may overflow, and it's required to add a record to its parent and so on. The overflowing root node will result in tree height growth.

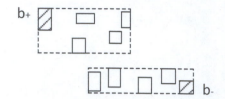

FIGURE 10.36: Choosing boxes b_+ and b_- from a set of boxes.

There are several strategies for splitting the node. One of them is based on selecting two bounding boxes b_+ and b_- (of all boxes in the node) such that putting them together in the same new node creates a very big bounding box. As a measure of how big the resulting box is using the following heuristic – we choose b_+ and b_- to minimize the following value $volume(union(b_+, b_-)) - volume(b_+) - volume(b_-)$. Here the $union(b_1, b_2)$ denotes union of bounding boxes b_1 and b_2 and *volume* means volume of the bounding box (see Fig. 10.36).

When such boxes b_+ and b_- are found, each of them becomes part of new node. For every other box we check to which group we should add a corresponding object to get a minimal increase of the node's bounding volume.

Below is python-style pseudo-code demonstrating the process of node splitting for an R-tree.

```python
def splitNode ( recs ):
  rp = recs [0]
  rm = recs [1]
  fun= 0

  for r1 in recs:
    for r2 in recs:
      b=merge (r1.box, r2.box).volume () -
        r1.box.volume () - r2.box.volume ()
      if b > f:
        rp=r1
        rm=r2
        f =b

  box1 =rp.box
  node1=[rp]
  box2 =rm.box
  node2=[rm]

  for r in recs:
```

```
if (r == rp) or (r == rm):
   continue

f1=merge( box1, r.box ).volume()−box1.volume()
f2=merge( box2, r.box ).volume()−box2.volume()

if f1 < f2:
   node1.append ( r )
   box1 = merge ( box1, r.box )
else:
   node2.append ( r )
   box2 = merge ( box2, r.box )

return (node1, node2)
```

10.9 Mixed structures

Each of the spatial indices described in this chapter has its own weak and strong points. So it's a good idea to combine them. For example, first we use a coarse uniform grid to partition objects into cells, then some other index (a kD-tree or BVH-tree) for each cell.

On the other hand, it is possible to use a quad-/oct-/kD-tree to perform the initial subdivision and then use a uniform grid for one part with a lot of tiny objects and BSP-trees for other parts (since we've reduced the number of objects and using BSP-trees locally will not cause big splitting).

What spatial indices combine depends on the set of objects and typical requests which the resulting structure is optimized for.

Chapter 11

Curves and surfaces: Geometric modeling

11.1 Representation of curves and surfaces

There are several forms in which a geometric curve can be specified. The simplest form for a 2D-curve is to define it via the function giving one coordinate (y) from the other (x)

$$y = f(x). \tag{11.1}$$

But this form has some limitations, e.g., we cannot represent some simple shapes like a circle using Equation (11.1). So very often a *parametric form* of the curve is used

$$\begin{cases} x = x(u), \\ y = y(u). \end{cases} \qquad (11.2)$$

Here the parameter u takes values in some range ($u \in [a, b]$); quite often this range is normalized to the segment $[0, 1]$. For a curve in 3D-space we just add one more coordinate equation to (11.2)

$$\begin{cases} x = x(u), \\ y = y(u), \\ z = z(u). \end{cases} \qquad (11.3)$$

Usually we require that functions $x(u)$, $y(u)$ and $z(u)$ to be continuous and have several continuous derivatives (i.e., to belong to some class $C^k[a, b]$).

The circle which we are unable to represent using explicit form (11.1) can be easily written in a parametric form as follows

$$\begin{cases} x = r \cos u, \\ y = r \sin u, 0 \le u \le 2\pi. \end{cases} \qquad (11.4)$$

Quite often curves are written using *polar coordinates* as in (11.5) (see Figure 11.1).

$$\begin{cases} x = r(\phi) \cos \phi, \\ y = r(\phi) \sin \phi, 0 \le \phi \le 2\pi. \end{cases} \qquad (11.5)$$

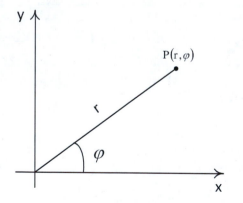

FIGURE 11.1: Polar coordinates.

Note that a parametric representation is not unique – if there is a parametric representation of the curve and some continuous and strongly monotonic function $u = u(v)$, then we can write the same curve using new parameter v

$$\begin{cases} x = x(u(v)), \\ y = y(u(v)), \\ z = z(u(v)). \end{cases} \tag{11.6}$$

The new parameter v takes values in a new range $[a', b']$ such that $u(a') = a$ and $u(b') = b$.

There is one more form of curve representation – an *implicit* equation. We can specify a 2D-circle as a set of all points (x, y) whose coordinates satisfy the equation

$$x^2 + y^2 = R^2. \tag{11.7}$$

In a general case an implicit form of a 2D-curve is given by the equation

$$F(x, y) = 0. \tag{11.8}$$

For the rest of this chapter we will be dealing mostly with parametric representations of curves in 2D and 3D. Such a representation will be written in a vector form

$$p = p(u), a \le u \le b. \tag{11.9}$$

Here the $p(u)$ is the function mapping segment $[a, b]$ into 2D- or 3D-space.

The surface just as a curve can be given by an explicit equation giving one coordinate from two others.

$$z = f(x, y) \tag{11.10}$$

Also we can use a parametric form of the surface but this time we need two parameters u and v

$$p = p(u, v), a \le u \le b, c \le v \le d. \tag{11.11}$$

And of course there is an implicit form of surface via equation of the following form

$$F(x, y, z) = 0. \tag{11.12}$$

For example, the sphere in 3D-space can be given by implicit equation $x^2 + y^2 + z^2 = R^2$.

Surfaces can be written in the *spherical coordinates*. In this case each point is defined by two angles (ϕ and θ) and a distance r to the coordinate origin (see Figure 11.2).

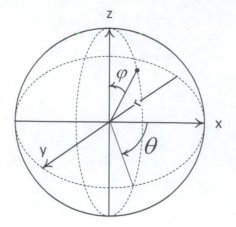

FIGURE 11.2: Spherical coordinates of the point.

$$\begin{cases} x(\theta, \phi) = r\sin\theta\cos\phi, \\ y(\theta, \phi) = r\sin\theta\sin\phi, \\ z(\theta, \phi) = r\cos\theta. \end{cases} \qquad (11.13)$$

The surface equation in spherical coordinates takes the form $r = r(\theta, \phi)$.

11.2 Elements of differential geometry, tangent space, curvature

11.2.1 Differential geometry of curves

Now we will work with 3D-curves and surfaces, and a 2D-case can be obtained by just throwing away (or setting to zero) a third component. We also will be mostly using a parametric representation of the curve in the vector form

$$p = p(u). \qquad (11.14)$$

Here the $p(u)$ is the function mapping segment of real numbers to 3D-vectors ($f : [a, b] \mapsto \mathbb{R}^3$). We will assume that $p(u)$ has at least one continuous derivative $p'(u)$.

Parameterization is called *regular* if $\|p'(u)\| \neq 0$ for all u from the range $[a, b]$. Parameterization $p = p(u)$ is called *natural* if $\|p'(u)\| = 1$ for all u from $[a, b]$.

The length of the arc of curve corresponding to $u_1 \leq u \leq u_2$ can be found via the integral

$$s = \int_{u_1}^{u_2} \|p'(u)\| du. \tag{11.15}$$

For natural parameterization the parameter s is the arc length – if we have two points $p_1 = p(s_1)$ and $p_2 = p(s_2)$ and $p(s)$ is natural parameterization then the length of curve between points p_1 and p_2 is equal to $|s_2 - s_1|$.

Vector $p'(u)$ is the tangent vector to the curve at point $p(u)$, but except for natural parameterization it is not normalized. So we can define a unit tangent vector $t(u)$ for the curve (provided the parameterization is regular) by the equation

$$t(u) = \frac{p'(u)}{\|p'(u)\|}. \tag{11.16}$$

If the function $p(u)$ has a non-zero second-order derivative $p''(u)$ then we can also define a unit binormal vector $b(u)$,

$$b(u) = \frac{[p'(u), p''(u)]}{\|[p'(u), p''(u)]\|}. \tag{11.17}$$

From the tangent and binormal vectors we can get a third vector – normal – as their cross product

$$t(u) = [b(u), t(u)]. \tag{11.18}$$

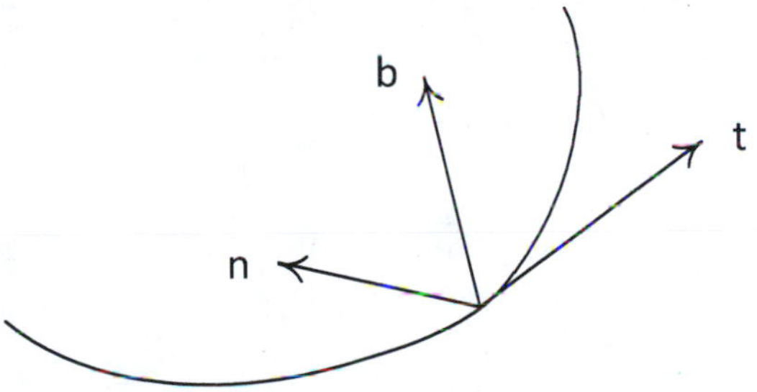

FIGURE 11.3: Frenet-Serret frame.

These three vectors $t(u)$, $n(u)$ and $b(u)$ form a basis in 3D-space and are called the *Frenet-Serret frame* (see Figure 11.3).

For natural parameterization the equations for the Frenet-Serret frame became simpler

$$t(u) = p'(u),$$

$$n(u) = \frac{p''(u)}{\|p''(u)\|},$$

$$b(u) = \frac{[p'(u), p''(u)]}{\|[p'(u), p''(u)]\|}. \tag{11.19}$$

An important property of the Frenet-Serret frame is that is does not depend on the curve parameterization – if we change parameterization then for every point of the curve we still get the same t, n and b vectors.

For the natural parameterization of the curve the *Frenet-Serret formulas* hold true.

$$\begin{pmatrix} t'(s) \\ n'(s) \\ b'(s) \end{pmatrix} = \begin{pmatrix} 0 & k_1(s) & 0 \\ -k_1(s) & 0 & k_2(s) \\ 0 & -k_2(s) & 0 \end{pmatrix} \cdot \begin{pmatrix} t(s) \\ n(s) \\ b(s) \end{pmatrix} \tag{11.20}$$

Here the $k_1(s)$ is the *curvature* of the curve and the $k_2(s)$ is the *torsion*.

Curvature and the torsion of the curve also do not depend on the parameterization of the curve. They can be defined (for any parameterization) by the following equation, provided the function $p(u)$ is smooth enough

$$k_1(u) = \frac{\|[p'(u), p''(u)]\|}{\|p'(u)\|^3},$$

$$k_2(u) = \frac{p'(u)p''(u)p'''(u)}{\|[p'(u), p''(u)]\|^3}. \tag{11.21}$$

Here the $p'(u)p''(u)p'''(u)$ denotes the mixed product of these three vectors, which can be defined as $(p'(u), [p''(u), p'''(u)])$.

11.2.2 Differential geometry of surfaces

Now consider the case of the parametrically defined surface in a 3D-space (11.11).

We will be dealing with smooth surfaces, so we require that function $p(u, v)$ has continuous partial derivatives of up to the second order on both u and v.

If we fix the value of one of the parameters, e.g., $v = v_0$ then we will get a parametric curve $p = p(u, v_0)$ in a 3D-space with a tangent vector $p'_u(u, v_0)$.

Also we can fix the value of other parameter, e.g., $u = u_0$ and get another curve $p = p(u_0, v)$ (passing through the same point (u_0, v_0)) with a tangent vector $p'_v(u, v_0)$ (see Figure 11.4).

So at any point of the surface we have two tangent vectors p'_u and p'_v. The parameterization is called *regular* if for all u and v we have $[p'_u, p'_v] \neq 0$.

Regular parameterization means that at no point these two tangent vectors

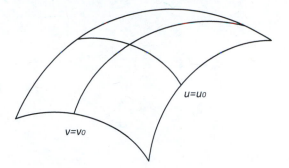

FIGURE 11.4: Two parametric curves on the surface.

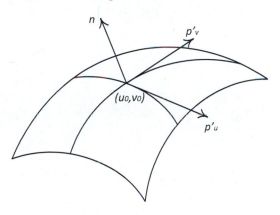

FIGURE 11.5: Tangent and normal vectors to the surface.

can be colinear, so at any point $p_0 = p(u_0, v_0)$ we can define the *tangent plane* to the surface – $(p - p_0, n) = 0$. The unit normal vector n to the surface is defined as the normalized cross-product of tangent vectors

$$n(u, v) = \frac{[p'_u(u, v), p'_v(u, v)]}{\|[p'_u(u, v), p'_v(u, v)]\|}. \tag{11.22}$$

For smooth-enough surfaces we can introduce the first and second fundamental forms of the surface written through the differentials of parameters

$$I = (dp, dp) = E\,du^2 + 2F\,du\,dv + G\,dv^2, \tag{11.23}$$

$$II = (d^2p, n) = L\,du^2 + 2M\,du\,dv + N\,dv^2. \tag{11.24}$$

The functions E, F, G, L, M and N are defined by the following equations

$$
\begin{aligned}
E &= \|p'_u\|^2, \\
F &= (p'_u, p'_v), \\
G &= \|p'_v\|^2, \\
L &= (p''_{uu}, n), \\
M &= (p''_{uv}, n), \\
N &= (p''_{vv}, n).
\end{aligned}
\tag{11.25}
$$

Note that always we have $EF - G^2 > 0$.

If we have some set Ω on the parametric plane (u, v) then the area of the surface corresponding to Ω can be computed via the integral

$$
S_\Omega = \int_\Omega \sqrt{EG - F^2} \, du \, dv.
\tag{11.26}
$$

If we fix some point $p_0 = p(u_0, v_0)$ on the surface then for any direction λ in a parametric plane (i.e., line coming through (u_0, v_0)) we get a curve coming through p_0. For this curve we can find its curvature at p_0 by the equation

$$
k(\lambda) = \frac{L du^2 + 2M du \, dv + N dv^2}{E du^2 + 2F du \, dv + G dv^2}.
\tag{11.27}
$$

There are only two possible cases – either curvature at this point does not depend on direction λ or it has only two extreme values – k_+ and k_-, called the *main curvatures* of the surface at p_0. Their product K is called the *Gauss curvature* and defined by the equation

$$
K = k_+ k_- = \frac{LN - M^2}{EG - F^2}.
\tag{11.28}
$$

Their sum H is called a *mean curvature* and defined by the equation

$$
H = \frac{NE - 2MF - LG}{EG - F^2}.
\tag{11.29}
$$

11.3 Bezier and Hermite curves and surfaces

One of the very often-used classes of curves and surfaces are Bezier and Hermite curves and surfaces.

11.3.1 Bezier curves

If we are given a set of points (called *control points*) $P_0, P_1, \cdots, P_m$ then we can define an elementary Bezier curve by the formula

$$p(u) = \sum_{i=0}^{m} B_i^m(u) P_i, 0 \leq u \leq 1. \tag{11.30}$$

Here the $B_i^m(u)$ are the Bernstein polynomials of the order m which are defined as follows

$$B_i^m(u) = \frac{m!}{i!(m-i)!} u^i (1-u)^{m-i}. \tag{11.31}$$

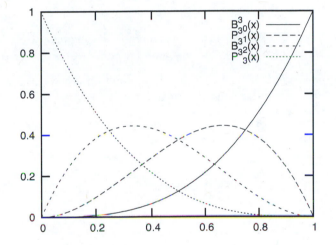

FIGURE 11.6: Bernstein polynomials of the third degree.

On the Figure 11.6 Bernstein polynomials of the third degree (u^3, $3u^2(1-u)$, $3u(1-u)^2$ and $(1-u)^3$) are shown.

The Bernstein polynomials have several important properties:

- they are non-negative on $[0, 1]$;

- their sum is equal to one ($\sum_{i=0}^{m} B_i^m(u) = 1$);

- the order of $B_i^m(u)$ is exactly m.

For the Bezier curve we can easily write down its derivatives from Equation (11.31):

$$p'(u) = m \sum_{i=0}^{m-1} (P_{i+1} - P_i) B_i^{m-1}(u), \tag{11.32}$$

$$p''(u) = m(m-1) \sum_{i=0}^{m-2} (P_{i+2} - 2P_{i+1} + P_i) B_i^{m-2}(u). \tag{11.33}$$

The Bezier curve has many useful properties:

- it is smooth (see (11.32));

- it starts at P_0 and ends at P_m $(p(0) = P_0, p(1) = P_m)$;

- it completely lies in the convex hull of its control points $P_0, P_1, \cdots, P_m$;

- it is symmetric, i.e., if we revert the order of the points the curve will be the same;

- at its start the Bezier curve is tangent to the segment $P_0 P_1$ and at the end it is tangent to the last segment $P_{m-1} P_m$ (see Figure 11.7);

- if all points $P_0, P_1, \cdots, P_m$ are on the same line then the corresponding Bezier curve will be lying in this line too;

- if all points $P_0, P_1, \cdots, P_m$ are in the same plane then the corresponding Bezier curve will be in this plane too.

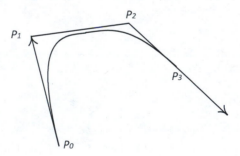

FIGURE 11.7: Bezier curve with control points P_0, P_1, P_2 and P_3.

One commonly used case of the Bezier curve is the cubic Bezier curve $(m = 3)$ (see Figure 11.8) which is defined by the equation

$$p(u) = (((1 - u)P_0 + 3uP_1)(1 - u) + 3u^2 P_2)(1 - u) + u^3 P_3. \tag{11.34}$$

This equation can be rewritten in a matrix form

FIGURE 11.8: Examples of Bezier curves of the third order.

$$p(u) = PMU. \tag{11.35}$$

Here the matrix P is built from the input points (they form its columns), matrix M is the fixed matrix of coefficients and vector U is composed of powers of u

$$M = \begin{pmatrix} 1 & -3 & 3 & 1 \\ 0 & 3 & -6 & 3 \\ 0 & 0 & 3 & -3 \\ 0 & 0 & 0 & 1 \end{pmatrix}, \tag{11.36}$$

$$P = \begin{pmatrix} P_0 & P_1 & P_2 & P_3 \end{pmatrix} = \begin{pmatrix} x_0 & x_1 & x_2 & x_3 \\ y_0 & y_1 & y_2 & y_3 \\ z_0 & z_1 & z_2 & z_3 \end{pmatrix}, \tag{11.37}$$

$$U = \begin{pmatrix} 1 \\ u \\ u^2 \\ u^3 \end{pmatrix}. \tag{11.38}$$

If we have many input points then it may be undesirable to build one large Bezier curve from all of them since we will get a polynomial of a large degree. So in this case we can build the resulting curve as a composite curve consisting of several low-order Bezier curves. In this case we must ensure proper conditions at interior points to make the resulting composite curve having the continuous derivative of first order.

Usually this *composite Bezier curve* is built from elementary cubic Bezier curves (see Figure 11.9).

To ensure continuity of first-order derivatives (so-called G^1 continuity) we need every three points $P_{3i-1}, P_{3i}, P_{3i+1}$ to be colinear (i.e., lie on some line).

To ensure continuity of second-order derivatives (so-called G^2 continuity) we need every five points $P_{3i-2}, P_{3i-1}, P_{3i}, P_{3i+1}, P_{3i+2}$ to be coplanar, i.e., lie in one plane.

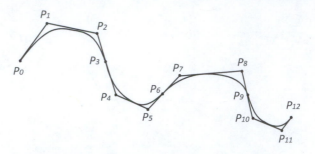

FIGURE 11.9: Composite Bezier curve.

11.3.2 Hermite curves

One more often-used class of curves is Hermite curves. Given two points P_0 and P_1 and two vectors Q_0 and Q_1 we can build an elementary cubic Hermite curve via the equation

$$p(u) = (1 - 3u^2 + 2u^3)P_0 = u^2(3 - 2u)P_1 + u(1 - u)^2 Q_0 - u^2(1 - u)Q_1, 0 \le u \le 1. \tag{11.39}$$

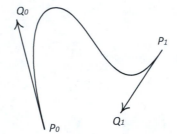

FIGURE 11.10: Cubic Hermite curve.

Like a Bezier curve, a cubic Hermite curve (see Figure 11.10) can be written in a matrix form

$$p(u) = GMU. \tag{11.40}$$

Here the matrix G is built from the input points P_0, P_1 and vectors Q_0, Q_1 (they form its columns), matrix M is the fixed matrix of coefficients and vector U is composed of powers of u

$$M = \begin{pmatrix} 1 & 0 & -3 & 2 \\ 0 & 0 & 3 & -2 \\ 0 & 1 & -2 & 1 \\ 0 & 0 & -1 & 1 \end{pmatrix}, \tag{11.41}$$

$$G = \begin{pmatrix} P_0 & P_1 & Q_0 & Q_1 \end{pmatrix}, \tag{11.42}$$

$$P = \begin{pmatrix} 1 \\ u \\ u^2 \\ u^3 \end{pmatrix}. \tag{11.43}$$

The Hermite curve starts at point P_0 ($p(0) = P_0$) and ends at P_1 ($p(1) = P_1$), tangent vector at P_0 coincides with Q_0 ($p'(0) = Q_0$), tangent vector at P_1 coincides with Q_1 ($p'(0) = Q_0$).

Equation (11.39) can be written both in a Bezier form and in a Hermite form:

$$
\begin{aligned}
p(u) =& B_0^3(u)P_0 + B_1^3(u)(P_0 + \tfrac{1}{3}Q_0) + B_2^3(u)(P_1 - \tfrac{1}{3}Q_1) + \\
& B_3^3(u)P_1, \\
p(u) =& H_0^3(u)P_0 + H_1^3(u)Q_0 + H_2^3(u)Q_1 + H_3^3(u)P_1.
\end{aligned}
\tag{11.44}
$$

Here the $H_i^3(u)$ are Hermite polynomials shown below

$$
\begin{aligned}
H_0^3(u) &= B_0^3(u) + B_1^3(u), \\
H_1^3(u) &= \frac{1}{3}B_1^3(u), \\
H_2^3(u) &= -\frac{1}{3}B_2^3(u), \\
H_3^3(u) &= B_2^3(u) + B_3^3(u).
\end{aligned}
\tag{11.45}
$$

If we have an array of points $P_0, \cdots, P_m$ and two non-zero vectors Q_0 and Q_m, then we can build a composite cubic Hermite curve as a union of m elementary Hermite curves.

Each elementary curve is defined by points P_{i-1}, P_i and vectors Q_{i-1}, Q_i. All points $P_0, \cdots, P_m$ are known, but only the first (Q_0) and the last (Q_m) tangent vectors are given.

So the remaining tangent vectors are found from the following system of equations

$$
\begin{cases}
Q_0 + 4Q_1 + Q_2 = -3P_0 + 3P_2, \\
Q_1 + 4Q_2 + Q_3 = -3P_1 + 3P_3, \\
\cdots \\
\\
Q_{m-3} + 4Q_{m-2} + Q_{m-1} = -3P_{m-3} + 3P_{m-1}, \\
Q_{m-2} + 4Q_{m-1} + Q_m = -3P_{m-2} + 3P_m.
\end{cases}
\tag{11.46}
$$

A composite cubic Hermite curve has the following properties:

- it is a C^2 curve (has a continuous curvature);

- it comes through all input points $P_0, \cdots, P_m$;

- tangent vectors Q_i are uniquely defined by input points and first and last tangent vectors Q_0 and Q_m.

11.3.3 Bezier surfaces

If we have a 2D-array of points $P_{ij}, i = 0, \cdots, m, j = 0, \cdots, n$, then we can build a Bezier surface in the same way we were building a Bezier curve

$$p(u,v) = \sum_{i=0}^{m} \sum_{j=0}^{n} B_i^m(u) B_j^n(v) P_{ij}, 0 \leq u \leq 1, 0 \leq v \leq 1. \tag{11.47}$$

From Equation (11.47) we can easily get first-order partial derivatives of the Bezier surface

$$p_u'(u,v) = m \sum_{i=0}^{m-1} \sum_{j=0}^{n} B_i^{m-1}(u) B_j^n(v)(P_{i+1,j} - P_{ij}), \tag{11.48}$$

$$p_v'(u,v) = n \sum_{i=0}^{m} \sum_{j=0}^{n-1} B_i^m(u) B_j^{n-1}(v)(P_{i,j+1} - P_{ij}). \tag{11.49}$$

As with Bezier curves the most important and widely used case is a bicubic Bezier surface ($m = n = 3$). It is defined by 16 control points P_{ij} and can be written in the following form:

$$p(u,v) = \sum_{i=0}^{3} B_i^3(u) \Big(\sum_{j=0}^{3} B_j^3(v) P_{ij} \Big). \tag{11.50}$$

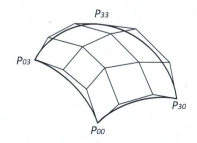

FIGURE 11.11: Bicubic Bezier surface.

A bicubic Bezier surface can be written in a matrix form just like a curve

$$p(u,v) = U^T M^T P M V. \tag{11.51}$$

The vectors U and V are composed of powers of u and v and matrix

$$M = \begin{pmatrix} 1 & -3 & 3 & 1 \\ 0 & 3 & -6 & 3 \\ 0 & 0 & 3 & -3 \\ 0 & 0 & 0 & 1 \end{pmatrix}. \tag{11.52}$$

The Bezier surface (patch) satisfies several useful properties just like the Bezier curve:

- it is smooth (has continuous derivatives);

- it is bounded by Bezier curves of corresponding order (i.e., $p(u,0), p(u,1), p(0,v), p(1,v)$ are elementary Bezier curves of order m and n, respectively);

- the Bezier surface completely lies in the convex hull of its control points P_{ij};

- if all points P_{ij} lie in the plane then the surface is a polygon in this plane.

We can get values of a surface and its derivative at each corner. Below are corresponding values for the corner $u = 0, v = 0$

$$\begin{aligned} p(0,0) &= P_{00}, \\ p'_u(0,0) &= m(P_{10} - P_{00}), \\ p'_v(0,0) &= n(P_{01} - P_{00}), \\ p''_{uv}(0,0) &= mn((P_{11} - P_{10}) - (P_{01} - P_{00}). \end{aligned} \tag{11.53}$$

From bicubic Bezier surfaces we can build composite surfaces. If we have two sets of control points $P_{ij}^{(1)}$ and $P_{ij}^{(2)}$ each defining its own bicubic Bezier surface $p^{(1)}$ and $p^{(2)}$, then if $P_{3j}^{(1)} = P_{0j}^{(2)}, j = 0, 1, 2, 3$ then both surfaces will share the same boundary Bezier curve $p^{(1)}(1,v) = p^{(2)}(0,v)$.

So in this case we already have a continuous surface. If we want it to be a C^1 surface, then additional conditions on control points are required:

- all triples $P_{2j}^{(1)}, P_{3j}^{(1)} = P_{0,j}^{(2)}, P_{1,j}^{(2)}$ should be colinear for all $j = 0, \cdots, 3$;

- expression $\dfrac{\|P_{3j}^{(1)} - P_{2j}^{(1)}\|}{\|P_{1j}^{(2)} - P_{0j}^{(2)}\|}$ must be constant for all j.

11.3.4   Hermite surfaces

We can introduce a bicubic Hermite surface using the equations

$$
\begin{cases}
x(u,v) = UMG_xM^TV^T, \\
y(u,v) = UMG_yM^TV^T, \\
z(u,v) = UMG_zM^TV^T,
\end{cases}
\tag{11.54}
$$

The matrices G_x, G_y and G_z define the properties of a Hermite surface at the corners. They have the same structure, so we will look at the structure of matrix G_x.

$$
G_x =
\begin{pmatrix}
x(0,0) & x(0,1) & x'_u(0,0) & x'_u(0,1) \\
x(1,0) & x(1,1) & x'_u(1,0) & x'_u(1,1) \\
x'_v(0,0) & x'_v(0,1) & x''_{uv}(0,0) & x''_{uv}(0,1) \\
x'_v(1,0) & x'_v(1,1) & x''_{uv}(1,0) & x''_{uv}(1,1)
\end{pmatrix}.
\tag{11.55}
$$

The upper-left 2×2 submatrix of G_x contains the x-coordinates of all four corners of the surface. The upper-right submatrix contains the tangent vector along u for all corners. The lower-left submatrix contains the tangent vector along v and the lower-right submatrix contains a *twist* at all four corners.

The matrix M for the bicubic Hermite surface is given by the equation

$$
M =
\begin{pmatrix}
1 & 0 & -3 & 2 \\
0 & 0 & 3 & -2 \\
0 & 1 & -2 & 1 \\
0 & 0 & -1 & 1
\end{pmatrix}.
\tag{11.56}
$$

11.4   Interpolation

Interpolation of some data is a quite often encountered task – we are given a set of values (u_i, y_i) of unknown function (or points in a 2D- or 3D-space), and we want to build a function of some simple enough class that comes through all of these points (see Figure 11.12).

Very close to interpolation is another task – when we want to build a function coming close enough to the given points. This kind of task arises when we have too much data usually containing some kind of errors (or noise) so we want a rather simple function "smoothing out" these errors (see Figure 11.13).

Usually we have a set (grid) of values (called *knots*) $a = u_0 < u_1 < \cdots < u_{m-1} < u_m = b$. The grid is called *uniform* if the distance between two neighboring knots is the same $u_{i+1} - u_i = h, i = 0, \cdots, m - 1$, where the h is a step of this grid. In this case any knot u_i can be written as $u_i = a + (i - 1)h$.

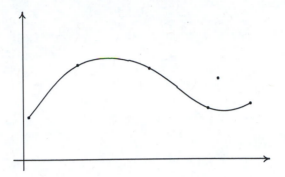

FIGURE 11.12: Function comes through given points.

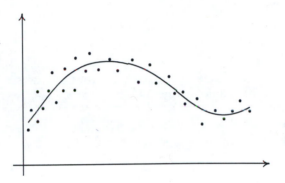

FIGURE 11.13: Smoothing function.

For every knot u_i we are given some value y_i. And the task of interpolation is to build a smooth function $s(u)$ such that for all i's $s(u_i) = y_i$.

Such a function is called a *spline* of degree p if

- on any segment $[u_i, u_{i+1}]$ this function is a polynomial of the order p (so it can be written as $s(u) = \sum_{k=0}^{p} a_k^i (u - u_i)^k$);

- $s(u) \in C^{p-1}[a, b]$.

The polynomial of degree p is defined by $p + 1$ coefficients. Therefore, if we have $m + 1$ knots then we will need $m(p + 1)$ coefficients to define each polynomial for each segment $[u_i, u_{i+1}]$.

From the condition $s(u) \in C^{p-1}$ we get conditions on derivatives $s^k(u_i - 0) = s^k(u_i + 0)$. Therefore, we get $p(m - 1)$ conditions on coefficients.

To fully define a spline we still need $(p + 1)m - p(m - 1) = m + p$ more conditions which will uniquely define all the coefficients. Since we are interpolating we get $m + 1$ conditions $s(u_i) = y_i$ which leaves us with only $p - 1$ conditions. Usually these conditions are set at the ends of the segment u_0 and u_m and called *boundary conditions*.

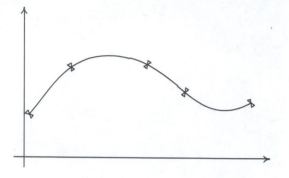

FIGURE 11.14: Steel spline.

The term *spline* comes from an early way of producing a smooth curve coming through given points used by engineers. They used a thin metal or wood strips forcing them to come through given points. A strip can come at any angle through the point. It was later shown that the strip takes a form corresponding to minimum energy. This steel or wooden strip was called a spline (see Figure 11.14).

Note that instead of using a separate polynomial on each segment $[u_i, u_{i+1}]$, we could always build one polynomial of degree m called a *Lagrange interpolation polynomial*

$$L_m(u) = \sum_{i=0}^{m} y_i \frac{\phi(u)}{(u - u_i)\phi'(u_i)}, \tag{11.57}$$

$$\phi(u) = \prod_{i=0}^{m} (u - u_i). \tag{11.58}$$

Lagrange's polynomial is simple and completely defined by a set of input pairs (u_i, y_i). It has continuous derivatives of any order.

But it also has several serious drawbacks making it unsuitable for large datasets:

- the order of the polynomial depends on the number of points;

- changes in any of the input points requires rebuilding the polynomial;

- adding a new point increases the order of the polynomial and requires its full rebuilding.

Note that Lagrange polynomials of a high degree may behave very badly and it was shown that increasing the number of knots on the segment may not result in an increased quality of interpolation.

So using splines usually proves to be a more convenient approach. In the next sections we will cover several of the mostly used spline types.

11.5   Splines

11.5.1   B-splines

B-splines (from *basic splines*) are splines with the given degree n which are defined by the Cox-de Boor equations (see Fig. 11.16)

$$b_{j,0} = \begin{cases} 1, u_j \le u < u_{j+1}, \\ 0, otherwise \end{cases}$$

$$b_{j,k}(u) = \frac{u - u_j}{u_{j+k} - u_j} b_{j,k-1}(u) + \frac{u_{j+k+1} - u}{u_{j+k+1} - u_j} b_{j+1,k-1}(u). \tag{11.59}$$

When the distance between neighboring nodes u_{j+1} and u_j is constant and does not depend on j the B-spline is called *uniform* and *non-uniform* otherwise.

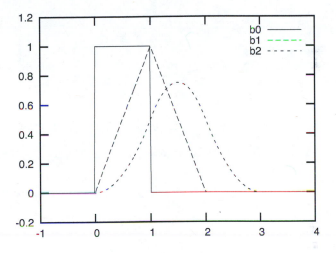

FIGURE 11.15: First three basis functions.

For uniform B-splines it is possible to write a non-recursive equation

$$b_{j,n}(u) = b_n(u - u_j). \tag{11.60}$$

The function $b_n(u)$ is defined by the equation

$$b_n(u) = \frac{n+1}{n} \sum_{i=0}^{n+1} \omega_{i,n} max(0, u - u_j)^n. \tag{11.61}$$

The scaling coefficients $\omega_{i,n}$ are as follows

$$\omega_{i,n} = \prod_{j=0, j \neq i}^{n+1} \frac{1}{u_j - u_i} \tag{11.62}$$

In Figure 11.16 you can see uniform cubic basic splines $\frac{(1-u)^3}{6}, \frac{3t^3 - 6t + 4}{6}, \frac{-3t^3 + 3t^2 + 3t + 1}{6}, \frac{t^3}{6}$.

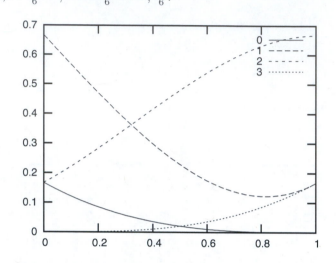

FIGURE 11.16: Basis functions of the third order.

When we have a set of control points $P_0, \cdots, P_{m-n-2}$ then the B-spline curve is defined by equation formula

$$B(u) = \sum_{i=0}^{m-n-2} P_i b_{i,n}(u), u \in [u_n, u_{m-n-1}]. \tag{11.63}$$

For the case of a uniform cubic B-spline curve we have

$$B(u) = \frac{(1-u)^3}{6} P_0 + \frac{3u^3 - 6u^2 + 4}{6} P_1 + \frac{-3u^3 + 3u^2 + 3u + 1}{6} P_2 + \frac{u^3}{6} P_2. \tag{11.64}$$

We can write (11.64) in a matrix form

$$B(u) = PMU,$$
$$P = (P_0\ P_1\ P_2\ P_3),$$
$$M = \frac{1}{6} \begin{pmatrix} 1 & -3 & 3 & 1 \\ 4 & 0 & -6 & 3 \\ 1 & 3 & 3 & -3 \\ 0 & 0 & 0 & 1 \end{pmatrix}. \qquad (11.65)$$

Basis uniform polynomials $b_{i,n}(u)$

- are non-negative $(b_{i,n}(u) \geq 0)$;

- their sum is equal to one.

Cubic B-spline curve $B(u)$ has several important properties (see Figure 11.17):

- it completely lies in the convex hull of its control points P_0, P_1, P_2, P_3 (but usually does not pass through them);

- the tangent vector at one end $(u = 0)$ is parallel to vector $P_0 P_2$;

- the tangent vector at the other end $(u = 1)$ is parallel to vector $P_1 P_3$.

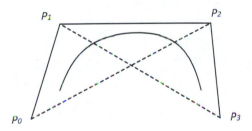

FIGURE 11.17: Cubic B-spline.

11.5.2 NURBS

A B-spline curve is defined as a weighted sum of its control points P_i. And the weights of these control points depend only on basis functions $b_{i,n}(u)$. But sometimes it becomes desirable to give some control point(s) more (or less) weight than other control points.

In order to do so we add to each control point P_i some weight w_i, and lose a very important property of B-spline – that sum of all weights is always equal to one. So we need to renormalize the blending functions in this way

$$B(u) = \frac{\sum_{i=0}^{m} w_i b_{i,m}(u)}{\sum_{i=0}^{m} w_i b_{i,m}(u)} P_i. \tag{11.66}$$

We can rewrite Equation (11.66) in a more common form of blending functions and control points

$$B(u) = \sum_{i=0}^{m} n_{i,m}(u) P_i, \tag{11.67}$$

$$n_{i,m}(u) = \frac{w_i b_{i,m}(u)}{\sum_{i=0}^{m} w_i b_{i,m}(u)}. \tag{11.68}$$

Note that the sum of the functions $n_{i,m}(u)$ is always equal to one.

Such a spline curve is called *Non-Uniform Rational B-Spline* or NURBS (see Figure 11.18).

NURBS curves admit a very simple geometric interpretation – if we add each weight w_i to the corresponding 3D-control point P_i, then we will obtain a 4D-homogeneous vector $P_i' = (x_i \ y_i \ z_i \ w_i)^T$.

For such 4D-control points we can build a B-spline and after coming from homogeneous coordinates to normal 3D-coordinates (i.e., by dividing all coordinates by the fourth coordinate) we will get Equation (11.67).

So NURBS curves can be considered as a generalization of traditional non-uniform B-splines giving more control over the shape of the curve.

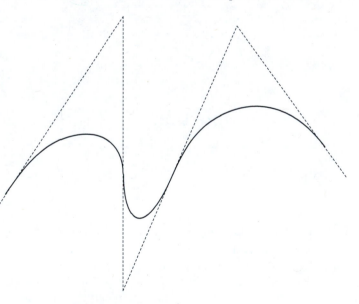

FIGURE 11.18: Example of a NURBS curve.

One important feature of NURBS is that they are invariant with respect to affine and perspective transforms. It means that if we build a NURBS by a set of control points and then transform the resulting curve it will be the same as a NURBS curve built from transformed control points.

Changing weights changes the influence of each control point and therefore the shape of the curve. Figure 11.19 shows the effect of changing the weight w_3 of the NURBS.

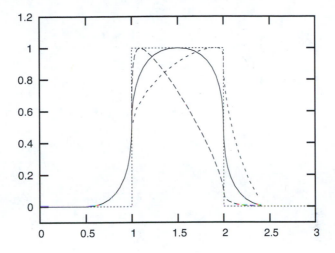

FIGURE 11.19: NURBS for different weights for the fourth control point.

11.5.3 Catmull-Rom splines

Catmull-Rom cubic splines curve for given control points P_0, P_1, P_2 and P_3 is defined so that the tangent at each inner point P_i can be found from the difference between neighboring points as $\tau(P_{i+1} - P_{i-1})$. The parameter τ is called a *tension* and usually is set to 0.5. Figure 11.20 shows how it affects the shape of the curve.

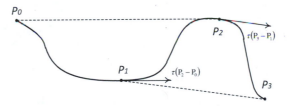

FIGURE 11.20: Catmull-Rom spline for points P_0, P_1, P_2 and P_3.

This spline curve can be written in a matrix form just as the other curves

$$B(u) = PMU, \tag{11.69}$$

$$P = (P_0 \; P_1 \; P_2 \; P_3), \tag{11.70}$$

$$M = \begin{pmatrix} 0 & -\tau & 2\tau & -\tau \\ 1 & 0 & \tau - 3 & 2 - \tau \\ 0 & \tau & 3 - 2\tau & \tau - 2 \\ 0 & 0 & -\tau & \tau \end{pmatrix}. \tag{11.71}$$

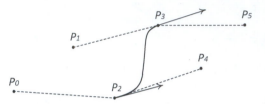

FIGURE 11.21: Catmull–Rom spline.

From Equation (11.69) we can easily get values and tangents at curve endpoints

$$\begin{aligned} B(0) &= P_1, \\ B(1) &= P_2, \\ B'(0) &= \tau(P_2 - P_0), \\ B'(1) &= \tau(P_3 - P_1). \end{aligned} \tag{11.72}$$

Note that the resulting curve may not lie in the convex hull of its control points P_0, P_1, P_2 and P_3.

If we have a group of control points $P_0, P_1, \cdots, P_m$ then for each quadruple of points $P_{i-1}, P_{i-1}, P_i, P_{i+1}$ we can build a Catmull-Rom spline curve from P_{i-1} to P_i. Since tangents at these points are defined by other control points, it means that all such curve segments link to each other forming a C^1-smooth spline curve.

11.6 Surfaces of revolution

One class of relatively easy and often-met surfaces is called *surfaces of revolution*. These surfaces are produced by rotating a curve around some line in 3D (see Figure 11.22).

Consider a 2D-curve $x = \phi(u), y = \psi(u), u \in [a, b]$. Now if we rotate that curve around a z-axis we will get a parametric surface, described by the equations

$$\begin{cases} x(u,v) = \phi(u)cosv, \\ y(u,v) = \phi(u)sinv, \\ z(u,v) = \psi(u). \end{cases} \tag{11.73}$$

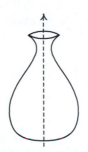

FIGURE 11.22: Surfaces of revolution.

Here the parameter u takes values in the range $[a,b]$ and parameter v – in the range $[0, 2\pi]$. From Equation (11.73) we can easily get tangent vectors

$$p'_u(u,v) = \begin{pmatrix} \phi'(u)cosv \\ \phi'(u)sinv \\ \psi'(u) \end{pmatrix},$$

$$p'_v(u,v) = \begin{pmatrix} \phi(u)(-sinv) \\ \phi(u)cosv \\ 0 \end{pmatrix}. \tag{11.74}$$

Knowing them we get a unit normal by normalizing their cross-product

$$n(u,v) = \frac{sign\phi}{\sqrt{\phi'^2 + \psi'^2}} \begin{pmatrix} \psi'(u)cosv \\ \psi'(u)sinv \\ \phi'(u) \end{pmatrix}. \tag{11.75}$$

11.7 Subdivision of curves and surfaces

If a curve (or a surface) is defined by a set of points then we can approximate that curve (or a surface) with a polyline (or polygon). Instead of

explicitly building a spline we may use various subdivision schemes to generate more points, making our curve (surface) to look smoother. Usually such
techniques are used to build good-looking surfaces from polygonal meshes.

11.7.1 Curve subdivision

For a polyline defined by points $P_0, P_1, \cdots, P_m$ we use these points to generate a new set of points $P'_0, P'_1, \cdots, P'_{2m}$ containing twice the initial number
of points and giving a "more refined" polyline.

Usually the rules for getting new points depend on whether the new point
index is even or odd, so two equations are used – one for even-numbered points
P'_{2i} and one for odd-numbered points P'_{2i+1}.

One of the simplest methods of curve subdivision is the *Doo-Sabin* method
defined by the equations

$$
\begin{cases}
P'_{2i} = \frac{3}{4}P_i + \frac{1}{4}P_{i+1}, \\
P'_{2i+1} = \frac{1}{4}P_i + \frac{3}{4}P_{i+1}.
\end{cases}
\tag{11.76}
$$

In Figure 11.23 the results of applying of rules (11.76) to the simple rectangle are shown.

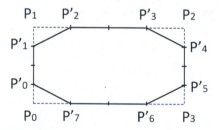

FIGURE 11.23: First iteration of the Doo-Sabin subdivision.

We can recursively apply the subdivision process many times, each time
refining our polyline, making it look like a smooth curve. In Figure 11.24 the
next two iterations on a rectangle are shown.

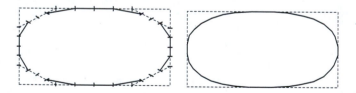

FIGURE 11.24: Next two iterations of the Doo-Sabin subdivision.

Another variant of curve subdivision is the well-known *Catmull-Clark* subdivision scheme based on the following rules

$$\begin{cases} P'_{2i} = \frac{1}{8}P_{i-1} + \frac{6}{8}P_i + \frac{1}{8}P_{i+1}, \\ P'_{2i+1} = \frac{1}{2}P_i + \frac{1}{2}P_{i+1}. \end{cases} \tag{11.77}$$

Note that the first equation of (11.77) can be written as a half-sum of two points

$$P'_{2i} = \frac{1}{2}\left(\frac{1}{4}P_{i-1} + \frac{3}{4}P_i\right) + \frac{1}{2}\left(\frac{3}{4}P_i + \frac{1}{4}P_{i+1}\right). \tag{11.78}$$

Figure 11.25 shows the result of applying the Catmull-Clark subdivision process to the rectangle from Figure 11.23.

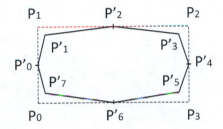

FIGURE 11.25: First iteration of the Catmull-Clark subdivision.

11.7.2   Surface subdivision

One of the classical surface subdivision schemes is the Catmull-Clark algorithm. It is performed on arbitrary polygonal meshes refining them.

The first step of this algorithm computes a *face point* F for every face of the mesh. A *face point* F is computed as an average of all vertices of the face (see Figure 11.26 a).

The next step processes edges. Usually each edge is shared between two faces. Then for each such edge these faces are determined and a new *edge point* R is computed as an average of four points – two endpoints of the edge and two face-points of the adjacent faces (see Figure 11.26 b).

Then each face-point is connected with the new edges with created edge points. After that we process original vertices.

If we have an original vertex P which belongs to k faces (and therefore to k edges) then we compute R – an average of all face-points of all these k faces and R – an average of midpoints of all k edges. After that, vertex P is moved to the point given by following formula

$$\frac{F + 3R + (k-3)P}{k}.$$

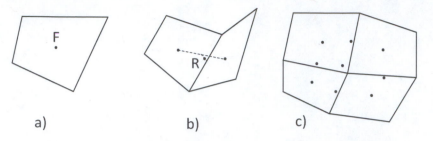

a)　　　　　　　　b)　　　　　　　　c)

FIGURE 11.26: Steps of the Catmull-Clark surface subdivision.

This procedure can be repeated many times, resulting in a polygonal surface (which looks like a smooth surface).

But Catmull-Clark subdivision produces quadriliterals (which are not flat polygons) and require information about adjacent faces. On the other side, the geometry which are fed into the GPUs is usually represented as a triangle mesh and each triangle is processed separately. Also for each triangle we know not only its vertices, but also unit normals at these vertices.

So for many real-time applications it is desirable to use a tessellation algorithm which can process subtriangles individually and independently. One such algorithm is the so-called *curved PN triangles*. In this algorithm, from vertices and normals of every triangle a cubic Bezier patch is built to generate new vertices. For generating normals a quadratic patch is used.

Let's look how this algorithm works. If we have a triangle with vertices P_0, P_1, P_2 and normals n_0, n_1, n_2 then we build a bicubic Bezier patch written with barycentric coordinates u, v, w $(u + v + w = 1, u, v, w \geq 0)$,

$$p(u, v, w) = \sum_{i+j+k=3} b_{ijk} \frac{3!}{i!j!k!} u^i v^j w^k. \tag{11.79}$$

All of the coefficients b_{ijk} of (11.79) are classified into three groups (see Figure 11.27):

- vertex coefficients $(b_{300}, b_{030}, b_{003})$;

- tangent coefficients $(b_{210}, b_{120}, b_{021}, b_{012}, b_{201}, b_{102})$;

- a center coefficient (b_{111}).

Since we want endpoints of our bicubic patch to coincide with vertices of the triangle, we trivially get equations for vertex coefficients

$$\begin{aligned} b_{300} &= P_0, \\ b_{030} &= P_1, \\ b_{003} &= P_2. \end{aligned} \tag{11.80}$$

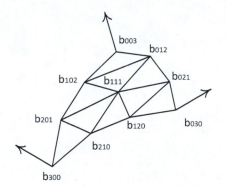

FIGURE 11.27: Control points for the bicubic patch.

Rules for computing tangent coefficients are more complicated. In order to find tangent coefficient b_{ijk}, we first compute an intermediate point $(iP_0 + jP_1 + kP_2)/3$.

Then in order to get b_{ijk} we project this intermediate point onto the tangent plane of the closest vertex (defined by the normal at the vertex). The tangent plane coming through the vertex P_i with the normal n_i is defined by equation $(p - P_i, n_i) = 0$. Projection of an arbitrary point p on this plane can be defined as follows

$$\pi_i(p) = p - (p - P_i, n_i)n_i. \tag{11.81}$$

So we get the following equation for tangent coefficients

$$
\begin{aligned}
b_{210} &= (2P_0 + P_1 - w_{01}n_0)/3, \\
b_{120} &= (2P_1 + P_0 - w_{10}n_1)/3, \\
b_{021} &= (2P_1 + P_2 - w_{12}n_1)/3, \\
b_{012} &= (2P_2 + P_1 - w_{21}n_2)/3, \\
b_{102} &= (2P_2 + P_0 - w_{20}n_2)/3, \\
b_{201} &= (2P_0 + P_2 - w_{02}n_0)/3.
\end{aligned}
\tag{11.82}
$$

Here the coefficients w_{ij} are defined by the next formula

$$w_{i,j} = (P_j - P_i, n_i). \tag{11.83}$$

The central coefficient b_{111} is computed by the formula

$$E = (b_{210} + b_{120} + b_{021} + b_{012} + b_{102} + b_{201})/6,$$
$$V = (P_0 + P_1 + P_2)/3,$$
$$b_{111} = E + \frac{1}{2}(E - v) = \frac{3}{2}E - \frac{1}{2}V. \tag{11.84}$$

For computing normals a quadratic function $n(u, v, w)$ is used (see Figure 11.28).

$$n(u, v, w) = \sum_{i+j+k=2} n_{ijk} u^i v^j w^k. \tag{11.85}$$

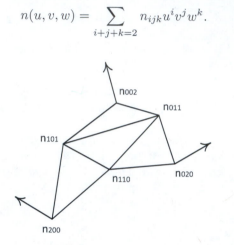

FIGURE 11.28: Normal control points.

The vertex $(n_{200}, n_{020}, n_{002})$ and tangent $(n_{110}, n_{101}, n_{011})$ coefficients are defined by the equations

$$n_{200} = n_0,$$
$$n_{020} = n_1,$$
$$n_{002} = n_2,$$
$$n_{110} = \frac{n_0 + n_1 - v_{01}(P_1 - P_0)}{\|n_0 + n_1 - v_{01}(P_1 - P_0)\|}, \tag{11.86}$$
$$n_{011} = \frac{n_1 + n_2 - v_{12}(P_2 - P_1)}{\|n_1 + n_2 - v_{12}(P_2 - P_1)\|},$$
$$n_{101} = \frac{n_2 + n_0 - v_{20}(P_0 - P_2)}{\|n_2 + n_0 - v_{20}(P_0 - P_2)\|}.$$

The v_{ij} coefficients are given by the following equation

$$v_{ij} = 2\frac{(P_j - P_i, n_i + n_j)}{\|P_j - P_i\|^2}. \tag{11.87}$$

When all coefficients (which can be computed for each triangle independently) are found, then we can create as many points inside the original triangle as we want.

In Chapter 14 we will see how this algorithm can be implemented using OpenGL 4.1 tessellation shaders.

Another variant of triangle tessellation which is very suitable for real-time applications is *Phong tessellation*. It is a shading method that linearly interpolates the normal across the polygon and then normalizes the result (since linear interpolation of unit vectors is usually a non-unit, it can even be a zero vector). This scheme uses a quadratic patch.

The basic idea of Phong tessellation is simple – we compute a new point P' using the linear interpolation of the vertices

$$P' = uP_0 + vP_1 + wP_2. \tag{11.88}$$

Each of the vertices P_0, P_1, P_2 defines its own tangent plane and we project P' onto each of them. Then these projections are blended together using the same weights u, v, w as in (11.88).

Using the projection function $\pi_i(p)$ from (11.82) we can write a new vertex P^*

$$P^* = u\pi_0(P') + v\pi_1(P') + w\pi_2(P') \tag{11.89}$$

We can introduce a blending factor α and use it to connect linear (P') and Phong interpolations

$$P^* = (1 - \alpha)P' + \alpha(u\pi_0(P') + v\pi_1(P') + w\pi_2(P')). \tag{11.90}$$

A normal vector for this point is found using the Phong shading method – we linearly interpolate normals and normalize the result

$$n^* = \frac{un_0 + vn_1 + wn_2}{\|un_0 + vn_1 + wn_2\|}. \tag{11.91}$$

Chapter 12

Basics of animation

Animation of objects (coming from the Latin word *anima*) deals usually with interpolation – we have positions and orientations given at several moments of time and we want to get new positions and orientations for an arbitrary moment of time.

This interpolation comes in two forms – coordinates (positions) interpolation and orientation interpolation.

12.1   Coordinates interpolation

For coordinates interpolation we have a set of known moments of time $t_0, t_1, \cdots, t_{n-1}$ and for each such moment t_i we know a position p_i. The goal is to build a smooth curve $p = p(t)$ such that $p(t_i) = p_i$ for $i = 0, \cdots, n-1$.

The simplest variant to achieve this is to use linear interpolation on each segment $[t_i, t_{i+1}]$. This variant requires minimal computations but the resulting curve will not be smooth (piecewise linear). Because of it, the movement will not look natural (see Figure 12.1).

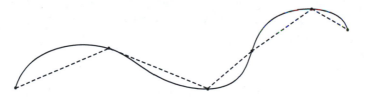

FIGURE 12.1: Smooth and piecewise linear interpolation.

In order to get good interpolation we should use some kind of spline interpolation covered in Chapter 11. We may use a composite bicubic spline or a B-spline of some order. One big advantage of using a B-spline curve is its locality property – changing some position p_j will not change all of the curve but only some neighboring part of it.

12.2 Orientation interpolation

Interpolation of orientations is more complex than interpolation of positions. Here we have a choice of how we store and process orientations – as a rotation matrix, Euler angles or quaternion.

Interpolation of rotation matrices is the worst choice – during it we will be getting matrices which are not rotation matrices, moreover we can even get a matrix whose determinant is zero.

Interpolation with Euler angles is slightly better (so quite often orientations are specified with Euler angles) but it can result in a *gimbal lock*.

The best way to do the interpolation is using unit quaternions – it is free from the problems of other forms and requires only three numbers (we are considering only unit quaternions).

If we have two quaternions q_0 and q_1, then we can simply use the function *slerp* defined in Chapter 4 (see (4.98)). But mostly we have more than two orientations – for each moment of time $t_i, i = 0, \cdots, n - 1$, we are given unit quaternion q_i and our goal is to build a smooth interpolation between the quaternions.

The usual trick is to build an analog of cubic interpolation for quaternions using the de Casteljau algorithm with t from the range $[0, 1]$ for every pair of quaternions q_i, q_{i+1}.

The quaternion cubic curve (just as normal curves in 2D/3D) is defined by four quaternions p, a, b and q, where quaternions a and b are some values used to control the shape of the curve.

At the first step we interpolate (using the *slerp* function) between p and q, getting an intermediate quaternion c. In the same way we interpolate between quaternions a and b thus getting intermediate quaternion d. And finally we interpolate between these intermediate quaternions c and d (see Figure 12.2.

This process can be described by the function *squad* given by (12.1)

$$squad(t, p, a, b, q) = slerp(2t(1 - t), slerp(t, p, q), slerp(t, a, b)). \quad (12.1)$$

It is easy to get values of *squad* at endpoints - $t = 0$ and $t = 1$

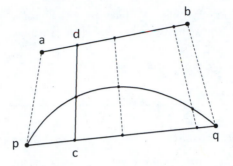

FIGURE 12.2: Cubic quaternion interpolation.

$$squad(0, p, a, b, q) = slerp(0, slerp(0, p, q), slerp(0, a, b,)) =$$
$$slerp(0, p, a) = p,$$
$$squad(1, p, a, b, q) = slerp(0, slerp(1, p, q), slerp(1, a, b,)) =$$
$$slerp(0, q, b) = q.$$

(12.2)

Also we can find derivatives by t at endpoints

$$squad'_t(0, p, a, b, q) = p\Big(log(p^{-1}q) + 2log(p^{-1}a)\Big),$$
$$squad'_t(1, p, a, b, q) = q\Big(log(p^{-1}q) - 2log(q^{-1}b)\Big).$$

(12.3)

In order to build a smooth cubic quaternion curve using the *squad* function for interpolating between adjacent quaternions q_i and q_{i+1}, we just need to find two such quaternions a_i and b_i that the resulting composite curve will have a continuous derivative (i.e., its derivative will be continuous at all q_i).

The obvious condition for it is given by the Equation (12.4) which should hold true for all $i = 0, \cdots, n-3$

$$squad'_t(1, q_i, a_i, b_i, q_{i+1}) = squad'_t(0, q_{i+1}, a_{i+1}, b_{i+1}, q_{i+2}).$$

(12.4)

One of the simple ways to get correct coefficients is to define a_i by the equation

$$a_i = q_i exp\Big(-\frac{log(q_i^{-1}q_{i+1}) + log(q_i^{-1}q_{i-1})}{4}\Big).$$

(12.5)

To interpolate between two quaternions q_i and q_{i+1} we can use the following function (it's not the unique solution but it usually gives good results)

$$S_i(t) = squad(t, q_i, a_i, a_{i+1}, q_{i+1}).$$

(12.6)

Note that this function uses t values from the range $[0, 1]$ for every index $i = 0, \cdots, n - 2$. To use the real-time values t_i we just need to remap t for every segment $[t_i, t_{i+1}]$ into the range $[0, 1]$.

12.3 Key-frame animation

The very term *key frame* comes from creating cartoons – usually there is a set of key frames drawn by leading artists while all intermediary frames are drawn based on these key frames by other artists. For computer animation this approach makes it easy to define an animation by just specifying the state at several moments of time and then using interpolation to get smooth animations.

The simplest way to animate some object (e.g., for computer games that object usually is a triangle mesh) is to select a set of moments of time $t_0, t_1, \cdots, t_m$ (*key frames*) and for each of them specify the state of the object being animated.

If we use this approach to animate a triangle mesh then for every moment t_j we store the coordinates of all vertices of the mesh as well as normals at all these vertices.

For any moment of time $t \in [t_i, t_{i+1}]$ we can use some form of interpolation, quite often the linear interpolation between two key frames was used.

Computer games, such as various First Person Shooters (FPS), for many years successfully used this approach. Often the linear interpolation was used to get positions of animated characters between key frames.

Linear interpolation is very easy and fast; for getting more realistic animation it is possible to use one of the methods from Chapter 11. But the main drawback of this approach is a big amount of data for any non-trivial animations, especially when we animate complex meshes consisting of large groups of triangles.

12.4 Skeletal animation

Most of complex animated models used in computer graphics, especially in games, are of human characters or some animals. It can be easily noted that animation of such models can be largely defined by animation of its skeleton (and various muscles).

Usually each point of skin is directly affected by several bones and in a much lesser degree by muscles (maybe except for facial animation muscles play the very important role and the number of muscles affecting the skin is very large).

Skeletal animation is a technique based on this observation. For this kind of animation all data is centered around the bones. There are not so many bones and usually they are organized hierarchically (each bone has a parent bone and several child bones) (see Figure 12.3).

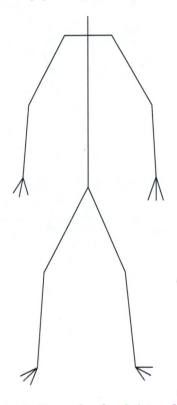

FIGURE 12.3: Example of a skeleton for a model.

For every vertex of the triangle mesh there is some prefixed number of bones, each with its own weight, which affect this vertex. Every bone defines some transform (usually this transform consists only of rotation and translation) and for every vertex the weighted sum of these transformations is used to define the position of the vertex during the animation.

Each vertex depends on a fixed set of bones with a fixed set of weights and these dependencies does not change in the course of animation, so for every model they are specified only once.

The animation is defined only for bones – it describes how bone transformations are changing during the course of animation. Knowing new transformations it is easy to compute new vertex positions; quite often it is done directly on the GPU.

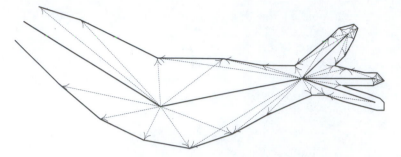

FIGURE 12.4: Example of skin affected by bones.

If every bone defines some transformation then it's possible to store this transform as a matrix, but since the transforms usually consist only of rotations and translations, it is more common and convenient to use a vector (for translation) and unit quaternion or Euler angles (for rotation). Instead of a matrix we can define such a transform only by six values (for a unit quaternion we need only three numbers).

Since bones are usually organized into the hierarchy, then any bone has a link to its parent bone (except the root bone) and transformation for every bone is usually given in terms of its parent bone.

To store animations of bones we can use a standard key-frame approach – it is very efficient since the number of bones is usually much smaller than the number of vertices in the mesh (see Figure 12.4).

12.5 Path following

One of the simple animations often used to control cameras in games and films is the *path following*. We want some object (e.g., a camera) to move along some path at the same time specifying the orientation of the object (where the camera should look).

To specify the path any of the spline curves can be used and orientation is given by introducing the *Center Of Interest (COI)* – the point at which a camera should be targeted (see Figure 12.5).

Note that the center of interest may also move along some path, so for every moment of time t we have its position defined as function $c(t)$. Then our object (camera) is moving along some other curve $p = p(t)$, so the direction (view vector) for the camera can be defined by the equation

$$v(t) = \frac{c(t) - p(t)}{\|c(t) - p(t)\|}. \tag{12.7}$$

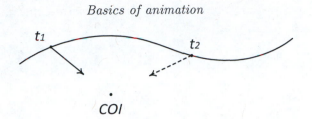

FIGURE 12.5: Tracking the center of interest.

In order to properly orient an object in space we need an additional vector; quite often it is the so-called *up direction* (defining where "up" should be for the object).

Usually it is desirable to have this up vector $u(t)$ to be close to some coordinate axis, e.g., the y-axis. But if we simply take $u_0 = (0,1,0)^T$ as our up vector then the chances are that it will not be orthogonal to our view vector (which is usually bad).

The common way is to define all these vectors in the following way

$$s(t) = [v(t), (0,1,0)^T],$$
$$u(t) = [s(t), v(t)].$$
(12.8)

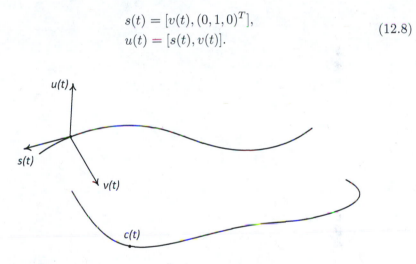

FIGURE 12.6: Frame for tracking center of interest.

Now we have a triple of mutually orthogonal vectors $v(t), u(t), s(t)$ which completely define the orientation of our camera in space as it moves along the path (see Figure 12.6).

Chapter 13

Lighting models

Lighting plays a great role in defining how objects will look. The more lighting details we are able to capture the more realistic objects will look. So if we want to render realistically looking models we need to account for lighting. In this chapter we will cover many various lighting models starting from the simplest ones.

All lighting models describe interactions of light with matter. A common scenario is shown in Figure 13.1 – we a have a point P on the plane made of some material which is illuminated from a given direction l and we want to know the amount of light that is reflected in some other direction v.

The light falling on a surface is usually scattered all over the upper hemisphere (see Figure 13.2). If material is transparent then some light is also scattered inside the material.

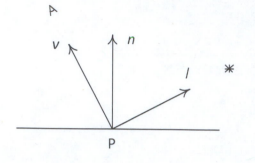

FIGURE 13.1: Common lighting environment.

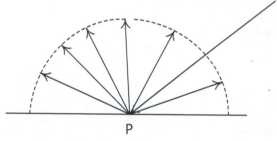

FIGURE 13.2: Scattering the light into the upper hemisphere.

13.1 Diffuse (Lambert) model

The simplest lighting model was created over a century ago for the perfectly diffuse case. This model assumes that falling light is uniformly scattered in all directions of the upper hemisphere (see Figure 13.2).

Therefore, the direction v to the observer has no influence and the only fact that matters is how much light is falling on a surface per unit area. This depends on a cosine of the angle of incidence θ – the angle between the normal to the surface n and the direction l from which light is falling (as shown in Figure 13.3).

Let's consider a parallel beam of light falling from the direction l at a point on the surface with a normal vector n. Then the lit area S on the surface is connected with the area S_{perp} of a perpendicular crossing of the ray with the standard cosine law (13.1)

$$S_{perp} = S\cos\theta \tag{13.1}$$

So the only factor which affects the reflected light is the cosine of the angle of incidence θ. In the case of unit vectors l and n this cosine is simple

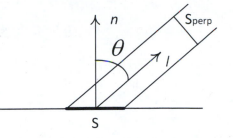

FIGURE 13.3: Area S lit by a beam of light on the surface.

the dot product of these vectors – (l, n). This model is usually described by the following equation:

$$I = CI_l max((n, l), 0). \tag{13.2}$$

Here C is the color of the surface (usually defined by an RGB triple) and I_l is the color and intensity of the light (also as an RGB triple). The *max* function is used to avoid negative values in the case when an angle of incidence θ is greater than $\pi/2$.

But using Equation (13.1) can result in unlit areas being completely black, so to avoid it an *ambient* term is usually introduced. This term is intended to model the *indirect illumination* – scattered light falling from all directions. Almost all real scenes include this kind of light and the ambient term is a simple and rude approximation to it.

So the lighting is assumed to be consisting from two parts – diffuse and ambient, each with its own weight (k_d and k_a). The ambient lighting is given by an RGB triple I_a. The resulting lighting is given by Equation (13.3)

$$I = k_a I_a + k_d C I_l max((n, l), 0). \tag{13.3}$$

Sometimes this model is modified by introducing a *bias value b* and the resulting model is called a *wrap-around* lighting model

$$I = k_a I_a + k_d C I_l \frac{1}{1+b} max((n, l) + b, 0). \tag{13.4}$$

13.2 Phong model

The Lambert model (13.4) does not support specular highlights which are often present on smooth surfaces. One of the simplest models to account for such highlights is the Phong lighting model. This model just adds a specular term to the diffuse lighting model with a weight k_s.

$$I = k_a I_a + k_d C I_l max((n,l),0) + k_s C_s I_l max((r,v),0)^p \qquad (13.5)$$

Here C_s is the color of the specular highlight, r is the vector l reflected relative to the normal n (see Figure 13.4) and p is the roughness coefficient – the bigger it is the more smooth the surface is. The v vector is the unit vector in the direction of the observer (also called an *eye vector*).

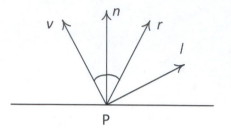

FIGURE 13.4: Vectors for the Phong lighting model.

The highlight color C_s for dielectrics usually is just white color, but for metals it usually coincides with the surface color C. The unit reflected vector r can be easily found from l and n, provided they are both of unit length:

$$r = 2n(n,l) - l. \qquad (13.6)$$

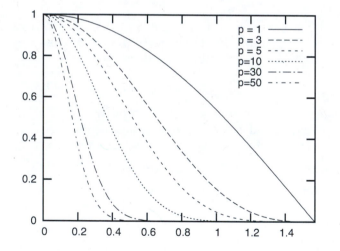

FIGURE 13.5: Plot of $cos^p \theta$ for various values of p.

Figure 13.5 shows the function $\cos^p \theta$ for various values of p.

13.3 Blinn-Phong model

Another often-used lighting model supporting specular highlights is the Blinn-Phong model, given by Equation (13.7).

$$I = k_a I_a + k_d C I_l max((n, l), 0) + k_s C_s I_l max((n, h), 0)^p \qquad (13.7)$$

Here the h is the unit halfway vector between l and v (see Figure 13.6)

$$h = \frac{l + v}{\|l + v\|}. \qquad (13.8)$$

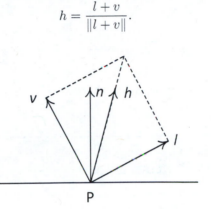

FIGURE 13.6: Vectors for the Blinn-Phong lighting model.

13.4 Ward isotropic model

One more model for adding specular highlights is the *Ward isotropic model*, where the specular term is given by the exponent (and therefore is faster to compute).

$$I = k_a I_a + k_d C I_l max((n, l), 0) + k_s C_s I_l e^{-k \tan \theta^2} \qquad (13.9)$$

Here k is the roughness coefficient and θ is the angle between vectors n and h (h is the halfway vector from the Blinn-Phong model (13.8)). This model can be written using the dot product (n, h) to avoid getting the angle and computing it's tangent.

$$I = k_a I_a + k_d C I_l max((n, l), 0) + k_s C_s I_l e^{-k \frac{1 - (n,h)^2}{(n,h)^2}} \qquad (13.10)$$

In Figure (13.7) you can see plot of $e^{-k tan \theta}$ for various values of k.

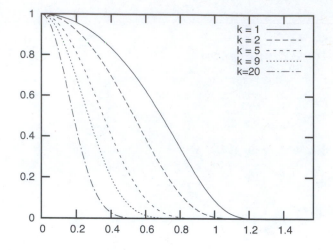

FIGURE 13.7: Plot of $e^{-ktan^2\theta}$ for various values of k.

13.5 Minnaert lighting

An interesting model for modeling the illumination of the Moon was proposed by Minnaert. It completely lacks a specular component (have you ever seen a specular highlight on the Moon?) and has an additional coefficient k to control the lighting

$$I = k_aI_a + k_dCI_l(n, l)^{1+k}(1 - (n, v))^{1-k}. \tag{13.11}$$

This model works fine not only for the Moon but renders some materials like velvet.

13.6 Lommel-Seeliger lighting

Another lighting model coming from astronomy, where it was used to model the lighting of asteroids, is the Lommel-Seeliger model. It also consists of only a diffuse term and can be used to render velvet and similar materials

$$I = k_aI_a + k_dCI_l\frac{max((n, l), 0)}{max((n, l), 0) + max((n, v), 0)}. \tag{13.12}$$

13.7   Rim lighting

In some cases it is important to emphasize the rim (contour line) of the object being lit. There is an easy trick to do so via adding one more term to the lighting equation.

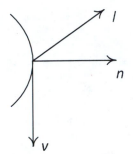

FIGURE 13.8: Vectors for the rim lighting term.

The rim is characterized with the vector v being nearly perpendicular to the normal vector n (see Figure 13.8). So the $1 - (n, v)$ can be used as a measure of how close the point is to the rim

$$I_{rim} = k_{rim} C_{rim} I_l (1 + b - max((n, v), 0))^p. \qquad (13.13)$$

Here the b is the small bias value and parameter p controls the sharpness of the rim. As it can be easily seen, the I_{rim} reaches maximal value when the view direction v is perpendicular to the normal n.

13.8   Distance attenuation

In real life the distance to the light source affects the lighting by the $1/d^2$ factor where d is the distance to the light source.

But in graphics, using $1/d^2$ to control lighting often leads to unrealistic looking lighting, so commonly another term is used to account for distance

$$f_{att}(d) = min(1, \frac{1}{a_c + a_l d + a_q d^2}). \qquad (13.14)$$

Here a_c, a_l and a_q are adjustable parameters which can be chosen to get the attenuation giving the most realistic results for the given scene ranging from a constant to an inverse quadratic model.

So adding distance attenuation into the Blinn-Phong model we will get the following lighting equation

$$I = k_a I_a + f_{att}(d) I_l (k_d C max((n, l), 0) + k_s C_s max((n, h), 0)^p). \qquad (13.15)$$

13.9 Reflection, Fresnel coefficient and its approximations

All the above models are just empirical guesses which give good visual appearance but have no serious physical grounds. One of the factors which should be taken into account if we want to get a more realistic lighting model is the physics of light reflection.

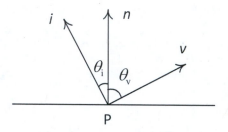

FIGURE 13.9: Reflection of light.

If we have an incident light falling at some point P from the direction i (see Figure 13.9) then the amount of light that will be reflected depends on both the angle of incidence θ_i and the wavelength λ.

This amount is described by the *Fresnel* coefficient $F_\lambda(\theta)$. The equation for it is rather complex and it depends on properties of material at point P, so usually some quick and simple approximations are used instead (see Figure 13.10).

The formulas below give the simplest variants of the Fresnel coefficient taking into account only the angle of incidence

$$F(\theta) = 1 - cos\theta, \qquad (13.16)$$

$$F(\theta) = \frac{1}{(1 + cos\theta)^8}. \qquad (13.17)$$

To take wavelength into account we can use the Fresnel value at zero incidence $F(0)$ which corresponds to the case of normal falling light. Usually

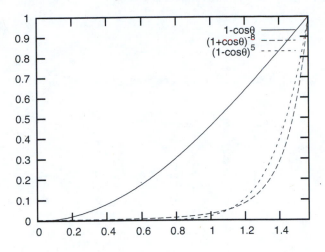

FIGURE 13.10: Plots of various Fresnel approximations.

we know the reflected color for this case which we take as $F(0)$. Then we can use Schlick's approximation:

$$F(\theta) = F(0) + (1 - F(0))(1 - cos\theta)^5. \qquad (13.18)$$

13.10 Strauss lighting model

Parameters used in many lighting models are not intuitive and often have no corresponding physical properties. The Strauss model (proposed in 1990) is based on four simple parameters. All of them take values from zero to one (a more general model used for ray tracing includes a fifth parameter – the index of the refraction of material).

Parameters of this model are:

- c – color of the surface as an RGB triple;

- s – smoothness of the surface, zero corresponds to a very rough surface, one corresponds to a perfect mirror;

- m – metallness of the surface, one corresponds to the metallic surface;

- t – transparency of the surface.

The illumination in the Strauss model is split into diffuse and specular parts

$$I = I_l(D + S). \tag{13.19}$$

Diffuse D and specular S terms are defined by the following equations:

$$D = Cmax((n, l), 0)(1 - ms)(1 - s^3)(1 - t),$$
$$S = C_s(-(h, v))^{\frac{3}{1-s}} R. \tag{13.20}$$

Other values used in this model are given by the following equations:

$$R = min(1, r + j(r + k))$$
$$r = (1 - t) - (1 - s^3)(1 - t)$$
$$j = fresnel((n, l))shadow((n, l))shadow((n, v)) \tag{13.21}$$
$$C_s = C_{white} + m(1 - fresnel((n, l)))(C - C_{white}).$$

Two functions $fresnel$ and $shadow$ are given by Equation (13.22)

$$fresnel(x) = \frac{\frac{1}{(x - k_f)^2} - \frac{1}{k_f^2}}{\frac{1}{(1 - k_f)^2} - \frac{1}{k_f^2}}, \tag{13.22}$$

$$shadow(x) = \frac{\frac{1}{(1 - k_s)^2} - \frac{1}{(x - k_s)^2}}{\frac{1}{(1 - k_s)^2} - \frac{1}{k_s^2}}.$$

Here the coefficient k is usually taken as 0.1, k_f as 1.12 and k_s as 1.01. The C_{white} is the vector $(1, 1, 1)$ (RGB triple corresponding to white color).

13.11   Anisotropic lighting

All previously described lighting models correspond to the *isotropic* case. A material (and a corresponding lighting model) is called isotropic if rotating the surface around the normal does not change the light visible at the point (see Figure 13.12).

However, there are materials which exhibit clear anisotropic behavior – rotating the surface around the normal significantly changes the visible color at the point. The simplest examples of such surfaces are the surface of a compact disc, brushed metal and hair.

Now we will describe the simplest anisotropic lighting model. Since what is seen at a given point changes with rotation around the normal n, we need

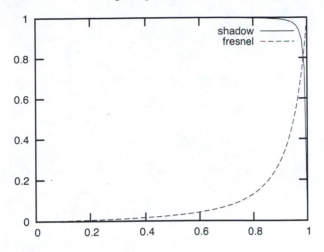

FIGURE 13.11: Plot of *shadow(x)* and *fresnel(x)* functions from the Strauss lighting model.

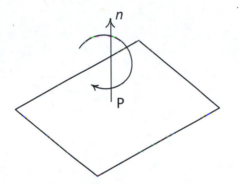

FIGURE 13.12: Rotating around the normal.

some other vector attached to the surface at P which we can use to track such rotation (it will be rotated when we rotate the surface around the normal).

Usually the so-called *tangent* vector t is introduced, which is orthogonal to the normal vector n. Then at any illuminated point we know both vectors, the normal n and the tangent t (see Figure 13.13).

Knowing t and n vectors we can build a third vector b called *binormal* as their cross-product

$$b = [t, n]. \tag{13.23}$$

The resulting triple n, t and b are mutually orthogonal and have unit length (provided n and t are both of unit length). Therefore, they form a basis in

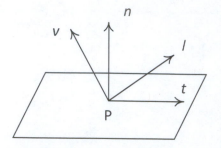

FIGURE 13.13: Vectors for anisotropic lighting.

3D-space. This basis is called a *tangent space basis*, vectors t and b form the *tangent plane*.

The simplest anisotropic model is based on a very simple concept – a surface is considered consisting of infinitesimally thin curves (hairs), whose direction at any point of the surface is given by the tangent vector (see Figure 13.14).

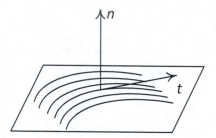

FIGURE 13.14: Surface with a tangent vector t at every point.

Many common anisotropic cases such as the surface of a compact disc or a brushed metal fit nicely into this model. The lighting model for such a surface is based on a lighting model for a single thin hair.

If we have such an infinitesimally thin hair and a point P on it, then we have a tangent vector t at it, but we cannot define a single normal vector n – any vector perpendicular to t can be used as a normal.

So the approach is to pick such vector n which will be perpendicular to t and which will give maximal value to some lighting model (e.g., the Blinn-Phong model).

Now we start with the diffuse term. We need to find such unit vector n that $(n, t) = 0$ and it gives maximal value to (n, l). In order to do it we split vector l into the sum of two components – one which is parallel to t (we denote it as l_t) and the other which is perpendicular to t (we denote it as l_n) (see Figure 13.15)

$$l = l_t + l_n. \tag{13.24}$$

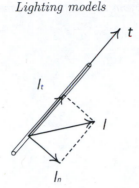

FIGURE 13.15: Lighting a hair.

Since l_t is parallel to t it is just a scaled vector t (by (l,t)), so if vectors t and l are unit vectors then we have the following equations for l_t and l_h

$$l_t = (l,t)t, \tag{13.25}$$
$$l_n = l - (l,t)t. \tag{13.26}$$

Then we can rewrite the expression we want to maximize as $(n,l) = (l_n,n)$ since l_t is perpendicular to n. It is evident that the vector which maximizes this dot product must be parallel to l_n, so we just have to normalize it

$$n = \frac{l_n}{\|l_n\|} = \frac{l - (l,t)t}{\|l - (l,t)t\|}. \tag{13.27}$$

We can find the length of l_n from the dot product

$$\|l - (l,t)t\|^2 = (l,l) - 2(l,t)^2 + (t,t)(l,t)^2 = 1 - (l,t)^2. \tag{13.28}$$

Therefore, we get the following values for vector n and its dot product:

$$n = \frac{l - (l,t)t}{\sqrt{1 - (l,t)^2}},$$
$$(l,n) = \frac{(l,l) - (l,t)^2}{\sqrt{1 - (l,t)^2}} = \sqrt{1 - (l,t)^2}. \tag{13.29}$$

So the diffuse component will have the following form:

$$I = k_d C I_l \sqrt{1 - (l,t)^2}. \tag{13.30}$$

In the same way we can find the maximal value of the specular part of the Blinn-Phong model and write the resulting lighting equation

$$I = k_a I_a + k_d C I_l \sqrt{1 - (l,t)^2} + k_s C_s I_l (1 - (h,t)^2)^{p/2}. \tag{13.31}$$

13.11.1   Ward anisotropic model

Another well-known anisotropic lighting model is Ward's anisotropic lighting model. It is characterized by coefficients k_t and k_b and it uses both tangent t and binormal b vectors.

$$I = k_a I_a + k_s C_s \exp - \big(k_t(h,t)^2\big) - \big(k_b(h,b)^2\big). \qquad (13.32)$$

13.12   Bidirectional Reflection Distribution Function (BRDF)

All of the above models are empirical – they are chosen to give a nice looking image but usually are not physically accurate. In order to define a physically accurate lighting model we need to introduce several important notions.

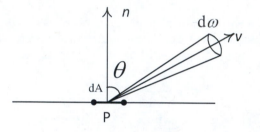

FIGURE 13.16: Energy falling on area dA from solid angle $d\omega$.

The *radiance* (usually denoted as E) is used to define the amount of light energy falling on a point P from a given direction ω (see Figure 13.16). It is defined as the energy flow $d\Phi$ (measured in Watts) per solid angle $d\omega$ per projected area dA^{proj}

$$E = \frac{d^2\Phi}{d\omega dA^{perp}}. \qquad (13.33)$$

The projected area dA^{proj} is obtained by projecting the differential area dA onto the direction of ω and they are connected by the already met cosine of the falling angle relationship (see Figure 13.17)

$$dA^{perp} = dA cos\theta. \qquad (13.34)$$

The radiance is measured by the Watts per steradian per meter squared $(W/(srm^2))$.

Then we can define the ratio of the power reflected in the given direction

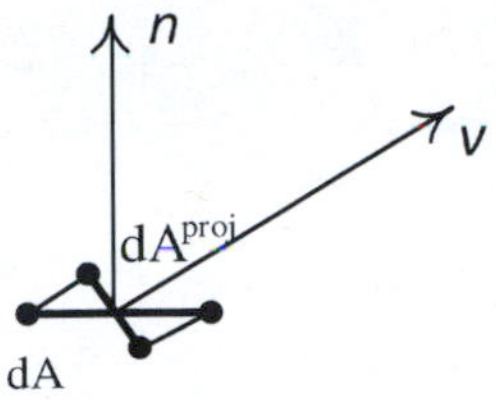

FIGURE 13.17: Surface area dA and projected area A^{proj}.

ω_o to the radiance $dL_i(\omega)$ falling at this point from direction ω_i (and through some solid differential angle $d\omega$). This ratio is called a *Bidirectional Reflection Distribution Function* (BRDF) $f_r(\omega_o, \omega_i)$

$$f_r(\omega_o, \omega_i) = \frac{dL_o(\omega_o)}{dE(\omega_i)} = \frac{dL_o(\omega_o)}{L_i(\omega_i)cos\theta_i d\omega_i}. \tag{13.35}$$

Here the function $L_i(\omega)$ describes lighting energy falling from direction ω. The BRDF is measured in inverse steradians.

If we know the light $L_i(\omega)$ falling at the point from all over the upper hemisphere then knowing the BRDF we can find the lighting energy reflected in a given direction ω_o by integrating over the upper hemisphere S_+

$$L_o(\omega_o) = \int_{S_+} f_r(\omega_o, \omega_i)L_i(\omega_i)cos\theta_i d\omega_i. \tag{13.36}$$

The BRDF usually depends on a wavelength λ – light with a different wavelength will be reflected differently.

Physically-based BRDFs obey several important properties.

First of all it obeys the *Helmholtz reciprocity principle* – if we revert the direction of light (i.e., swap ω_i and ω_o) then the BRDF will not change:

$$f_r(\omega_o, \omega_i) = f_r(\omega_i, \omega_o), \forall \omega_i, \omega_o. \tag{13.37}$$

Also the BRDF should obey the *energy conservation law* – a surface cannot reflect more energy than it receives:

$$\int_{S_+} f_r(\omega_o, \omega_i)cos\theta_i d\omega_i \leq 1, \forall \omega_o. \tag{13.38}$$

For the Lambert lighting model the corresponding BRDF is just a constant $f_r(\omega_o, \omega_i) = \frac{\rho}{\pi}$. Here the π is the normalization constant since we're integrating it over the upper hemisphere (whose area is equal to pi).

13.13 Oren-Nayar model

There are several lighting models which are based on physics and which satisfy several important physical principles such as energy conservation. Usually all such models are based on a *microfacet surface model*. Under this model the surface is considered as composed of tiny facets which do satisfy some very simple lighting model (see Figure 13.18). The orientations of such facets (*microfacets*) are considered to be random with some given distribution.

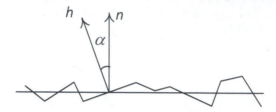

FIGURE 13.18: Microfaceted model, normal to the surface n and the normal to the facet h.

For every such microfacet there is a normal to the microfacet itself (usually denoted as h) and a normal to the surface n. The distribution of microfacets is usually given in terms of probability density function $D(\alpha)$ for the angle α between vectors h and n.

The Oren-Nayar model (first published in 1992) enhances the standard Lambert shading model. It considers the surface to be composed of tiny ideal diffuse facets.

But for such surfaces we encounter the fact that direction to the viewer matters, unlike the pure Lambertian model.

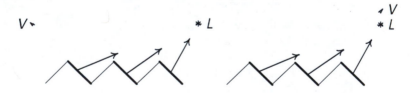

FIGURE 13.19: Dependence of the lighting on the viewer position.

As you can see in Figure 13.19, the position of the observer E affects the visible lighting. On the right the observer sees mostly lit faces, but on the left the observer sees mostly unlit faces. So the position affects whether the same surface lit with the same light source L will be considered as either lit or unlit.

For this model the Gaussian distribution with a parameter σ and a zero mean (13.39) is used to model the distribution of the faces

$$D(\alpha) = Ce^{-\frac{\alpha^2}{\sigma^2}}. \tag{13.39}$$

Here C is the normalization constant which ensures that integral over all possible angles α will be equal to one.

The parameter σ corresponds to the roughness of the surface, $\sigma = 0$ corresponds to the ideally smooth (diffuse) surface, and the bigger values of σ correspond to rough surfaces.

The complete Oren-Nayar model, while being physically correct, is very complex; it takes into account such complex phenomena as light inter-reflections between facets. Such complexity prevents it from being used in real-time applications, but there is a simplified version of this model, which can work in realtime. This simplified model is shown below

$$I = max(\cos\theta, 0)(A + Bmax(0, \cos(\phi_v - \phi_l)))\sin\alpha\tan\beta. \tag{13.40}$$

The parameters A, B and the angles α and β are defined by the following equations:

$$
\begin{aligned}
A &= 1 - 0.5\frac{\sigma^2}{\sigma^2 + 0.33}, \\
B &= 0.45\frac{\sigma^2}{\sigma^2 + 0.09}, \\
\alpha &= min(\theta_l, \theta_v), \\
\beta &= max(\theta_l, \theta_v).
\end{aligned}
\tag{13.41}
$$

Here the θ_l and θ_v are the angles between normal vector n and the vectors l and v, respectively. And the angle $\phi_l - \phi_v$ is the angle between projections of l and v onto the tangent plane (see Figure 13.20).

To compute the required $\cos(\phi_v - \phi_l)$ we need first to project vectors v and l onto the tangent plane getting vectors v_p and l_p (see Figure 13.20)

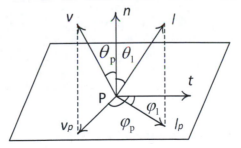

FIGURE 13.20: Polar angles for the Oren-Nayar lighting model.

$$v_p = v - n(n, v),$$
$$l_p = l - n(n, l). \tag{13.42}$$

Then we compute lengths of these projections and cosine from their dot product

$$||v_p||^2 = ||v||^2 - 2(n, v)^2 + ||n||^2(n, v)^2 = 1 - (n, v)^2,$$
$$||l_p||^2 = 1 - (n, l)^2,$$
$$cos(\phi_l - phi_v) = \frac{(v_p, l_p)}{||v_p||||l_p||}. \tag{13.43}$$

Therefore, we get:

$$cos(\phi_l - \phi_v) = \frac{(v, l) - (n, l)(n, v)}{\sqrt{(1 - (n, v)^2)(1 - (n, l)^2)}}. \tag{13.44}$$

Note that angles θ_l and θ_v are always in the range $[0, \pi/2]$. Therefore, both sines and cosines of these angles are non-negative. Since both sine and tangent in this range are monotonously increasing functions then we get:

$$sin(min(\theta_l, \theta_v)) = min(\sin \theta_l, \sin \theta_v),$$
$$tan(max(\theta_l, \theta_v)) = max(\tan \theta_l, \tan \theta_v). \tag{13.45}$$

13.14 Cook-Torrance model

Another well-known lighting model based on the microfacet model is the Cook-Torrance lighting model (originally published in 1981). It is also physically-based and it gives very good results for metallic surfaces. This model uses the Fresnel term to accurately model light reflected and the geometry term to model *facet masking* and *facet shadowing* (see Figure 13.21).

This model targets strong reflections and considers the surface to be composed of tiny ideal mirrors (unlike the Oren-Nayar model).

The geometry term (*Geometry Attenuation Factor, GAF*) accounts for facets shadowing (blocking light to) other facets from the light source (Figure 13.21 right) and also facets masking other facets from being fully seen by an observer (Figure 13.21 left).

This geometry term is given by the following equation:

Masking   **Shadowing**

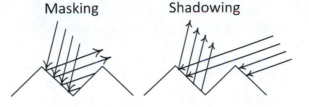

FIGURE 13.21: Masking and shadowing.

$$G = min\Big(1, \frac{2(n,h)(n,v)}{(v,h)}, \frac{2(n,h)(n,l)}{(v,h)}\Big). \qquad (13.46)$$

The Cook-Torrance model uses Beckman's distribution function $D_B(\alpha)$ to model surface roughness; the parameter m controls the roughness

$$D_B(\alpha) = \frac{1}{m^2 \cos^4 \alpha} \exp -(\frac{\tan \alpha}{m})^2. \qquad (13.47)$$

Note that we can avoid computing the angle α by using the dot product the following way

$$\tan^2 \alpha = \frac{sin^2\alpha}{cos^2\alpha} = \frac{1 - cos^2\alpha}{cos^2\alpha} = \frac{1 - (n,h)^2}{(n,h)^2}. \qquad (13.48)$$

Using it we can rewrite the Beckman distribution function as:

$$D_B(\alpha) = \frac{1}{m^2(n,h)^4\alpha} \exp -(\frac{1 - (n,h)^2}{(n,h)^2m^2}). \qquad (13.49)$$

The overall lighting for the Cook-Torrance model is given by the Equation (13.50)

$$I = I_l max(0, (n,l)) \frac{F(\theta)GD_B(\alpha)}{(n,l)(n,v)}. \qquad (13.50)$$

The Cook-Torrance illumination model gives very realistically looking metals. Also there are several tricks to lower the amount of required computations so it can be used in real-time applications.

13.15   Ashikhmin-Shirley model

Ashikhmin and Shirley proposed an anisotropic model also using a microfacet surface model. It is based on four simple and intuitive parameters and is easier to compute than the Cook-Torrance model.

This model uses an anisotropic distribution function $D(\alpha)$ of the following form (here the t and b are the tangent and binormal vectors)

$$D(\alpha) = \sqrt{(e_t + 1)(e_b + 1)} max(0, (n, h))^{e_t cos^2 \phi_h + e_b sin^2 \phi_h}. \qquad (13.51)$$

We can rewrite this equation getting sine and cosine of angle ϕ_h from the following dot products – (h, t) and (h, b)

$$D(\alpha) = \sqrt{(e_t + 1)(e_b + 1)} max(0, (n, h))^{\frac{e_t (h,t)^2 + e_b (h,b)^2}{1 - (n,h)^2}}. \qquad (13.52)$$

The Ashikhmin-Shirley model is written as a sum of diffuse and specular parts:

$$I = max(0, (n, l)) I_l (I_d + I_s). \qquad (13.53)$$

These parts are given by the following equations

$$
\begin{aligned}
I_s &= \frac{D(\alpha)}{8\pi} \frac{F(\theta, C_s)}{(v, h) max((n, l), (n, v))}, \\
I_d &= \frac{28}{23\pi} C_d (1 - C_s) \left(1 - (1 - \frac{(n, v)}{2})^5\right) \left(1 - (1 - \frac{(n, l)}{2})^5\right).
\end{aligned}
\qquad (13.54)
$$

This model also uses the Schlick approximation to the Fresnel term (13.16) with $F(0) = C_s$.

So as you can see the model depends on two colors – C_d (diffuse) and C_s (specular) and two coefficients – e_t and e_b. The case of equal coefficients $e_t = e_b$ gives an isotropic version of the Ashikhmin-Shirley model.

13.16 Image-Based Lighting (IBL)

All the above models work with the case of a small amount of point (or directional) light sources.

But in reality the light is falling from all directions of the upper hemisphere. It is clearly seen when we need to render a landscape – the light comes not only from the Sun, but also from the sky. And the sky gives a good deal of total illumination (see Figure 13.22).

So in reality we do not have point light sources but rather light falling from all directions. Then knowing both illumination and the BRDF we can get light leaving at given direction ω_o by Equation (13.48). But for real-time

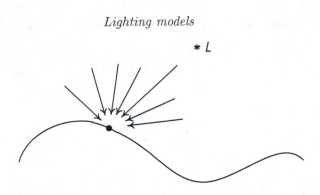

FIGURE 13.22: A point being lit from the sky and the Sun.

applications it is now impossible to compute such an integral for every pixel, even for very simple BRDFs.

Quite often other approaches are used for representing the falling illumination and the integral is approximated with something more suitable for real-time applications.

One group of such approaches is called an *Image-Based Lighting (IBL)*. In this approach the illumination is given by special images (often computed in realtime). Then such images are blurred and just a few samples weighted by BRDF are taken and summed (instead of computing a full integral (13.48)).

The simplest approach of such kind (which was among others used in the Half-Life 2 game) is called *ambient cubes*.

An ambient cube is just a cube located at some point of space and oriented along coordinate axes. Each face has some color associated with it, so in fact the cube is just a location in space and six colors attached to its faces (see Figure 13.23).

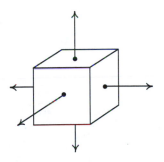

FIGURE 13.23: Ambient cube.

Then we can build vector l from the current point to the center of this ambient cube and compute weighted sum of its faces' colors to approximate light coming from direction l.

It gives some rough approximation of color coming from a given direction.

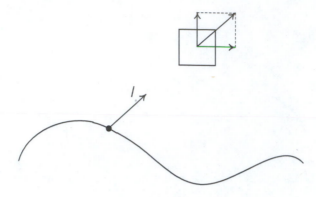

FIGURE 13.24: Usage of the ambient cube.

Usually a group of such ambient cubes is used, so when we have a point then we pick a few (2–3) nearest cubes and from them get approximate lighting.

To get accuracy with this method we often need many such cubes (usually arranged in a grid, see Figure 13.25); all of them are updated once in several frames (the frequency of the update usually depends on the distance to the observer).

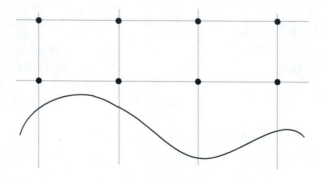

FIGURE 13.25: Grid of ambient cubes.

This method captures such effects as global illumination from the sky, ambient illumination inside a building and so on. But all points and directed light sources (such as the Sun) are processed the normal way.

Another approach is using such cubes too, but this time each face of the cube instead of a single color contains an image, associated with it. The image is what will be seen if we place a camera at the center of the cube such that a face becomes the image plane of the camera (in fact this is the way images for such cubes are computed)(see Figure 13.26).

Such a cube can capture more details than an ambient cube but since we do not want to process every texel of the associated image, the image is blurred so we can take just a few texels from it.

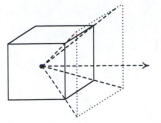

FIGURE 13.26: Camera for a face of an environment cube.

Then to approximate light coming from the given direction we pick a value from a corresponding face and location in the image and weight it with the BRDF.

Since these cubes (environment cubes) can capture more details, we usually need a much smaller amount of them to get an approximation to falling light.

Of course environment cubes as well as ambient cubes give only an approximation suitable to capture the effects which are difficult to capture by other means. All point and directional lights are processed the normal ways. But nevertheless they get some kind of global illumination feeling in the scene.

13.17 Spherical harmonics and their usage for lighting

If we have some point in a scene then its illumination from all directions $I(\omega)$ is just a function defined on a unit sphere S.

Now if we look at functions defined on the unit sphere S then we can see that they have some common points with vectors – we can add them and we can multiply them by a number. If we require that such functions be square integrable (these functions form the $L^2(S)$ function space) then we can define a dot product between any two of them by integrating their product over the surface of the sphere

$$(f,g) = \int_S f(\omega)g(\omega)dS. \tag{13.55}$$

From the dot product we can define a norm of such a function as a $\sqrt{(f,f)}$. Such a dot product and a norm satisfy all properties of their 2D/3D-analogs.

Note that this integral can be written using spherical coordinates the following way

$$(f,g) = \int_0^{2\pi} \int_0^{\pi} f(\theta, \phi)g(\theta, \phi) \sin \theta d\theta d\phi. \tag{13.56}$$

All functions from $L^2(S)$ form a linear (or vector) space. We can think of creating a basis for this space. But here we have a small surprise – this space has an infinite dimension.

So we should use an infinite number of basis functions $e_i(\omega), i = 0, 1, ...$ Then we can write down function $f(\omega)$ as a infinite weighted sum of basis functions:

$$f(\omega) = \sum_{i=0}^{\infty} f_i e_i(\omega) \qquad (13.57)$$

The basis $e_i(\omega), i = 0, 1, ...$ (just as in the 2D/3D-case) is called an *orthonormal* if any function from it has a unit length (i.e., $\|e_i\| = 1$) and the dot product of different basis functions is zero ($(e_i, e_j) = 0, i \neq j$).

For an orthonormal basis we can easily get coefficients f_i for expansion (13.57) just as a dot product with basis functions

$$f_i = (f, e_i) = \int_S f(\omega) e_i(\omega) dS. \qquad (13.58)$$

It can be shown that $\lim_{n \to \infty} \|f - \sum_{i=0}^{n} f_i e_i\| = 0$. It means that if we take several first members of this expansion then we get a good enough estimate to f

$$f \approx \sum_{i=0}^{n} f_i e_i(\omega).$$

Now if we have two functions $f(\omega)$ and $g(\omega)$ given by their expansions $f = \sum_{i=0}^{\infty} f_i e_i$ and $g = \sum_{i=0}^{\infty} g_i e_i$ then we can get their dot product without computing an integral of the unit sphere S

$$(f, g) = \int_S f(\omega) g(\omega) dS = \sum_{i=0}^{\infty} f_i g_i. \qquad (13.59)$$

Now if we take several first elements from (13.59) then we will get an approximation to the integral (13.55)

$$(f, g) \approx \sum_{i=0}^{n} f_i g_i.$$

If we have a linear space then we can introduce a linear operator. A very simple way to do it is to define a *kernel* function $k(\omega_1, \omega_2)$ and use integration as shown in (13.60)

$$(Af)(\omega) = \int_S k(\omega, \omega')f(\omega')dS. \qquad (13.60)$$

Then for any basis function $e_i(\omega)$ we can get an expansion of Ae_i using the basis

$$Ae_i(\omega) = \sum_{j=0}^{\infty} a_{ij}e_j(\omega). \qquad (13.61)$$

Here the a_{ij} are just some numbers defining the linear operator (13.60). Using (13.61) we can get the expansion of Af

$$(Af)(\omega) = \sum_{i=0}^{\infty}\sum_{j=0}^{\infty} f_i a_{ij}e_j(\omega). \qquad (13.62)$$

Thus, we can get an approximation of the Af just by limiting both sums to the first n

$$(Af)(\omega) \approx \sum_{i=0}^{n}\sum_{j=0}^{n} f_i a_{ij}e_j(\omega) = \sum_{j=0}^{n}\left(\sum_{i=0}^{n} f_i a_{ij}\right)e_j(\omega). \qquad (13.63)$$

If we look at the illumination integral (13.48) then we can now note that it looks just as the Equation (13.60), except that we're now integrating on the whole unit sphere S instead of the upper hemisphere S_+.

If we find a good orthonormal basis $e_i(\omega)$ then we can approximate all lighting with just a few coefficients (the few are usually from 4 up to 36) and get rid of functions and integrals.

Note that for the diffuse lighting (which is a very common case) the BRDF is constant and all we need to do is to get the expansion of $max(cos\theta, 0)$ via the basis functions

$$\int_S max(cos\theta), 0)e_i(\omega)dS = c_i, i = 0, 1, ... \qquad (13.64)$$

So the diffuse lighting can be approximated as a $\sum_{i=0}^{n} f_i c_i$, where f_i are describing the falling from hemisphere light.

But in order to use all of this we need an orthonormal basis for $L^2(S)$. One of the most well-known (and often used) orthonormal basis for $L^2(S)$ are the *spherical harmonics*.

Spherical harmonics are the functions $y_l^m(\theta, \phi)$ which are defined by the following equations

$$y_l^m(\theta, \phi) = \begin{cases} \sqrt{2}K_l^m \cos(m\phi)P_l^m(\cos\theta), m > 0 \\ \sqrt{2}K_l^m \sin(-m\phi)P_l^{-m}(\cos\theta), m < 0 \\ K_l^0 P_l^0(\cos\theta), m = 0. \end{cases} \tag{13.65}$$

Here the index l defines the *band* and for each band l the index m takes values from $-l$ to l. Parameter K_l^m is the normalizing coefficient (to ensure the norm of each function will be equal to one) and is given by Equation (13.66)

$$K_l^m = \sqrt{\frac{(2l+1)(l-|m|)!}{4\pi(l+|m|)!}}. \tag{13.66}$$

And the $P_l^m(x)$ are the *associated Legendre polynomials*. These polynomials are defined by the following equations

$$\begin{aligned} &P_l^m(x)(l-m) = x(2l-1)P_{l-1}^m(x) - (l+m-1)P_{l-2}^m(x), \\ &P_m^m(x) = (-1)^m(2m-1)!!(1-x^2)^{m/2}, \\ &P_{m+1}^m(x) = x(2m+1)P_m^m(x). \end{aligned} \tag{13.67}$$

Below you can see two first bands of these polynomials

$$\begin{aligned} P_0^0(x) &= 1, \\ P_1^0(x) &= x, \\ P_1^1(x) &= -\sqrt{(1-x^2)}, \\ P_2^0(x) &= \frac{1}{2}(3x^2 - 1), \\ P_2^1(x) &= -3x\sqrt{1-x^2}, \\ P_2^2(x) &= 3(1-x^2). \end{aligned} \tag{13.68}$$

In Figure 13.27 you can see these functions plotted in the range $[-1, 1]$.

Since spherical harmonics are defined as $P_l^m(\cos\theta)$ corresponding bands are shown below as a functions of θ

$$\begin{aligned} P_0^0(\cos\theta) &= 1, \\ P_1^0(\cos\theta) &= \cos\theta, \\ P_1^1(\cos\theta) &= -\sin\theta, \\ P_2^0(\cos\theta) &= \frac{1}{2}(3\cos^2\theta - 1), \\ P_x^1(\cos\theta) &= -3\sin\theta\cos\theta, \\ P_2^2(\cos\theta) &= 3\sin^2\theta. \end{aligned} \tag{13.69}$$

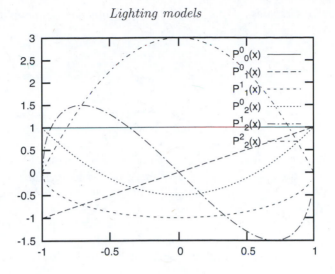

FIGURE 13.27: First three bands of $P_l^m(x)$.

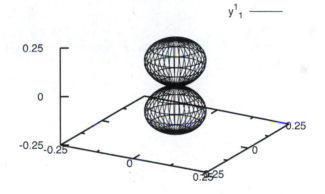

FIGURE 13.28: Plot of spheric harmonic with $l = 1$ and $m = 0$.

Therefore, if we have a function $y(\theta, \phi)$ defined on a unit sphere (see Figure 13.27) (if it is defined only on a hemisphere we can just mirror it to the other hemisphere or define as zero in the other hemisphere) then we can approximate it by several bands of spherical harmonics

$$f(\theta, \phi) \approx \sum_{l=0}^{n} \sum_{m=-l}^{l} f_i^m y_l^m(\theta, \phi). \tag{13.70}$$

Here the f_l^m are coefficients of expansions defined by the following integrals:

$$f_l^m = \int_S f(\theta, \phi) y_l^m(\theta, \phi) dS = \int_0^{2\pi} \int_0^{\pi} f(\theta, \phi) y_l^m(\theta, \phi) sin\theta d\theta d\phi. \quad (13.71)$$

One important property of spherical harmonics is connected with rotation. If we have some rotation matrix R and a function $f(\omega)$ defined on S then we can define a new function on the sphere just as $g(\omega) = f(R\omega)$.

It turns out that there is a connection between expansion coefficients of "rotated" function g and coefficients of function f – coefficients of each band of g are produced by multiplying coefficients of the corresponding band for original function f by a special rotation matrix for this band. Note that for band l there are $2l+1$ coefficients and therefore the rotation matrix for it will be $(2l+1) \times (2l+1)$.

Usually only 2–3 first bands of spherical harmonics expansion are used, e.g., CryEngine 3 uses only the first two bands (4 coefficients) for computing global illumination in realtime.

Spherical harmonics can be used to approximate a lighting environment and/or visible color due to the lighting environment. For example, the CryEngine 3 uses a grid of points. For each of those points it stores 4 coefficients (corresponding to two first bands) describing light falling on it from all sides.

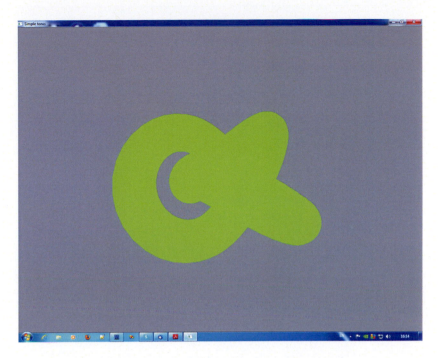

FIGURE 1.1: Simple torus rendered in one color.

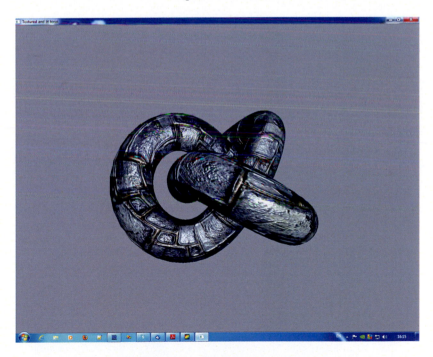

FIGURE 1.2: Textured and lit torus.

FIGURE 14.1: Lambert lighting of the knot.

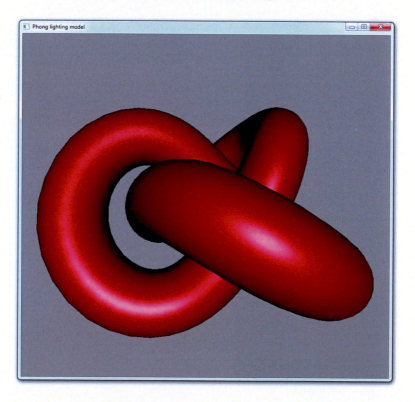

FIGURE 14.2: Phong lighting of the knot.

FIGURE 14.3: Blinn-Phong lighting of the knot.

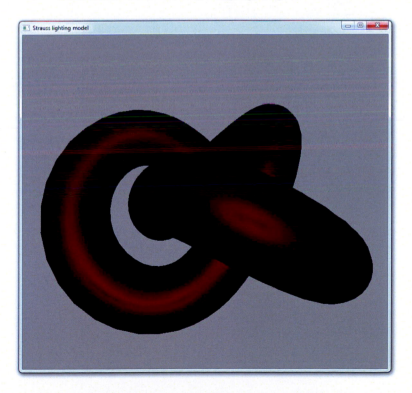

FIGURE 14.4: Strauss lighting of the knot.

FIGURE 14.5: Oren-Nayar lighting of the knot.

FIGURE 14.6: Cook-Torrance lighting of the knot.

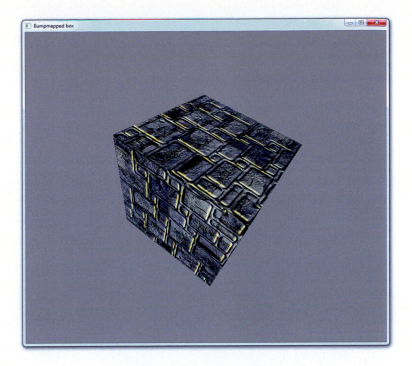

FIGURE 16.10: Bumpmapped box.

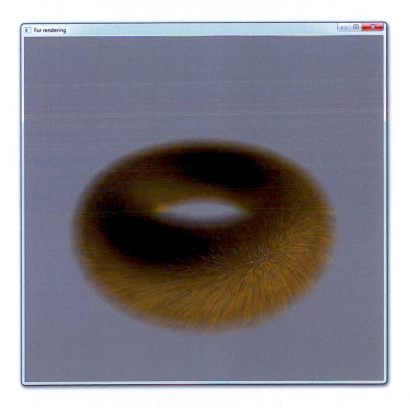

FIGURE 16.13: Fur torus.

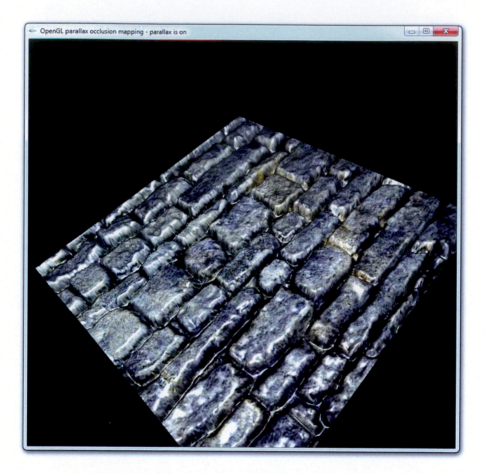

FIGURE 16.19: Quad rendered with parallax occlusion mapping.

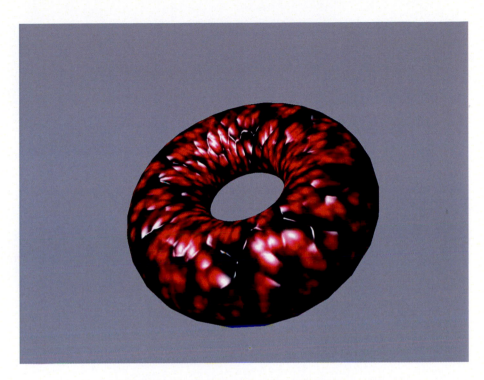

FIGURE 18.20: Organic-looking object.

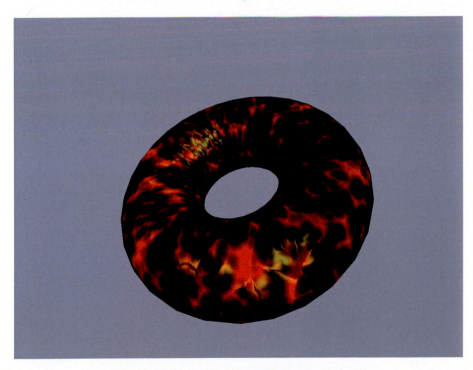

FIGURE 18.21: One more organic-looking object.

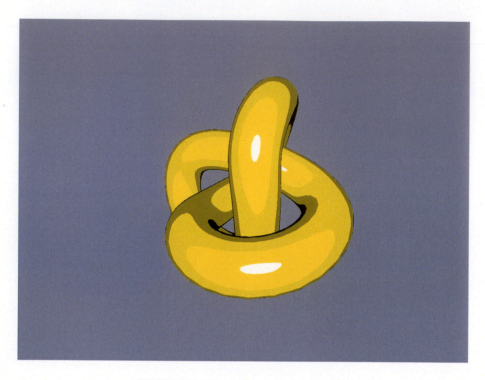

FIGURE 19.1: Cartoon rendering.

FIGURE 19.2: Watercolor rendering.

Chapter 14

Advanced OpenGL

In this chapter we will cover some advanced OpenGL features, including geometry shaders, tessellation, OpenGL ES 2 and WebGL.

14.1   Implementation of lighting models

Here we will cover how some of the lighting models covered in Chapter 13 can be implemented with OpenGL shaders.

14.1.1   Lambert model

We will start with the simplest lighting model – the Lambert model. For this model to be evaluated at every fragment we need to know for every fragment following two vectors – unit normal n and unit vector to light source l.

A normal vector can be taken from the the per-vertex normal values – they will be interpolated across primitives, so all we need is to pass them from the vertex shader to the fragment shader and normalize them (since interpolating unit vectors can result in vectors which are not unit). Note that normal should be transformed using the normal matrix, i.e., the inverted transpose of the upper-left 3×3 of the model-view matrix. We will pass this matrix as uniform to the vertex shader.

The direction to the light can be computed in the vertex shader from the light source position. Then we again pass this value to the fragment shader and normalize before using it.

In a simple example we hard-code coefficients k_a and k_d into the fragment shader (instead of making them uniform variables which are passed to the shader at runtime).

— vertex

```
#version 330 core

uniform mat4 proj;
uniform mat4 mv;
uniform mat3 nm;
uniform vec3 light;   // light  position

layout (location = 0) in vec3 pos;
layout (location = 2) in vec3 normal;

out vec3 n;      // normal
out vec3 l;      // direction  to  light

void main(void)
{
    vec4 p = mv * vec4 ( pos, 1.0 );

    gl_Position   = proj * p;
    n             = normalize ( nm * normal );
    l             = normalize ( light − p.xyz );
}
```

— fragment

```
#version 330 core

in vec3 n;
in vec3 l;

out vec4 color;
```

```
void main ( void )
{
   vec3   n2   = normalize ( n );
   vec3   l2   = normalize ( l );
   float  diff = max ( dot ( n2, l2 ), 0.0 );
   vec4   clr  = vec4 ( 0.7, 0.1, 0.1, 1.0 );
   float  ka   = 0.2;
   float  kd   = 0.8;

   color = ( ka + kd*diff ) * clr ;
}
```

The object we will light using the Lambert model will be a mesh representing a knot. Below is the C++ code for the corresponding window class.

```
class    MeshWindow : public GlutRotateWindow
{
   Program       program;
   BasicMesh  *  mesh;
   vec3          eye;
   vec3          light;

public:
   MeshWindow () : GlutRotateWindow( 200, 200, 400, 400,
                                      "Lambert_lighting_model" )
   {
      if ( !program.loadProgram ( "lambert.glsl" ) )
      {
         printf ( "Error_building_program:_%s\n",
                     program.getLog ().c_str () );
         exit   ( 2 );
      }

      program.bind ();

      mesh  = createKnot  ( 1, 4, 120, 30 );
      eye   = vec3 ( 3, 3, 3 );
      light = vec3 ( 5, 5, 5 );
   }
```

Our *redisplay* method sets model-view and normal matrices for the program and calls the *render* method of the mesh.

```
void MeshWindow :: redisplay ()
{
   mat4 mv = getRotation  ();
   mat3 nm = normalMatrix ( mv );
```

```
glClear ( GL_COLOR_BUFFER_BIT | GL_DEPTH_BUFFER_BIT );

program.bind ();
program.setUniformMatrix ( "mv" , mv );
program.setUniformMatrix ( "nm" ,  nm );

mesh -> render ();

program.unbind ();
}
```

To better show how lighting works we add the *idle* method, which will be moving our light source on a trajectory around our mesh. Note that for our animation we are using physical time since the program start, which makes the rate of our animation independent of the computer the program is run on.

```
void MeshWindow :: idle ()
{
    float angle = 4 * getTime ();

    light.x = 8*cos ( angle );
    light.y = 8*sin ( 1.4 * angle );
    light.z = 8 + 0.5 * sin ( angle / 3 );

    program.bind ();
    program.setUniformVector ( "light", light );
    program.unbind ();

    glutPostRedisplay ();
}
```

Below you can see the screenshot of the mesh lit with the Lambert model (Figure 14.1).

14.1.2   Phong lighting model

The main difference in the Phong lighting model is that we need not only unit normal n and direction to the light source l, but we also need unit direction from the fragment to the camera v. It can be easily computed in the vertex shader and then passed to the fragment shader.

In the fragment shader after normalizing input vectors we can compute the reflected vector r; note that we don't need to normalize it since the formula used from unit vectors always produces unit vectors.

Corresponding shaders are shown below.

```
— vertex
```

FIGURE 14.1 (See color insert.): Lambert lighting of the knot.

```
#version 330 core

uniform mat4 proj;
uniform mat4 mv;
uniform mat3 nm;
uniform vec3 eye;          // eye position
uniform vec3 light;        // light position

layout(location = 0) in vec3 pos;
layout(location = 2) in vec3 normal;

out vec3 n;
out vec3 v;
out vec3 l;

void main(void)
{
    vec4 p = mv * vec4 ( pos, 1.0 );

    gl_Position  = proj * p;
    n            = normalize ( nm * normal );
    v            = normalize ( eye - p.xyz );
    l            = normalize ( light - p.xyz );
}
```

```
— fragment
#version 330 core

in        vec3 n;
in        vec3 v;
in        vec3 l;

out vec4 color;

void main(void)
{
    vec3   n2   = normalize ( n );
    vec3   l2   = normalize ( l );
    float  nl   = dot(n2, l2);
    vec3   r    = (2.0*nl) * n2 - l2;
    float  diff = max ( nl, 0.0 );
    float  spec = pow ( max ( dot ( n2, r ), 0.0 ), 50.0 );
    vec4   clr  = vec4 ( 0.7, 0.1, 0.1, 1.0 );
    float  ka   = 0.2;
    float  kd   = 0.8;
    float  ks   = 0.5;

    color = (ka + kd*diff)*clr + ks*vec4(spec);
}
```

In Figure 14.2 you can see the resulting image.

14.1.3   Blinn-Phong lighting model

In Figure 14.3 the knot is lit using the Blinn-Phong lighting model. Corresponding shaders are very similar to the Phong shaders – the main difference is using the h vector instead of r. The halfway vector h is computed in the vertex shader and then passed to the fragment shader where it is normalized and used to compute the specular highlight.

```
— vertex

#version 330 core

uniform mat4 proj;
uniform mat4 mv;
uniform mat3 nm;
uniform vec3 eye;      // eye position
uniform vec3 light;    // light position
```

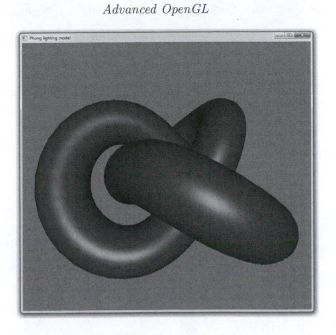

FIGURE 14.2 (See color insert.): Phong lighting of the knot.

FIGURE 14.3 (See color insert.): Blinn-Phong lighting of the knot.

```
layout(location = 0) in vec3 pos;
layout(location = 2) in vec3 normal;
```

```glsl
out vec3 n;
out vec3 v;
out vec3 l;
out vec3 h;

void main(void)
{
    vec4 p = mv * vec4 ( pos, 1.0 );

    gl_Position  = proj * p;
    n            = normalize ( nm * normal );
    v            = normalize ( eye - p.xyz );
    l            = normalize ( light - p.xyz );
    h            = normalize ( v + l );
}

-- fragment
#version 330 core

in vec3 n;
in vec3 v;
in vec3 l;
in vec3 h;

out vec4 color;

void main(void)
{
    vec3  n2   = normalize ( n );
    vec3  l2   = normalize ( l );
    vec3  h2   = normalize ( h );
    float nl   = dot(n2, l2 );
    float diff = max ( nl, 0.0 );
    float spec = pow ( max ( dot ( n2, h2 ), 0.0 ), 50.0 );
    vec4  clr  = vec4 ( 0.7, 0.1, 0.1, 1.0 );
    float ka   = 0.2;
    float kd   = 0.8;
    float ks   = 0.5;

    color = (ka + kd*diff)*clr + ks*vec4(spec);
}
```

14.1.4   Strauss lighting model

For the Strauss lighting model we again can use the vertex shader from the Phong lighting model since the changes will be only in the fragment shader. Here we will pass smoothness, metallness and transparency via uniform variables which can be changed in the application via key presses.

So the declaration of our window class will look as shown below.

```
class MeshWindow : public GlutRotateWindow
{
    Program     program;
    BasicMesh * mesh;
    vec3        eye;
    vec3        light;
    float       smooth;
    float       metal;
    float       transp;

public:
    MeshWindow () : GlutRotateWindow( 200, 200, 400, 400,
                                        "Strauss_lighting_model" )
    {
        if ( !program.loadProgram ( "strauss.glsl" ) )
        {
            printf ( "Error_building_program:_%s\n",
                    program.getLog ().c_str () );
            exit    ( 2 );
        }

        program.bind ();

        mesh  = createKnot ( 1, 4, 120, 30 );
        eye   = vec3 ( 5, 5, 5 );
        light = vec3 ( 5, 5, 5 );

        smooth = 0.5;
        metal  = 1.0;
        transp = 0.3;

        printf ( "Use_+_and_-_keys_to_change_smoothness\n" );
        printf ( "Use_*_and_/_keys_to_change_metallness\n" );
        printf ( "Use_[_and_]_keys_to_change_transparency\n" );
    }
```

The *keyTyped* method is not shown here as it is trivial – use the key to increment/decrement the corresponding value and clamp this value to the $[0, 1]$ range.

The fragment shader is very convenient to introduce *shadow* and *fresnel* as separate functions. This shader is just straightforward implementation of equations for the Strauss lighting model.

```glsl
#version 330 core

uniform float sm;
uniform float mtl;
uniform float tr;

in   vec3 n;
in   vec3 v;
in   vec3 l;
in   vec3 h;
out  vec4 color;

float fresnel ( float x, float kf )
{
   float dx  = x - kf;
   float d1  = 1.0 - kf;
   float kf2 = kf * kf;

return (1.0 / (dx * dx) - 1.0 / kf2) /
       (1.0 / (d1 * d1) - 1.0 / kf2 );
}

float shadow ( float x, float ks )
{
   float dx  = x - ks;
   float d1  = 1.0 - ks;
   float ks2 = ks * ks;

   return (1.0 / (d1*d1) - 1.0 / (dx * dx) ) /
          (1.0 / (d1 * d1) - 1.0 / ks2 );
}

void main (void)
{
   const vec4  diffColor = vec4 ( 1.0, 0.0, 0.0, 1.0 );
   const vec4  specColor = vec4 ( 1.0, 1.0, 0.0, 1.0 );
   const float k  = 0.1;
   const float kf = 1.12;
   const float ks = 1.01;

   vec3  n2 = normalize ( n );
   vec3  l2 = normalize ( l );
```

```
vec3   v2 = normalize ( v );
vec3   h2 = reflect    ( 12 , n2 );
float  nl = dot( n2, 12 );
float  nv = dot( n2, v2 );
float  hv = dot( h2, v2 );
float  f  = fresnel( nl, kf );
float  s3 = sm * sm * sm;

        // diffuse term
float  Rd   = ( 1.0 - s3 ) * ( 1.0 - tr );
vec4   diff = nl * ( 1.0 - mtl * sm ) * Rd * diffColor;

        // inputs into the specular term
float  r       = (1.0 - tr) - Rd;
float  j       = f * shadow ( nl, ks ) * shadow ( nv, ks );
float  reflect = min ( 1.0, r + j * ( r + k ) );
vec4   C1      = vec4 ( 1.0 );
vec4   Cs      = C1 + mtl * (1.0 - f) * (diffColor - C1);
vec4   spec    = Cs * reflect * pow ( -hv, 3.0 / (1.0 - sm) );

        // composite the final result , ensuring
diff  = max ( vec4 ( 0.0 ), diff );
spec  = max ( vec4 ( 0.0 ), spec );
color = diff + spec*specColor;
}
```

In Figure 14.4 the resulting image is shown.

14.1.5 Normalized Phong and Blinn-Phong models

The standard Phong and Blinn-Phong models do not obey the energy conservation law – the corresponding integral is not equal to one. But these models can be easily normalized.

A normalized Phong lighting model is shown below

$$I = k_a I_a + k_d C I_l max((n, l), 0) + k_s C_s I_l \frac{n+1}{2\pi} max((r, v), 0)^p. \quad (14.1)$$

And the corresponding normalized equation for the Blinn-Phong is shown below

$$I = k_a I_a + k_d C I_l max((n, l), 0) + k_s C_s I_l \frac{n+8}{8\pi} max((n, h), 0)^p. \quad (14.2)$$

Shaders for these models are not shown but you can find them on the CRC website.

FIGURE 14.4 (See color insert.): Strauss lighting of the knot.

14.1.6   Oren-Nayar lighting model

We can use our vertex shader from the Phong model as our vertex shader for the Oren-Nayar lighting model. It just computes vectors n, l and v and passes them to the fragment shader.

To compute $cos(\theta_v - \theta_l)$ we will project l and v vectors onto the tangent plane and after their normalization the dot product will give us the required cosine.

```
vec3   l2 = normalize ( l );
vec3   n2 = normalize ( n );
vec3   v2 = normalize ( v );
float  nl = dot ( n2, l2 );
float  nv = dot ( n2, v2 );
vec3   lProj = normalize ( l2 - n2 * nl );
vec3   vProj = normalize ( v2 - n2 * nv );
float  cx    = max ( dot ( lProj, vProj ), 0.0 );
```

Then we need to compute $sin\alpha \cdot tan\beta$ where α and β are given by (13.41). Since we are interested only in the case when both input angles are in the $[0, \pi/2]$ range, we will use the property that cosine function is monotonously decreasing in this range and therefore we get the equations

$$cos\alpha = max(cos\theta_v, cos\theta_l), \tag{14.3}$$

$$cos\beta = min(cos\theta_v, cos\theta_l). \tag{14.4}$$

Knowing cosines of both angles and that they are angles in the $[0, \pi/2]$ range we can find required functions from these cosines

$$sin\alpha \tan\beta = \sqrt{\frac{(1 - cos^2\alpha)(1 - cos^2\beta)}{cos^2\beta}}. \tag{14.5}$$

Now we can write a fragment shader for the Oren-Nayar lighting model as shown below.

```
#version 330 core

in vec3 v;
in vec3 l;
in vec3 n;

out vec4 color;

void main( void )
{
    vec4   clr    = vec4 ( 0.7, 0.1, 0.1, 1.0 );
    float  roughness = 3.0;

    vec3   l2   = normalize( l );
    vec3   n2   = normalize( n );
    vec3   v2   = normalize( v );
    float  nl   = dot( n2, l2 );
    float  nv   = dot( n2, v2 );
    vec3   lProj   = normalize(l2 - n2 * nl);
    vec3   vProj   = normalize(v2 - n2 * nv);
    float  cx     = max(dot( lProj, vProj), 0.0);
    float  cosAlpha = max(nl, nv);
    float  cosBeta  = min(nl, nv);
    float  ca2      = cosAlpha*cosAlpha;
    float  cb2      = cosBeta*cosBeta;
    float  dx       = sqrt((1.0 - ca2)*(1.0 - cb2)/
                       (cb2+0.001));
    float  r2       = roughness * roughness;
    float  a        = 1.0 - 0.5 * r2 / (r2 + 0.33);
    float  b        = 0.45 * r2 / ( r2 + 0.09 );
```

```
    color = max( nl ,  0.0 ) * c * (a + b * cx * dx );
}
```

In Figure 14.5 the resulting image is shown.

FIGURE 14.5 (See color insert.): Oren-Nayar lighting of the knot.

14.1.7   Cook-Torrance lighting model

For this shader we will also use the Phong vertex shader, but the fragment shader will be completely different. First we need to use some approximation for Fresnel – we will use the Schlick approximation and we compute the Beckman distribution using (13.49).

Since these are just plain equations written in the GLSL, we won't go into details and show the fragment shader.

```
#version 330 core

in vec3 v;
in vec3 l;
in vec3 n;

out vec4 color;

void main( void )
{
```

```
float roughness = 0.09;
vec4  r0   = vec4 ( 1.0, 0.92, 0.23, 1.0);
vec4  clr  = vec4 ( 0.7, 0.1, 0.1, 1.0 );
vec3  l2   = normalize(l);
vec3  n2   = normalize(n);
vec3  v2   = normalize(v);
vec3  h    = normalize(l2 + v2);
float nh   = dot(n2, h);
float nv   = dot(n2, v2);
float nl   = dot(n2, l2);
float r2   = roughness * roughness;
float nh2  = nh * nh;
float ex   = -(1.0 - nh2)/(nh2 * r2);
float d    = pow(2.7182818284, ex ) /
                 (r2*nh2*nh2);
vec4  f    = mix(vec4(pow(1.0-nv, 5.0)), vec4(1.0), r0);
float x    = 2.0 * nh / dot(v2, h);
float g    = min(1.0, min (x * nl, x * nv));
vec4  ct   = f*(d * g / nv);
float diff = max(nl, 0.0);
float ks   = 0.5;

color = diff * clr + ks * ct;
}
```

Note how the surface lit with the Cook-Torrance lighting model differs from the Phong or Blinn-Phong models (see Figure 14.6).

14.1.8   Ashikhmin-Shirley lighting model

For this lighting model we will need not only normal to the surface n but also tangent t and binormal b. Note that all these vectors are transformed by the same upper-left 3×3 submatrix of the model-view matrix.

```
#version 330 core

layout(location = 0) in vec3 pos;
layout(location = 2) in vec3 normal;
layout(location = 3) in vec3 tangent;
layout(location = 4) in vec3 binormal;

uniform vec3 light;
uniform vec3 eye;
uniform mat4 proj;
uniform mat4 mv;
uniform mat3 nm;
```

FIGURE 14.6 (See color insert.): Cook-Torrance lighting of the knot.

```
out vec3 l;
out vec3 h;
out vec3 v;
out vec3 t;
out vec3 b;
out vec3 n;

void main( void )
{
  vec4 p = mv * vec4 ( pos, 1.0 );

  gl_Position  = proj * p;

  n = normalize (nm * normal);
  t = normalize (nm * tangent);
  b = normalize (nm * binormal);
  l = normalize (light - p.xyz);
  v = normalize (eye    - p.xyz);
  h = normalize (l + v);
}
```

In the fragment shader we normalize all input vectors and compute corresponding dot products. The diffuse and specular terms are computed exactly

following Equations (13.54). Note that A should in fact be computed not in a shader but in a calling application; here it just wastes resources.

```glsl
#version 330 core

in vec3 l;
in vec3 h;
in vec3 v;
in vec3 t;
in vec3 b;
in vec3 n;

out vec4 color;

uniform float mx, my;
uniform float ks, kd;
uniform float r0;
uniform vec4  specular;

#define PI 3.1415926

void main( void )
{
  vec4  clr = vec4 ( 0.7, 0.1, 0.1, 1.0 );
  vec3  n2  = normalize( n );
  vec3  t2  = normalize( t );
  vec3  b2  = normalize( b );
  vec3  l2  = normalize( l );
  vec3  h2  = normalize( h );
  vec3  v2  = normalize( v );
  float nv  = max(0.0, dot(n2, v2));
  float nl  = max(0.0, dot(n2, l2));
  float nh  = max(0.0, dot(n2, h2));
  float hl  = max(0.0, dot(h2, l2));
  float t1h = dot(b2, h2 );
  float t2h = dot(t2, h2 );

                 // calculate diffuse
  float    rd = (28.0/(23.0*PI)) *
               (1.0 - pow(1.0 - 0.5*nv, 5.0)) *
               (1.0 - pow(1.0 - 0.5*nl, 5.0));

                 // calculate specular
  float    A = sqrt((mx + 1.0) * (my + 1.0) /
               (8.0 * PI));
  float    B = pow(nh, (mx*t1h*t1h + my*t2h*t2h)/
```

```
                      (1.0 - nh*nh));
  float    F  = (r0 + (1.0 - r0) * pow(1.0 - hl, 5.0))/
                (hl * max(nv, nl));
  float    rs = A * B * F;

  color = nl * ( clr * kd * ( 1.0 - ks ) * rd +
           specular * ks * rs );
}
```

14.2   Geometry shaders

The vertex shader processes individual vertices. It has no information about which form the primitive current vertex belongs to or about other vertices of the current primitive. This allows to process vertices in parallel achieving a high rendering speed.

But there are cases which can benefit from the ability to process individual primitives. Such an ability is present in OpenGL 3 in the form of *geometry shaders* (see Figure 14.7).

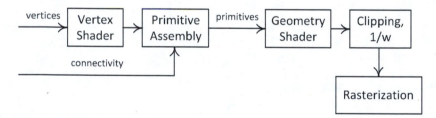

FIGURE 14.7: Place of geometry shader in the pipeline.

Geometry shaders receive vertices after they have been processed by the vertex shader but this shader is called *per-primitive* rather than per-vertex and have access to all vertices of the primitive. It can receive primitives of the type specified in the shader itself. Possible primitive types are shown in Table 14.1.

The last two primitive types – lines and triangles with adjacency – are new primitive types. For these types the primitive includes information about adjacent vertices (see Figure 14.8).

There are strip versions of these primitives which are shown on Figures 14.9 and 14.10.

The type of input primitive is defined in the geometry shader using a *layout* directive. The following example shows how to specify in a geometry shader that its input primitives are triangles;

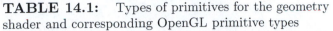

TABLE 14.1: Types of primitives for the geometry shader and corresponding OpenGL primitive types

Shader type	OpenGL types
points	GL_POINTS
lines	GL_LINES, GL_LINE_STRIP, GL_LINE_LOOP
triangles	GL_TRIANGLES, GL_TRIANGLE_FAN, GL_TRIANGLE_STRIP
lines_adjacency	GL_LINES_ADJACENCY, GL_LINE_STRIP_ADJACENCY
triangle_adjacency	GL_TRIANGLE_ADJACENCY, GL_TRIANGLE_STRIP_ADJACENCY

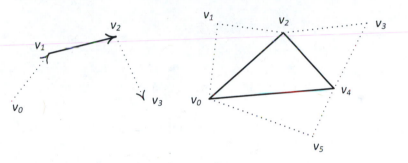

FIGURE 14.8: Line and triangle with adjacency.

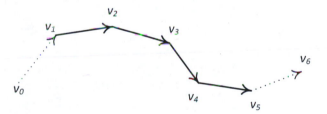

FIGURE 14.9: Line strip with adjacency.

```
layout (triangles) in;
```

From the application the type of input primitive can be found by using the **glGetProgramiv** command with a parameter GL_GEOMETRY_INPUT_TYPE from a linked program object.

```
glGetIntegeriv ( program, GL_GEOMETRY_INPUT_TYPE,
                &inType );
```

In the geometry shader the type of output primitives is also specified with the maximum number of vertices which the geometry shader can emit per

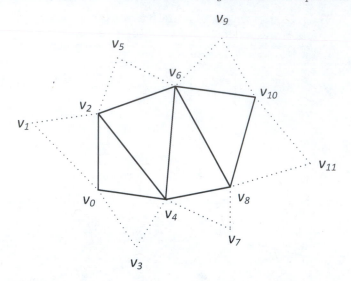

FIGURE 14.10: Triangle strip with adjacency.

invocation. Only three types of output primitives are supported – *points, line_strip* and *triangle_strip*.

layout (triangle_strip , max_vertices=4) **out;**

The next piece of code shows how to get these values from a linked program object.

```
glGetIntegeriv ( program , GL_GEOMETRY_OUTPUT_TYPE,
                            &outType );
glGetIntegeriv ( program , GL_GEOMETRY_VERTICES_OUT,
                            &maxVertices );
```

It is possible for a geometry shader to be called several times for every input primitive. This is also specified in the geometry shader source.

layout (triangles_adjacency , invocations = 5) in;

The geometry shader has several standard input variables:

- *gl_in* – an array containing values for every vertex of the primitive;

- *gl_PrimitiveIDIn* – a primitive sequence number generated by **glDraw** calls;

- *gl_InvocationID* – an instance number of the primitive when the geometry shader is called several times per input primitive.

The *gl_in* is an array of standard vertex attributes:

- *gl_Position* – vertex coordinates generated by vertex shader;

- *gl_PointSize* – size of the point, used for points rasterizing;

- *gl_ClipDistance[ ]* – an array of distance from the vertex to all user-defined clipping planes.

The length of *gl_in* array can be found as *gl_in.length()*. The geometry shader has access to uniform variables and all vertex shader outputs. Because the geometry shader has access to all vertices of the primitive, the vertex shader outputs should be declared as arrays.

For example, suppose that in the vertex shader we have the following output variable declaration.

out vec3 vertexNormal;

Then in order to access this variable in the geometry shader it should be declared in it as an array.

in vec3 vertexNormal [];

Also the geometry shader has several built-in output variables – *gl_Position*, *gl_PointSize* and *gl_ClipDistance[ ]*, *gl_PrimitiveID*, *gl_Layer* and *gl_ViewportIndex*. Note that all these variables correspond to one vertex and after a call of **EmitVertex** producing an output vertex their values become undefined.

The output variable of a geometry shader (and of a vertex shader as well) can be declared with a *flat* qualifier. In this case it will not be interpolated during rasterization and the value of the first or the last vertex of the primitive (the so-called *provoking vertex*) will be passed to the fragment shader.

out vec3 vertexNormal;
flat out vec3 faceNormal;

Most of standard output variables of the geometry shader corresponds to the fields of *gl_in* array items. Also the geometry shader can write into the *gl_Layer* output variable. This will select a layer from a texture array or a face of the cubemap (bound as a color attachment to the user-defined framebuffer object) that this primitive should be rendered into.

Writing into the *gl_ViewportIndex* selects a viewport for the rendering of this primitive (this variable is available only since OpenGL 4.1).

The geometry shader outputs a vertex by calling the **EmitVertex** function. After all vertices of the primitive have been generated, a call of the **EndPrimitive** function emits a primitive consisting of these vertices.

Below is a simple geometry shader that just copies all input triangles into the output.

```
#version 330 core

layout (triangles) in;
layout (triangle_strip, max_vertices=3) out;
```

```
void main ()
{
  for ( int i = 0; i < gl_in.length (); i++ )
  {
    gl_Position = gl_in [i].gl_Position;
    EmitVertex ();
  }
  EndPrimitive ();
}
```

A geometry shader can be successfully used for tasks like:

- compute per-primitive values (e.g., face normal);

- cull primitives (if the geometry shader does not output primitive it is culled);

- change the type of the primitive;

- create a small amount of new geometry.

The geometry shader can create new primitives, but it is usually a bad idea to use it for generating many new primitives like tessellation.

Our first example of geometry shader usage will be rendering of *billboards*. A billboard is a quad always parallel to the plane we are projecting onto. Usually a billboard is specified by a single point and a size. Then the geometry shader can construct two triangles forming a quad from point and size.

A common application for billboards are various particle systems when many animated billboards are used to render various visual effects.

The usual way of constructing a billboard is by using up and right directions – if we have a camera, which is doing the projection, then there are three vectors defining its orientation in space – view direction, up direction and right direction.

If we add to the vector any linear combination of up and right vectors we will get the vector which is in the same plane as the origin vector and this plane is parallel to the plane we are projecting onto. So we use up and right vectors scaled by billboard size to build the three vertices required to build a quad from our point.

To make things easier it will be passing in the vertex buffer 4D-vectors where the first three components define the location of the billboard in space and the remaining component defines the size of the billboard. This way we can have many billboards of different sizes.

The declaration of the corresponding window class and its constructor are shown below. The *vertices* array defines billboards. In the constructor we load shaders, create and fill with data corresponding vertex buffer and vertex array objects.

```
#define NUM_VERTICES   3
#define VERTEX_SIZE    (4*sizeof(float))

static float vertices [NUM_VERTICES * 4] =
{
  0,  -1,  0,  1,
  1,   0,  0,  2,
  0,   1,  1,  3
};

class    MeshWindow : public GlutRotateWindow
{
  Program      program;
  VertexArray  vao;
  VertexBuffer buf;
  vec3         eye;

public:
  MeshWindow() : GlutRotateWindow( 200, 200, 400, 400,
                                   "Billboards" )
  {
    if ( !program.loadProgram ( "geom-1.glsl" ) )
    {
      printf ( "Error_loading_shader:_%s\n",
               program.getLog ().c_str () );
      exit ( 1 );
    }

    program.bind ();
    vao.create  ();
    vao.bind    ();
    buf.create  ();
    buf.bind    ( GL_ARRAY_BUFFER );
    buf.setData ( NUM_VERTICES * VERTEX_SIZE, vertices,
                  GL_STATIC_DRAW );
    program.setAttrPtr ( "posSize", 4, VERTEX_SIZE,
                         (void *) 0 );
    buf.unbind  ();
    vao.unbind  ();
    program.unbind ();

    eye = vec3 ( 5, 5, 5 );
  }
```

The *redisplay* method passes up and right vectors to the shader program and calls **glDrawArrays** to draw the points defining billboards.

```
void redisplay ()
{
    glClear ( GL_COLOR_BUFFER_BIT | GL_DEPTH_BUFFER_BIT );

    mat4 mv = getRotation ();
    vec3 viewDir = vec3 ( 0, 0, 1 );
    vec3 sideDir = vec3 ( 0, 1, 0 );
    vec3 upDir   = vec3 ( 1, 0, 0 );

    program.bind ();
    program.setUniformMatrix ( "mv",    mv );
    program.setUniformVector ( "up",    upDir );
    program.setUniformVector ( "right", sideDir );

    vao.bind ();
    glDrawArrays ( GL_POINTS, 0, NUM_VERTICES );
    vao.unbind ();
    program.unbind ();
}
```

The vertex shader for this example is trivial – it transforms the given point with model-view and projection matrices. Also it extracts billboard size from the passed-in data and passes it to the geometry shader.

```
#version 330 core

uniform mat4 proj;
uniform mat4 mv;

in  vec4  posSize;  // position in xyz, size in w
out float size;

void main(void)
{
    gl_Position  = proj * mv * vec4 ( posSize.xyz, 1.0 );
    size         = 0.5 * posSize.w;
}
```

The geometry shader receives points as its input and produces triangles – for every invocation it will generate six vertices. It receives transformed vertex in homogeneous coordinates, splits them into *xyz* and *w* parts and uses them to generate two triangles using the given vertex and billboard size.

```
#version 330 core

layout (points) in;
layout (triangle_strip, max_vertices = 6) out;
```

```
uniform vec3 up;
uniform vec3 right;

in   float size [];

void main ()
{
  vec3   u = up * size [0];
  vec3   r = right * size [0];
  vec3   p = gl_in [0]. gl_Position.xyz;
  float w = gl_in [0]. gl_Position.w;

       // 1st triangle
  gl_Position = vec4 ( p - u - r, w );
  EmitVertex ();

  gl_Position = vec4 ( p - u + r, w );
  EmitVertex ();

  gl_Position = vec4 ( p + u + r, w );
  EmitVertex    ();
  EndPrimitive ();

       // 2nd triangle
  gl_Position = vec4 ( p + u + r, w );
  EmitVertex    ();

  gl_Position = vec4 ( p + u - r, w );
  EmitVertex ();

  gl_Position = vec4 ( p - u - r, w );
  EmitVertex    ();
  EndPrimitive ();
}
```

The fragment shader is not shown here – it can do anything from outputting a single color for every fragment to using some texture to produce relevant color.

Our next example of using a geometry shader instead of billboards will generate quads (as before, each quad will be represented by a pair of triangles), which are bisectors between two directions. One direction will be the direction to the camera and the other direction will be specified as a uniform vector.

The vertex shader differs from the previous example – it also computes the normalized vector v to the camera.

```
#version 330 core

uniform mat4 proj;
uniform mat4 mv;
uniform vec3 eye;      // eye position

in   vec4  posSize;    // position in xyz, size in w
out  float size;
out  vec3  v;

void main(void)
{
    gl_Position  = proj * mv * vec4 ( posSize.xyz, 1.0 );
    size         = 0.5 * posSize.w;
    v            = -normalize ( gl_Position.xyz );
}
```

The corresponding geometry shader is shown below – the main difference with the previous example is that it uses different direction vectors to define the plane quad should belong to.

First direction vector f is defined as a bisector of the given direction (to the Sun) and direction to the camera v. Second direction vector g is defined by the cross-product of vector f and direction to the Sun. It can be easily seen that both of those vectors define a plane which is a bisector between v and Sun directions.

```
#version 330 core

layout (points) in;
layout (triangle_strip , max_vertices = 6) out;

uniform vec3 sun;          // sun direction

in float size [];
in vec3  v     [];

void main ()
{
    vec3  p  = gl_in [0].gl_Position.xyz;
    vec3  vn = v [0];

            // bisector of v and sun
    vec3  f  = normalize ( vn + sun ) * size [0];
    vec3  g  = normalize ( cross ( f, sun ) ) * size [0];
    float w  = gl_in [0].gl_Position.w;
```

```
                // 1st triangle
       gl_Position = vec4 ( p - g - f, w );
       EmitVertex ();

       gl_Position = vec4 ( p - g + f, w );
       EmitVertex ();

       gl_Position = vec4 ( p + g + f, w );
       EmitVertex    ();
       EndPrimitive ();

                // 2nd triangle
       gl_Position = vec4 ( p + g + f, w );
       EmitVertex    ();

       gl_Position = vec4 ( p + g - f, w );
       EmitVertex ();

       gl_Position = vec4 ( p - g - f, w );
       EmitVertex    ();
       EndPrimitive ();
}
```

As an example of geometry shader usage we study a case of extruding a contour line for the input primitives. A *contour line* is the line where normal is perpendicular to the direction of the observer. If we use a triangle with normals specified at vertices then we interpolate the normal across the triangle and can locate a segment from one edge to another such that the interpolated normal on this segment will be perpendicular to the view direction.

So in the vertex shader we compute a dot product of the normal and view direction for every vertex.

```
// vertex shader
#version 330 core

uniform mat4 proj;
uniform mat4 mv;
uniform mat3 nm;
uniform vec3 eye;

in   vec3   pos;
in   vec3   normal;
out  vec3   n;
out  vec3   v;
out  float  s;
```

```
void main (void)
{
    vec3 p = vec3 ( mv * vec4 ( pos, 1.0 ) );

    gl_Position  = mv * vec4 ( pos, 1.0 );
    n            = nm * normal;
    v            = normalize ( vec3 ( eye ) - p );
    s            = dot ( n, v );
}
```

Then in the geometry shader we check whether all three dot products for the triangle vertices have the same sign (we check the sign with small tolerance values to account for numerical inaccuracies). If all three dot products have the same sign then we simply copy the primitive to the output – it cannot contain a segment of the contour line. Otherwise we have two edges of the triangle such that signs of dot products at the ends of these edges differ. Then we can use linear interpolation to locate a point on each of these edges where these dot products will be zero (see Figure 14.11). These two points form a segment of the contour line. We copy the input triangle to an output one and output two additional triangles forming a quad based on this segment and interpolated normals at its ends.

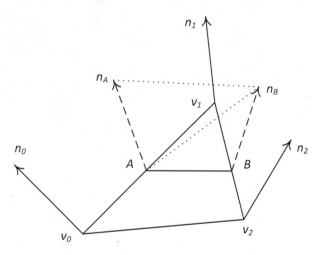

FIGURE 14.11: Extruding a contour segment.

```
// geometry shader
#version 330 core

#define EPS      0.001

layout (triangles) in;
```

```
layout (triangle_strip, max_vertices = 9) out;

uniform mat4 proj;
uniform float finSize;

in  vec3 n [];
in  vec3 v [];

int signWithTolerance ( float v )
{
  if ( v > EPS )
    return 1;

  if ( v < -EPS )
    return -1;

  return 0;
}

int addPoint ( float f0, int i0, float f1, int i1,
               inout vec4 points [4],
               inout vec3 normals [4], int count )
{
              // parameter across edge,
              // t*f0 + (1-t)*f1 = 0
  float t = f1 / ( f1 - f0 );

  points  [count]   = mix ( gl_in [i1].gl_Position,
                            gl_in [i0].gl_Position, t );
  normals [count++] = finSize * normalize (
                            mix ( n [i1], n [i0], t ) );

  return count;
}

void main ()
{
  float f0 = dot ( v [0], n [0] );
  float f1 = dot ( v [1], n [1] );
  float f2 = dot ( v [2], n [2] );
  int   s0 = signWithTolerance ( f0 );
  int   s1 = signWithTolerance ( f1 );
  int   s2 = signWithTolerance ( f2 );

              // emit source triangle
```

```
for ( int i = 0; i < 3; i++ )
{
   gl_Position = proj * gl_in [i].gl_Position;

   EmitVertex ();
}

EndPrimitive ();
        // now check for fins
        // quick exit for common cases
if ( s0 == 1 && s1 == 1 && s2 == 1 )
   return;

if ( s0 == -1 && s1 == -1 && s2 == -1 )
   return;

bool on01 = s0 * s1 <= 0;
bool on02 = s0 * s2 <= 0;
bool on12 = s1 * s2 <= 0;

        // locate edges that contain contour points
vec4 points  [4];
vec3 normals [4];
int  count = 0;

if ( on01 )
   count = addPoint ( f0, 0, f1, 1, points,
                            normals, count );

if ( on02 )
   count = addPoint ( f0, 0, f2, 2, points,
                            normals, count );

if ( on12 )
   count = addPoint ( f1, 1, f2, 2, points,
                            normals, count );

if ( count >= 2 )   // emit quad from edge
{
   gl_Position = proj*points [0];
   EmitVertex ();

   gl_Position = proj*( points [0]+vec4 (normals [0] ,0.0));
   EmitVertex ();
```

```
    gl_Position = proj*points [1];
    EmitVertex ();
    EndPrimitive ();

    gl_Position = proj*(points[0]+vec4(normals[0],0.0));
    EmitVertex ();

    gl_Position = proj*(points[1]+vec4(normals[1],0.0));
    EmitVertex ();

    gl_Position = proj*points[1];
    EmitVertex ();
    EndPrimitive ();
  }
}
```

In Figure 14.12 you can see the resulting image of a torus with contour line extruded.

FIGURE 14.12: Extruded contour line.

TABLE 14.2: Transform feedback primitive modes

Mode	Possible OpenGL types	Description
GL_POINTS	GL_POINTS	Stores vertex attributes
GL_LINES	GL_LINES, GL_LINE_STRIP, GL_LINE_LOOP	Stores each line segment as a pair of vertices
GL_TRIANGLES	GL_TRIANGLES, GL_TRIANGLE_FAN, GL_TRIANGLE_STRIP	Stores each triangle as three vertices

14.3 Transform feedback

Usually all transformed (in vertex and geometry shaders) vertices go to the primitive assembly and rasterization stages. In OpenGl 3 it is possible to store the processed vertices in one or several buffer objects (see Figure 14.13).

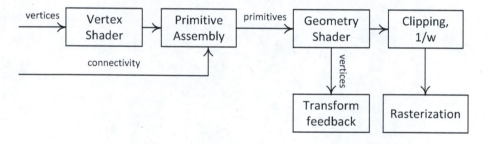

FIGURE 14.13: Transform feedback in the pipeline.

This *transform feedback* mode takes vertices from one or several buffer objects, processes them with vertex and geometry (if this shader is present) shaders and stores processed vertices (before clipping) in the other set of buffer objects.

Commands **glBeginTransformFeedback** and **glEndTransformFeedback** are used to start and finish the transform feedback mode.

void glBeginTransformFeedback (GLenum primitiveMode);
void glEndTransformFeedback ();

The parameter *mode* specifies the type of primitives to be stored. Table 14.2 lists possible values for this parameter and corresponding OpenGL primitive types.

After the command **glBeginTransformFeedback** all generated primitives will be stored in specified buffer objects. Primitive types should correspond to the *mode* parameter; incomplete primitives are not stored.

Every call to the **glBeginTransformFeedback** command should have a closing call to **glEndTransformFeedback**.

The vertices are stored into buffer objects bound to the GL_TRANS-FORM_FEEDBACK_BUFFER target. The buffers are bound by calling **glBindBufferRange** or **glBindBufferPos** commands with the target set to GL_TRANSFORM_FEEDBACK_BUFFER and to the index specifying the vertex attribute to be stored in this buffer.

There are two ways of storing vertex attributes in the transform feedback mode – GL_INTERLEAVED_ATTRIBS and GL_SEPARATE_ATTRIBS.

In the GL_INTERLEAVED_ATTRIBS mode all specified attributes are stored into one buffer object and in GL_SEPARATE_ATTRIBS each attribute is stored in its own buffer object.

To specify the output mode and attributes which should be stored, the **glTransformFeedbackVaryings** command is used.

```
void glTransformFeedbackVaryings (
          GLuint program ,
          GLsizei count ,
          const char ** names ,
          GLenum bufferMode );
```

Parameter *names* specifies an array of zero-terminated attribute names. The *count* parameter specifies the number of attributes in the *names* array and the *bufferMode* parameter specifies the storing mode GL_INTERLEAVED_ATTRIBS or GL_SEPARATE_ATTRIBS.

Note that this command can be called only for linked programs and there should not be duplicates in the *names* array. There are limitations to the number of stored attributes for each of two possible modes.

```
int maxInterlevedAttrs , maxSeparateAttrs ;

glGetIntegerv (
     GL_MAX_TRANSFORM_FEEDBACK_INTERLEAVED_COMPONENTS,
     &maxInterleavedAttrs );
glGetIntegerv (
     GL_MAX_TRANSFORM_FEEDBACK_SEPARATE_ATTRIBS,
     &maxSeparateAttrs );
```

Entering the transform feedback mode does not disable primitive rasterization and rendering. To disable the primitive rasterization command **glDisable** with an argument equal to GL_RASTERIZER_DISCARD should be called.

Now let's see how transform feedback can be used to create a particle simulation in the GPU. In this simulation every particle is defined by position and velocity. Particles will be moving under the gravity force and inside a box. When a particle touches the sides of the box it is reflected and the absolute value of its velocity is decreased by a damping factor.

It can be seen that we easily get the next iteration of particle based on its state in the previous moment of time, but it will be very difficult (if even possible) to write an analytical solution based only on a particle's initial state and time.

So for this case we will be using two shader programs – one will be using the vertex shader and transform feedback mode to compute a new state for every particle and the second will be using the particle state to render all particles.

The vertex shader for the particle animation is shown below.

```glsl
#version 330 core

uniform mat4    proj;
uniform mat4    mv;
uniform float   dt;
uniform vec3    boxSize;

layout (location = 0) in vec3 pos;
layout (location = 1) in vec3 vel;

out vec3 newPos;
out vec3 newVel;

void main(void)
{
    const vec3 acc  = vec3 ( 0, -0.02, 0 );
    const float damp = 0.9;

    bool        refl = false;

    gl_Position = proj * mv * vec4 ( pos, 1.0 );
    newPos      = pos + dt * vel;
    newVel      = vel + acc * dt;

        // check for collision
    if ( abs ( newPos.x ) >= boxSize.x )
    {
        newPos   -= dt * vel;
        newVel.x = -newVel.x;
        refl     = true;
    }

    if ( abs ( newPos.y ) >= boxSize.y )
    {
        newPos   -= dt * vel;
        newVel.y = -newVel.y;
        refl     = true;
```

```
}

if ( abs ( newPos.z ) >= boxSize.z )
{
  newPos  -= dt * vel;
  newVel.z = -newVel.z;
  refl     = true;
}

if ( refl )
  newVel *= damp;
}
```

To keep data for all particles we will use the ping-pong technique – two buffers will contain positions and velocities from the previous frame and we will store new positions and velocities into another two buffers. In the next frame we will swap these buffer pairs.

So we will have two velocities buffers, two position buffers and two vertex array objects to keep the buffer state. All of them will be organized into arrays.

```
VertexArray   vao      [2];
VertexBuffer  posBuf   [2];   // positions
VertexBuffer  velBuf   [2];   // velocities
int           ind;            // index for arrays
```

Buffers *posBuf[ind]* and *velBuf[ind]* will contain the state of all particles at the previous frame (or the initial state at the start of the application). We will use transform feedback to compute a new state and store it into *posBuf[ind^1]* and *velBuf[ind^1]*.

After buffer objects are filled with a new state the *ind* variable is flipped (*ind ^= 1*) and we perform rendering from buffers *posBuf[ind]* and *velBuf[ind]*.

Below is the declaration of our window class and its constructor are shown.

```
#define NUM_PARTICLES    5000

class MeshWindow : public GlutRotateWindow
{
  float         lastTime;
  vec3          eye;
  int           ind;
  vec3          p [NUM_PARTICLES];
  vec3          v [NUM_PARTICLES];
  Program       program;
  VertexArray   vao [2];
  VertexBuffer  posBuf [2], velBuf [2];

public:
```

```
MeshWindow ()  :  GlutRotateWindow ( 200, 200, 400, 400,
                                    "Transform_feedback" )
{
  if ( !program.loadProgram ( "tf3.glsl" ) )
  {
    printf ( "Error_loading_shader:_%s\n",
                  program.getLog ().c_str () );
    exit    ( 1 );
  }

  lastTime = 0;
  eye      = vec3 ( 3, 3, 3 );
  ind      = 0;

  initParticles ();

  program.bind ();
  program.transformFeedbacksVars ( "newPos;newVel",
                                  GL_SEPARATE_ATTRIBS );
  program.relink ();
  program.unbind ();

  for ( int i = 0; i < 2; i++ )
  {
    vao [i].create ();
    vao [i].bind   ();

    posBuf [i].create     ();
    posBuf [i].bind       ( GL_ARRAY_BUFFER );
    posBuf [i].setData    ( NUM_PARTICLES * sizeof ( vec3 ),
                            p, GL_STATIC_DRAW );
    posBuf [i].setAttrPtr ( 0, 3, sizeof ( vec3 ),
                            (void *) 0 );

    velBuf [i].create     ();
    velBuf [i].bind       ( GL_ARRAY_BUFFER );
    velBuf [i].setData    ( NUM_PARTICLES * sizeof ( vec3 ),
                            v, GL_STATIC_DRAW );
    velBuf [i].setAttrPtr ( 1, 3, sizeof ( vec3 ),
                            (void *) 0 );
    vao [i].unbind        ();
  }
}
```

Here we specify which output variables of the vertex shader will be written into vertex buffers and in which mode – in our case we are using separate buffers (GL_SEPARATE_ATTRIBS). To specify this we use the *transform-FeedbacksVars* method of our **Program** class – it receives a list of semicolon-separated output names and mode. Note that after this method we should relink our program object using the *relink* method.

Method *initParticles* initializes arrays of particle positions with the coordinate origin and array of particle velocities with random values in the $[-0.1, 0.1]$ range.

```
void initParticles ()
{
  for ( int i = 0; i < NUM_PARTICLES; i++ )
  {
    p [i] = vec3 ( 0, 0, 0 );
    v [i] = vec3 ( randUniform ( -0.1, 0.1 ),
                   randUniform ( -0.1, 0.1 ),
                   randUniform ( -0.1, 0.1 ) );
  }
}
```

The *redisplay* method performs two tasks – it saves new attributes in vertex buffers and performs rendering of particles. The last task is performed due to the fact that we do not disable rasterizing; therefore, the same shader program (and rendering code) is used both for transform feedback and rendering.

```
void redisplay ()
{
  float t  = getTime ();
  mat4  mv = getRotation ();

  glClear ( GL_COLOR_BUFFER_BIT | GL_DEPTH_BUFFER_BIT );

  program.bind ();
  program.setUniformMatrix ( "mv", mv );
  program.setUniformFloat  ( "dt", t - lastTime );

  posBuf [ind^1].bindBase ( GL_TRANSFORM_FEEDBACK_BUFFER, 0 );
  velBuf [ind^1].bindBase ( GL_TRANSFORM_FEEDBACK_BUFFER, 1 );

  glBeginTransformFeedback ( GL_POINTS );

  vao [ind].bind ();

  glDrawArrays ( GL_POINTS, 0, NUM_PARTICLES );

  vao [ind].unbind ();

  glEndTransformFeedback ();
```

```
program . unbind ( );

lastTime = t ;
}
```

Our animation code in C++ is very simple – since we already use physical time in the *redisplay* method we only need to switch which buffers contain new data and request window redisplay.

```
void idle ()
{
  ind ^= 1;

  glutPostRedisplay ( );
}
```

Corresponding vertex and fragment shaders are shown below.

— vertex

```
#version 330 core

uniform mat4   proj ;
uniform mat4   mv ;
uniform float  dt ;
uniform vec3   boxSize ;

layout ( location = 0) in vec3 pos ;
layout ( location = 1) in vec3 vel ;

out vec3 newPos ;
out vec3 newVel ;

void main ( void )
{
        // gravity acceleration
  const vec3   acc   = vec3 ( 0, −0.02, 0 );

        // damping for each reflection
  const float damp = 0.9 ;

  bool        refl = false ;

  gl_Position = proj * mv * vec4 ( pos , 1.0 );
  newPos      = pos + dt * vel ;
  newVel      = vel + acc * dt ;
```

```
        // if collision then
        // return to state before collision
    if ( abs ( newPos.x ) >= boxSize.x )
    {
      newPos  -= dt * vel;
      newVel.x = -newVel.x;
      refl     = true;
    }

    if ( abs ( newPos.y ) >= boxSize.y )
    {
      newPos  -= dt * vel;
      newVel.y = -newVel.y;
      refl     = true;
    }

    if ( abs ( newPos.z ) >= boxSize.z )
    {
      newPos  -= dt * vel;
      newVel.z = -newVel.z;
      refl     = true;
    }

    if ( refl )  // there was reflection
      newVel *= damp;
}

-- fragment

#version 330 core

out vec4 color;

void main(void)
{
        color = vec4 ( 1.0, 1.0, 0.0, 1.0 );
}
```

As you can see in this example, we are easily animating and rendering thousands of the particles entirely on the GPU. Later we will cover how such animation on the GPU can be achieved using OpenCL.

FIGURE 14.14: Particle animation.

14.4 Multiple Render Targets (MRT)

A fragment shader can output several values – it is sufficient to declare several output variables.

out vec4 color1;
out vec4 color2;

If we will attach two color attachments to the framebuffer object then after rendering, the first attachment will contain values of *color1* output and the second attachment will contain values of *color2* output.

To specify draw buffers into which fragment shader outputs are written, we need to use the **glDrawBuffers** command.

void glDrawBuffers (GLsizei n, **const** GLenum * bufs);

Here *n* is a parameter number of buffers in *bufs* array. Every element of *bufs* can be either GL_NONE or one of the constants GL_COLOR_ATTACH-MENTi. Below the basic scheme of rendering into two colorbuffers is shown – create the framebuffer, create the textures and attach them to the framebuffer; select the framebuffer and color attachments during rendering.

Below you can see a snippet of code showing how to create the framebuffer and setup MRT rendering.

```
    // declare frame buffer and textures
FrameBuffer buffer ( width, height,
```

```
                        FrameBuffer :: depth32 );
Texture    * tx1, * tx2;
. . .
    // setup buffer
buffer.create ();
buffer.bind    ();

tx1 = buffer.createColorTexture ();
tx2 = buffer.createColorTexture ();

buffer.attachColorTexture ( tx1, 0 );
buffer.attachColorTexture ( tx2, 1 );
buffer.unbind ();
```

The following snippet of code shows how to perform actual rendering into two separate textures simultaneously.

```
    // setup rendering
GLenum  buffers [] = { GL_COLOR_ATTACHMENT0,
                       GL_COLOR_ATTACHMENT1 };
buffer.bind ();

glDrawBuffers ( 2, buffers );

reshape ( buffer.getWidth (), buffer.getHeight () );

    // now do render
. . .
buffer.unbind ();
```

We will be using MRT rendering in the special effects chapter (Chapter 16) writing our deferred renderer.

14.5 Uniform blocks and uniform buffers

Setting uniform values for the program object is a costly operation so it is better to reduce the number of such calls. For this purpose we can use so-called *uniform blocks*. Using them we can update a whole group of uniform variables in one command.

In addition to commands setting uniform variables individually there is another way – *uniform blocks*. A uniform block is a named group of uniform variables as shown below.

uniform Lighting

```
{
  vec4   diffColor;
  vec4   specColor;
  float  specPower;
};
```

Inside a shader all these uniform variables can be referenced without specifying a uniform block name (e.g., *diffColor*) as if they were regular uniform variables.

It is possible to explicitly specify the type of memory layout for a uniform block – **packed, shared** or **std140**. The first format is most effective in packing variables but the exact memory layout of the block depends on the implementation; unused shader variables can be dropped.

Another memory layout (**shared**) which is used by default, also provides implementation defined packing but it is guaranteed that if we have several shaders with the same uniform block then memory layout for this block will be the same.

The last layout (**std1240**) explicitly defines the rules for memory layout; the resulting layout is portable and does not depend on the implementation.

The exact memory layout of a uniform block is important because all data for a uniform block is provided by the buffer object bound to the GL_UNIFORM_BUFFER target. So it is possible to set the contents of the whole uniform block with just a few commands and share these contents with other shaders.

Every uniform block is identified in the program by its index which is obtained by calling the **glGetUniformBlockIndex** command.

```
void glGetUniformBlockIndex ( GLuint program,
                              const char * blockName );
```

The **glGetActiveUniformBlockiv** command gets information about the uniform block, such as the number of variables in it and total size of the block.

```
void glGetActiveUniformBlockiv ( GLuint program,
                                 GLuint blockIndex,
                                 GLenum pname,
                                 GLint * param );
```

The following snippet of code shows how to get the size of the uniform block named "Lighting" and number of uniform variables in it.

```
GLuint blockIndex = glGetUniformBlockIndex ( program,
                                             "Lighting" );
GLint   blockSize , numUniforms;

glGetActiveUniformBlockiv ( program, blockIndex,
    GL_UNIFORM_BLOCK_DATA_SIZE, &blockSize );
```

```
glGetActiveUniformBlockiv ( program, blockIndex,
    GL_UNIFORM_BLOCK_ACTIVE_UNIFORMS, &numUniforms );
```

Every uniform variable within the block has its own index and using this index it is possible to get memory offset and size for the variable. The following snippet of code shows how to get offsets and sizes of all variables of the "Lighting" uniform block.

```
const char * names [] =
{
    "diffColor", "specColor", "specPower"
};

GLuint index    [3]; // index for every uniform
GLint  offset   [3]; // offset for every uniform
GLint  size     [3]; // size for every uniform

glGetUniformIndices   ( program, 3, names, index );
glGetActiveUniformsiv ( program, 3, index,
                        GL_UNIFORM_OFFSET, offset );
glGetActiveUniformsiv ( program, 3, index,
                        GL_UNIFORM_SIZE,   size );
```

A uniform buffer providing data for a uniform block should be bound to the indexable target GL_UNIFORM_BUFFER. After this, the command **glUniformBlockBinding** sets a uniform buffer bound to a particular index as the data source for a uniform block with the given block index.

```
void glUniformBlockBinding ( GLuint program,
                             GLuint blockIndex,
                             GLuint bufferBindIndex );
```

Introduced earlier, class Program provides support for uniform blocks via the methods **indexForUniformBlock**, **uniformBlockSize**, **uniformBlockBinding**, **uniformBlockActiveUniforms**, **getUniformBlockVar** and **bindBufferToIndex**.

The code below shows how to set all values for uniform block "Lighting".

```
void setupUbo ( VertexBuffer& buf, int bindingPoint,
    const vec4& dColor, const vec4& sColor, float specPwr )
{
    static const char * names [3] =
    {
        "diffColor", "specColor", "specPower"
    };

    static GLuint index   [3];  // index for every variable
    static int    offset  [3];
```

```
static GLuint blockIndex;
static int    blockSize;
static bool   inited = false;

if ( !inited )
{
    inited     = true;
    blockIndex = program.indexForUniformBlock( "Lighting" );
    blockSize  = program.uniformBlockSize( blockIndex );

    glGetUniformIndices  ( program.getProgram (), 3,
                           names, index );
    glGetActiveUniformsiv( program.getProgram (), 3,
                           index, GL_UNIFORM_OFFSET, offset );

        // init with zero's
    byte  * buffer = new byte [blockSize];

    memset ( buffer, 0, blockSize );

    buf.create    ();
    buf.bindBase ( GL_UNIFORM_BUFFER, bindingPoint );
    buf.setData  ( blockSize, buffer, GL_STREAM_DRAW );

    delete buffer;
}

buf.bindBase ( GL_UNIFORM_BUFFER, bindingPoint );
program.bindBufferToIndex ( blockIndex, bindingPoint );

byte  * ptr = (byte *) buf.map ( GL_WRITE_ONLY );

memcpy ( ptr + offset [0], &dColor.x, 16 );
memcpy ( ptr + offset [1], &sColor.x, 16 );
memcpy ( ptr + offset [2], &specPwr, 4   );

buf.unmap ();
}
```

One of the benefits of uniform blocks is that it changes values of a group of uniform variables with just a single call and shares these values between several programs.

14.6 Tessellation

The geometry shaders can generate new primitives but they work slowly when generating many new primitives. So for the purpose of generating many new primitives hardware tessellation was created. The support of hardware tessellation was added to OpenGL 4 but we can use it in OpenGL 3.3 as an OpenGL extension.

For this purpose two new shader types – the *tessellation control* shader and *tessellation evaluation* shader – were added and the pipeline has been changed to support tessellation (see Figure 14.15).

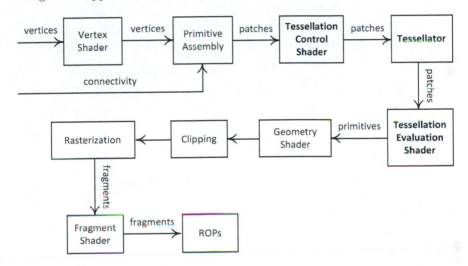

FIGURE 14.15: Programmable pipeline with tessellation.

Tessellation works only with primitives of a new primitive type added to OpenGL – patches (GL_PATCHES). A patch can contain many vertices, e.g., for splines it may contain all control points. A number of vertices per patch should be specified either in the tessellation control shader or (if this shader is absent) in an application via the **glPatchParameteri** command.

```
glPatchParameteri ( GL_PATCH_VERTICES, 4 );
glDrawArrays      ( GL_PATCHES, 0, count );
```

Tessellation is performed by two shaders and the hardware tessellator.

The tessellation control shader (GL_TESS_CONTROL_SHADER) is called separately for every vertex of the input patch, but it (like the geometry shader) has full access to all patch vertices. This shader provides parameters for the hardware tessellator and tessellation evaluation shader. A number of vertices per patch in the shader is specified in the **layout** directive.

```
layout (vertices=3) out;
```

All output values of the vertex shader are passed to the tessellation control shader as arrays; array size is omitted. So if in the vertex shader we have an output variable called *normal* of the **vec3** type, then in the tessellation control shader in order to access it we should declare it as an input array.

```
in vec3 normal [];
```

From a linked program object the number of vertices per patch can be queried using the **glGetProgramiv** command.

```
glGetProgramiv ( program ,
                 GL_TESS_CONTROL_OUTPUT_VERTICES,
                 &numVertices );
```

The tessellation control shader takes as its input the following standard variables:

- *gl_in* – an array, as in a geometry shader;

- *gl_PatchVerticesIn* – a number of vertices per patch;

- *gl_PrimitiveID* – a sequential number if primitive generated by **glDraw** commands;

- *gl_InvocationID* – a vertex number for the current primitive.

The shader also has several standard output variables:

- *gl_out* – an output array for vertices;

- *gl_TessLevelOuter* – an array of 4 floating-point numbers;

- *gl_TessLevelInner* – an array of 2 floating-point numbers.

The shader writes vertex data into the *gl_out* array and its own output variables. Also the shader should write values in the *gl_TessLevelOuter* and *gl_TessLevelInner* arrays.

The first of these arrays (*gl_TessLevelOuter*) controls how the border of the primitive should be subdivided. The second array (*gl_TessLevelInner*) controls the subdivision of the interior part of the patch.

The tessellation control shader can introduce its own per-vertex and per-primitive output variables. Per-primitive output variables should have the *patch* specifier. Per-vertex output variables should be declared as arrays.

```
out vec2 myVar [];          // per-vertex output
patch out float faceVal;    // per-primitive output
```

If any of the tessellation outer levels is less than or equal to zero then the whole patch is discarded.

The simplest tessellation control shader is shown below. It simply copies input vertex coordinates to output and sets tessellation levels (only once for the primitive).

```
#version 420 core

layout ( vertices=3 ) out;
uniform float level;    // global level of tessellation

void main ()
{
  gl_out [gl_InvocationID]. gl_Position =
      gl_in [gl_InvocationID]. gl_Position;

  if ( gl_InvocationID == 0 )
  {
    gl_TessLevelInner [0] = level;
    gl_TessLevelInner [1] = level;
    gl_TessLevelOuter [0] = level;
    gl_TessLevelOuter [1] = level;
    gl_TessLevelOuter [2] = level;
  }
}
```

Note that the tessellation control shader has full access to all inputs and outputs for every vertex of the patch, so it is possible to access outputs for another vertex of the patch.

But this can result in subtle errors because the order in which patch vertices will be processed by the tessellation control shader is undefined.

So the tessellation control shader can call a barrier synchronization function *barrier()*. When the tessellation control shader reaches the call of this function, it stops processing the current vertex and waits till this function is called for all vertices of the patch. Only after that does the vertex processing continue.

If the shader wants to access some outputs for other vertices it should write values for its own vertex and then call a *barrier* function. Only after this can it safely access written outputs for all other vertices.

The tessellation evaluation shader specifies type of tessellation in its **layout** directive. Only three types of tessellation are supported – **triangles**, **quads** and **isolines** (see Figure 14.16).

In the same **layout** directive the type of edge subdivision (**equal_spacing**, **fractional_even_spacing** and **fractional_odd_spacing**) can be specified and ordering of the output vertices (**cw** or **ccw**) can be specified too.

```
layout ( triangles , equal_spacing , ccw) in;
```

The hardware tessellator for every input patch according to a specified tessellation type generates new primitives which are passed to the tessellation evaluation shader. For every vertex of generated primitive, special coordinates specifying location of the vertex in the original patch are computed and passed

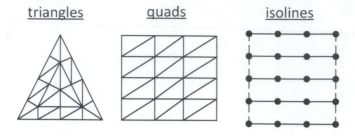

FIGURE 14.16: Types of tessellation.

to the shader. These coordinates are either standard 2D-coordinates or 3D-barycentric coordinates.

For tessellation it is possible not to specify the tessellation control shader. In this case tessellation inner and outer levels should be set by the application by executing the **glPatchParameterfv** command.

glPatchParameterfv (GLenum pname,
                     const GLfloat * values);

If *pname* is equal to GL_PATCH_DEFAULT_OUTER_LEVEL then the *values* parameter points to an array of four floating-point values specifying tessellation outer levels.

If *pname* is equal to GL_PATCH_DEFAULT_INNER_LEVEL then the *values* parameter points to an array of two floating-point values specifying tessellation inner levels.

For the **quads** tessellation mode all four outer levels are used; for the **triangles** tessellation mode only the first three values are used; and for the **isolines** mode only the first two outer levels are used.

Outer tessellation levels specify for the edges of the corresponding primitive (triangle or a quad) to how many parts should be split. But the exact number of parts into which edge will be split depends on both the outer tessellation levels and chosen type of edge tessellation.

If we have selected the **equal_spacing** subdivision type then corresponding to the edge the outer level will be clamped to the $[1, max]$ segment. Here the max is the implementation defined maximum tessellation level which can be obtained by calling the **glGetIntegerv** command with the GL_MAX_TESS_GEN_LEVEL parameter.

glGetIntegerv (GL_MAX_TESS_GEN_LEVEL, &maxLevel);

After clipping, the outer tessellation level will be rounded up to the nearest integer value n and corresponding edge will split into n equal parts.

If the edge subdivision type is **fractional_even_spacing** then the outer level will be clipped by the $[2, max]$ segment and then rounded up to the nearest even integer n.

For the **fractional_odd_spacing** tessellation type, the outer level is clipped by the $[1, max - 1]$ segment and is rounded up to the nearest odd integer n.

If obtained integer n is equal to one, then the corresponding edge is not subdivided at all. Otherwise the edge is split into $n - 2$ equal-sized parts and two additional parts (total n parts). Lengths of the additional parts are equal and they are located symmetrically relative to the endpoints of the edge.

The ratio of the lengths of additional parts to the lengths of equal-sized parts is a monotonic function of $n - f$, where f is the clamped outer tessellation level.

The tessellator generates primitives with vertices ordered either clockwise (**cw**) or counterclockwise (**ccw**) according to the specification in the **layout** directive. By default, vertices are ordered counterclockwise and ordering is relative to the generated coordinates.

It is possible to specify in the layout directive of the tessellation evaluation shader the **point_mode** option which forces the tessellator to output points as output primitive.

layout (triangles , equal_spacing , point_mode) **in ;**

Now we look how each primitive type (triangles, quads and isolines) is tessellated.

Tessellation of the triangle starts with building a set of nested triangles (see Figure 14.17).

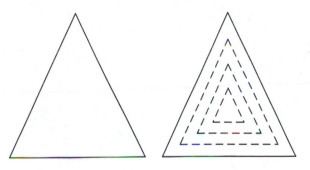

FIGURE 14.17: Nested triangles.

If after clipping and rounding all tessellation levels are equal to one, then one triangle is generated and its vertices will have the following barycentric coordinates – $(0, 0, 1)$, $(0, 1, 0)$ and $(1, 0, 0)$.

If the inner level is equal to one but at least one of the outer levels is greater than one then the innner level is treated as equal to $1 + \epsilon$ and it is rounded to 1 or 2 according to the spacing mode.

To build a set of nested triangles, first inner tessellation level is clamped and rounded producing some integer value n. Then all three edges of the triangle are split into n equal parts.

If $n = 2$ then we get a degenerate inner triangle (see Figure 14.18, right).

Otherwise, from subdivision points nearest to source triangle vertices, lines perpendicular to triangle edges are built. Their intersection points inside of the triangle gives three points from which a new triangle inside of the current one is built (see Figure 14.18 left).

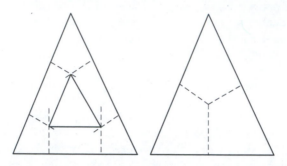

FIGURE 14.18: Building of an inner triangle.

If $n = 3$ then the process of building nested triangles is stopped, otherwise edges of the constructed inner triangle are split into $n - 2$ equal parts and the process of building an inner triangle is repeated.

After all nested triangles are built, the space between these triangles is split and filled with triangles based on edge split points.

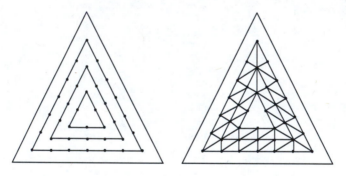

FIGURE 14.19: Filling areas between triangles.

The last step of tessellation is filling the area between the original triangle and the first nested triangle. For this area the equal-sized subdivision of edges of the original triangle is discarded and these edges are split using corresponding outer levels and subdivision types, each edge using its own outer level. After this, the area is filled by the triangles built on edge subdivision points.

Every vertex for all generated triangles gets its own barycentric coordinates (u, v, w) uniquely identifying the position of the vertex in the subdivided triangle.

Quad tessellation is much simpler. Two vertical edges (corresponding to

$u = 0$ and $u =)$ are split into edges defined by the first inner tessellation level number of equal-sized parts. Then two horizontal edges (corresponding to $v = 0$ and $v = 1$) are split too, but this time the number of produced parts is defined by the second inner level.

After this we get a block of rectangles and every inner rectangle (i.e., not touching the edges of the original quad) is split into two triangles (see Figure 14.20).

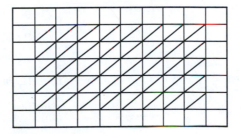

FIGURE 14.20: Quad tessellation.

Then every quad edge of the source quad is subdivided accordingly to four outer tessellation levels (each edge gets its own level) and spacing type and remaining space is filled with triangles based on subdivision points. Every vertex gets its own coordinates (u, v) $(u, v \in [0, 1])$.

For isolines tessellation mode a quad is converted to a set of horizontal (i.e., $v = const$) polylines (see Figure 14.21). At first step of tessellation vertical edges ($u = 0$ and $u = 1$) are split into equal-sized parts, the number of which is determined by the second outer subdivision level. For this mode, the spacing type is simply ignored. The subdivision points define horizontal edge ($v = const$) which are split using the first outer subdivision level. As a result, this tessellation produces a set of segments; vertices of these segments get their own coordinates (u, v) just like quad tessellation.

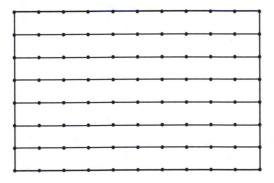

FIGURE 14.21: Isolines tessellation.

Note that for quad and triangle tessellation, the outer tessellation level is set for every edge. It avoids cracks when we are tessellating a triangle or a quad mesh – we only want to ensure that every edge shared by two primitives will get the same outer tessellation level.

A tessellation evaluation shader (GL_TESS_EVALUATION_SHADER) is separately called for every vertex of primitive created by the tessellator. This shader receives coordinates (u, v) or (u, v, w) in the *gl_TessCoord* input variable. Also it has access to the following input variables:

- *gl_in* – an output vertices of tessellation control shader for all patch vertices;

- *gl_PatchVerticesIn* – a number of vertices in the source patch;

- *gl_PrimitiveID* – a primitive number from the **glDraw** command;

- *gl_TessLevelInner* – an array of inner tessellation levels as set by the tessellation control shader;

- *gl_TessLevelOuter* – an array of outer tessellation levels.

The shader receives outputs of the tessellation control shader and in order to be used they should be declared as arrays. The results of the tessellation evaluation shader should be written into the following variables – *gl_Position*, *gl_PointSize* and *gl_ClipDistance*.

A simple tessellation evaluation shader which uses vertex barycentric coordinates to interpolate original vertices is shown below.

```
#version 420 core

layout ( triangles , equal_spacing ) in;

void main ()
{
   gl_Position = gl_TessCoord.x * gl_in [0].gl_Position +
                 gl_TessCoord.y * gl_in [1].gl_Position +
                 gl_TessCoord.z * gl_in [2].gl_Position;
}
```

The hardware tessellator can be used to create polygonal approximations to various spline surfaces. The next example uses tessellation to create a polygonal approximation to the bicubic Bezier surface. Bicubic Bezier surface is defined by 16 control points B_{ij}, which form a patch. The tessellation control shader just passes patch vertices and sets the tessellation level; tessellation evaluation shader computes vertex coordinates using control points and vertex coordinates *gl_TessCood*.

The *vertices* array is shown below containing all 16 control points for our Bezier path.

```
#define  PATCH_SIZE            16   // 16 control points
#define  VERTEX_SIZE           (3*sizeof(float))
#define  NUM_VERTICES          (PATCH_SIZE)

static const float vertices [PATCH_SIZE * 3] =
{
    -2.0f,  -2.0f,  0.0f,    // P00*
    -1.0f,  -2.0f,  1.0f,    // P10
     1.0f,  -1.0f,  2.0f,    // P20
     2.0f,  -2.0f,  0.0f,    // P30*
    -2.0f,  -1.0f,  1.0f,    // P01
    -1.0f,  -1.0f,  1.0f,    // P11
     2.0f,   0.0f,  1.0f,    // P21
     2.0f,  -1.0f,  2.0f,    // P31
    -3.0f,   0.0f,  1.0f,    // P02
    -1.0f,  -1.5f,  1.0f,    // P12
     0.0f,   0.0f,  0.0f,    // P22
     1.0f,   1.0f,  1.0f,    // P32
    -2.0f,   2.0f,  0.0f,    // P03*
    -1.5f,   3.0f,  2.0f,    // P13
     1.0f,   3.0f,  2.0f,    // P23
     2.0f,   2.0f,  0.0f     // P33*
};
```

The window class declaration and constructor are shown in the listing below.

```
class MeshWindow : public GlutRotateWindow
{
    int           inner;   // inner tess. level
    int           outer;   // outer tess. level
    vec3          eye;
    VertexBuffer  buf;
    VertexArray   vao;
    Program       program;

public:
    MeshWindow () : GlutRotateWindow ( 200, 200, 400, 400,
                          "Bezier_tesselation_demo" )
    {
        if ( !program.loadProgram ( "bezier.glsl" ) )
        {
            printf ( "Error_loading_shader:_%s\n",
                    program.getLog ().c_str () );
            exit    ( 1 );
        }
```

```
inner = 2;
outer = 2;
eye   = vec3 ( 3, 3, 4 );

program.bind  ();
vao.create    ();
vao.bind      ();
buf.create    ();
buf.bind          ( GL_ARRAY_BUFFER );
buf.setData       ( NUM_VERTICES * VERTEX_SIZE, vertices,
                    GL_STATIC_DRAW );
program.setAttrPtr ( "position", 3, VERTEX_SIZE,
                     (void *) 0 );
vao.unbind        ();
program.unbind    ();

updateCaption ();
}
```

The *redisplay* method sets for the program object the model-view matrix, uniforms inner and outer, which represent inner and outer tessellation levels for our shaders and sets the patch size. After this, we set the polygon mode to render only polygon outlines and perform actual rendering.

```
void redisplay ()
{
    glClear ( GL_COLOR_BUFFER_BIT | GL_DEPTH_BUFFER_BIT );

    mat4 mv = getRotation ();

    program.bind  ();
    program.setUniformMatrix ( "mv", mv );
    program.setUniformInt    ( "inner", inner );
    program.setUniformInt    ( "outer", outer );
    program.setPatchSize     ( PATCH_SIZE );

    vao.bind ();
    glPolygonMode ( GL_FRONT_AND_BACK, GL_LINE );
    glDrawArrays  ( GL_PATCHES, 0, NUM_VERTICES );
    vao.unbind ();
    program.unbind ();
}
```

We also use the *keyTyped* method to change inner and outer tessellation levels using the keyboard.

```
void keyTyped ( unsigned char key, int modifiers,
```

```
                        int x, int y )
{
    if ( key == 27 || key == 'q' || key == 'Q' ) // quit requested
        exit ( 0 );

    if ( key == '+' )
        inner++;
    else
    if ( key == '-' && inner > 1 )
        inner --;

    if ( key == '*' )
        outer++;
    else
    if ( key == '/' && outer > 1)
        outer --;

    if ( key == '+' || key == '-' || key == '/' || key == '*' )
        updateCaption ();

    glutPostRedisplay ();
}
```

The vertex shader is very simple in our case – it just transforms the vertex using model-view and projection matrices.

```
#version 410 core

uniform mat4 proj;
uniform mat4 mv;

in vec3 position;

void main(void)
{
    gl_Position = proj * mv * vec4 ( position, 1.0 );
}

-- tesscontrol

#version 420 core

uniform int inner;
uniform int outer;

layout (vertices = 16) out;
```

```
void main(void)
{
  gl_TessLevelInner [0] = inner;
  gl_TessLevelInner [1] = inner;
  gl_TessLevelOuter [0] = outer;
  gl_TessLevelOuter [1] = outer;
  gl_TessLevelOuter [2] = outer;
  gl_TessLevelOuter [3] = outer;

  gl_out [gl_InvocationID].gl_Position =
        gl_in [gl_InvocationID].gl_Position;
}

—— tesseval

#version 420 core

layout(quads, equal_spacing) in;

void main(void)
{
  float x = gl_TessCoord.x;
  float y = gl_TessCoord.y;
  vec4  u = vec4 ( 1.0, x, x*x, x*x*x );
  vec4  v = vec4 ( 1.0, y, y*y, y*y*y );
  mat4  b = mat4 ( 1,   0,   0, 0,
                  -3,   3,   0, 0,
                   3,  -6,   3, 0,
                  -1,   3,  -3, 1 );

  vec4  bu = b * u; // vector or Bernstein polynoms at u
  vec4  bv = b * v; // vector or Bernstein polynoms at v

  vec4 p00 = gl_in [ 0].gl_Position;
  vec4 p10 = gl_in [ 1].gl_Position;
  vec4 p20 = gl_in [ 2].gl_Position;
  vec4 p30 = gl_in [ 3].gl_Position;
  vec4 p01 = gl_in [ 4].gl_Position;
  vec4 p11 = gl_in [ 5].gl_Position;
  vec4 p21 = gl_in [ 6].gl_Position;
  vec4 p31 = gl_in [ 7].gl_Position;
  vec4 p02 = gl_in [ 8].gl_Position;
  vec4 p12 = gl_in [ 9].gl_Position;
  vec4 p22 = gl_in [10].gl_Position;
```

```
vec4 p32 = gl_in [11].gl_Position;
vec4 p03 = gl_in [12].gl_Position;
vec4 p13 = gl_in [13].gl_Position;
vec4 p23 = gl_in [14].gl_Position;
vec4 p33 = gl_in [15].gl_Position;

gl_Position =
    bu.x*(bv.x*p00 + bv.y*p01 + bv.z*p02 + bv.w*p03)+
    bu.y*(bv.x*p10 + bv.y*p11 + bv.z*p12 + bv.w*p13)+
    bu.z*(bv.x*p20 + bv.y*p21 + bv.z*p22 + bv.w*p23)+
    bu.w*(bv.x*p30 + bv.y*p31 + bv.z*p32 + bv.w*p33);
}
```

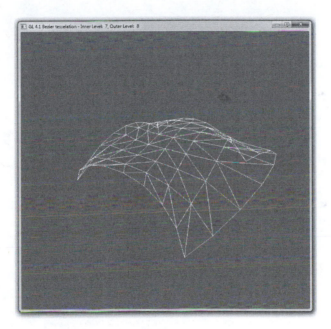

FIGURE 14.22: Tessellated Bezier patch.

Also we can implement Phong tessellation using the tessellation shader. As in the previous example, the tessellation control shader prepares data for tessellation and the tessellation evaluation shader computes the resulting vertex attributes – position and normal.

```
— vertex

#version 420 core

uniform mat4 mv;
```

```glsl
uniform mat3 nm;

in   vec3 position;
in   vec3 normal;
out  vec3 n;

void main(void)
{
  gl_Position = mv * vec4 ( position , 1.0 );
  n           = normalize ( nm * normal );
}

-- tesscontrol

#version 420 core

uniform int inner;
uniform int outer;

in   vec3 n  [];
out  vec3 nn [];

layout(vertices = 3) out;

void main(void)
{
  gl_TessLevelInner [0] = inner;
  gl_TessLevelInner [1] = inner;
  gl_TessLevelOuter [0] = outer;
  gl_TessLevelOuter [1] = outer;
  gl_TessLevelOuter [2] = outer;
  gl_TessLevelOuter [3] = outer;

  gl_out [gl_InvocationID].gl_Position =
           gl_in [gl_InvocationID].gl_Position;
  nn      [gl_InvocationID]              =
           n [gl_InvocationID];
}

-- tesseval

#version 420 core

uniform mat4 proj;
```

```
in vec3 nn [];

layout(triangles, equal_spacing) in;

void main(void)
{
  float u = gl_TessCoord.x;
  float v = gl_TessCoord.y;
  float w = gl_TessCoord.z;

  vec4 p  = u * gl_in [0].gl_Position +
            v * gl_in [1].gl_Position +
                 w * gl_in [2].gl_Position;
  vec3 n  = normalize ( u*nn [0] + v*nn [1] + w*nn [2] );
  vec4 p0 = p-dot(p.xyz-gl_in [0].gl_Position.xyz, nn[0]) *
            vec4 ( nn [0], 0.0 );
  vec4 p1 = p-dot(p.xyz-gl_in [1].gl_Position.xyz, nn[1]) *
            vec4 ( nn [1], 0.0 );
  vec4 p2 = p-dot(p.xyz-gl_in [2].gl_Position.xyz, nn[2]) *
            vec4 ( nn [2], 0.0 );

  gl_Position = proj * ( u * p0 + v * p1 + w * p2 );
}
```

The listing below shows how we can implement curved PN-triangles using hardware tessellation. The vertex shader traditionally is very simple – it just transforms vertex position and vertex normal. The task of the tessellation control shader is to compute Bezier coefficients for positions and normals. All these coefficients are declared as **patch** because they are per-patch. Note that the input patch in this case is the triangle with normals specified at vertices.

In order to simplify the computations of these coefficients, several function are introduced. Just as in our other examples, we use one inner tessellation level and one outer tessellation level specified as uniform values. However, this can be easily changed – here we use one inner and one outer coefficient just for simplicity.

The tessellation evaluation shader uses barycentric coordinates to compute actual vertex position and normal using coefficients for Bezier patches computed in the tessellation evaluation shader.

```
-- vertex

#version 420 core

uniform mat4 mv;
uniform mat3 nm;
```

```
in   vec3 position ;
in   vec3 normal ;
out vec3 n ;

void main ( void )
{
        gl_Position = mv * vec4 ( position , 1.0 );
        n           = normalize ( nm * normal );
}

— tesscontrol

#version 420 core

uniform int inner ;
uniform int outer ;

in   vec3 n [];

patch out vec3 b_300 ; // Bezier patch coefficients for
patch out vec3 b_030 ; // vertices
patch out vec3 b_003 ;
patch out vec3 b_210 ;
patch out vec3 b_120 ;
patch out vec3 b_021 ;
patch out vec3 b_012 ;
patch out vec3 b_102 ;
patch out vec3 b_201 ;
patch out vec3 b_111 ;

patch out vec3 n_200 ; // Bezier coefficients for normals
patch out vec3 n_020 ;
patch out vec3 n_002 ;
patch out vec3 n_110 ;
patch out vec3 n_011 ;
patch out vec3 n_101 ;

layout ( vertices = 3) out ;

float w ( int i , int j )
{
  return dot ( gl_in [ j ]. gl_Position . xyz −
               gl_in [ i ]. gl_Position . xyz , n [ i ]);
}
```

```
vec3 bb ( int i , int j )
{
  return (2.0*gl_in [i]. gl_Position.xyz +
          gl_in  [j]. gl_Position.xyz −
          w ( i , j ) * n [i]) / 3.0;
}

float lengthSq ( const vec3 v )
{
  return dot ( v, v );
}

vec3 nn ( int i , int j )
{
  vec3 dv  = gl_in [j]. gl_Position.xyz −
             gl_in [i]. gl_Position.xyz;
  vec3 vij = 2.0*( dv, n [i] + n [j] ) / lengthSq ( dv );
  vec3 nij = n [i] + n [j] − vij * dv;

return normalize ( nij );
}

void main(void)
{
  gl_TessLevelInner  [0] = inner;
  gl_TessLevelInner  [1] = inner;
  gl_TessLevelOuter  [0] = outer;
  gl_TessLevelOuter  [1] = outer;
  gl_TessLevelOuter  [2] = outer;
  gl_TessLevelOuter  [3] = outer;

  gl_out [gl_InvocationID]. gl_Position =
         gl_in [gl_InvocationID]. gl_Position;

  b_300 = gl_in [0]. gl_Position.xyz;
  b_030 = gl_in [1]. gl_Position.xyz;
  b_003 = gl_in [2]. gl_Position.xyz;

  b_210 = bb ( 0, 1 );
  b_120 = bb ( 1, 0 );
  b_021 = bb ( 1, 2 );
  b_012 = bb ( 2, 1 );
  b_102 = bb ( 2, 0 );
  b_201 = bb ( 0, 2 );
  b_111 = 1.5*(b_210+b_120+b_021+b_012+b_102+b_201)/6.0 −
```

```
       0.5*(gl_in [0].gl_Position.xyz+gl_in [1].
       gl_Position.xyz+gl_in [2].gl_Position.xyz) / 3.0;

  n_200 = n [0];
  n_020 = n [1];
  n_002 = n [2];
  n_110 = nn ( 0, 1 );
  n_011 = nn ( 1, 2 );
  n_101 = nn ( 2, 0 );
}


-- tesseval

#version 420 core

uniform mat4 proj;

in vec3 nn [];
out vec3 normal;

patch in vec3 b_300; // Bezier patch coefficients for vertices
patch in vec3 b_030;
patch in vec3 b_003;
patch in vec3 b_210;
patch in vec3 b_120;
patch in vec3 b_021;
patch in vec3 b_012;
patch in vec3 b_102;
patch in vec3 b_201;
patch in vec3 b_111;


patch in vec3 n_200; // Bezier coefficients for normals
patch in vec3 n_020;
patch in vec3 n_002;
patch in vec3 n_110;
patch in vec3 n_011;
patch in vec3 n_101;

layout(triangles, equal_spacing) in;

void main(void)
{
  float u = gl_TessCoord.x;
  float v = gl_TessCoord.y;
  float w = gl_TessCoord.z;
```

```
vec3   p = (b_300*u + 3.0*b_210*v + 3.0*b_201*w)*u*u +
           (b_030*v + 3.0*b_120*u + 3.0*b_021*w)*v*v +
           (b_003*w + 3.0*b_012*v + 3.0*b_102*u)*w*w +
           6.0*b_111*u*v*w;
vec3   n = n_200*u*u + n_020*v*v + n_002*w*w +
           2.0*n_110*u*v + 2.0*n_011*v*w +
           2.0*n_101*u*w;

gl_Position = proj * vec4 ( p, 1.0 );
normal      = normalize ( n );
}
```

In Figure 14.23 you can see the image of the PN-triangle rendered with the inner and outer tessellation level of five.

FIGURE 14.23: Curved PN-triangle rendered with tessellation.

14.7 OpenGL ES 2

OpenGL ES is a version of OpenGL targeted at mobile devices such as mobile phones, tablets and other such devices. It exists now in three major versions – 1, 2 and 3.

OpenGL 1 is targeted at mobile devices with a fixed rendering pipeline (like first generation iPhones) and OpenGL ES 2 is targeted at mobile devices with a programmable pipeline (such as the iPad and iPhone 4).

OpenGL ES 1.0 is based on OpenGL 1.5 with a cleaned interface and many elements removed. Many of the removed elements are deprecated in OpenGL 3.

For performance reasons, OpenGL ES 1 does not support double precision floating-point values but supports 32-bit fixed-point values in a 16.16 format. For many floating-point functions, versions which take fixed-point arguments were added. The corresponding OpenGL type is called **GLfixed** and **GLclampx** and it has the type suffix "x".

Immediate mode support was totally removed from all versions of OpenGL ES and all rendering is performed via **glDraw** commands taking vertex data from vertex arrays.

OpenGL ES 1 comes in two profiles – *Common* and *Common-Lite*. In the Common-Lite profile the floating-point type is completely removed and replaced with the fixed-point type.

Common-Lite profile commands use only "i" and "x" type suffixes with the exception of the **glColor4ub** command. The common profile uses only suffixes "f", "i" and "x" (with the same exception).

OpenGL ES does not support the following primitive types – GL_QUADS, GL_QUAD_STRIP and GL_POLYGON and commands **glVertex, glTexCoord**.

OpenGL ES 2 is based on OpenGL 2 with some of the functionality removed. OpenGL ES 2 supports only the Common profile and has a limited support of fixed type – usually a device with a programmable pipeline has a good support of floating-point operations. As with OpenGL ES 1, this version does not support the immediate mode and performs rendering only from vertex arrays. The set of supported primitives is the same as in OpenGL ES 1.

However, OpenGL ES 2 does support only generic vertex attributes specified by **glVertexAttrib** and **glVertexAttribPointer** commands (GLint and GLuint types in these commands are not supported).

Commands **glMultiDrawArrays** and **glMultDrawElements** are not supported as in the OpenGL ES 1. Support of the buffer objects is also the same as in OpenGL ES 1.

As you can see, OpenGL ES 2 is somewhat similar to OpenGL 3 with some functionality limited or removed.

OpenGL ES 2 supports 2D-textures and cubemaps. It also supports textures whose size is not a power of two but this support is limited - mipmaps for such textures are not supported and the only supported wrap mode for them is GL_CLAMP_TO_EDGE. All texture minification and magnification filters from OpenGL 2 are supported.

Alpha test is not supported. Alpha blending is supported and command **glBlendEquation** supports only the following functions – GL_FUNC_ADD,

GL_FUNC_SUBTRACT and GL_FUNC_REVERSE_SUBTRACT. Command **glBlendColor** and corresponding blend modes are supported.

Note that due to the absence of fixed pipeline in order to render anything, the vertex and fragment shaders should be supplied.

OpenGL ES 2 and OpenGL ES 3 uses the same GLSL shading language but with some small differences. First per-vertex inputs of the vertex shader are declared as **attribute** (instead of **in** in OpenGL 3). Outputs of the vertex shader and corresponding inputs of the fragment shader are declared as **varying**.

```
attribute  vec4  pos;
attribute  vec2  texCoord;
varying    float  f;
```

One more feature of shading language for OpenGL ES is the precision qualifiers. You should specify what precision should be used for various variables. There are three available precision qualifiers – **high** (high precision), **mediump** (medium precision) and **lowp** (low precision).

```
varying mediump vec2  texCoord;
lowp vec4  color;
highp vec4  coords;
```

Also using the **precision** statement you can specify the default precision for some type – in the shader snippet below, the float-type medium precision is selected. It means that if you have not specified the precision of a float variable then the default precision of **mediump** will be used.

```
precision mediump float;
lowp vec4  color;     // will have low precision
vec4  coords;         // will have medium precision
```

Using precision qualifiers allows the shading language compiler to perform various optimizations which can have a big influence on the performance; this is very important for mobile devices.

We will be using some OpenGL ES shaders in the next section devoted to WebGL.

14.8 WebGL

WebGL provides a way of using OpenGL right from your browser (note that Internet Explorer does not currently support WebGL; for WebGL you should use Chrome, Firefox or Safari). It is built upon OpenGL ES 2 and provides full access to OpenGL commands from java-script and renders directly into canvas element of the web page.

Because WebGL is based on OpenGL ES 2, it has no standard attributes and no support for standard matrix operations. There are several java-script libraries which can be used to make using WebGL easier. We will be using *sylvester.js* for matrix and vector operations (available at *http://sylvester.jcoglan.com/*) and *glUtils.js* libraries.

If we want to render in the browser we need to provide some initialization function which will be called on loading the web page and a canvas element into which we will rendering.

```
<script type "text/javascript" src="sylvester.js"></script>
<script type "text/javascript" src="glUtils.js"></script>
<body onload = "webGLStart();">
<P>
<canvas id="canvas" style="border:_none;"
  width = "500" height="500"></canvas>
```

In a function which will be called on page loading we should locate the corresponding canvas element and WebGL will create a context for it. After this, we should load and compile shaders, prepare textures, buffers and clear the area. Also we can set up a timer to call rendering code several times per second.

```
var gl;

function webGlStart()
{
  if ( !canvas )
    alert("Could not initialise canvas, sorry :-(");

  try {
    gl = canvas.getContext("webgl");

    if ( !gl )
        gl = canvas.getContext("experimental-webgl");

    gl.viewportWidth  = canvas.width;
    gl.viewportHeight = canvas.height;
  } catch(e) {}

  if ( !gl )
    alert("Could not initialise WebGL, sorry :-(");

  gl.viewport(0, 0, canvas.width, canvas.height );
  gl.clearColor(0.0, 0.0, 0.0, 1.0);
  gl.clearDepth(1.0);
  gl.enable(gl.DEPTH_TEST);
  gl.depthFunc(gl.LEQUAL);
}
```

Note that we try to get context using the name "webgl". However, some browsers do not support it, so if we failed to obtain context this way we try to get context using old name "experimental-webgl".

As you can see from the body of this function the standard OpenGL functions like **glEnable** or **glClearDepth** are replaced by calling corresponding methods of created canvas – **gl.enable** and **gl.clearDepth**.

Since in OpenGL ES 2 there is no fixed-pipeline support in order to render something, we need a vertex and fragment shader which will be passed as elements of the page. Below two simple shaders are shown as they are embedded into the page.

```
<script id="shader-vs" type="x-shader/x-vretex">
    attribute vec3 vertexPos;
    attribute vec4 vertexColor;

    uniform mat4 mvMatrix;
    uniform mat4 prMatrix;

    varying vec4 color;

    void main ()
    {
      glPosition = prMatrix * mvMatrix *
                     vec4 ( vertexPos, 1.0 );
      color     = vertexColor;
    }
</script>
<script id="shader-fs" type="x-shader/x-fragment">
    precision highp float;
    varying    vec4   color;

    void main ()
    {
      gl_FragColor = color;
    }
</script>
```

We will put some command java-script code dealing with initialization, loading of shaders and textures and doing several matrix operations into a separate file which can be shared between several examples.

The first function in our utility script will get an OpenGL canvas and perform OpenGL initialization.

```
function getGl ( canvas )
{
  if ( !canvas )
    alert("Could not initialise canvas, sorry :-(");
```

```
try {
  gl = canvas.getContext("webgl");

  if ( !gl )
    gl = canvas.getContext("experimental-webgl");

  gl.viewportWidth  = canvas.width;
  gl.viewportHeight = canvas.height;
} catch(e) {}

if ( !gl )
  alert("Could not initialise WebGL, sorry :-(");

gl.viewport(0, 0, canvas.width, canvas.height );
gl.clearColor(0.0, 0.0, 0.0, 1.0);
gl.clearDepth(1.0);
gl.enable(gl.DEPTH_TEST);
gl.depthFunc(gl.LEQUAL);

return gl;
}
```

The function *getShader* loads the shader from a specified section of an HTML source and compiles it. In the case of a compile error an alert is shown.

```
function getShader ( gl, id )
{
  var shaderScript = document.getElementById ( id );

  if (!shaderScript)
    return null;

  var str = "";
  var k   = shaderScript.firstChild;

  while ( k )
  {
    if ( k.nodeType == 3 )
      str += k.textContent;

    k = k.nextSibling;
  }

  var shader;
```

```
if ( shaderScript.type == "x-shader/x-fragment" )
  shader = gl.createShader ( gl.FRAGMENT_SHADER );
else if ( shaderScript.type == "x-shader/x-vertex" )
  shader = gl.createShader ( gl.VERTEX_SHADER );
else
  return null;

gl.shaderSource(shader, str );
gl.compileShader(shader);

if (!gl.getShaderParameter(shader, gl.COMPILE_STATUS))
{
  alert(gl.getShaderInfoLog(shader ));
  return null;
}

return shader;
}
```

The next function – *loadProgram* – creates a new program object, loads and compiles vertex and fragment shaders for it, attaches them to the program object and perform link. As before, an alert is shown in case of an error.

```
function loadProgram ( gl, vertId, fragId )
{
  var fragmentShader = getShader ( gl, vertId );
  var vertexShader   = getShader ( gl, fragId );
  var shaderProgram  = gl.createProgram ();

  gl.attachShader(shaderProgram, vertexShader );
  gl.attachShader(shaderProgram, fragmentShader );
  gl.linkProgram(shaderProgram);

  if (!gl.getProgramParameter(shaderProgram,
       gl.LINK_STATUS))
  {
    alert("Could not initialise shaders");

    return null;
  }

  return shaderProgram;
}
```

Since we will be using matrices in our code, it is convenient to use a function for working with matrix uniforms.

```
function setMatrixUniform ( gl, program, name, mat )
{
  var loc = gl.getUniformLocation ( program, name );

  gl.uniformMatrix4fv ( loc,   false,
                        new Float32Array (mat.flatten ()));
}
```

The next two functions are responsible for texture creation. The function *loadImagetexture* creates a texture object and sets a callback for it so that when the texture image is loaded that image will be set for a corresponding OpenGL texture object.

```
function createGLTexture(gl, image, texture)
{
  gl.enable(gl.TEXTURE_2D);
  gl.bindTexture(gl.TEXTURE_2D, texture);
  gl.pixelStorei(gl.UNPACK_FLIP_Y_WEBGL, true);
  gl.texImage2D(gl.TEXTURE_2D, 0, gl.RGBA, gl.RGBA,
                gl.UNSIGNED_BYTE, image);
  gl.texParameteri(gl.TEXTURE_2D, gl.TEXTURE_MAG_FILTER,
                   gl.LINEAR);
  gl.texParameteri(gl.TEXTURE_2D, gl.TEXTURE_MIN_FILTER,
                   gl.LINEAR_MIPMAP_LINEAR);
  gl.texParameteri(gl.TEXTURE_2D, gl.TEXTURE_WRAP_S,
                   gl.REPEAT);
  gl.texParameteri(gl.TEXTURE_2D, gl.TEXTURE_WRAP_T,
                   gl.REPEAT);
  gl.generateMipmap(gl.TEXTURE_2D)
  gl.bindTexture(gl.TEXTURE_2D, null);
}

function loadImageTexture(gl, url)
{
  var texture = gl.createTexture();
  texture.image = new Image();
  texture.image.onload = function() { createGLTexture(gl,
               texture.image, texture) }
  texture.image.src = url;

  return texture;
}
```

Now let's see what we need to render a triangle with color specified at its vertices using WebGL. First of all we need to load our shaders.

```
function initShaders ()
{
  shaderProgram = loadProgram ( gl , "shader-vs", "shader-fs" );
  gl.useProgram(shaderProgram);

  vertexPositionAttribute =
      gl.getAttribLocation(shaderProgram , "aVertexPosition");
  gl.enableVertexAttribArray(vertexPositionAttribute);

  vertexColorAttribute =
      gl.getAttribLocation(shaderProgram , "aVertexColor");
  gl.enableVertexAttribArray(vertexColorAttribute);
}
```

Since WebGL performs all rendering using buffer objects containing vertices and indices, we need to create and initialize corresponding buffer objects (we will create global variables *posBuf* and *colorBuf* for keeping these objects in).

```
function initBuffers ()
{
  posBuffer = gl.createBuffer ();
  gl.bindBuffer ( gl.ARRAY_BUFFER, posBuffer );
  var vertices = [
    0.0,   1.0,   0.0,
   -1.0,  -1.0,   0.0,
    1.0,  -1.0,   0.0
  ];
  gl.bufferData( gl.ARRAY_BUFFER, new Float32Array (vertices),
                 gl.STATIC_DRAW);
  posBuffer.itemSize = 3;
  posBuffer.numItems = 3;

  colorBuffer = gl.createBuffer ();
  gl.bindBuffer ( gl.ARRAY_BUFFER, colorBuffer );
  var colors = [
    1.0, 0.0, 0.0, 1.0,
    0.0, 1.0, 0.0, 1.0,
    0.0, 0.0, 1.0, 1.0,
  ];
  gl.bufferData( gl.ARRAY_BUFFER, new Float32Array (colors),
                 gl.STATIC_DRAW);
  colorBuffer.itemSize = 4;
  colorBuffer.numItems = 3;
}
```

As you can see, when we load the data from java-script arrays into buffer objects, we use special object **Float32Array**, which prepares an array of items in memory.

Also we will use several other globals for keeping program objects, attributes locations and two matrices we will be using instead of the modelview (*mvMatrix*) and projection (*prMatrix*) matrices in the fixed pipeline. In working with these matrices we will use the *sylvester* library.

```
var gl;
var mvMatrix;
var prMatrix;
var shaderProgram;
var vertexPositionAttribute;
var vertexColorAttribute;
var posBuffer;
var colorBuffer;
```

Then we will provide java-script analogs and common OpenGL matrix commands using the variables *mvMatrix* and *prMatrix*:

```
function loadIdentity()
{
    mvMatrix = Matrix.I(4);
}

function multMatrix(m)
{
    mvMatrix = mvMatrix.x(m);
}

function mvTranslate(v)
{
    var m = Matrix.Translation($V([v[0],v[1],v[2]])).ensure4x4();

    multMatrix(m);
}

function perspective(fovy, aspect, znear, zfar)
{
    prMatrix = makePerspective(fovy, aspect, znear, zfar);
}
```

And now we are ready to write the function that will render a triangle into a canvas element.

```
function drawScene()
{
    gl.clear    ( gl.COLOR_BUFFER_BIT | gl.DEPTH_BUFFER_BIT );
```

```
perspective  ( 45, 1.0, 0.1, 100.0 );
loadIdentity ();
mvTranslate  ( [0.0, 0.0, -5.0] );

gl.bindBuffer(gl.ARRAY_BUFFER, posBuffer);
gl.vertexAttribPointer(vertexPositionAttribute,
        posBuffer.itemSize, gl.FLOAT, false, 0, 0);

gl.bindBuffer(gl.ARRAY_BUFFER, colorBuffer);
gl.vertexAttribPointer(vertexColorAttribute,
        colorBuffer.itemSize, gl.FLOAT, false, 0, 0);

setMatrixUniforms ();
gl.drawArrays(gl.TRIANGLES, 0, posBuffer.numItems);
gl.flush ();
}
```

Our next example will render a rotating textured cube. For it we will need the *mvRotate* function and of course the **initBuffers** function should be rewritten to create buffers for texture coordinates instead of colors.

```
function mvRotate(ang, v)
{
    var arad = ang * Math.PI / 180.0;
    var m    = Matrix.Rotation(arad,
                    $V([v[0],v[1],v[2]])).ensure4x4();

    multMatrix(m);
}

function initBuffers()
{
    cubeVertexPositionBuffer = gl.createBuffer();
    gl.bindBuffer(gl.ARRAY_BUFFER,
            cubeVertexPositionBuffer);
    vertices = [
        // Front face
     -1.0, -1.0,  1.0,
      1.0, -1.0,  1.0,
      1.0,  1.0,  1.0,
     -1.0,  1.0,  1.0,

        // Back face
     -1.0, -1.0, -1.0,
     -1.0,  1.0, -1.0,
      1.0,  1.0, -1.0,
```

```
    1.0,  -1.0,  -1.0,

        // Top face
 -1.0,   1.0,  -1.0,
 -1.0,   1.0,   1.0,
  1.0,   1.0,   1.0,
  1.0,   1.0,  -1.0,

        // Bottom face
 -1.0,  -1.0,  -1.0,
  1.0,  -1.0,  -1.0,
  1.0,  -1.0,   1.0,
 -1.0,  -1.0,   1.0,

        // Right face
  1.0,  -1.0,  -1.0,
  1.0,   1.0,  -1.0,
  1.0,   1.0,   1.0,
  1.0,  -1.0,   1.0,

        // Left face
 -1.0,  -1.0,  -1.0,
 -1.0,  -1.0,   1.0,
 -1.0,   1.0,   1.0,
 -1.0,   1.0,  -1.0,
];
gl.bufferData(gl.ARRAY_BUFFER,
        new Float32Array(vertices),   gl.STATIC_DRAW);
cubeVertexPositionBuffer.itemSize = 3;
cubeVertexPositionBuffer.numItems = 24;

cubeVertexTextureCoordBuffer = gl.createBuffer();
gl.bindBuffer(gl.ARRAY_BUFFER, cubeVertexTextureCoordBuffer);
var textureCoords = [
        // Front face
  0.0, 0.0,
  1.0, 0.0,
  1.0, 1.0,
  0.0, 1.0,

        // Back face
  1.0, 0.0,
  1.0, 1.0,
  0.0, 1.0,
  0.0, 0.0,
```

```
      // Top face
  0.0 , 1.0 ,
 ·0.0 , 0.0 ,
  1.0 , 0.0 ,
  1.0 , 1.0 ,

      // Bottom face
  1.0 , 1.0 ,
  0.0 , 1.0 ,
  0.0 , 0.0 ,
  1.0 , 0.0 ,

      // Right face
  1.0 , 0.0 ,
  1.0 , 1.0 ,
  0.0 , 1.0 ,
  0.0 , 0.0 ,

      // Left face
  0.0 , 0.0 ,
  1.0 , 0.0 ,
  1.0 , 1.0 ,
  0.0 , 1.0 ,
];
gl . bufferData ( gl . ARRAY_BUFFER,
        new Float32Array ( textureCoords ) , gl . STATIC_DRAW ) ;
cubeVertexTextureCoordBuffer . itemSize = 2;
cubeVertexTextureCoordBuffer . numItems = 24;

cubeVertexIndexBuffer = gl . createBuffer ( ) ;
gl . bindBuffer ( gl . ELEMENT_ARRAY_BUFFER,
        cubeVertexIndexBuffer ) ;
var cubeVertexIndices = [
  0, 1, 2,      0, 2, 3,     // Front face
  4, 5, 6,      4, 6, 7,     // Back face
  8, 9, 10,     8, 10, 11,   // Top face
  12, 13, 14,   12, 14, 15,  // Bottom face
  16, 17, 18,   16, 18, 19,  // Right face
  20, 21, 22,   20, 22, 23   // Left face
]
gl . bufferData ( gl . ELEMENT_ARRAY_BUFFER,
      new Uint16Array ( cubeVertexIndices ) ,  gl . STATIC_DRAW ) ;
cubeVertexIndexBuffer . itemSize = 1;
cubeVertexIndexBuffer . numItems = 36;
}
```

Also we need to modify vertex and fragment shaders. And after that, our final part – the **drawScene** function is shown below.

```
function drawScene()
{
  gl.clear(gl.COLOR_BUFFER_BIT | gl.DEPTH_BUFFER_BIT)

  perspective  ( 45, 1.0, 0.1, 100.0 );
  loadIdentity ();
  mvTranslate ( [0.0, 0.0, -7.0] );
  mvRotate    ( xRot, [1, 0, 0] );
  mvRotate    ( yRot, [0, 1, 0] );

  gl.bindBuffer(gl.ARRAY_BUFFER, cubeVertexPositionBuffer);
  gl.vertexAttribPointer(shaderProgram.vertexPositionAttribute,
        cubeVertexPositionBuffer.itemSize, gl.FLOAT, false, 0, 0);

  gl.bindBuffer(gl.ARRAY_BUFFER, cubeVertexTextureCoordBuffer);
  gl.vertexAttribPointer(shaderProgram.textureCoordAttribute,
        cubeVertexTextureCoordBuffer.itemSize, gl.FLOAT, false, 0, 0);

  gl.activeTexture(gl.TEXTURE0);
  gl.bindTexture(gl.TEXTURE_2D, crateTexture);
  gl.uniform1i(shaderProgram.samplerUniform, 0);

  gl.bindBuffer(gl.ELEMENT_ARRAY_BUFFER, cubeVertexIndexBuffer);
  setMatrixUniforms();
  gl.drawElements(gl.TRIANGLES, cubeVertexIndexBuffer.numItems,
                  gl.UNSIGNED_SHORT, 0);

  xRot += 0.6;
  yRot += 0.3;
}
```

Next, we need to modify our **webGLStart** function to set up animation.

```
function webGLStart()
{
  var canvas = document.getElementById("canvas");

  gl              = getGl ( canvas );
  createTexture = loadImageTexture ( gl, "block.bmp" );

  initShaders ();
  initBuffers ();
  setInterval ( drawScene, 15 );
}
```

Chapter 15

GPU image processing

One of the areas (outside of 3D-graphics) where GPUs can be very effective is *image processing*. Usually we have one or several images and want to change the input image in some way (or to combine several images). Besides, we can have two images and want to build a transition from one image to another. Image processing includes tasks such as image magnification/minification and image warping.

15.1   Sampling, aliasing, filters

All image processing requires sampling of the texture, i.e., reading values from it. But thinking of texture as just a discrete array of texels can result in *aliasing*.

To understand why it can be, let's consider a simple testcase – the sampling of a sine function. We will take a function $sin(\pi x)$ and sample this function at points $x_i = i \cdot \Delta x$. The sampling rate is defined by Δx and we will take it to be equal to 3/2 (see Figure 15.1).

Now let's look only at the samples taken and see whether we can restore the original function from these samples (see Figure 15.2). But from the taken samples it looks like our function is not $sin(\pi x)$ but $sin(-\pi x/3)$ (see Figure 15.3).

Our problem is that we have used too big a step Δx compared to the period of the function T equal to 2.

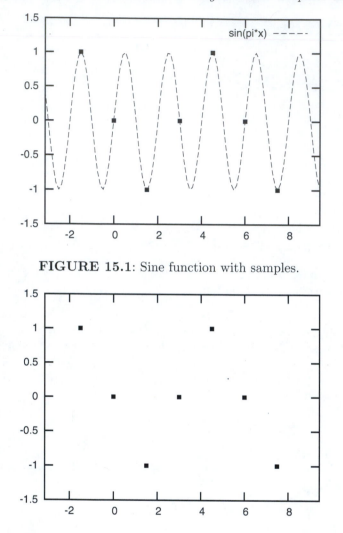

FIGURE 15.1: Sine function with samples.

FIGURE 15.2: Set of sample points for the sine function.

In an area of mathematics called *sampling theory* there is a theorem called the *Nyquist limit* (or the *Nyquist-Shannon sampling theorem*). It states that if our original function (which is sampled) contains no frequencies higher or equal to ω then it can be restored from samples taken at a rate less then $1/(2\omega)$.

For our sine function its period T is equal to 2, therefore it has a frequency equal to $1/T = 0.5$ Hz. So we should sample it at a rate less than $1/(2 \cdot 0.5) = 1$, but our sampling rate is bigger so conditions of the Nyquist theorem are not met.

Now if we have some function that is not a sine or cosine, we can apply

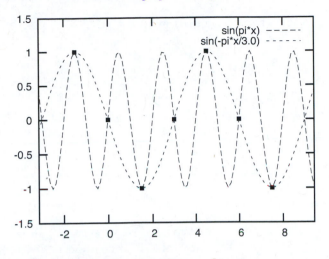

FIGURE 15.3: Restore functions.

the Fourier transform and from it we will see what frequencies are present in the spectrum of this function.

Usually a function has all frequencies and we need to remove high frequencies before sampling if we ever want to restore this function. It is usually achieved by filtering the function with some type of smoothing kernel.

Now let's look at how texture mipmaps are built and what they are. Each successive mipmap level is in fact doubling the distance between individual samples (texels) and it is clear that sooner or later we will get aliasing artifacts – they can be clearly seen when we set the minification filter to GL_NEAREST.

In order to avoid them for every layer of mipmap, we are averaging the values from the previous level. This averaging is just a filter which suppresses high frequencies and helps us to get rid of aliasing artifacts.

Usually filters for an image processing are based on *convolution* with some kernel. A filter for a function of one scalar variable with a kernel $k(x)$ is given by the formula

$$f(x) = \int_{-\infty}^{\infty} k(t)f(x-t)dt. \tag{15.1}$$

If instead of a function we have a 1D-image (array) of values $a_i, i = 0, \ldots, n-1$, then the convolution kernel is also a 1D-array and the filtering itself is done according to

$$a_i' = \sum_{j=-N}^{N} k_j a_{i-j}. \tag{15.2}$$

The N defines the size of the kernel, which is $(2N+1)$. For a two-dimensional image a kernel is defined by $(2N+1)(2M+1)$ matrix k_{ij} and the filtering itself is given by the formula

$$a'_{ij} = \sum_{l=-N}^{N} \sum_{m=-M}^{M} k_{l,m} a_{i-l,j-m}. \qquad (15.3)$$

So for many cases the image filter is represented as a matrix k_{ij}.

15.2 Sepia effect

One of the simplest effects is turning a color image into shades of gray (or some other color). For this we just mix RGB components with appropriate weights. Usually these weights are $(0.3, 0.59, 0.11)$. Therefore, we can convert RGB color to brightness using a dot product of the weights vector and the RGB vector.

In photography the *sepia* effect is obtained by using a filter with glass of some color. As a result we obtain an image in the shades of this color.

In order to implement the sepia effect in the shader, we just need to multiply the color of the filter by computed brightness. The main part of this filter is the fragment shader; the vertex shader will just set up data for rasterization and interpolation.

So we set up a parallel projection and draw a rectangle that will map to our viewport. It will be easier to perform image processing if the source image is a texture rectangle – we can address this texture using normal texel coordinates.

Shown below is the corresponding vertex shader.

```
#version 330 core

layout (location = 0) in vec4 pos;

out vec2 tex;

void main (void)
{
    tex         = pos.zw;
    gl_Position = vec4( pos.xy, 0.0, 1.0 );
}
```

The corresponding fragment shader is shown below.

```
#version 330 core

uniform samplerRect image;
```

```
in   vec2 tex;
out vec4 color;

const vec3 lum = vec3( 0.3, 0.59, 0.11 );
const vec4 c   = vec4( 1.0, 0.89, 0.54, 1.0 );

void main(void)
{
  vec3 texel = texture( image, tex ).rgb;

  color = c * dot( texel, lum );
}
```

15.3 Effects based on color transformations

It is possible to create interesting image filters by using HSV color space and performing pixel transformations in this space. Working with the HSV color space we can easily change saturation of the image and locate some specific color independently of its brightness and saturation.

Here we will write a shader which desaturates all image texels except yellow and red texels. For those texels the saturation will be increased.

As our first step we should convert color of the current texel into the HSV color space, which can be easily done using the fragment shader shown below.

```
vec3 rgbToHsv ( const in vec3 c )
{
  float mn    = min( min( c.r, c.g ), c.b );
  float mx    = max( max( c.r, c.g ), c.b );
  float delta = mx - mn;
  float h, s, v;

  v = mx;

  if ( mx > 0.001 )
  {
    s = delta / mx;

    if ( abs( c.r - mx ) < EPS )
      h = ( c.g - c.b ) / delta;
    else
    if ( abs( c.g - mx ) < EPS )
```

```
        h = 2.0 + ( c.b − c.r ) / delta;
      else
        h = 4.0 + ( c.r − c.g ) / delta;
  }
  else
  {
    s = 0.0;
    h = 0.0;
  }

  return vec3( h / 6.0, s, v );
}
```

After this we can simply check whether the pixel is yellow or red by checking whether its hue is close to the hue of yellow $(1/6)$ or to the hue of red (0 or 1).

If the hue of the current pixel is close to 0, $1/6$ or 1 then we increase its saturation by multiplying it on the constant c_1, otherwise we desaturate it by multiplying the saturation by the constant c_2. The corresponding fragment of code is shown below.

```
#version 330 core

#define EPS 0.05

in    vec2 tex;
out vec4 color;

uniform samplerRect mainTex;

void main (void)
{
  const float c1 = 1.2;
  const float c2 = 0.2;

  vec3 c   = texture ( mainTex, tex ).rgb;
  vec3 hsv = rgbToHsv( c );

  if ( abs(hsv.x)<EPS || abs(hsv.x−1.0/6.0)<EPS ||
       abs(hsv.x−1.0)<EPS )
    hsv.y *= c1;
  else
    hsv.y *= c2;

  color = vec4 ( hsvToRgb ( hsv ), 1.0 );
}
```

The last part of the shader is converting color from the HSV color space back to the RGB color space.

```
vec3     hsvToRgb ( const in vec3 c )
{
    float  h = c.x;
    float  s = c.y;
    float  v = c.z;
    vec3   res;

    if ( s < 0.001 )
        return vec3 ( v, v, v );

    h *= 6.0;

    float  fi = floor( h );
    int    i  = int( fi );
    float  f = h - fi;
    float  p = v * ( 1.0 - s );
    float  q = v * ( 1.0 - s * f );
    float  t = v * ( 1.0 - s * ( 1.0 - f ) );

    if ( i == 0 )
        return vec3 ( v, t, p );

    if ( i == 1 )
        return vec3 ( q, v, p );

    if ( i == 2 )
        return vec3 ( p, v, t );

    if ( i == 3 )
        return vec3 ( p, q, v );

    if ( i == 4 )
        return vec3 ( t, p, v );

    return vec3 ( v, p, q );
}
```

15.4   Edge detect filters

An edge detection filter locates discontinuities in the source image. There are many different edge detect filters, but all of them are based on the approximation of derivatives.

The simplest approximation is the symmetric approximation of first-order derivatives using the following kernels

$$D_x = \begin{pmatrix} -1 & 0 & 1 \end{pmatrix},$$ (15.4)

$$D_y = \begin{pmatrix} 1 \\ 0 \\ -1 \end{pmatrix}.$$ (15.5)

A more accurate filter is based on Prewitt's kernel (see Figure 15.4)

$$P_x = \begin{pmatrix} -1 & 0 & 1 \\ -1 & 0 & 1 \\ -1 & 0 & 1 \end{pmatrix},$$ (15.6)

$$P_y = \begin{pmatrix} 1 & 1 & 1 \\ 0 & 0 & 0 \\ -1 & -1 & -1 \end{pmatrix}.$$ (15.7)

FIGURE 15.4: Result of edge detecting using Prewitt's kernel.

The Sobel filter gives good results too (see Figure 15.6)

$$S_x = \begin{pmatrix} -1 & 0 & 1 \\ -2 & 0 & 2 \\ -1 & 0 & 1 \end{pmatrix},$$ (15.8)

FIGURE 15.5: Original Lena image.

$$S_y = \begin{pmatrix} 1 & 2 & 1 \\ 0 & 0 & 0 \\ -1 & -2 & -1 \end{pmatrix}. \qquad (15.9)$$

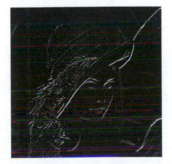

FIGURE 15.6: Result of edge detection with the Sobel filter.

Instead of approximations of first-order derivatives we can use a Laplacian operator which is based on second-order derivatives (see Figure 15.7).

$$L_1 = \begin{pmatrix} 0 & -1 & 0 \\ -1 & 4 & -1 \\ 0 & -1 & 0 \end{pmatrix}, \qquad (15.10)$$

$$L_2 = \begin{pmatrix} -1 & -1 & -1 \\ -1 & 8 & -1 \\ -1 & -1 & -1 \end{pmatrix}. \qquad (15.11)$$

It is really simple to implement such filters as shaders. The fragment shader for Laplacian is shown below.

FIGURE 15.7: Result of application of the Laplacian filter.

```glsl
#version 330 core

uniform samplerRect image;

in   vec2 tex;
out vec4 color;

const vec4 lum = vec4 ( 0.3, 0.59, 0.11, 0.0 );

float l ( in vec2 tx )
{
  return dot( lum, texture ( image, tx ) );
}

void main(void)
{
  mat3 m = mat3 (  0.0, -1.0,  0.0,
                  -1.0,  4.0, -1.0,
                   0.0, -1.0,  0.0 );

  float v = m[0][0]*l( vec2( tex.x - 1, tex.y - 1 ) ) +
            m[1][0]*l( vec2( tex.x,     tex.y - 1 ) ) +
            m[2][0]*l( vec2( tex.x + 1, tex.y - 1 ) ) +
            m[0][1]*l( vec2( tex.x - 1, tex.y ) ) +
            m[1][1]*l( vec2( tex.x,     tex.y ) ) +
            m[2][1]*l( vec2( tex.x + 1, tex.y ) ) +
            m[0][2]*l( vec2( tex.x - 1, tex.y + 1 ) ) +
            m[1][2]*l( vec2( tex.x,     tex.y + 1 ) ) +
            m[2][2]*l( vec2( tex.x - 1, tex.y + 1 ) ) );

  color = vec4 ( v );
}
```

15.5 Emboss filter

One often-used effect is *emboss*. It can be treated as a biased derivative of the image brightness in some direction. We can write emboss as a matrix filter using the matrix E

$$E = \begin{pmatrix} 2 & 0 & 0 \\ 0 & -1 & 0 \\ 0 & 0 & -1 \end{pmatrix}. \tag{15.12}$$

In Figure 15.8 you can see the result of applying the emboss filter to the image.

FIGURE 15.8: Emboss filter.

Since the matrix for the emboss filter has only three non-zero coefficients, we can write it without using the matrix as it is shown below.

```
#version 330 core

uniform samplerRect image;

in   vec2 tex;
out vec4 color;

const vec4 lum = vec4 ( 0.3, 0.59, 0.11, 0.0 );

void main(void)
{
    mat3 m = mat3 (  2.0,    0.0,    0.0,
                     0.0,   -1.0,    0.0,
                     0.0,    0.0,   -1.0 );
```

```
float  v =
    2.0*dot(lum,  texture(image,  vec2(tex.x−1,  tex.y−1)))−
    dot(lum,  texture(image,  vec2(tex.x,     tex.y)))−
    dot(lum,  texture(image,  vec2(tex.x−1,  tex.y+1)));

color = vec4 ( v + 0.5 );
}
```

15.6   Blur filters, Gaussian blur, separable filters

Another common matrix filter is *blur*. The blur filter suppresses high frequencies in the image and makes it look "blurry".

The simplest blur filter just averages values in the neighborhood of the texel, like the filter does with the matrix from (15.13). Such filters with all matrix elements equal to the same value are called *box filters*.

$$B = \begin{pmatrix} 1/9 & 1/9 & 1/9 \\ 1/9 & 1/9 & 1/9 \\ 1/9 & 1/9 & 1/9 \end{pmatrix}. \tag{15.13}$$

But in many cases the Gaussian filter provides much better suppression of high frequencies and it is usually used for blur. In the simplest case, Gaussian blur (with the 3×3 kernel) is defined by the matrix G from the formula

$$G = \frac{1}{16} \cdot \begin{pmatrix} 1 & 2 & 1 \\ 2 & 4 & 2 \\ 1 & 2 & 1 \end{pmatrix}. \tag{15.14}$$

Gaussian filters have a much bigger kernel and elements of the kernel can be defined by the formula

$$g_{ij} = C \cdot e^{-k^2(i^2+j^2)}, i, j = -N, \cdots, N. \tag{15.15}$$

Here C is a normalization constant, which is just the inverse of the sum of all filter coefficients. Usually such filters with big kernel sizes make using Equation (15.3) very inefficient because it requires $(2N+1)^2$ textures access for a single texel.

So Gauss filtering is performed separately – one horizontal pass and one vertical pass only $4N+2$ texture accesses per input texel. Equation (15.16) shows why this can be done

$$a'_{lm} = \sum_{i=-N}^{N} \sum_{j=-N}^{N} Ce^{-k^2(i^+ j^2)} a_{l+i,m+j} =$$

$$\sum_{i=-N}^{N} \sum_{j=-N}^{N} (\sqrt{C}e^{-k^2 i^2})(\sqrt{C}e^{-k^2 j^2}) a_{l+i,m+j} =$$

$$\sum_{i=-N}^{N} \sqrt{C}e^{-k^2 i^2} \left(\sum_{j=-N}^{N} \sqrt{C}e^{-k^2 j^2} a_{l+i,m+j} \right) =$$

$$\sum_{i=-N}^{N} \sqrt{C}e^{-k^2 i^2} b_{l+i,m}.$$

(15.16)

Here the elements b_{ij} are defined by the following formula

$$b_{lm} = \sum_{j=-N}^{N} \sqrt{C}e^{-k^2 j^2} a_{l,m+j}.$$

(15.17)

As you can see, these elements are the result of applying a vertical blur to the source image. In order to perform a 2D-Gaussian blur it is sufficient to perform two 1D-blurs – one horizontal blur and one vertical blur.

A simple python script is shown below, which builds a shader to perform 1D-blur for a given kernel size.

```
import sys , math, string

    # 1d Gaussian distribution , s is standard deviation
def gaussian ( x, s ):
  return math.exp ( -x*x/(2*s*s) )

    # return array normalized of coefficients for kernal size k
def buildCoeffs ( k, s ):
  coeffs = []
  sum    = -1.0
  for x in range ( k + 1 ):
    c    = gaussian ( float ( x ), s )
    sum += 2*c
    coeffs.append ( c )

    # renormalize coeffs
  for x in range ( k + 1 ):
    coeffs [x] = coeffs [x] / sum

  return coeffs

def genVertexShader ( k, s ):
  return """#version 330 core
```

```
in    vec2  texCoord;
out   vec2  tex;

uniform  mat4  mv;
uniform  mat4  proj;

void  main(void)
{
   gl_Position = proj * mv * gl_Vertex;
   tex         = texCoord;
}\n\n"""

def genFragmentShader ( k, s, d1, d2 ):
   coeffs = buildCoeffs ( k, s )
   shd0  = "#version_330_core\n\nin__vec2_tx;\nout_vec4_color;\n"
   shd1  = " uniform _____sampler2D_imageMap;\n\n" ;
   shd2  = " void_main_(void)\n{\n\tvec2_tx__=_tex;\n"
   shd3  = "\tvec2_dx__=_vec2_(%f,%f);\n" % ( d1, d2 )
   shd4  = "\tvec2_sdx_=_dx;\n"
   shd5  = "\tvec4_sum_=_texture(_imageMap,_tx_)_*_%f;\n\n"
                        % coeffs [0]
   shd   = shd0 + shd1 + shd2 + shd3 + shd4 + shd5

   for x in range ( 1, k + 1 ):
      shd = shd + ( "\tsum_+=_(texture(_imageMap,_tx_+_sdx_)_+_"
            shd = shd + "texture2D_(_mainTex,_tx_-_sdx_)_)*_%f;_\n"
                        % coeffs [x] )
      shd = shd + "\tsdx_+=_dx;\n"

   return shd + "\n\tcolor_=_sum;\n}\n"

def getOpts ():
   opt  = ""
   opts = {}

   for s in sys.argv [1:]:
      if s [0] == '-':
         opt = s [1:]
      else:
         opts [opt] = s
         opt         = ""

   return opts

if __name__ == "__main__":
   s    = 3.0
   k    = 7
   name = "b-y"
```

```python
if len ( sys.argv ) > 1:
    if sys.argv [1] == '-h' or sys.argv [1] == '-?':
        print "Gaussian_blure_shader_generator"
        print "Options:"
        print "     -s n          _set_the_S_constant"
        print "     -k n          _set_the_kernel_radius"
        print "     -f_filename _-_set_the_output_filename"
        sys.exit ( 0 )

    opts = getOpts ()

    if opts.has_key ( "s" ):
        s = string.atof ( opts ["s"] )

    if opts.has_key ( "k" ):
        k = string.atoi ( opts ["k"] )

    if opts.has_key ( "f" ):
        name = opts ["f"]

vert = genVertexShader ( k, s )
frag = genFragmentShader ( k, s, 0.0, 1.0 / 512.0 )
f1   = open ( name + ".vsh", "w" )
f1.write ( vert )
f1.close ()
f2   = open ( name + ".fsh", "w" )
f2.write ( frag )
f2.close ()
print "Shaders_%s_and_%s_have_been_successfully_generated" %
    ( name + ".vsh", name + ".fsh" )
```

An example of a generated filter is shown below.

```glsl
#version 330 core

in   vec2 tx;
out vec4 color;
uniform sampler2D imageMap;

void main (void)
{
    vec2 tx  = tex;
    vec2 dx  = vec2 (0.000000,0.001953);
    vec2 sdx = dx;
    vec4 sum = texture( imageMap, tx )*0.134598;

    sum += (texture( imageMap, tx + sdx ) +
            texture( mainTex, tx - sdx ) )*0.127325;
```

```
sdx  +=  dx;
sum  +=  (texture( imageMap,  tx + sdx ) +
          texture( mainTex,  tx - sdx ) )*0.107778;
sdx  +=  dx;
sum  +=  (texture( imageMap,  tx + sdx ) +
          texture( mainTex,  tx - sdx ) )*0.081638;
sdx  +=  dx;
sum  +=  (texture( imageMap,  tx + sdx ) +
          texture( mainTex,  tx - sdx ) )*0.055335;
sdx  +=  dx;
sum  +=  (texture( imageMap,  tx + sdx ) +
          texture( mainTex,  tx - sdx ) )*0.033562;
sdx  +=  dx;
sum  +=  (texture( imageMap,  tx + sdx ) +
          texture( mainTex,  tx - sdx ) )*0.018216;
sdx  +=  dx;
sum  +=  (texture( imageMap,  tx + sdx ) +
          texture( mainTex,  tx - sdx ) )*0.008847;
sdx  +=  dx;

color  =  sum;
}
```

The kernel for the Gaussian blur is not the only one kernel which can be
replaced by two 1D-filters.

A filter kernel k_{ij} is called *separable* if it can be written as

$$k_{ij} = a_i \cdot b_j. \qquad (15.18)$$

If a kernel is separable, then filtering with this kernel can be replaced by
separate horizontal and vertical passes using a_i and b_j as kernels for each pass.
Clearly, the Gaussian kernel is separable with $a_i = b_i = \sqrt{C}exp(-k^2 i^2)$.

15.7   Old-film effect

One more nice effect which can be done quite easily using the shaders is
the "old-film effect". We will try to make an image look like it is from a very
old film played in the cinema.

This effect is used to process a set of images or a video.

What factors contribute to the "old film" look and feel?

The first contributing factor is that the image is in a grayscale. Another
factor is that the image always jerks and its brightness constantly changes.
An image also has random scratches and blips on it.

We have already covered how to construct a greyscale image. We just need to add some random value to its texture coordinates and some random factor controlling its brightness.

GLSL does not have a random number generator, but we can use the sum of several high frequency sines and cosines of time. If their frequencies are high enough we will get nearly random values for every frame.

To add some scratches and blips to the image we will simply use two prepared textures whose texture coordinates will be randomly changed.

All texture coordinates jerking and changes of brightness will be computed in the vertex shader and then passed to the fragment one. The corresponding vertex shader is shown below.

```
#version 330 core

layout(location = 0) in vec4 pos;

uniform float time;

out vec2    shudder;
out float   brightness;
out vec2    blipCoord;
out vec2    scratchCoord;
out vec2    tex;

void main(void)
{
    shudder      = 0.0015 * vec2( sin( time*81.23 ),
                              cos( time*73.123 ) );
    brightness   = clamp( 3.0 * sin( time*177.123 ),
                      0.7, 1.0 );
    blipCoord    = vec2( sin( 313.744*time ) +
                      cos( 122.337*time ),
                      cos( 73.435*time )+sin( 170.773*time ) );
    scratchCoord = vec2( 0.01*cos( 171.578*time ),
                      0.2*sin( 213.4264*time ) );
    tex          = pos.zw;
    gl_Position  = vec4( pos.xy, 0.0, 1.0 );
}
```

The task of the fragment shader is simply to convert an image to grayscale and apply scratches, blips and brightness changes.

```
#version 330 core

uniform float        time;

uniform samplerRect image;
```

```glsl
uniform sampler2D     scratchMap;
uniform sampler2D     blipMap;

in  vec2   shudder;
in  float  brightness;
in  vec2   blipCoord;
in  vec2   scratchCoord;
in  vec2   tex;

out vec4 color;

const vec3 luminance = vec3 ( 0.3, 0.59, 0.11 );

void main (void)
{
    ivec2 sz       = textureSize( image );
    vec2  size     = vec2( float( sz.x ), float( sz.y ));
    vec2  tx       = tex / size;
    vec4  clr      = texture( image,
                              tex+shudder*size );
    vec4  scratch = texture( scratchMap,
                              tx+scratchCoord );
    vec4  blip     = texture( blipMap,
                              tx + blipCoord );

    color = vec4( dot( clr.rgb, luminance ))*
                  brightness * scratch * blip, 1.0 );
}
```

15.8   Sharpness filter

This is a simple filter which add sharpness to the image. It is based on the following matrix kernel

$$S = \begin{pmatrix} -1 & -1 & -1 \\ -1 & 9 & -1 \\ -1 & -1 & -1 \end{pmatrix}. \tag{15.19}$$

The corresponding filter is shown below (note that the filter is applied to all color channels instead of brightness).

```glsl
#version 330 core
```

```
uniform samplerRect image;

in   vec2 tex;
out vec4 color;

void main(void)
{
    mat3 m = mat3 (  -1.0,  -1.0,  -1.0,
                     -1.0,   9.0,  -1.0,
                     -1.0,  -1.0,  -1.0 );

    color = m[0][0]*texture(image,  vec2(tex.x-1, tex.y - 1))+
            m[1][0]*texture(image,  vec2(tex.x,   tex.y - 1))+
            m[2][0]*texture(image,  vec2(tex.x+1, tex.y - 1))+
            m[0][1]*texture(image,  vec2(tex.x-1, tex.y))+
            m[1][1]*texture(image,  vec2(tex.x,   tex.y))+
            m[2][1]*texture(image,  vec2(tex.x+1, tex.y))+
            m[0][2]*texture(image,  vec2(tex.x-1, tex.y+1 ))+
            m[1][2]*texture(image,  vec2(tex.x,   tex.y+1 ))+
            m[2][2]*texture(image,  vec2(tex.x-1, tex.y+1 ));
}
```

15.9   Image denoising, bilateral filter

One of the most often-encountered tasks in image processing is *image denoising*, i.e., removing high frequency noise from the given image.

Since we want to remove high frequency noise, we need to apply some blur filter. The simplest variant is to use a Gaussian blur. But using it will smudge boundaries between colors and create colors leaking.

So instead of a Gaussian kernel a bilateral filter is often used. For every texel it takes into account how much colors of samples taken differ from the color of the current texel. The bigger the difference, the lesser the sample will contribute into the final sum.

The kernel for bilateral filtering for the pixel with coordinates p_0 and color c_0 is shown below.

$$k(p) = C \cdot exp(-k_1 \|p - p_0\|^2) \cdot exp(-k_2 \|c(p) - c_0\|^2). \qquad (15.20)$$

Note that this kernel is not separable; however, usually we can treat it as if it was separable.

Below is shown a shader of one pass of bilateral filtering (assuming the kernel is separable).

```glsl
#version 330   core

in   vec2 tex;
out vec4 color;

uniform float kl;
uniform float k2;
uniform samplerRect imageMap;

void main ()
{
    int    n   = 4;
    vec4   c0  = texture( imageMap, tex );
    vec4   clr = vec4( 0.0 );
    float  sum = 0.0;

    for ( int i = 0; i < n; i++ )
    {
        vec4   c  = texture( imageMap, tex + vec2 ( 0.0, i ) );
        vec3   dc = c.rgb - c0.rgb;
        float  w  = exp( -kl*i*i - k2*dot( dc, dc ) );

        clr += w * c;
        sum += w;
    }

    color = clr / sum;
}
```

Chapter 16

Special effects in OpenGL

16.1   Reflections

In many cases we need to create a convincing-looking reflection on a planar
or nearly planar surface. We will start with the case when we have an infinite
reflecting plane and want to compute reflection on it. In order to obtain a
reflection of objects in the plane we can simply reflect the camera relative to
this surface and render objects using the reflected camera.

After reflection was done we restore the original camera and render other
objects (see Figure 16.1).

If the reflected surface is a polygon then we need to clip the reflection to
this polygon. It can be easily done with the stencil buffer – we disable writing
to all buffers except stencil, set the stencil operation to the increment mode
and render the reflecting polygon. Then all visible pixels corresponding to this
polygon will be marked in the stencil buffer, and to clip the reflection we just
need to set the stencil test to reject all unmarked pixels.

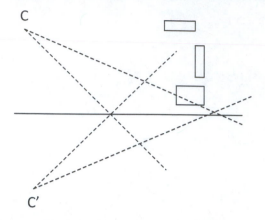

FIGURE 16.1: Creating a reflection using reflected camera C'.

```
glColorMask   ( GL_FALSE, GL_FALSE, GL_FALSE, GL_FALSE );
glDepthMask   ( GL_FALSE );
glStencilFunc ( GL_ALWAYS, 0, 255);
glStencilTest ( GL_KEEP, GL_FALSE, GL_INCR );

drawPolygon ();

glStencilMask ( 0 );
glColorMask   ( GL_TRUE, GL_TRUE, GL_TRUE, GL_TRUE );
glStencilFunc ( GL_EQUAL, 1, 255 );
glStencilTest ( GL_KEEP, GL_KEEP, GL_KEEP );

renderReflection ();
```

But quite often the reflecting plane is water and its surface contains ripples, so it is not a plane mirror. However, we can ignore it and render the reflected image into the texture – we need only use the framebuffer object with 2D-texture attached to it.

After we have reflection stored in the texture, we can render the reflecting polygon. The corresponding shader will apply some distortion to the texture coordinates, which will result in the image looking like a rippled surface reflecting objects.

But there is one catch – we cannot simply apply a reflected image to the polygon as if it was a normal texture. The reason for this is that while obtaining this image we have already performed a perspective transformation to it. If we render it as a standard texture, this will result in perspective transformation being applied two times.

The correct way of applying the reflection texture is to project it onto the surface of the polygon. Imagine that at the camera location we have a projector which projects a reflected image onto the polygon (see Figure 16.2).

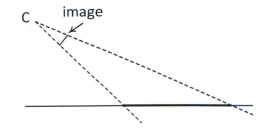

FIGURE 16.2: Projecting an image onto the polygon.

In order to perform such a projection we can use the product of model-view and projection matrices, which were used for rendering reflection into the texture. Then we apply this matrix to the vertex coordinates of the polygon. But because this matrix will map all coordinates into the $[-1, 1]$ range and since the texture coordinates should be in the $[0, 1]$ range, we need to apply a scale by $(0.5, 0.5, 0.5)^T$ and translation by $(0.5, 0.5, 0.5)^T$ to get the correct matrix that will transform vertices of the source polygon into the texture coordinates. Also do not forget to apply perspective division to the computed texture coordinates.

In order to modify texture coordinates creating the ripples effect, we can use 3D-texture containing the noise values (more on noise in Chapter 18). We will use source vertex coordinates modified by time to get the noise value. After this, the noise value will be added to texture coordinates for accessing the reflection texture.

Below are the vertex and fragment shaders for rendering rippled water.

```
— vertex

#version 330 core

uniform mat4 mv;
uniform mat4 proj;
uniform mat4 mirrorMat;

layout ( location = 0 ) in vec3 position;

out vec4 pos;
out vec2 tex;

void main(void)
{
    gl_Position = proj * mv * vec4( position, 1.0 );
```

```
    pos                = mirrorMat * vec4( position , 1.0 );
}
```

—— fragment

```
#version 330 core

uniform sampler2D image;
uniform sampler3D noiseMap;
uniform float     time;

in   vec4 pos;
out vec4 color;

void main(void)
{
    vec3 ncoord = vec3( pos.x, pos.y + 0.1*time, pos.z ) * 3.1;
    vec3 noise  = texture( noiseMap, ncoord ).rgb;

    color = 0.7*texture(image, pos.xy/pos.w + 0.05*noise.xy);
}
```

16.2   Volumetric/Layered fog

A fixed pipeline supports an automatic application of fog to the objects. It is computed per-vertex from the distance between a vertex and camera/observer. After the fog value is computed it is interpolated across the primitive and applied to its fragments.

This can be easily done with a programmable pipeline. But quite often another type of fog is needed – a *layered fog*. This fog forms a layer in the scene (see Figure 16.3).

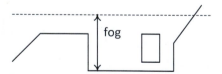

FIGURE 16.3: Layered fog.

Note that the fog bounding plane can cross other polygons so we cannot use per-vertex fog calculations and should perform them in the fragment shader.

To determine the amount of fog to be applied to the fragment we build a ray through the camera and fragment and determine the length of the part of the ray which is in the fog volume (see Figure 16.4).

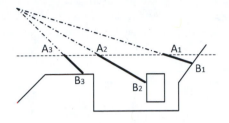

FIGURE 16.4: Segments in fog.

To get this length, before applying such a fog, we can copy the contents of the depth buffer into the texture and then render the polygon which bounds the fog layer. The z-coordinate of a fragment defines the point where the ray enters the fog layer (A_i) and the corresponding value from the texture with z-values defines the point where the ray pierces some scene object (B_i).

To compute the amount of fog to be applied for the current fragment, we need to know the distance between these two points. We can use the fact that both points are located on the same ray from the camera and therefore the following equality holds

$$\|A_i - B_i\| = \|A_i \cdot (1 - \frac{B_{i,z}}{A_{i,z}})\| = \|A_i\| \cdot \left(1 - \frac{B_{i,z}}{A_{i,z}}\right). \qquad (16.1)$$

In order to use (16.2) we need 3D-coordinates from the vertex shader of the current fragment.

```
#version 330 core

uniform mat4 mv;
uniform mat4 proj;

layout ( location = 0 ) in vec3 position;

out vec2 tex;
out vec3 pos;

void main(void)
{
    pos           = (mv * vec4 ( position , 1.0 )).xyz;
    gl_Position = proj * mv * vec4 ( position , 1.0 );
}
```

The corresponding fragment shader uses the interpolated A_i value passed from the vertex shader, takes the corresponding distance from the texture with depth values and computes the required distance. There are several variants on how this distance can be mapped to the fog value, but we will use an exponential law – the fog level is computed as $exp(-k \cdot distance)$.

This is shown below (computing the linear z_{eye} from the values of the depth buffer will be covered in the section on deferred rendering).

```glsl
#version 330 core

uniform sampler2DRect    depthMap;
uniform float            fogDensity;
uniform vec3             fogColor;

in   vec3  pos;
out vec4  color;

void main(void)
{
    float  zSample = texture ( depthMap, gl_FragCoord.xy ).x;
    float  zNear   = 0.1;
    float  zFar    = 100.0;

    zSample = zFar*zNear / (zSample*(zFar - zNear) - zFar);

    float  alpha = abs(zSample - pos.z)*fogDensity;

    color = vec4 ( fogColor, alpha );
}
```

This type of fog is just alpha-blended in the already rendered geometry.

16.3   Billboards, particle systems, soft particles

One type of the frequently used objects in games are *billboards*. The billboard is a polygon (usually a rectangle) which always faces the camera, i.e., orthogonal to the camera's view direction (see Figure 16.5).

The billboard can be defined by just one point (e.g., its lower left corner) and its size (width and height). All other points are produced by adding to this point's scaled camera's *up* and *right* vectors.

There are several ways how it can be done.

We simply send all four vertices for each sprite with the same position but different texture coordinates. Then the vertex shader changes position

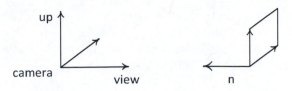

FIGURE 16.5: Billboard and camera.

for every vertex of the billboard according to passed texture coordinates and camera's *up* and *right* vectors passed as uniforms.

```
#version 330 core

uniform mat4   mv;
uniform mat4   proj;
uniform vec3   up;
uniform vec3   right;
uniform float  time;

layout ( location = 0 ) in vec3 position;
layout ( location = 1 ) in vec2 texCoord;

out vec2 tex;

void main(void)
{
    float c   = cos ( time );
    float s   = sin ( time );
    vec3  pos = vec3( position.x*c - position.z*s,
                      position.y,
                      position.x*s + position.z*c );

    pos += texCoord.x*right + texCoord.y*up;

    gl_Position = proj * mv * vec4( pos, 1.0 );
    tex         = texCoord;
}
```

In the vertex shader the vertex coordinates are animated (they rotate in the *y*-plane using a *time* variable to define the angle) and after animation passed vertex positions are modified with *up* and *right* directions. The texture coordinates are used here to define how the vertex should be moved using *up* and *right* vectors.

We can keep positions and texture coordinates in two separate vertex buffers so when we need to change positions we do not affect texture coordinates. But in this approach we have to send all four vertices for each billboard knowing that one vertex will be enough.

Another way to create billboards is sending points and converting them in the geometry shader into billboards.

— vertex

```
#version 330 core

layout ( location = 0 ) in vec3 position;
layout ( location = 1 ) in vec2 texCoord;

void main(void)
{
        gl_Position = vec4 ( position , 1.0 );
}
```

— geometry

```
#version 330 core

layout (points) in;
layout (triangle_strip , max_vertices = 6) out;

uniform mat4   mv;
uniform mat4   proj;
uniform vec3   up;
uniform vec3   right;
uniform float  time;

out vec2 texCoord;

void main (void)
{
  vec3   pos = gl_in [0].gl_Position.xyz;
  float  w   = gl_in [0].gl_Position.w;
  float  c   = cos ( time );
  float  s   = sin ( time );
  vec3   p   = vec3( pos.x*c − pos.z*s,
                     pos.y,
                     pos.x*s + pos.z*c );

  texCoord    = vec2( 0.0, 0.0 );
  gl_Position = proj*mv*vec4( p, w );
  EmitVertex ();
```

```
texCoord     = vec2( 1.0, 0.0 );
gl_Position = proj*mv*vec4( p + right, w );
EmitVertex ();

texCoord     = vec2( 1.0, 1.0 );
gl_Position = proj*mv*vec4( p + up + right, w );
EmitVertex    ();
EndPrimitive ();       // 1st triangle

texCoord     = vec2( 0.0, 0.0 );
gl_Position = proj*mv*vec4( p, w );
EmitVertex    ();

texCoord     = vec2( 1.0, 1.0 );
gl_Position = proj*mv*vec4( p + up + right, w );
EmitVertex ();

texCoord     = vec2( 0.0, 1.0 );
gl_Position = proj*mv*vec4 ( p + up, w );
EmitVertex    ();
EndPrimitive ();       // 2nd triangle
}
```

The most often-used application of billboards is rendering of *particle systems*. A particle system is a set of points where each point has its own position, velocity, size, color and other attributes. The particle movements are defined by some simple law, e.g., gravity.

Usually each particle is rendered as a textured billboard: positions, velocities and other particle parameters are updated either by CPU or GPU.

Particle systems are used to create many effects such as smoke, fire, explosions, rain, etc.

A particle system can contain many small particles or a lesser amount of big particles. And when we are rendering big particles we can encounter artifacts as shown in the Fig. 16.6

These artifacts appear when the billboard crosses scene polygons, and we see it as if the billboard is cut.

For such cases the *soft particles* provide a good alternative. The main idea behind soft particles is to treat each particle as a volumetric object, like a sphere or box instead of a polygon.

Such a particle is rendered as a simple polygon, but the fragment shader modulates its opacity based on the distance between the polygon and the scene objects.

For every fragment of the polygon we build a ray from the camera to find the thickness of the particle.

We compare the depth of the particle fragment with the corresponding

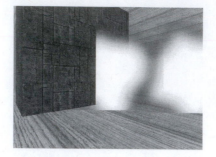

FIGURE 16.6: Artifacts for big particles.

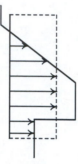

FIGURE 16.7: Soft particle as the volume.

value from the depth buffer (usually we copy the contents of the depth buffer into a depth texture and take depth values from it).

If the depth of the particle is greater than the depth from the depth buffer, then we discard the fragment – it won't be visible. Otherwise, we modulate the alpha component of the fragment's color by scaled distance between these two values.

Soft particles differ from ordinary particles only in the modulation of the alpha component in the fragment shader.

```
#version 330 core

uniform sampler2DRect depthMap;
uniform sampler2D      particleMap;

in  vec2 tex;
out vec4 color;

void main(void)
{
    float zSample = texture ( depthMap, gl_FragCoord.xy ).x;
```

```
vec4   c        = texture ( particleMap , tex );
float zNear    = 0.1;
float zFar     = 100.0;

if ( c.r < 0.02 )
   discard ;

float d1 = zFar*zNear /(zSample *(zFar − zNear) − zFar);
float d2 = zFar*zNear /(gl_FragCoord.z*(zFar − zNear)
                       − zFar);
float d = min( 0.5, abs( d1 − d2 )*0.3 );

c.a *= d*c.r ;

color = c ;
}
```

16.4   Bumpmapping

Bumpmapping is a technique (proposed in 1978 by J. Blinn) to simulate microrelief of the surface (bumps, wrinkles) without modifying the actual geometry.

To achieve this effect, the normal of the polygon n is perturbed for every fragment and the lighting is computed with this perturbed normal. Initially the microrelief of the surface was given by the *height map* – the texture representing the heightfield over the polygon (see Figure 16.8)

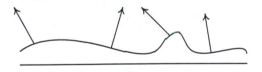

FIGURE 16.8: Height field.

When such a texture is applied to the surface, finite differences are used to compute normal. But now used normal maps which contain already computed normals. Since the length of every normal is equal to one, then $(n + 1)/2$ will produce a 3D-vector that can be treated as a color. So every normal is encoded as color by using Equation (16.2)

$$c = \frac{1}{2}(n + 1). \tag{16.2}$$

The color c from the normal map is converted back to normal n using the inverse transformation

$$n = 2c - 1. \tag{16.3}$$

Note that due to texture filtering the n vector computed by (16.3) may be not unit and has to be normalized.

A *height* or a *normal* map is used to define normal at every fragment resulting from polygon rasterization.

But if we want to pack normals into the texture (normal map) what coordinate system should we use for storing these normals? All standard spaces such as world or object space are not a good choice – they require complex transformations for every fragment of the normal and prevent us from using the same normal map with other polygons (this also relates to the moving polygons).

Usually normals for the normal maps are given in the *tangent space*. A tangent space is defined by tangent vector t, binormal b and normal n. Each of these vectors has unit length and is orthogonal to the other two vectors (see Figure 16.9).

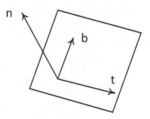

FIGURE 16.9: Tangent space for a polygon.

So a tangent space is defined separately for every polygon by adding tangent and binormal vectors to the already specified normal. When normals in tangent space are stored in the normal map, we can use this normal map for every polygon we want (provided we know tangent and binormal vectors for it).

If we have a triangle $v_0 v_1 v_2$ with texture coordinates (p, q) specified for every vertex, then we can compute tangent t, binormal b and the normal n vectors.

Unit normal n is defined by a cross-product of two edge directions

$$n = \frac{v_2 - v_0, v_1 - v_0}{\|v_2 - v_0, v_1 - v_0\|}. \tag{16.4}$$

We need two vectors t' and b' such that if vertex v_i has texture coordinates (p_i, q_i) then the following equations are true

$$\begin{cases} v_1 - v_0 = (p_1 - p_0)t' + (q_1 - q_0)b', \\ v_2 - v_0 = (p_2 - p_0)t' + (q_2 - q_0)b'. \end{cases} \qquad (16.5)$$

It is a linear system with 6 unknowns and 6 equations. Its solution can be written as

$$\begin{pmatrix} t'_x & t'_y & t'_z \\ b'_x & b'_y & b'_z \end{pmatrix} = \frac{1}{(p_1 - p_0)(q_2 - q_0) - (p_2 - p_0)(q_1 - q_0)} \cdot A \cdot B \qquad (16.6)$$

The matrices A and B are given by equations below

$$A = \begin{pmatrix} q_2 - q_0 & -(q_1 - q_0) \\ -(p_2 - p_0) & p_1 - p_0 \end{pmatrix}, \qquad (16.7)$$

$$B = \begin{pmatrix} v_{1x} - v_{0x} & v_{1y} - v_{0y} & v_{1z} - v_{0z} \\ v_{2x} - v_{0x} & v_{2y} - v_{0y} & v_{2z} - v_{0z} \end{pmatrix}. \qquad (16.8)$$

After we have found these vectors we just need to apply the Gram-Schmidt algorithm to make vectors orthogonal to each other and to normal n

$$\begin{cases} t = t' - (n, t')n, \\ b = b' - (n, b)b - (t', b)t' \frac{1}{\|t'\|^2}. \end{cases} \qquad (16.9)$$

The final step is normalization of t and b, after which we will have our tangent space basis ready for a given triangle.

```
void    computeTangents ( BasicVertex& v0,
                          const BasicVertex& v1,
                          const BasicVertex& v2 )
{
    vec3 e0( v1.pos.x−v0.pos.x, v1.tex.x−v0.tex.x,
            v1.tex.y−v0.tex.y );
    vec3 e1( v2.pos.x−v0.pos.x, v2.tex.x−v0.tex.x,
            v2.tex.y−v0.tex.y );
    vec3 cp = cross( e0, e1 );

    if ( fabs( cp.x ) > EPS )
    {
        v0.t.x = −cp.y / cp.x;
        v0.b.x = −cp.z / cp.x;
    }
    else
    {
        v0.t.x = 0;
        v0.b.x = 0;
```

```
        }

    e0.x = v1.pos.y - v0.pos.y;
    e1.x = v2.pos.y - v0.pos.y;
    cp   = cross ( e0, e1 );

    if ( fabs( cp.x ) > EPS )
    {
       v0.t.y = -cp.y / cp.x;
       v0.b.y = -cp.z / cp.x;
    }
    else
    {
       v0.t.y = 0;
       v0.b.y = 0;
    }

    e0.x = v1.pos.z - v0.pos.z;
    e1.x = v2.pos.z - v0.pos.z;
    cp   = cross ( e0, e1 );

    if ( fabs( cp.x ) > EPS )
    {
       v0.t.z = -cp.y / cp.x;
       v0.b.z = -cp.z / cp.x;
    }
    else
    {
       v0.t.z = 0;
       v0.b.z = 0;
    }

    if ( dot( cross( v0.t, v0.b ), v0.n ) < 0 )
       v0.t = -v0.t;
}
```

Since normal vector n is used in the dot products with other vectors (such as l and v), to compute lighting we need to convert these vectors into the tangent space. The best place for such a conversion is the vertex shader which will pass all vectors in the tangent space to the fragment shader.

A vertex shader is shown below which for every vector takes normal, tangent and binormal and produces l and v vectors in the tangent space.

```
#version 330 core

uniform vec3 lightPos;
```

```
uniform vec3 eyePos;
uniform mat4 mv;
uniform mat4 pr;
uniform mat3 nm;

in vec3 normal;
in vec3 tangent;
in vec3 binormal;
in vec2 texCoord;

out vec3 l;
out vec3 v;
out vec2 tex;

void main ()
{
   vec3 p  = vec3( mv * gl_Vertex );
   vec3 l1 = normalize( lightPos - p );
   vec3 v1 = normalize( eyePos - p );
   vec3 n  = nm * normal;
   vec3 t  = nm * tangent;
   vec3 b  = nm * binormal;

            // convert l1 and v1 into tangent space
   l   = vec3( dot(l1,t), dot(l1,b), dot(l1,n) );
   v   = vec3( dot(v1,t), dot(v1,b), dot(v1,n) );
   tex = texCoord;
   gl_Position = pr * mv * gl_Vertex
}
```

Then in the fragment shader we just fetch normal from the normal map, normalize all participating vectors and compute lighting.

```
#version 330 core

in vec3 l;
in vec3 v;
in vec2 tex;

out vec4 color;

uniform sampler2D bumpMap;
uniform sampler2D diffuseMap;
uniform float     specPower;

void main ()
```

```
{
    vec3    n     = texture( bumpMap, tex ).rgb;
    vec4    c     = texture( diffuseMap , tex );
    vec3    n2    = normalize( 2.0*n − vec3( 1.0 ) );
    vec3    l2    = normalize( l );
    vec3    v2    = normalize( v );
    vec3    h2    = normalize( l + v );
    float   spec = pow( max( dot( n2, h2 ), 0.0 ), specPower );

    color = c * max( dot(n2, l2), 0.0 ) + vec4( spec );
}
```

In Figure 16.10 the bumpmapped box is shown.

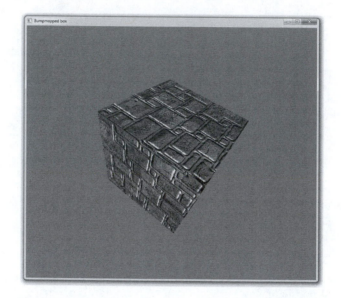

FIGURE 16.10 (See color insert.): Bumpmapped box.

16.5   Reflection and refraction, environment mapping

Cubemaps can be used to imitate reflection on a reflective complex object with a very simple shader.

If a cubemap was produced by rendering a scene onto each face, i.e., it captures a scene as seen from some point, then this cubemap can be used to imitate a reflection just by computing the reflected vector for every fragment and using this reflection vector to fetch color from the cube map. This method gives an approximation to true reflection, but for complex and/or moving objects it is very difficult to see the difference. This method is called *environment mapping*.

All we need is a direction to the observer v and a normal vector n in the fragment shader. Then we can compute reflected vector r (see the fragment shader below) using built-in function *reflect*.

```
#version 330 core

in vec3 n;
in vec3 v;

out vec4 color;

samplerCube envMap;

void main ()
{
    vec3 r = reflect ( normalize (v), normalize (n) );

    color = texture ( envMap, r );
}
```

We can easily combine environment mapping with bumpmapping – the only difference is that we do everything in tangent space and get a normal n from the normal map. This is called EMBM (*Environment Mapped Bumpmapping*).

```
#version 330 core

in        vec3 n;
in        vec3 v;
in   vec2 tex;
out vec4 color;

uniform sampler2D    bumpMap;
uniform samplerCube cubeMap;

void main (void)
{
    vec3 n  = 2.0*(texture ( bumpMap, tex ).rgb - vec3 ( 0.5 ));
    vec3 v2 = normalize ( v );
    vec3 n2 = normalize ( n );
    vec3 r  = reflect ( v2, n2 );

    color = texture ( cubeMap, r );
```

}

We can use this approach to imitate not only reflection but a refraction too (but only a single refraction). If we have a transparent object (e.g., glass) then for every fragment we can compute not only a reflected vector but a refracted vector as well. Then we fetch two values from the cubemap – one for reflected direction and the other for refracted direction. These values are combined using the Fresnel term.

In order to make it look more realistic we could use the fact that the refraction coefficient depends on the wavelength λ. So we can take three different refraction coefficients (for red, green and blue) and use the build-in **refract** function to compute three refracted vectors r_R, r_G and r_B.

Then we fetch three color values from the cubemap. From each of these colors we take only one component and add them together to form a refracted color.

```glsl
#version 330 core

in   vec3 n;
in   vec3 v;
out vec4 color;

uniform samplerCube cubeMap;

void main(void)
{
    const vec3 eta = vec3 ( 0.9, 0.92, 0.94 );

    vec3  v2 = normalize( v );
    vec3  n2 = normalize( n );
    vec3  r  = reflect( v2, n2 );
    vec3  tr = refract( -v2, n2, eta.r );
    vec3  tg = refract( -v2, n2, eta.g );
    vec3  tb = refract( -v2, n2, eta.b );
    vec3  refractionColorRed   = texture( cubeMap, tr ).rgb;
    vec3  refractionColorGreen = texture( cubeMap, tg ).rgb;
    vec3  refractionColorBlue  = texture( cubeMap, tb ).rgb;
    vec3  refractionColor      = vec3 ( refractionColorRed.r,
                                        refractionColorGreen.g,
                                        refractionColorBlue.b );

    float f  = pow ( max ( 0, dot ( v2, n2 ) ), 5.0 );

    color = texture( cubeMap, r )*(1.0-f) +
            vec4( refractionColor, 1.0 )*f;
}
```

16.6 Fur rendering

Rendering of objects covered with fur is complicated by the fact that fur is really a volumetric phenomena. It is the volume of space filled with densely packed fur hairs.

Rendering each hair individually (as a polyline) is not used (but there are several demos using this approach) and a much simpler approach is often taken.

Suppose we have a sphere and want to render this sphere covered with fur. Then we could render a series of semitransparent nested spheres with a small distance between them. They will fill some volume around the source sphere (see Figure 16.11).

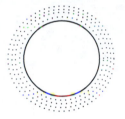

FIGURE 16.11: Nested shells for a sphere.

Now to create the hair look, we need to apply to each of the nested spheres (called *shells*) a texture. This texture will have non-transparent texels marking each hair, all other texels are transparent.

If we alpha-blend shells with such a texture we will get an image looking like a fur ball, provided the distance between successive shells is small enough (see Figure 16.12).

By offsetting texture coordinates on the shells we can create a fur whose hairs are not perpendicular to the sphere like they are combed. Modifying texture coordinates we can create the appearance of combed fur, animated fur and so on.

FIGURE 16.12: Shells forming hairs.

The next way to make our fur look real is to apply some lighting to the shells. In Chapter 10 we built a lighting model for individual hair (13.31). This model is based on the hair tangent vector t.

In the simplest case when we have straight hairs, the tangent vector will coincide with the normal to the sphere. However, if we are modifying texture coordinates then the tangent vector will be bent in a direction defined by changes to texture coordinates.

The simple fragment shader shown below performs rendering of the shells.

```
in  vec2  tex;
in  vec3  l;
in  vec3  v;
in  vec3  t;
in  vec3  b;
in  vec3  n;

out vec4  color;

uniform sampler2D shellMap;
uniform vec2    dtex;
uniform float  kd;
uniform float  ks;

void main()
{
   vec4 c = texture( shellMap, tex );

   if ( c.a < 0.01 )
        discard;

   vec3   t2 = normalize( n + dtex.x*t + dtex.y*b );
   vec3   l2 = normalize( l );
   vec3   h2 = normalize( l + v );
   float  tl = dot( t2, l2 );
   float  th = dot( t2, h2 );

   color = c*sqrt(1.0 - tl*tl)*kd +
           vec4(1.0)*pow(1.0 - th*th, 35.0 )*ks;
}
```

One more thing can be done to increase the quality of the fur image – extrude from a contour line the quads textured with the image of hairs. Such an extrusion was covered in the section about geometric shaders.

In Figure 16.13 you can see the resulting image.

FIGURE 16.13 (See color insert.): Fur torus.

16.7   Parallax, relief and cone step mapping

The bumpmapping covered earlier is used very often to show microrelief of the surface without modifying surface geometry. But there are other methods of showing microrelief which are not connected with lighting or reflection. A group of such methods is based on the *parallax effect*.

The simplest of such methods is called *parallax mapping*. It changes the texture coordinates of the fragment using a heightfield specifying the microrelief.

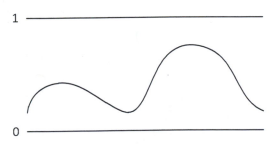

FIGURE 16.14: Microrelief defined by a heightfield.

If we have a surface with microrelief defined by a heightfield (see Figure 16.14), then we can use this microrelief to change texture coordinates depending on the angle at which we are looking on this surface.

Consider a point A on the surface seen from a direction given by unit vector v (see Figure 16.15). If the surface has no relief, then we take texture coordinates T_0 corresponding to A.

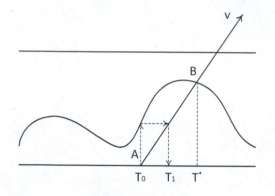

FIGURE 16.15: Parallax effect.

However, if there is some relief defined by a heightfield then we should use point B with a texture coordinate T^* corresponding to the intersection of the heightfield with a ray from point A in direction v.

This effect – dependence of the texture coordinates on the viewing direction, is called *parallax*. The simplest variant of taking parallax into account is to use height at point A to define new texture coordinates T_1 from T_0

$$T_1 = T_0 + h\frac{v_{xy}}{v_z}. \qquad (16.10)$$

Of course it does not give a true solution (T^*), but if we adjust texture coordinates using (16.10) it will be sufficient to create a parallax effect. Note that usually a height value h is scaled and biased before substituting into equation (16.10).

It can be simply implemented in a fragment shader, but note that all computations are performed in the tangent space.

```
#version 330 core

in vec3 v;
in vec2 tex;

out vec4 color;

uniform sampler2D heightMap;
uniform sampler2D diffMap;
```

```
uniform float        scale;
uniform float        bias;

void main()
{
    float h = scale*(1.0 − texture(heightMap, tex).a)+bias;
    vec2  t = tex − v.xy * (h/v.z);

    color = texture( diffMap, t );
}
```

This method gives only an approximation to the true intersection point B and when $|v_z|$ is close to zero it produces noticeable artifacts. To cope with them it is possible to completely skip division by v_z. The corresponding method is called *parallax with offset limiting*

$$T_1 = T_0 + h \cdot v_{xy}. \qquad (16.11)$$

We can improve parallax mapping by using *steep parallax mapping*. It just splits the height range into slices and then checks the height at A_i – the points of slice intersection with a ray from A in the direction v.

As soon as we have found a couple of successive points A_i and A_{i+1} such that one of them is below the heightfield and the other is above it, we stop checking and use the first point below the heightfield to define new texture coordinates (see Figure 16.16).

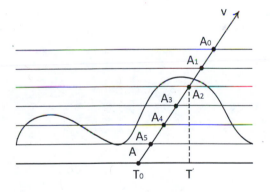

FIGURE 16.16: Steep parallax mapping.

This algorithm can be easily implemented in a fragment shader as shown below.

```
#version 330 core

in vec3 v;
in vec2 tex;
```

```glsl
out vec4 color;

uniform sampler2D heightMap;
uniform sampler2D diffMap;

void main()
{
  const float numSteps = 10;

  float step   = 1.0 / numSteps;
  vec2  dtex   = vt.xy * (scale*step/vt.z);
  float height = 1.0;
  vec2  tx     = tex;
  float h      = texture( heightMap, tx ).a;

  while( h < height )
  {
    height -= step;
    tx     += dtex;
    h       = texture( heightMap, tx ).a
  }
  color = texture( diffMap, tx );
}
```

This method gives good results but at grazing angles the separate layers can be seen (see Figure 16.17).

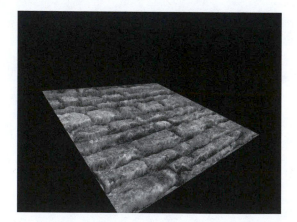

FIGURE 16.17: Layers in steep parallax mapping.

To avoid such artifacts we need to use both found points A_i and A_{i+1} and use some method to more accurately approximate the point of intersection of the ray with the heightfield. For example, we can use several iterations of binary subdivision to improve accuracy.

But there is a much simpler approach called *parallax occlusion mapping* (POM) which can be used to get a good approximation to the intersection. When segment A_iA_{i+1} piercing the heightfield is found we can assume that height along this segment is a linear function; therefore, we can find the intersection of the heightfield with this segment (see Figure 16.18)

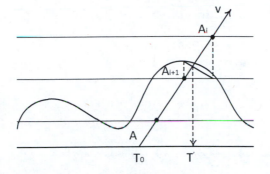

FIGURE 16.18: Finding an approximate intersection in parallax occlusion mapping.

The fragment shader implementing this approach is shown below.

```
#version 330 core

in vec3 v;
in vec2 tex;

out vec4 color;

uniform sampler2D heightMap;
uniform sampler2D diffMap;

void main()
{
   const float numSteps = 10;

   float step   = 1.0 / numSteps;
   vec2  dtex   = vt.xy * (scale*step/vt.z);
   float height = 1.0;
   vec2  tx     = tex;
   float h      = texture( heightMap, tx ).a;

   while( h < height )
   {
```

```
    height  -= step;
    tx      += dtex;
    h        = texture( heightMap, tx ).a
}

vec2  tPrev = tx - dtex;
float hPrev = texture( heightMap, tPrev ).a-(height+step);
float hCur  = h - height;
float w     = hCur/(hCur - hPrev);

tx    = mix( tx, tPrev, w );
color = texture( diffMap, tx );
}
```

In Figure 16.19 the rendered quad with parallax occlusion mapping is shown.

FIGURE 16.19 (See color insert.): Quad rendered with parallax occlusion mapping.

Parallax occlusion mapping usually works well and produces the correct image, but it can miss small details as shown in Figure 16.20.

There are several methods which never miss an intersection but they are iterative and require special texture. One of these methods is called *cone step mapping* and it is based on a very simple idea – from every point on the heightfield we build a cone such that it never pierces the heightfield. Each

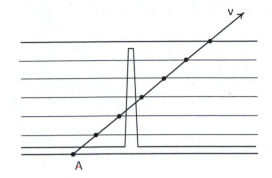

FIGURE 16.20: POM missing detail in an intersection.

such cone is defined by its half-angle whose tangent is stored in the texture (usually this half-angle is limited to $\pi/4$).

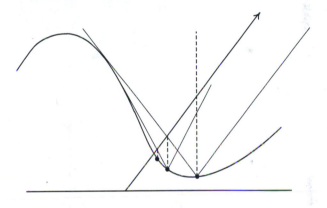

FIGURE 16.21: Cone step mapping.

Then iterations are built very simply. If we have some point A_i, then we find the intersection of the cone built at this point with a ray. This intersection point becomes a new approximation point; we build a cone at it, find its intersection with a ray and so on (see Figure 16.21).

But in some cases this method can very slowly converge to the intersection. So there is a modification of this method which converges much faster. In the original algorithm the cone cannot pierce the heightfield. A modified algorithm, called *relaxed cone step mapping*, allows for the cone to pierce the heightfield but provides a ray from the cone's origin that cannot intersect the heightfield more than once.

When we are using this method we must check that the ray may pierce the heightfield, but only once. So we check whether a new point is below the heightfield and if so it means that we have found the segment containing only one intersection (see Figure 16.22). Then we can use either the approach

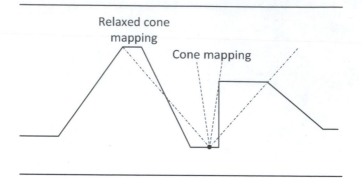

FIGURE 16.22: Relaxed cone step mapping vs. cone step mapping.

from parallax occlusion mapping or binary subdivision to get a more accurate approximation to the intersection point.

16.8   Sky rendering, Perez all-weather model

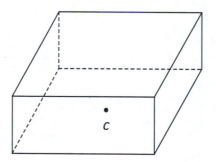

FIGURE 16.23: Hemicube around the camera.

There are several ways to render a sky. The simplest one is to use a prepared cubemap texture with a sky image. Then we render a big enough hemicube (or a hemisphere) around the camera position and use the cubemap texture to provide colors for it (see Figure 16.23).

This method can result in a high quality sky but it depends on the quality of original cubemaps. Also produced sky is static.

We can have several cubemaps – one for the sky and one or more for the clouds. The clouds cubemaps can be animated. But this will not change the time of the day which affects the coloring of the sky.

Another approach to rendering the sky uses the same hemicube or hemisphere but colors computed for its fragments are based on some sky model. One of such models is the *Perez all-weather model*. This model allows to change the sun position and also has the parameter called *turbidity*, which affects the resulting coloring.

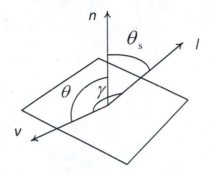

FIGURE 16.24: Angles for the Perez model.

The Perez model gives the color of the sky in Yxy color space as a function of three angles – θ, θ_S and γ: θ is the angle between the direction to the point on the sky and the up direction, θ_S is the angle between the direction to the Sun and the up direction and γ is the angle between the direction to the Sun and the direction to the point on the sky.

The model introduces the $F(\theta, \gamma)$ function which is used in color computations

$$F(\theta, \gamma) = \left(1 + Ae^{B/cos\theta}\right)\left(1 + Ce^{D\gamma} + Ecos^2\gamma\right). \qquad (16.12)$$

Parameters A, B, C, D and E depend on the turbidity T and define atmospheric properties.

According to this model a color of point on the sky corresponding to angles θ_S, θ and γ is defined by the formulae

$$\begin{cases} Y = Y_z \frac{F(\theta,\gamma)}{F(0,\theta_S)}, \\ x = x_z \frac{F(\theta,\gamma)}{F(0,\theta_S)}, \\ y = y_z \frac{F(\theta,\gamma)}{F(0,\theta_S)}. \end{cases} \qquad (16.13)$$

The $Y_z x_z y_z$ is the color at zenith. This color is defined by the following equations

$$\begin{cases} Y_z = (4.0453T - 4.9710)tan\chi - 0.2155T + 2.4192 \\ x_z = t \cdot \begin{pmatrix} 0.00166 & -0.00375 & 0.00209 & 0 \\ -0.02903 & 0.06377 & -0.03202 & 0.00394 \\ 0.11693 & -0.21196 & 0.06052 & 0.25886 \end{pmatrix} \Theta, \\ y_z = t \cdot \begin{pmatrix} 0.00275 & -0.0061 & 0.00317 & 0 \\ -0.04214 & 0.0897 & -0.04153 & 0.00516 \\ 0.15346 & -0.26756 & 0.0667 & 0.26688 \end{pmatrix} \Theta, \\ t = (T^2 \ T \ 1), \\ \Theta = \begin{pmatrix} \theta_S^3 \\ \theta_S^2 \\ \theta_S \\ 1 \end{pmatrix}. \end{cases} \qquad (16.14)$$

Here the angle χ is defined by the formula

$$\chi = (\frac{4}{9} - \frac{T}{120})(\pi - 2\theta_S). \qquad (16.15)$$

Each color component of Yxy has its own set of coefficients A, B, C, D and E

$$\begin{pmatrix} A_Y \\ B_Y \\ C_Y \\ D_Y \\ E_Y \end{pmatrix} = \begin{pmatrix} 0.1787 & -1.4630 \\ -0.3554 & 0.4275 \\ -0.0227 & 5.3251 \\ 0.1206 & -2.5771 \\ -0.0670 & 0.3703 \end{pmatrix} \begin{pmatrix} T \\ 1 \end{pmatrix}, \qquad (16.16)$$

$$\begin{pmatrix} A_x \\ B_x \\ C_x \\ D_x \\ E_x \end{pmatrix} = \begin{pmatrix} -0.0193 & -0.2592 \\ -0.0665 & 0.0008 \\ -0.0004 & 0.2125 \\ -0.0641 & -0.8989 \\ -0.0033 & 0.0452 \end{pmatrix} \begin{pmatrix} T \\ 1 \end{pmatrix}, \qquad (16.17)$$

$$\begin{pmatrix} A_y \\ B_y \\ C_y \\ D_y \\ E_y \end{pmatrix} = \begin{pmatrix} -0.0167 & -0.2608 \\ -0.0950 & 0.0092 \\ -0.0079 & 0.2102 \\ -0.0441 & -1.6537 \\ -0.0109 & 0.0529 \end{pmatrix} \begin{pmatrix} T \\ 1 \end{pmatrix}. \qquad (16.18)$$

Computing the color of the given point of the sky can be done in the vertex shader and interpolated during rasterization. The corresponding vertex shader is shown below.

```glsl
in vec2 texCoord;

out vec2 tex;
out vec3 v;
out vec3 l;
out vec3 pos;
out vec3 colorYxy;

uniform mat4  mv;
uniform mat4  proj;
uniform vec4  sunPos;
uniform vec4  eyePos;
uniform float turbidity;

vec3 perezZenith( float t, float thetaSun )
{
    const float pi = 3.1415926;
    const vec4 cx1 = vec4(0,0.00209,-0.00375,0.00165);
    const vec4 cx2 = vec4(0.00394,-0.03202,0.06377,-0.02903);
    const vec4 cx3 = vec4(0.25886,0.06052,-0.21196,0.11693);
    const vec4 cy1 = vec4(0.0,0.00317,-0.00610,0.00275);
    const vec4 cy2 = vec4(0.00516,-0.04153,0.08970,-0.04214);
    const vec4 cy3 = vec4(0.26688,0.06670,-0.26756,0.15346);

    float t2    = t*t;
    float chi   = (4.0/9.0 - t/120.0 )*(pi - 2.0*thetaSun );
    vec4  theta = vec4 ( 1, thetaSun, thetaSun*thetaSun,
                         thetaSun*thetaSun*thetaSun );

    float Y = (4.0453*t-4.9710)*tan(chi)-0.2155*t+2.4192;
    float x = t2*dot(cx1, theta)+t*dot(cx2, theta) +
              dot(cx3, theta);
    float y = t2*dot(cy1, theta)+t*dot(cy2, theta) +
              dot(cy3, theta);

    return vec3( Y, x, y );
}

vec3  perezFunc(float t, float cosTheta, float cosGamma)
{
    float gamma      = acos( cosGamma );
    float cosGammaSq = cosGamma * cosGamma;
    float aY =  0.17872 * t - 1.46303;
    float bY = -0.35540 * t + 0.42749;
    float cY = -0.02266 * t + 5.32505;
```

```
float  dY =    0.12064 * t − 2.57705;
float  eY = −0.06696 * t + 0.37027;
float  ax = −0.01925 * t − 0.25922;
float  bx = −0.06651 * t + 0.00081;
float  cx = −0.00041 * t + 0.21247;
float  dx = −0.06409 * t − 0.89887;
float  ex = −0.00325 * t + 0.04517;
float  ay = −0.01669 * t − 0.26078;
float  by = −0.09495 * t + 0.00921;
float  cy = −0.00792 * t + 0.21023;
float  dy = −0.04405 * t − 1.65369;
float  ey = −0.01092 * t + 0.05291;

return vec3 (
   (1.0+aY*exp(bY/cosTheta))*(1.0+cY*exp(dY*gamma)+
   eY*cosGammaSq),
   (1.0+ax*exp(bx/cosTheta))*(1.0+cx*exp(dx*gamma)+
   ex*cosGammaSq),
   (1.0+ay*exp(by/cosTheta))*(1.0+cy*exp(dy*gamma)+
   ey*cosGammaSq) );
}

vec3   perezSky( float t, float cosTheta,
                 float cosGamma, float cosThetaSun )
{
   float  thetaSun = acos          ( cosThetaSun );
   vec3   zenith   = perezZenith( t, thetaSun );
   vec3   clrYxy   = zenith*perezFunc(t, cosTheta, cosGamma)/
                     perezFunc(t, 1.0, cosThetaSun);

   clrYxy [0] *= smoothstep ( 0.0, 0.1, cosThetaSun );

   return clrYxy;
}

void main(void)
{
   pos              = 0.1 * gl_Vertex.xyz;
   v                = normalize( (gl_Vertex−eyePos).xyz );
   l                = normalize( sunPos.xyz );
   colorYxy         = perezSky( turbidity, max(v.z, 0.0)+0.05,
                                dot( l, v ), l.z );
   tex              = texCoord;
   gl_Position      = proj * mv * gl_Vertex;
}
```

Since the resulting Y value can be large, we need to apply simple transformation to ensure it will be in the $[0,1]$ range

$$Y^* = 1 - exp\left(-\frac{Y}{25}\right).\qquad(16.19)$$

After this, we convert the resulting Yxy color to an RGB color space and return it.

```
in vec3 v;
in vec3 l;
in vec3 colorYxy;

out vec4 color;

vec3     convertColor()
{
  vec3   clrYxy = vec3 ( colorYxy );

  clrYxy [0] = 1.0 - exp ( -clrYxy [0] / 25.0 );

  float ratio = clrYxy [0] / clrYxy [2];
  vec3  XYZ;
                // convert to XYZ
  XYZ.x = clrYxy [1] * ratio;
  XYZ.y = clrYxy [0];
  XYZ.z = ratio - XYZ.x - XYZ.y;
                // convert to RGB
  const vec3 rCoeffs = vec3(3.240479,-1.53715,-0.49853 );
  const vec3 gCoeffs = vec3(-0.969256,1.875991,0.041556);
  const vec3 bCoeffs = vec3(0.055684,-0.204043,1.057311);

  return vec3(dot(rCoeffs, XYZ), dot(gCoeffs, XYZ),
             dot(bCoeffs, XYZ) );
}

void main ()
{
  color = vec4( clamp( convertColor(), 0.0, 1.0 ), 1.0 );
}
```

16.9   Screen-Space Ambient Occlusion (SSAO)

FIGURE 16.25: Ambient occlusion.

One of the tricks which can add a feeling of global illumination to the image is *ambient occlusion*. It shows which part of the hemisphere around a given point is not blocked by nearby objects (see Figure 16.25). A point in the plane with no objects near it has an ambient occlusion equal to zero, while a point located in some deep crevice has ambient occlusion close to one.

Ambient occlusion of the point characterizes how much of the ambient light can reach this point. Direct computing of an ambient occlusion is a slow process and usually cannot be done in realtime. However, there are several methods producing approximations of ambient occlusion which can work in realtime.

One of such methods is *Screen-Space Ambient Occlusion* (SSAO). It uses a depth buffer to compute the approximate value of ambient occlusion for every pixel.

For every texel P from the depth buffer we can compute the z_{eye} coordinate of a corresponding fragment in the eye (camera) space from the value in the depth buffer by the following formula (in this equation d is the value from the depth buffer)

$$z_{eye} = \frac{z_{far} \cdot z_{near}}{d \cdot (z_{far} - z_{near}) - z_{far}}. \tag{16.20}$$

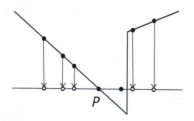

FIGURE 16.26: Estimating the ambient occlusion at P.

Then we can compute the approximated ambient occlusion using texels from the neighborhood of P. We will take several (usually between 8 and 16) sample points near P, find z_{eye} for each sample and use them to estimate how they occlude point P (see Figure 16.26).

Approximate attenuation is computed as

$$a(P) = \frac{1}{N} \sum_{i=0}^{N} \frac{1}{1 + d_i^2}.$$ (16.21)

The resulting value of (16.21) shows how much point P is attenuated by samples P_i. The d_i is given by the following equation

$$d_i = \begin{cases} 0, z_i - z < 0, \\ max\left(\frac{z_i - z}{z_{scale}}(2 - \frac{z_i - z}{z_{scale}}), 0\right), z_i - z \geq 0. \end{cases}$$ (16.22)

Here z_i is the z coordinate of the i-th sample in the eye coordinate space and z_{scale} is the scale factor controlling maximum distance at which the sample can affect attenuation at P.

Since we have no random function in GLSL we will use a prebuilt table of offsets from P. Then based on current texture coordinates we will extract a random unit vector from a small texture containing such vectors and use it to reflect offsets. Thus, nearby points will get a different set of offsets and if we use a small enough texture with unit vectors it will completely fit into the texture cache of the GPU.

The corresponding fragment shader is shown below. Here *depthMap* is a texture with values from the depth buffer; *randMap* is a texture with random unit vectors. Uniform *radius* controls the neighborhood of P where samples are taken from.

```
#version 330 core

uniform sampler2DRect depthMap;
uniform sampler2D      rotateMap;

in   vec2 tex;
out  vec4 color;

void main(void)
{
    const float zFar      = 100.0;
    const float zNear     = 0.1;
    const float attScale  = 1.0;
    const float radius    = 40;
    const float distScale = 0.25;
    const float bias      = 0.45;

    vec4 rndTable [8] = vec4 [8]
    (
        vec4 ( -0.5, -0.5, -0.5, 0.0 ),
        vec4 (  0.5, -0.5, -0.5, 0.0 ),
```

```
      vec4 ( −0.5,   0.5,  −0.5, 0.0 ),
      vec4 (   0.5,   0.5,  −0.5, 0.0 ),
      vec4 ( −0.5,  −0.5,   0.5, 0.0 ),
      vec4 (   0.5,  −0.5,   0.5, 0.0 ),
      vec4 ( −0.5,   0.5,   0.5, 0.0 ),
      vec4 (   0.5,   0.5,   0.5, 0.0 )
);

float  zSample = texture ( depthMap, gl_FragCoord.xy ).x;
float  z       = zFar*zNear / (zSample*(zFar − zNear) − zFar);
float  att     = 0.0;
vec3 plane     = 2.0*texture( rotateMap, gl_FragCoord.xy/4.0)
                 .xyz− vec3( 1.0 );

for ( int i = 0; i < 8; i++ )
{
    vec3   sample  = reflect( rndTable [i].xyz, plane );
    float zSample = texture( depthMap, gl_FragCoord.xy +
                                radius*sample.xy/z ).x;

    zSample = zFar*zNear/(zSample*(zFar − zNear) − zFar);

    float  dist = max ( zSample − z, 0.0 ) / distScale;
    float  occl = 15.0 * max ( dist * (2.0 − dist), 0.0 );

    att += 1.0 / ( 1.0 + occl*occl );
}

att   = clamp ( att/8.0 + 0.45, 0.0, 1.0 ) * attScale;
color = vec4 ( att );
}
```

To hide noise the results of this shader need to be blurred.

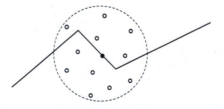

FIGURE 16.27: Using random points distributed in the sphere.

There are several other variants on how to compute ambient occlusion in screenspace. The simplest is to just pick samples in the small sphere around P and find how much of them are hidden with respect to the depth buffer.

Then the ration of hidden points to all points minus 0.5 will show how much this point is occluded (see Figure 16.27).

Another variant can be used if we have not only the depth map of the scene but also a normal map, i.e., for every point on the screen we have the eye-space normal. Such rendering methods and *deferred rendering* and *light prepass rendering* build a normal map for computing lighting, but we can also use it for computing ambient occlusion.

We need to restore coordinates of the original point P in the eye-space, restoring coordinates for every sample point P_i. If v_i is the eye-space vector from P to P_i and n is the eye-space normal at P, then we modulate the attenuation term to the i-th sample by $max((v_i, n), 0)$ (see Figure 16.28). You will find information about how to restore the eye-space coordinate from a depth buffer value in the section on deferred shading.

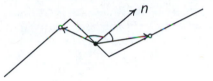

FIGURE 16.28: Using normals to control sample occlusion.

16.10   Modeling depth of field

Another effect which can be easily implemented is a *depth of field*. According to the laws of optics no lens (or a group of lenses) can produce an image with all objects sharp and in focus unless the lens diameter is zero. So when we make photographs or a movie there will always be objects out of focus.

Every camera has some distance (*focal distance*) at which all objects are in focus and objects not on this plane are out of focus (blurred). The further the object is from the focal plane the more it is blurred.

In computer graphics we usually use a camera model with a zero diameter lens. However, in many cases it is desirable to mimic real lenses and imitate such blurring. Such an effect is called *depth of field*.

If we take some distance d from the camera then every single point corresponds to a circle on an image plane called *circle of confusion* (COC). We will use the simplified equation of the radius of this circle of confusion

$$r_{coc} = \frac{|focalDepth - d|}{focalRange}.$$ (16.23)

Here the *focalDepth* is the distance at which objects are not blurred (the

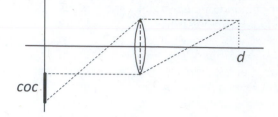

FIGURE 16.29: Circle of confusion.

radius of the corresponding circle of confusion is zero) and *focalRange* param-eter scales the circle of confusion.

Then during scene rendering we will output the biased signed radius of the circle of confusion (it differs from Equation (16.23) in that it does not use an absolute value of $focalDepth - d$ but the value itself) into an alpha channel

$$alpha = clamp(0.5 + scale \cdot \frac{focalDepth - d}{focalRange}, 0, 1). \qquad (16.24)$$

The corresponding fragment shader is shown below.

```
#version 330 core

uniform sampler2D imageMap;
uniform float focalDistance, focalRange;

in    vec2   tex;
in    float  z;
out   vec4   color;

void main(void)
{
    float blur = clamp(0.5+(focalDistance+z)/focalRange,
                       0.0,  1.0);

    color = vec4( texture( imageMap, tex ).rgb,  blur );
}
```

Then we can apply blur to the resulting image with a blur radius depending on the alpha value. For such blurring we will use a group of offsets with Poisson distribution.

When the radius of the circle of confusion is small, 8–12 samples will provide sufficient quality. However, for big values of radius this number of samples is insufficient. In order to keep our fragment shader small and quick we will downsample (4×4) the image and blur it.

At the filtering stage we will be taking samples both from the original image and from our downsampled and blurred image. These samples will be lerped based on the radius of the circle of confusion – for values near zero we will be giving more weight to the samples from the original image and for a large radius – to the samples from downsampled and blurred image.

Simple blurring of the image according to the circle of confusion can lead to noticeable artifacts when a bright object, which is closer to the camera than the current point, falls into the circle of confusion.

So we will multiply each sample which is closer to the camera by some factor reducing its contribution to the resulting color (leak reduction).

All this is done in the fragment shader shown below. The *image* and *imageLow* are original image and downsampled blurred image, correspondingly. Uniform variable *radiusScale* controls size of the circle of confusion.

```
#version 330 core

uniform sampler2D inputMap;
uniform sampler2D inputLowMap;

in   vec2   tex;
out  vec4   color;

void main(void)
{
    vec2   poisson [] = vec2 [8] (
            0.0,  0.0,  0.527837,  -0.85868,
           -0.040088,   0.536087,  -0.670445,  -0.179949,
           -0.419418,  -0.616039,  0.440453,  -0.639399,
           -0.757088,   0.349334,  0.574619,   0.685879 );

    float  radiusScale = 0.02;
    vec4   c     = texture( inputMap, tex );
    float  blur  = abs( c.a - 0.5 );
    float  cd    = c.a;
    float  discRadius = blur * radiusScale;
    vec4   tapLow, tapHigh, tap;

    c = vec4 ( 0.0 );

    for ( int i = 0; i < 8; i++ )
    {
        tapHigh = texture( inputMap,    tex+poisson [i]*discRadius );
        tapLow  = texture( inputLowMap, tex+poisson [i]*discRadius );
        blur    = abs(tapHigh.a - 0.5);
        tap     = mix( tapHigh, tapLow, blur );

        if ( tap.a >= cd )   // apply leaking reduction
           blur = 1.0;

        c.rgb += tap.rgb * blur;
```

```
   c.a    += blur;
}

color = c / c.a;
}
```

16.11 High Dynamic Range (HDR) rendering

Dynamic range is the ratio of the maximal value to the minimal non-zero value. The dynamic range of brightness for colors represented as RGB is rather low (since we are using only 8 bits per component). But the dynamic range we encounter in real life can be very large (e.g., 100,000:1). The human eye accommodates to various brightness levels and has a high dynamic range.

If we limit ourselves to the standard RGB color cube $[0, 1]^3$, we are seriously limiting our dynamic range. There can be very bright colors, e.g., $(1, 1, 10)$ is a very bright blue color. But if we stick to the RGB cube then it will clamped to $(1, 1, 1)$ which is a white color.

So if we want to use very bright colors we should not limit ourselves to the RGB cube and select a color format working with much greater levels of brightness. The floating-point format GL_RGBA_16F is just what we need. It keeps color components with enough precision and color values can be much bigger than one.

So we should render a scene into the texture of such a format. There can be very dark colors and very bright colors. To this image we can apply effects and later use *tone mapping* to map these HDR colors to normal range colors in order to show them on the monitor.

One of the standard effects applied to the HDR images is *bloom* – we copy bright parts of the image into a separate image (quite often this image is downsampled) and apply a Gaussian blur to it. Then the blurred image is added to the original one. Blurring enlarges bright areas and they may cover some of the not-bright parts of the image.

Shown below the fragment shader downsamples an original image selecting bright areas (and making black all other areas). After this pass we should apply the 2-pass Gaussian blur to create the downsampled image.

```
#version 330 core

uniform samplerRect image;
uniform float       threshold;

in  vec2 texCoords;
out vec4 color;
```

```
void main ()
{
    const vec3 lum = vec3 ( 0.27, 0.67, 0.06 );

    vec4  c = texture( image, texCoords );

    if ( dot ( c, lum ) < threshold )
        color = vec4 ( 0.0 );
    else
        color = c;
}
```

The next step adds a blurred bright image to the original image with some weight and performs *tone mapping*. There are several possible tone mapping operators which can be successfully used.

The simplest tone mapping operator applies function $y = x/(x+1)$ to each image component. It can be seen that this function will always map every image component into the $[0, 1]$ range.

Another tone mapping operator is performed using the exponent function – every component is transformed by function $y = 1 - exp(-kx)$ where the coefficient k is a positive constant controlling tone mapping.

One more tone mapping operator is given by the equation

$$\begin{cases} y = \frac{6.2x'^2 + 0.5x'}{6.2x'^2 + 1.7x' + 0.06}, \\ x' = max(x - 0.004, 0). \end{cases} \qquad (16.25)$$

```
#version 330 core

uniform samplerRect  image;
uniform float         threshold;

in   vec2 texCoords;
out  vec4 color;

void main ()
{
    vec4 c  = texture( image, texCoords );
    vec4 cp = max ( c - vec4 ( 0.004 ), 0.0 );
    vec4 cq = 6.2 * cp * cp;

    color = (cq + 0.5*cp)/
            (cq + 1.7*cp + vec4 ( 0.06 ) );
}
```

16.12   Realistic water rendering

In this section we will look at how a water surface can be rendered. We won't be using the Tessendorf model since it is based on the Fourier transform. Instead we will use a noise-based approach (noise function and its application will be covered in Chapter 18).

Consider a point P on the water surface with unit normal n. The unit direction to the camera is v and the unit direction to the light source (Sun) is l (see Figure 16.30).

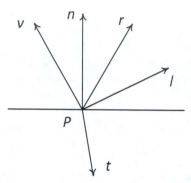

FIGURE 16.30: Reflected and refracted rays.

From vectors v and n we can find a reflected vector r and transmitted vector t. Both of these vectors contribute some colors with weights $F(\theta)$ and $1 - F(\theta)$, respectively.

Now let's see what factors contribute to the resulting color we see at point P. First, such a factor is the color of the water itself. It depends on the angle θ; for $\theta = 0$ we get a dark blue color c_1 and for θ close to $\pi/2$ we get a lighter green-blue color c_2. So for water color we can use the following equation

$$c_w(\theta) = c_1 cos\theta + c_2(1 - cos\theta).$$

This color corresponds to the t vector and has a weight equal to $1 - F(\theta)$. The reflected vector r adds reflected color (usually the sky from a cubemap) with weight $F(\theta)$. Also lighting contributes the specular part $max((r,l), 0)^k$.

Therefore, the resulting equation with all participating terms is shown below

$$C = c_w(\theta)(1 - F(\theta)) + F(\theta)c_{sky} + max((r, l), 0)^k. \tag{16.26}$$

Animation of water can be done at two levels – we can animate vertices of the water mesh by using several octaves of noise. Also in the fragment shader we can animate the normal vector using the same noise texture.

16.13   Deferred rendering

All lighting shaders considered before dealt with only one light source. But quite often in games we need many light sources. In this case we either get a very big and slow shader or we have many separate passes where each pass applies lighting from a single light source. Both of these approaches are very ineffective since they have the overall complexity $O(N \cdot L)$ where N is a number of objects in the scene and L is a number of light sources in the scene.

A common tendency in games is that both of these parameters constantly grow – we want to have highly detailed scenes with a lot of light sources. Quite often additional light sources are used to mimic global illumination.

Deferred shading or *deferred rendering* (opposed to standard or *forward rendering*) decouples geometric complexity of the scene from the lighting and achieves an overall complexity $O(N + L)$.

Deferred rendering renders all objects into the *G-buffer* (or geometry buffer). Then additional passes use this buffer to apply lighting to the scene. Geometric complexity takes place only in the process of the creation of a G-buffer. All lighting is based on G-buffer contents and depends only on light sources.

And what information for every pixel should the G-buffer contain so that we will be able to compute lighting from a given light source? For every pixel we need its 3D-coordinates to compute l and v vectors. Also we need a normal n.

In the simplest case we can use for the G-buffer two GL_RGBA_16F textures. The first will contain the position of the fragment in RGB components and the second will contain the normal in RGB components, both in the eye space (see Figure 16.31).

FIGURE 16.31: Simplest G-buffer structure.

Then in a lighting pass we render a screen-sized quad covering all pixels and for every pixel compute lighting from its position and normal. We can apply many light sources, each will add its lighting to the scene.

This approach can be easily implemented in OpenGL shaders. Below is shown first pass shaders which fill the geometry buffer with data. Corresponding vertex and fragment shaders for the geometry pass are shown below.

—— vertex

```glsl
#version 330 core

uniform mat4 mv;
uniform mat4 proj;
uniform mat3 nm;

layout ( location = 0 ) in vec3 pos;
layout ( location = 1 ) in vec2 texCoord;
layout ( location = 2 ) in vec3 normal;

out vec2 tex;
out vec3 n;
out vec4 p;

void main(void)
{
    tex         = texCoord;
    n           = nm * normal;
    p           = mv * vec4 ( pos, 1.0 );
    gl_Position = proj * p;
}

-- fragment

#version 330 core

in   vec2 tex;
in   vec3 n;
in   vec4 p;
out vec4 color [2];

void main(void)
{
    color [0] = vec4 ( p.xyz, 1.0 );
    color [1] = vec4 ( n, 1.0 );
}
```

The shaders applying the lighting from a light source with a given location will appear as shown below.

```glsl
-- vertex

#version 330 core

layout (location = 0) in vec4 pos;
```

```
out vec2 tex;

void main(void)
{
   tex          = pos.zw;
   gl_Position = vec4 ( pos.xy, 0.0, 1.0 );
}
```

— fragment

```
#version 330 core

uniform sampler2D posMap;
uniform sampler2D normalMap;
uniform vec4       light;

in   vec2 tex;
out vec4 color;

void main(void)
{
   vec3   p  = texture( posMap,    tex ).xyz;
   vec3   n  = texture( normalMap, tex ).xyz;
   vec3   l  = normalize( light.xyz − p );
   vec3   v  = normalize( −p );
   vec3   h  = normalize( l + v );
   float  diff = max( 0.2, dot ( l, n ) );
   float  spec = pow( max ( 0.0, dot ( h, n ) ), 40.0 );

   color = vec4( vec3( diff + spec ), 1.0 );
}
```

In this simple example we use untextured objects. So now we will see how we can add the support of texturing and bumpmapping.

For this we need to add diffuse color and specular power to the G-buffer. So the resulting G-buffer will contain 3 textures as shown in Figure 16.32.

One more change is connected with bumpmapping. Normal maps contain normals in the tangent space. But in deferred rendering all lighting is computed in the eye-space, so in the fragment shader of the first pass we need to convert the normal from the tangent space to the eye-space using the tangent space basis for the current primitive.

— vertex

```
#version 330 core
```

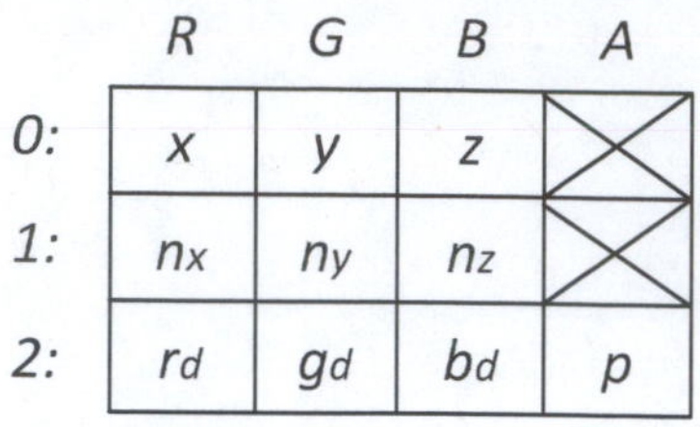

	R	G	B	A
0:	x	y	z	✕
1:	nx	ny	nz	✕
2:	rd	gd	bd	p

FIGURE 16.32: G-Buffer structure with support of textures.

```
uniform mat4 mv;
uniform mat4 proj;
uniform mat3 nm;

layout ( location = 0 ) in vec3 pos;
layout ( location = 1 ) in vec2 texCoord;
layout ( location = 2 ) in vec3 normal;
layout ( location = 3 ) in vec3 tangent;
layout ( location = 4 ) in vec3 binormal;

out vec2 tex;
out vec3 n;
out vec3 t;
out vec3 b;
out vec4 p;

void main(void)
{
    tex         = texCoord;
    n           = nm * normal;
    t           = nm * tangent;
    b           = nm * binormal;
    p           = mv * vec4 ( pos, 1.0 );
    gl_Position = proj * p;
}

-- fragment

#version 330 core

uniform sampler2D diffMap;
uniform sampler2D bumpMap;

in  vec2 tex;
```

```
in    vec3 n;
in    vec3 b;
in    vec3 t;
in    vec4 p;
out vec4 color [3];

void main(void)
{
    const float specPower = 70.0;

    vec4 c  = texture( diffMap, tex );
    vec3 nt = normalize( 2.0*texture( bumpMap, tex ).rgb -
                         vec3( 1.0 ) );

    color [0] = vec4 ( p.xyz, 1.0 );
    color [1] = vec4 ( nt.x*t + nt.y*b + nt.z*n, 1.0 );
    color [2] = vec4 ( c.rgb, specPower );
}
```

The lighting shader is changed only a little – it just takes diffuse color and specular power from the G-buffer.

```
— vertex

#version 330 core

layout(location = 0) in vec3 pos;
layout(location = 1) in vec2 texCoord;

uniform mat4 mv;
uniform mat4 proj;

out vec4 pp;
out vec2 tex;

void main(void)
{
    tex          = texCoord;
    pp           = mv * vec4 ( pos.xyz, 1.0 );
    gl_Position = proj * pp;
}

— fragment

#version 330 core
```

```
uniform sampler2D  posMap;
uniform sampler2D  normalMap;
uniform sampler2D  diffMap;
uniform vec4       light;

in   vec4 pp;
in   vec2 tex;
out  vec4 color;

void main(void)
{
   float z  = texture ( posMap,    tex ).z;
   vec3  p  = pp.xyz * z / pp.z;
   vec3  n  = texture( normalMap, tex ).xyz;
   vec4  c  = texture( diffMap, tex );
   vec3  l  = normalize ( light.xyz - p );
   vec3  v  = normalize ( -p );
   vec3  h  = normalize ( l + v );
   float diff = max ( 0.2, max( 0.0, dot ( l, n ) ) );
   float spec = pow ( max ( 0.0, dot ( h, n ) ), c.a );

color = vec4 ( diff*c.rgb + vec3( spec ), 1.0 );
}
```

The serious problem with the G-buffer is that it can be very big and require a great deal of memory bandwidth from the GPU. So to decrease the amount of memory used, we can optimize the G-buffer from Fig 16.32.

First of all we don't need all three coordinates – the z-coordinate is sufficient to restore x and y. Keeping all three components of the unit normal is also not required – since we know that the length of the normal is always equal to one, we can restore the third component (except for its sign) from the first two components.

Let's see how we can get all three eye-space coordinates from only z_{eye}. To achieve this we will render a quad with z equal to one whose edges are an intersection of the plane $z = 1$ with the viewing frustum.

If the vertex shader passes interpolate eye coordinates to the fragment shader, then in order to restore all three eye-space coordinates from z_{eye} we need to multiply passed coordinates by the z_{eye} value from the G-buffer (see Figure 16.33). It is because both the interpolated position and the corresponding point for which we have a z-coordinate lie on the same ray from the camera position and the interpolated coordinates will have a z-coordinate equal to 1.

There are several variants for how we can safely encode unit normal in two numbers. Knowing both n_x and n_y we can easily get $n_z = \pm\sqrt{1 - n_x^2 - n_y^2}$, but we don't know the sign of n_z and it can be any sign due to the usage of bump maps.

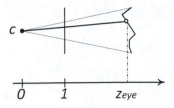

FIGURE 16.33: Locating the original location of a point in eye-space.

So when encoding normal we will check the sign of n_z, and if it is negative we will add 3 to the n_x moving it out of the $[-1, 1]$ range into the $[2, 4]$ range.

```
vec2 encodeNormal ( in vec3 normal )
{
    if ( normal.z < 0.0 )
        return vec2 ( normal.x + 3.0, normal.y );

    return normal.xy;
}
```

In order to restore normal we check whether n_x lies in the $[-1, 1]$ segment. If it is so, the sign of n_z is positive and $n_z = \sqrt{1 - n_x^2 - n_y^2}$. Otherwise, we know that the sign of n_z is negative and we need to subtract 3 from n_x and after this get n_z with a negative sign.

```
vec3 decodeNormal ( in vec2 nn )
{
    if ( nn.x > 1.5 )                       // negative n.z
    {
        float nx = nn.x - 3.0;
        float nz = -sqrt( 1.0 - nx*nx - nn.y*nn.y );

        return vec3( nx, nn.y, nz );
    }

    return vec3 ( nn.x, nn.y,
                  sqrt ( 1.0 - nn.x*nn.x - nn.y*nn.y ) );
}
```

So we have come to the following G-buffer structure shown in Figure 16.34. It contains z_{eye}, two normal components, gloss k_s, specular power p and diffuse color. We can easily put into an alpha channel of the first texture not one value k_s but two values, e.g., k_s and emission or k_s and material index, and so on.

Corresponding fragment shaders for the first pass are shown below.

—— vertex

	R	G	B	A
0:	z_{eye}	n_x	n_y	k_s
1:	r_d	g_d	b_d	p

FIGURE 16.34: Optimized G-buffer layout.

```
#version 330 core

uniform mat4 mv;
uniform mat4 proj;
uniform mat3 nm;

layout ( location = 0 ) in vec3 pos;
layout ( location = 1 ) in vec2 texCoord;
layout ( location = 2 ) in vec3 normal;
layout ( location = 3 ) in vec3 tangent;
layout ( location = 4 ) in vec3 binormal;

out vec2 tex;
out vec3 n;
out vec3 t;
out vec3 b;
out vec4 p;

void main(void)
{
    tex         = texCoord;
    n           = nm * normal;
    t           = nm * tangent;
    b           = nm * binormal;
    p           = mv * vec4 ( pos, 1.0 );
    gl_Position = proj * p;
}

-- fragment

#version 330 core

uniform sampler2D diffMap;
uniform sampler2D bumpMap;

in  vec2 tex;
```

```glsl
in   vec3 n;
in   vec3 b;
in   vec3 t;
in   vec4 p;
out vec4 color [2];

vec2 encodeNormal ( in vec3 normal )
{
    if ( normal.z < 0.0 )
      return vec2 ( normal.x + 3.0, normal.y );

    return normal.xy;
}

void main(void)
{
    const float specPower = 70.0;
    const float ks        = 0.7;

    vec4 c  = texture( diffMap, tex );
    vec3 nt = normalize( 2.0*texture( bumpMap, tex ).rgb -
                      vec3( 1.0 ) );
    vec2 nn = encodeNormal ( nt.x*t + nt.y*b + nt.z*n );

    color [0] = vec4 ( p.z, nn.x, nn.y, ks );
    color [1] = vec4 ( c.rgb, specPower );
}
```

The lighting vertex and fragment shaders are also changed as shown below.

—— vertex

```glsl
#version 330 core

layout (location = 0) in vec3 pos;
layout (location = 1) in vec2 texCoord;

uniform mat4 mv;
uniform mat4 proj;

out vec4 pp;
out vec2 tex;

void main(void)
{
    tex           = texCoord;
```

```
  pp            = mv * vec4 ( pos.xyz, 1.0 );
  gl_Position = proj * pp;
}

— fragment

#version 330 core

uniform sampler2D normalMap;
uniform sampler2D diffMap;
uniform vec4      light;

in   vec4 pp;
in   vec2 tex;
out vec4 color;

vec3 decodeNormal ( in vec2 nn )
{
  if ( nn.x > 1.5 )                    // negative n.z
  {
    float nx = nn.x - 3.0;
    float nz = -sqrt( 1.0 - nx*nx - nn.y*nn.y );

    return vec3( nx, nn.y, nz );
  }

  return vec3 ( nn.x, nn.y,
                sqrt ( 1.0 - nn.x*nn.x - nn.y*nn.y ) );
}

void main(void)
{
  vec4   c1 = texture ( normalMap, tex );
  float z  = c1.x;
  float ks = c1.w;
  vec3   p  = pp.xyz * z / pp.z;
  vec3   n  = normalize(decodeNormal ( c1.yz ));
  vec4   c2 = texture( diffMap, tex );
  vec3   l  = normalize ( light.xyz - p );
  vec3   v  = normalize ( -p );
  vec3   h  = normalize ( l + v );
  float diff = max ( 0.2, max( 0.0, dot ( l, n ) ) );
  float spec = pow ( max( 0.0, dot ( h, n ) ), c2.a );

  color = vec4 ( diff*c2.rgb + vec3( spec ), 1.0 );
```

}

One more optimization which we can use is computing z_{eye} from the values in the depth buffer. To see how this can be done we write how z and w components are transformed by the perspective projection matrix

$$\begin{pmatrix} z_p \\ w_p \end{pmatrix} = \begin{pmatrix} m_{33} & m_{34} \\ -1 & 0 \end{pmatrix} \begin{pmatrix} z_{eye} \\ 1 \end{pmatrix}. \tag{16.27}$$

After perspective division we will get the d' value from the $[-1, 1]$ interval

$$d' = \frac{z_p}{w_p} = -m_{33} + \frac{m_{34}}{z_{eye}}. \tag{16.28}$$

Now we substitute values for m_{33} and m_{34} into (16.28) and get the following equation for d' as a function of z_{eye}

$$d'(z_{eye}) = \frac{1}{z_{far} - z_{near}} \left(z_{far} + z_{near} + 2\frac{z_{far}z_{near}}{z_{eye}} \right). \tag{16.29}$$

But we need to remap this value from the $[-1, 1]$ range into the $[0, 1]$ range before storing it into the depth buffer. The resulting value d, which is written into the depth buffer, is given by the following formula

$$d(z_{eye}) = \frac{1 + d'(z_{eye})}{2} = \frac{1}{z_{far} - z_{near}\left(z_{far} + \frac{z_{far}z_{near}}{z_{eye}} \right)}. \tag{16.30}$$

Inverting Equation (16.30) we get the equation for z_{eye} from the value in the depth buffer d

$$z_{eye} = \frac{z_{far}z_{near}}{d \cdot (z_{far} - z_{near}) - z_{far}}. \tag{16.31}$$

Now let's see how we can optimize lighting calculations. The simplest way is to draw a fullscreen squad so the fragment shader will be executed for every pixel and compute lighting for it.

But this approach is not efficient – most of the lights have a limited area of influence. Usually this area is either a sphere or a clipped cone. For such a light source we can simply draw front faces of the sphere or a clipped cone. It will ensure that the fragment shader will be called only for fragments which can be lit by the given light source.

And even this step can be optimized more. As iseen in Figure 16.35 we need to process only those fragments of the back faces of the sphere/cone for which the depth test has failed.

We can use stencil buffer to mark corresponding pixels and this pass will be very quick because we disable any writing into the color buffers and depth buffer and will modify only the stencil buffer. The shader, which is used for such a pass, is very simple and lightweight.

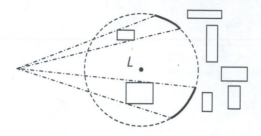

FIGURE 16.35: Parts of the sphere which require processing.

After this pass we use a lighting shader and configure the stencil test to skip all unmarked pixels. As a result we have replaced an expensive lighting pass for all pixels on the screen with a very cheap stencil pass and expensive pass but on a fewer number of pixels which is a win.

Usually deferred rendering does not handle transparent objects. But there is a simple enough trick which can render several transparent objects.

For this we need to keep the alpha value in the G-buffer and when we render a transparent surface we discard all fragments whose screen y-coordinate is even. Thus, in the resulting G-buffer we will have information about the transparent object (in odd lines) and the covered objects (in even lines).

Then we apply all the lighting in the usual way. But after we need one more pass which checks whether the current pixel or a pixel above belongs to the transparent surface. If it is, we perform blending of the colors of the transparent surface and covered surface (which is the pixel above it).

The fragment shader for a corresponding pass is shown below.

```glsl
#version 330 core

in   vec2 tex;
out vec4 color;

uniform sampler2DRect colorMap;

void main ()
{
    vec4   c  = texture( colorMap, tex );
    vec4   c2 = texture( colorMap, tex + vec2( 0.0, 1.0 ) );
    float  a  = c.a;
    float  a2 = c2.a;

    if ( a2 < 1.0 - EPS )
        color = mix( c, c2, a2 );
    else
    if a < 1.0 - EPS )
```

```
    color = mix( c2, c, a );
}
```

16.14   Light prepass rendering

Light Prepass (LPP) rendering is a rendering approach close to deferred rendering but it uses a small G-buffer. It requires that the G-buffer should contain only z_{eye} and normal n for every pixel which can be easily stuffed into a single GL_RGBA_16F texture (see Figure 16.36).

	R	G	B	A
0:	nx	ny	nz	Zeye

FIGURE 16.36: Structure of the G-buffer for light prepass rendering.

After all geometry has been rendered into the G-buffer, the lighting is computed and accumulated into the special lighting buffer. The equations below show how color and alpha components of the lighting buffer are computed.

$$\begin{cases} L_{RGB} = \sum_i I_i \cdot max((n, l_i), 0) \cdot att(d_i), \\ L_A = \sum_i lum(I_i) \cdot max((n, l_i), 0) \cdot max((n, h_i), 0)^k \cdot att(d_i). \end{cases} \tag{16.32}$$

Here I_i is color and brightness of the i-th light source, l_i is a direction to the i-th light source, h_i is a half-vector between v and l_i, d_i is a distance to the i-th light source and $att(d)$ is a distance attenuation function.

After all lights have been processed and we have the lighting buffer ready, all geometry is rendered again. This time during this rendering we simply apply lighting from the lighting buffer on the objects being rendered.

The diffuse part of the lighting is kept in the RGB components of the lighting buffer and specular component S is computed using the equation

$$S = chromaticity \cdot \sum_i lum(I_i \cdot max((n, l_i), 0) \cdot max((n, h_i), 0)^k \cdot att(d_i)).$$

$$\tag{16.33}$$

So the specular part is just a chromaticity value multiplied by brightness accumulated in the alpha component of the lighting buffer. The required chromaticity for specular lighting is computed from the diffuse part of the lighting buffer

$$chromaticity = \frac{\sum_i I_i \cdot max((n, l_i), 0) \cdot att(d_i)}{lum(\sum_i I_i \cdot max((n, l_i), 0) \cdot att(d_i))}. \tag{16.34}$$

In light prepass rendering we just trade the decreased size of the G-buffer for an extra geometry pass.

Both the deferred rendering and the light prepass rendering can render hundreds of light sources on modern GPUs.

16.15   Ambient cubes

One of the ways we can add indirect illumination is using an ambient cube. Each ambient cube contains six color values corresponding to its sides. Such a cube is placed in space and periodically updated.

The update of such a cube consists of rendering local objects into some small buffer and downsampling it to a 1×1 size.

If we have a group of ambient cubes in space then we can approximate ambient lighting on some point by picking one or several closest ambient cubes and picking color values from them.

This method was used in the Half-Life 2 game for indirect illumination of dynamic objects (all static geometry in this game was illuminated using prebuilt light maps).

16.16   Reflective shadow maps

A *Reflective Shadow Map* (RSM) is one of the ways to provide an approximation to indirect lighting. It is based on a very simple observation – all texels in the shadow map can be thought of as secondary light sources which illuminate nearby pixels.

If we have sufficient data for every RSM pixel (we need to have a 3D-position p corresponding to this pixel, normal n_p at it and the reflected radiant flux Φ_p, stored in several texture maps), then for every visible pixel we can add illumination from nearby RSM pixels.

An RSM pixel with a position p_r, normal n_r and flux Φ_r adds to the fragment with position p and a normal n an amount of light which is given by the equation

$$E_p(p, n) = \Phi_r \frac{max((p - p_r, n_r), 0) \cdot max((p_r - p, n), 0)}{\|p - p_r\|^4}. \tag{16.35}$$

Then we can take a group of samples (defined in the screenspace) and compute the lighting they contribute to the point p. Note that this method completely ignores the visibility between p and p_r. It was found that in order to produce realistic results the number of samples should be close to 300–400.

It is evident that this amount of samples per pixel cannot be taken for every pixel of the image. Therefore, the algorithm uses a highly downsampled image (up to 32×32 or 64×64) and computes an indirect lighting with a large amount of samples from the RSM.

Then for every pixel of the whole image, the four nearest pixels from the downsampled image are located and a distance check between the current point and all of them is performed. Normals at the current point and these four samples are also checked. If we have found that three or all four samples are close to the current point and their normals are close to the normal at the current pixel, then bilinear interpolation of the indirect lighting is performed. Otherwise, the current pixel is marked as requiring a full computation.

After this pass for all marked pixels their indirect lighting is computed directly by taking 300–400 samples and summing their lighting.

The described approach takes too many samples for pixels and strongly depends on interpolation (consider a bumpmapped surface, for which the normals check will surely fail) to be used in a serious product, but the very idea of the shadow map being the set of secondary lights has been successfully used in several other algorithms.

16.17 Splatting indirect illumination

One of the methods based on the RSM idea is *splatting indirect illumination*. The main difference between this approach and a previous one is that the previous approach was used to *gather* indirect lighting from RSM pixels, while this approach *splats* indirect illumination in the screenspace.

For the approach, a group of secondary light sources is selected and for every such secondary light source its lighting is distributed on nearby pixels using a *splat*. A splat is just a quad whose size depends on the brightness of the source with a light source at its center.

A fragment shader used for rendering splats computes for every covered pixel the illumination from a corresponding secondary light source. In this method a much smaller number of secondary light sources is used – usually 64 or less and they are carefully distributed in the screenspace.

All lighting calculations are done using the deferred rendering approach.

Chapter 17

Basics of GPGPU

GPGPU (General Purpose computations on GPUs) is a quickly growing area of using GPUs for solving a wide variety of non-graphical problems. GPGPU uses the GPU for solving various complex problems in much less time than traditional solving that using the CPU would require.

17.1   What is GPGPU?

Modern GPUs are in fact massively parallel devices with thousands of processing cores. They outperform traditional CPUs by an order of magnitude (in the number of floating-point operations per second, *Flops*).

When the evolution of GPUs led to the creation of programmable GPUs providing much more floating-point operations per second than traditional CPUs, the first attempts to use the GPU for not only graphical problems (such as sorting, fast Fourier transform, particle system dynamics and so on) appeared.

In these early attempts graphics APIs like OpenGL were used to get access to the GPU and all massively parallel computations were performed using fragment shaders.

Even such a complicated approach allowed implementation of various algorithms on the GPU and to achieve sufficient performance. However, these attempts were limited because they worked through purely graphical APIs not targeted for computing problems. These limitations included:

- the necessity to use graphics API;

- limited memory model;

- the inability of cooperation between computing different elements.

So there was a need of specialized APIs targeted at using the GPU as a massively parallel computing device. Two of the most successful emerged APIs specially designed for GPGPU are OpenCL and CUDA (Compute Unified Device Architecture).

CUDA supports only NVidia GPUs but provides an easy start, has very good documentation and tools, and uses modified C++ to write code for the GPUs.

OpenCL (Open Computing Language) is a multivendor cross-platform API which can be used not only with GPUs but also with other computing devices such as traditional processors, IBM Cell, DSPs (Digital Signal Processors) and so on.

Both of these APIs provide good integration with OpenGL so it is possible to perform computing using OpenCL (or CUDA) and then use results of these computations directly in OpenGL (without copying data back to the CPU memory) for rendering.

17.2 Basics of OpenCL

OpenCL (Open Computing Language) is an open and cross-platform standard for parallel computing on heterogeneous devices. OpenCL was initially developed by Apple Inc. and is now managed by the Khronos Group (version 1.0 of OpenCL was published at the end of 2008).

OpenCL consists of C-like language and an API for programming devices. OpenCL allows to program for CPUs, GPUs, Cell processors, DSPs and many other devices.

Here we will look at the basics of OpenCL and write several simple programs for performing computations on the GPU.

OpenCL is based on the following generalized models:

- platform model

- memory model

- execution model

- programming model.

In an OpenCL platform model each platform (provided by some vendor) consists of a host (CPU) connected to one or more *computing devices* (see Figure 17.1).

Each computing device consists of one or more *computing units* and each computing unit contains several *processing elements*. All computations are performed on processing elements.

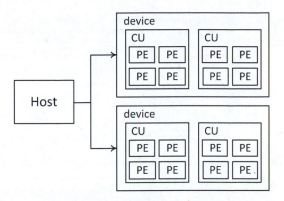

FIGURE 17.1: OpenCL platform model.

To get all available platforms the command **clGetPlatformIDs** should be used.

```
cl_int clGetPlatformIDs( cl_uint numEntries ,
                         cl_platform_id * platforms ,
                         cl_uint * numPlatforms );
```

The following snippet of C++ code shows how to get information about available platforms (see Table 17.2).

```
cl_platform_id  platform;
cl_device_id    device;
cl_uint         err;

err = clGetPlatformIDs( 1, &platform , NULL );

if ( err != CL_SUCCESS )
{
  printf ( "Error_obtaining_OpenCL_platform.\n" );

  return −1;
}

err = clGetDeviceIDs( platform , CL_DEVICE_TYPE_GPU, 1,
                  &device , NULL );

if ( err != CL_SUCCESS )
{
  printf ( "Error_obtaining_OpenCL_device.\n" );

  return −1;
}
```

TABLE 17.1: Supported device types in OpenCL

Device Type	Description
CL_DEVICE_TYPE_CPU	Host CPU
CL_DEVICE_TYPE_GPU	GPU device
CL_DEVICE_TYPE_ACCELERATOR	Dedicated OpenCL accelerator (g.e. IBM Cell Blade)
CL_DEVICE_TYPE_DEFAULT	Default OpenCL device type
CL_DEVICE_TYPE_ANY	All available OpenCL devices

TABLE 17.2: Possible values for parameter *pname* in the call of **clGetPlatformInfo**

Device Type	Description
CL_PLATFORM_PROFILE	Returns the profile name supported by the implementation.
CL_PLATFORM_VERSION	Returns OpenCL version string.
CL_PLATFORM_NAME	String containing the platform name.
CL_PLATFORM_VENDOR	String containing platform vendor.
CL_PLATFORM_EXTENSIONS	String containing space-separated list of supported OpenCL extensions.

To get information about a platform the **clGetPlatformInfo** command is used.

```
cl_int clGetPlatformInfo ( cl_platform_id platform,
                           cl_platform_info pname,
                           size_t valueBufSize,
                           void * valueBuf,
                           size_t * valueSize );
```

Parameter *pname* specifies what property of platform should be returned in *valueBuf* and *valueSize* parameters. Possible values of *pname* are shown in Table 17.2.

The following code gets all available platforms and prints platform and vendor names.

```
#include        <stdio.h>
#include        <stdlib.h>
#include        <CL/cl.h>

int main ( int argc, char * argv [] )
{
    cl_uint numPlatforms;
    cl_int   err = clGetPlatformIDs ( 0, NULL, &numPlatforms );

    if ( err != CL_SUCCESS )
    {
        printf ( "No_OpenCL_platform_found.\n" );
```

```
    exit    ( 1 );
}

cl_platform_id * platforms = new cl_platform_id [numPlatforms];

err = clGetPlatformIDs ( numPlatforms , platforms , &numPlatforms );

if ( err != CL_SUCCESS )
{
  printf ( "Error_getting_OpenCL_platform_found.\n" );
  exit    ( 1 );
}

for ( int i = 0; i < numPlatforms; i++ )
{
  char buf1 [1024];
  char buf2 [1024];

  clGetPlatformInfo ( platforms [i], CL_PLATFORM_NAME,
                          sizeof(buf1), buf1, NULL );
  clGetPlatformInfo ( platforms [i], CL_PLATFORM_VENDOR,
                          sizeof(buf2), buf2, NULL );

  printf ( "Platform:_%s\nVendor__:_%s\n", buf1, buf2 );
}

return 0;
}
```

For a given platform, command **clGetDeviceIDs** returns a list of all available devices for a given platform. To get information about a device, command **clGetDeviceInfo** is used.

```
cl_int clGetDeviceIDs( cl_platform_id platform ,
                       cl_device_type deviceType ,
                       cl_uint numEntries ,
                       cl_device_id * devices ,
                       cl_uint * numDevices );


cl_int clGetDeviceInfo( cl_device_id device ,
                        cl_deviceInfo pname,
                        size_t valueBufSize ,
                        void * valueBuf ,
                        size_t * valueSize );
```

A snippet of code for dumping information about a device is shown below.

```
err = clGetDeviceIDs ( platform , CL_DEVICE_TYPE_GPU, 1,
                       &device , NULL );
```

```
if ( err != CL_SUCCESS )
{
  printf ( "No_OpenCL_device_found.\n" );
  exit    ( 1 );
}

cl_ulong         sizGlobal , sizConst , sizLocal ;

clGetDeviceInfo( device , CL_DEVICE_NAME, sizeof(buf1),
                 buf1 , NULL );
clGetDeviceInfo( device , CL_DEVICE_GLOBAL_MEM_SIZE,
                 sizeof(sizGlobal),
                 &sizGlobal , NULL );
clGetDeviceInfo( device , CL_DEVICE_MAX_CONSTANT_BUFFER_SIZE,
                 sizeof(sizConst), &sizConst , NULL );
clGetDeviceInfo( device , CL_DEVICE_LOCAL_MEM_SIZE,
                 sizeof(sizLocal),
                 &sizGlobal , NULL );

printf ( "Name__:_%s\nGlobal_mem:_%d\nConstant__:%d\nLocal_:_%d\n" ,
         buf1 , sizGlobal , sizConst , sizLocal );
```

OpenCL implements a *stream processing model*. All OpenCL applications include *kernels* which are executed on devices (and are written in OpenCL language) and a host program which controls execution of kernels on devices.

A kernel is launched for every element of the N-dimensional computation domain (*ND-range*)($N = 1, 2, 3$). Each element of this domain is called a *work-item*. Each work-item executes the same kernel. Work-items can be considered as parallel threads executing the kernel.

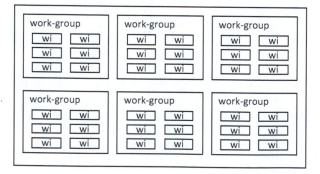

FIGURE 17.2: Structure of the ND-range.

All work-items are grouped into *work-groups* (see Figure 17.2). A work-group can be a 1/2/3-dimensional array of work-items. OpenCL supports interaction of work-items belonging to the same work-group via local memory and synchronization.

OpenCL supports the following types of memory – global, constant, local and private (see Figure 17.3).

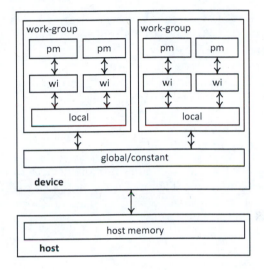

FIGURE 17.3: OpenCL memory hierarchy.

Global memory (corresponding memory qualifier is _global) is the memory of the device (e.g., DRAM for GPUs). It is available for reading and writing to all work-items, however it is usually slow.

Constant memory (the corresponding memory qualifier is __constant) is an area of global memory which can be cached and it is available to all work-items only for reading. Due to caching this kind of memory may be faster than global.

Local memory (the corresponding memory qualifier is _local) is fast memory which is allocated per work-group and all work-items of a work-group can read and write it.

Private memory (the corresponding memory qualifier is _private) is memory allocated per work-item. Every work-item has its own private memory which it can read and write.

A program running on a host creates a context. Context can be thought of as an environment for controlling OpenCL objects and resources. Context contains the following resources:

- devices
- kernels
- program objects

- memory objects

- command queue.

OpenCL context is created by calling the **clCreateContext** function.

```
cl_context clCreateContext(
        const cl_context_properties * props,
        cl_uint numDevices,
        const cl_device_id * devices,
        void (CL_CALLBACK *notify)(const char *errInfo,
                const void * privateInfo,
                size_t cb, void * userData),
        void * userData,
        cl_int * errCode );
```

This command creates context for one or more devices specified by *numDevices* and *devices* parameters. The parameter *notify* passes a callback which will be called to report errors in the created context. Note that this callback can be called asynchronously.

The host uses *command queue* to control devices. Each device needs its own command queue.

The following commands are placed into the command queue:

- kernel execution commands

- memory commands

- synchronization commands.

Commands placed into the command queue are executed asynchronously. They can be executed *in-order* and *out-of-order* (the command can start without waiting for a previous command to complete).

A command queue for the device is created by the **clCreateCommandQueue** command.

```
cl_command_queue clCreateCommandQueue(
                cl_context context, cl_device_id device,
                cl_command_queue_properties props,
                cl_int * errCode );
```

Below the simple example of creating a command queue for already existing context and device is shown.

Parameter *props* specifies properties for the command queue. It is a bit field and the only options supported now are CL_QUEUE_OUT_OF_ORDER_EXEC_MODE_ENABLE (to allow out-of-order execution of commands) and CL_QUEUE_PROFILING_ENABLED (enable profiling of commands).

TABLE 17.3: Vector data types in OpenCL language and host API

Scalar type	VectorType, N=2,3,4,8,16	Corresponding host type
char	charN	cl_charN
uchar	ucharN	cl_ucharN
short	shortN	cl_shortN
ushort	ushortN	cl_ushortN
int	intN	cl_intN
uint	uintN	cl_uintN
long	longN	cl_longN
ulong	ulongN	cl_ulongN
float	floatN	cl_floatN

```
cl_int            err;
cl_command_queue  queue = clCreateCommandQueue (
                    context , device , NULL, &err );

if ( err != CL_SUCCESS )
{
  printf ( "Error_creating_OpenCL_command_queue.\n" );
  exit    ( 1 );
}
```

All OpenCL kernels are written in a modified C99 language. From C99 the following features were removed:

- function pointers

- bit-fields

- variable length arrays

- recursion

- standard headers.

To the language vector types (see Table 17.3), work-item and work-group functions, synchronization commands and address space qualifiers were added.

It is possible to use x-, y-, z- and w-components for indexing into vector types. Also **lo** and **hi** can be used to get the lower and upper part of the vector. It is possible to get all even components by **even** index and all odd – by **odd**. Vector components can also be indexed by number in the **sN** format where N is one hex digit, e.g., **v.sF**.

```
float4  f  = (float4)(1.0f, 2.0f, 3.0f, 4.0f);
float2  f1 = f.zx;
uint4   u  = (uint4)(0);
float2  lo = f.lo;      // f.xy
float2  ev = f.even;    // f.xz
float   ff = f.s3;      // f.z
```

TABLE 17.4: Functions for getting information for work-items and work-groups

Function	Description
get_num_groups(idx)	ND-range size in work-groups
get_local_size(idx)	work-group size in work-items
get_group_id(idx)	global index of current work-group
get_local_id(idx)	local index of work-item in the work-group
get_global_id(idx)	global index of work-item in the ND-range
get_global_size(idx)	size of ND-range in work-items

A kernel is a function declared with the *kernel* specifier. The kernel can have only void return type and get information about the ND-range, current work-item and work-group by using functions from Table 17.4. Note that all functions from this table return information along a specified dimension.

OpenCL provides synchronization functions *barrier, fence, read_mem_fence* and *write_mem_fence*.

```
void barrier        ( cl_mem_fence_flags flags );
void mem_fence      ( cl_mem_fence_flags flags );
void read_mem_fence ( cl_mem_fence_flags flags );
void write_mem_fence ( cl_mem_fence_flags flags );
```

A call of a *barrier* function blocks the current work-item until all work-items in the work-group reached this call. It queues a memory fence to ensure that all memory operations to local or global memory issued before this command are visible to all work-items.

The *flags* parameter specifies the memory address space and can be set to a combination of the following flags – CL_LOCAL_MEM_FENCE and CL_GLOBAL_MEM_FENCE.

The call of *fence, read_mem_fence* and *write_mem_fence* ensures that all memory operations issued before this call are visible to all work-items.

A simple OpenCL kernel is shown below – it takes its global index, maps it to float point values, computes the sine of this value and stores it in the given area of global memory.

```
__kernel void test ( __global float * a, int n )
{
   int idx = get_global_id ( 0 );

   if ( idx < n )
     a [idx] = sin ( idx * 3.1415926f / 1024.0f );
}
```

To load and execute this kernel we need to create a program object from the kernel source. To do so we will use the **clCreateProgramWithSource** command.

```
cl_program clCreateProgramWithSource(
             cl_context context, cl_uint count,
             const char ** strings,
             const size_t * lengths,
             cl_int * errCode );
```

As you can see, this command is very close to the corresponding OpenGL command – it takes an array of zero-terminated strings. As with OpenGL we can pass all source as one big string.

After the program object has been created we need to compile and build it by using the **clBuildProgram** command.

```
cl_int clBuildProgram(
             cl_program program,
             cl_uint numDevices,
             const cl_device_id * devices,
             const char * options,
             void(*notify)(cl_program, void*),
             void * userData );
```

In this call we can pass an options string (e.g. "-D MY_DEF") to the OpenCL compiles in the *options* parameter and specify a callback.

A **clGetProgramBuildInfo** command gets a build log for the program objects.

```
cl_int clGetProgramBuildInfo(
             cl_program program,
             cl_device_id device,
             cl_program_build_info pname,
             size_t paramBufSize,
             void * paramBuf,
             size_t * paramSize );
```

Specifying CL_PROGRAM_BUILD_LOG as a *pname* we will get the build log. To get the size of the build log we can call this command specifying *paramBufSize* and *paramBuf* as zeros.

After the program has been successfully built, we can create a kernel object calling the **clCreateKernel** command.

```
cl_kernel clCreateKernel( cl_program program,
                          const char * kernelName,
                          cl_int * errCode );
```

OpenCL kernels can process only data that are stored in the device memory. So we need to pass data arrays from host memory to the device and vice versa.

For this we will use OpenCL memory buffer objects. Such objects are created by a call to the **clCreateBuffer** command.

```
cl_mem clCreateBuffer ( cl_context context ,
                        cl_mem_flags flags ,
                        size_t size , void * hostPtr ,
                        cl_int * errCode );
```

We will be using only the following memory flags –

- CL_MEM_READ_WRITE – memory can be read and written by device

- CL_MEM_WRITE_ONLY – memory will be written by device

- CL_MEM_READ_ONLY – memory will be read by device

- CL_MEM_COPY_HOST_PTR – copy memory from *hostPtr* into device memory.

Since our first kernel only writes to the device memory, we will use the CL_MEM_WRITE_ONLY flag.

We can pass a pointer to the host data and add the flag CL_MEM_COPY_HOST_PTR to the *flags* parameter. In this case the contents of host memory pointed to by *hostPtr* will be copied to the device (global) memory. It is possible to specify NULL as the *hostPtr* and then use **clEnqueueWriteBuffer** command to enqueue the memory copy operation from host memory to device memory.

```
cl_int clEnqueueWriteBuffer (
            cl_command_queue queue ,
            cl_mem buffer ,
            cl_bool blockingWrite ,
            size_t offset ,
            size_t numBytes ,
            const void * hostPtr ,
            cl_uint numEvents ,
            const cl_event * waitList ,
            cl_event * event );
```

This command adds to the command queue memory copy operation from host to device memory. Parameter *blockingWrite* indicates whether this copying operation is blocking (CL_TRUE) or not-blocking (CL_FALSE). If this operation is not-blocking then this command returns immediately; however, the memory pointed to by *hostPtr* cannot be reused until the event specified by *event* parameter is complete.

The command **clWaitForEvents** waits until all specified events are complete.

```
cl_int clWaitForEvents ( cl_uint numEvents ,
                         const cl_event * eventList );
```

Also it is possible to asynchronously check the status of the command associated with a given event by using the **clGetEventInfo** command with a parameter *pname* equal to CL_EVENT_COMMAND_EXECUTION_STATUS. If the returned value is CL_COMPLETE, then the corresponding command has been successfully completed.

```
cl_int clGetEventInfo (
            cl_event event ,
            cl_event_info pname ,
            size_t paramValueSize ,
            void * paramValue ,
            size_t * paramValueSizeRet );
```

In order to run the kernel we need to set kernel arguments using the **clSetKernelArg** command.

```
cl_int clSetKernelArg( cl_kernel kernel ,
                       cl_int argIndex ,
                       size_t argSize ,
                       const void * argPtr );
```

After all kernel arguments have been set we launch a kernel by calling the **clEnqueueNDRangeKernel** command. In this call we specify information about the ND-range we want our kernel executed on.

```
cl_int clEnqueueNDRangeKernel(
            cl_command_queue queue ,
            cl_kernel kernel ,
            cl_uint workDim ,
            const size_t * globalWorkOffset ,
            const size_t * globalSize ,
            const size_t * localSize ,
            cl_uint numEvents ,
            const cl_event * waitList ,
            cl_event * event );
```

Parameters *queue* and *kernel* specify the command queue and the kernel which should be executed. Parameter *workDim* specifies the number of dimensions for work-items in the ND-range. Parameter *globalWorkOffset* is not used now and should be set to NULL. Parameter *globalSize* is an array of values specifying the size of the ND-range for all used dimensions. Parameter *localSize* is an array too, but this array specifies the size of a work-group in the work-items for any used dimension.

If we want to create a 2D ND-range, then we specify *workDim* equal to 2 and *globalSize* and *localSize* will be arrays containing two elements.

In the **clEnqueueNDRangeKernel** command it is possible to specify a set of events which must be completed before starting the kernel execution. Parameter *event* specifies an event which will be associated with this kernel launch. We can check whether the kernel execution is completed by checking this event.

After this we need to get our data back using **clEnqueueReadBuffer**, which adds to the command queue memory copy operation from the device memory to the specified location in host memory.

```
cl_int  clEnqueueReadBuffer (
            cl_command_queue  command_queue,
            cl_mem  buffer,
            cl_bool  blockingRead,
            size_t  offset,  size_t  cb,
            void * ptr,
            cl_uint  numEvents,
            const  cl_event * eventWaitList,
            cl_event * event );
```

Note that this command can be blocking or notblocking depending on the *blockingRead* parameter.

Now we are ready to write the code which will run our first kernel and read the results. The first function in our code will be similar to that of the OpenGL example – load the kernel from a file. All other code does what we have already covered – get a platform and device, create a context and queue, create a buffer and load and prepare a kernel for execution. After that we set kernel arguments and launch the kernel. When the kernel has finished, we read data from global memory (of the GPU) to the CPU memory.

```
#include <stdio.h>
#include <stdlib.h>
#include <CL/cl.h>

#define N  (1024*1024)

const char * loadFile ( const char * fileName )
{
    printf ( "Loading %s\n", fileName );

    FILE * file = fopen ( fileName, "rb" );

    if ( file == NULL )
    {
        printf ( "Error opening %s\n", fileName );

        return NULL;
    }

    fseek ( file, 0, SEEK_END );
```

```
size_t size = ftell ( file );

if ( size < 1 )
{
    fclose ( file );
    printf ( "Error_loading_file_%s\n", fileName );

    return NULL;
}

char * buf = (char *) malloc ( size + 1 );

fseek ( file, 0, SEEK_SET );

if ( fread ( buf, 1, size, file ) != size )
{
    fclose ( file );
    free   ( buf );
    printf ( "Error_loading_file_%s\n", fileName );

    return NULL;
}

fclose ( file );

buf [size] = '\0';

return buf;
}

int main ( int argc, char * argv [] )
{
    cl_platform_id platform;
    cl_device_id   device;
    cl_int         err = clGetPlatformIDs ( 1, &platform,
                                    NULL );

    if ( err != CL_SUCCESS )
    {
        printf ( "No_OpenCL_platform_found.\n" );

        exit ( 1 );
    }

    err = clGetDeviceIDs ( platform, CL_DEVICE_TYPE_GPU, 1,
```

```
                              &device , NULL );

  if ( err != CL_SUCCESS )
  {
    printf ( "No_OpenCL_device_found.\n" );

    exit ( 1 );
  }

  cl_context context = clCreateContext( NULL, 1, &device ,
                                NULL, NULL, &err );

  if ( err != CL_SUCCESS )
  {
    printf ( "Error_creating_OpenCL_context.\n" );

    exit ( 1 );
  }

  cl_command_queue queue = clCreateCommandQueue (
                          context , device , NULL, &err );

  if ( err != CL_SUCCESS )
  {
    printf ( "Error_creating_OpenCL_command_queue.\n" );

    exit ( 1 );
  }

  float * buf = new float [N];
  int      n   = N;

  cl_mem outBuf = clCreateBuffer ( context ,
          CL_MEM_WRITE_ONLY, N*sizeof ( float ),
          NULL, &err );

  if ( err != CL_SUCCESS )
  {
    printf ( "Error_creating_OpenCL_memory_buffer.\n" );

    exit ( 1 );
  }

  const char * source = loadFile ( "test.cl" );
```

```
if ( source == NULL )
{
  printf ( "Error_loading_kernel_source.\n" );

  exit ( 1 );
}

cl_program program = clCreateProgramWithSource(
                     context, 1, &source, NULL, &err );

if ( err != CL_SUCCESS )
{
  printf ( "Error_creating_OpenCL_program.\n" );

  exit ( 1 );
}

if ( clBuildProgram( program, 1, &device,
                     NULL, NULL, NULL ) != CL_SUCCESS )
{
  size_t logSize;

  clGetProgramBuildInfo ( program, device,
                     CL_PROGRAM_BUILD_LOG, 0, NULL,
                 &logSize );

  char * str = new char [logSize + 1];

  clGetProgramBuildInfo ( program, device,
                     CL_PROGRAM_BUILD_LOG, logSize,
                 str, NULL );

  printf ( "Error_building_program:\n%s\n", str );

  delete str;

  exit ( 1 );
}

cl_kernel kernel = clCreateKernel( program, "test",
                                   &err );

if ( err != CL_SUCCESS )
{
  printf ( "Error_creating_OpenCL_kernel.\n" );
```

```
    exit ( 1 );
}

clSetKernelArg( kernel , 0, sizeof(outBuf), &outBuf );
clSetKernelArg( kernel , 1, sizeof(n),       &n );

size_t localSize  = 512;   // work-items per work-group
size_t globalSize = N;     // total  work-items

err = clEnqueueNDRangeKernel( queue, kernel , 1, NULL,
            &globalSize , &localSize , 0, NULL, NULL );

if ( err != CL_SUCCESS )
{
   printf ( "Error_launcing_OpenCL_kernel.\n" );

   exit ( 1 );
}

err = clEnqueueReadBuffer( queue, outBuf, CL_TRUE, 0,
            N*sizeof(float), buf, 0, NULL, NULL );

if ( err != CL_SUCCESS )
{
   printf ( "Error_getting_array_back.\n" );

   exit ( 1 );
}

printf ( "%f_%f\n", buf [0] , buf[1024] );

delete buf;
free ( (void *)source );
                              // release  resources
clReleaseKernel( kernel );
clReleaseCommandQueue( queue );
clReleaseContext( context );
clReleaseMemObject( outBuf );

return 0;
}
```

Note that the multiple **clRelease** commands free the allocated resources. In this example we did not pass any array from the CPU to the device.

TABLE 17.5: Corresponding termins between CUDA and OpenCL

OpenCL	CUDA
work item	thread
work group	block
ND-range	grid
local memory	shared memory

But it can be easily done using the **clEnqueueWriteBuffer** in the same way as we have read values from the device.

17.3 Basics of CUDA

CUDA (*Compute Unified Device Architecture*) is an NVidia API and language for performing computations on NVidia GPUs. The basic ideas behind CUDA are very close to that of OpenCL but there is a difference in terminology (see Table 17.5).

Besides in CUDA you can write all your code (for both the CPU and GPU) in a single file using extended C++ language (it means that you can use several C++ features such as templates). The provided compiler **nvcc** separates the host code from the device code, compiles the device code, uses an external compiler for the host code and produces a single executable.

Instead of memory buffers in CUDA you can directly allocate the GPU memory using the **cudaMalloc** command and perform copy operations using the **cudaMemcpy** function.

In CUDA the C++ language special directive for launching a kernel was added. Below there is our OpenCL example written using CUDA. Note that it is much shorter and easier to understand than OpenCL.

```
#include <stdio.h>

__global__ void test ( float * data, int n )
{
    int idx = blockIdx.x * blockDim.x + threadIdx.x;

    if ( idx < n )
        data [idx] = sinf ( idx * 3.1415926f / 1024.0f );
}

int main ( int argc, char * argv [] )
```

```
{
    int  n         = 16 * 1024 * 1024;
    int  numBytes = n * sizeof ( float );

            // allocate host memory
    float * a = new float [n];

            // allocate device memory
    float * dev = NULL;

    cudaMalloc ( (void**)&dev, numBytes );

        .   // set kernel launch configuration
    dim3 threads = dim3(512, 1);
    dim3 blocks  = dim3(n / threads.x, 1);

            // copy to the GPU memory
    cudaMemcpy ( dev, a, numBytes, cudaMemcpyHostToDevice );

            // run the kernel text
    test <<<blocks, threads>>>(dev, n);

            // copy results to CPU memory
    cudaMemcpy ( a, dev, numBytes, cudaMemcpyDeviceToHost );

            // release resources
    cudaFree    ( dev    );

    delete a;

    return 0;
}
```

17.4   Basics of linear algebra in OpenCL

Now we will study the case of matrix multiplication using the GPU.

Let N be an integer, multiple of 16 and A and B are two $N \times N$ matrices and we want to compute the matrix $C = A \cdot B$ (their product).

An element of matrix C can be written as follows

$$c_{ij} = \sum_{k=0}^{N-1} a_{ik} \cdot b_{kj}. \tag{17.1}$$

We can easily implement (17.1) as an OpenCL kernel. The obvious choice is to use one work-item per one element of matrix C and have a 2D ND-range composed of 16×16 work-groups.

The corresponding OpenCL kernel is shown below.

```
#define BLOCK_SIZE 16

__kernel void matrixMul( __global float * a,
                         __global float * b,
                         __global float * c, int n )
{
    int   x    = get_global_id(0);
    int   y    = get_global_id(1);
    float sum  = 0.0f;
    int   aOffs = y * n;
    int   bOffs = x;

    for ( int i = 0; i < n; i++ )
    {
       sum += a[aOffs + i] * b [bOffs];
       bOffs += n;
    }

    c[get_global_id(1) * n + get_global_id(0)] = sum;
}
```

Now let's take a single work-item and analyze how many arithmetic operations and how many loads from global memory it performs.

A single work-item executes $2N$ arithmetic operations and $2N$ reads from global memory. But arithmetic operations are very quick and reading from global memory has a large latency measured by hundreds of cycles. So our kernel is *memory bound* – its performance is affected by memory accesses rather than ALU (Arithmetic Logic Unit) operations.

Since we have a bottleneck in reading from global memory in this kernel, let's look at what data is read by work-groups from each matrix.

It can be easily seen that the work-items of a single work-group read from matrix A is a $N \times 16$ submatrix A' and from matrix B – $16 \times N$ submatrix B' (see Figure 17.4).

However, both of these submatrices contain only $32 \cdot N$ elements while all work-items of the work-group perform $16 \cdot 16 \cdot 2 \cdot N = 512N$ reads.

It means that every element from these submatrices is read 16 times by

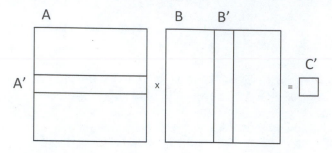

FIGURE 17.4: Submatrices used by a single work-group.

different work-items of the work-group. Since local memory usually has a small latency, we could use it to avoid the redundant global memory reads.

Usually the amount of local memory available to a work-group is not big so we cannot put both submatrices A' and B' into the local memory. Instead we will split these submatrices into 16×16 square submatrices A'_i and B'_i (see Figure 17.5). The submatrix C' corresponding to the entire work-group can be written as

$$C' = \sum_{i=0}^{N/16} A'_i \cdot B'_i. \tag{17.2}$$

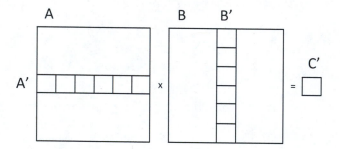

FIGURE 17.5: Computing C' as a sum of multiple small matrix products.

Thus, we need only two 16×16 matrices in local memory (i.e., $16 \cdot 16 \cdot sizeof(float) = 1024$ bytes) per the work-group.

Our kernel operates in the following way:

1. Set result to zero.

2. Read A'_i and B'_i from global memory into local memory.

3. Synchronize.

4. Compute product $A'_i \cdot B'_i$ and add it to the result.

5. Synchronize.

6. If not all submatrices A_i' and B_i' have been processed, increment i and go to step 2.

7. Save the result.

In step 2 every work-item reads one element from A_i' and one element from B_i' and stores them in local memory. The barrier synchronization is needed because before computing the $A_i' \cdot B_i'$ product we must ensure that all needed elements have been read into the local memory. Also after computing the submatrices product and before loading new submatrices we must ensure that all work-items finished computing the product and current data in local memory can be overridden.

The resulting OpenCL kernel is shown below.

```
#define BLOCK_SIZE 16
#define AS(i,j)    as[j+i*BLOCK_SIZE]
#define BS(i,j)    bs[j+i*BLOCK_SIZE]


__kernel void matrixMul( __global float * a,
                         __global float * b,
                         __global float * c,
                         __local  float * as,
                         __local  float * bs,
                         int n )
{
  int bx = get_group_id(0);
  int by = get_group_id(1);
  int tx = get_local_id(0);
  int ty = get_local_id(1);

  int   ai    = n * BLOCK_SIZE * by;
  int   aEnd  = ai + n - 1;
  int   aStep = BLOCK_SIZE;
  int   bi    = BLOCK_SIZE * bx;
  int   bStep = BLOCK_SIZE * n;
  int   offs  = n * ty + tx;
  float sum = 0.0f;

  for ( ; ai <= aEnd; ai += aStep, bi += bStep )
  {
        // load the matrices from
        // global to shared memory
    AS(ty, tx) = a[ai + offs];
    BS(ty, tx) = b[bi + offs];
```

```
        // make sure the matrices are loaded
    barrier(CLK_LOCAL_MEM_FENCE);

        // multiply the matrices
    for ( int k = 0; k < BLOCK_SIZE; k++ )
      sum += AS(ty, k) * BS(k, tx);

        // make sure that the computation is done
    barrier(CLK_LOCAL_MEM_FENCE);
  }

  c[get_global_id(1) * n + get_global_id(0)] = sum;
}
```

Note that the kernel receives pointers to local memory blocks as its arguments. The calling code should pass NULL to the **clSetKernelArg** as a pointer, but specify the correct size of a local memory block. The corresponding C++ code is shown below.

```
int main ( int argc, char * argv [] )
{
  cl_platform_id  platform;
  cl_device_id    device;
  cl_int          err = clGetPlatformIDs( 1,
                             &platform, NULL );

  if ( err != CL_SUCCESS )
  {
    printf ( "No_OpenCL_platform_found.\n" );

    exit ( 1 );
  }

  err = clGetDeviceIDs( platform, CL_DEVICE_TYPE_GPU,
                             1, &device, NULL );

  if ( err != CL_SUCCESS )
  {
    printf ( "No_OpenCL_device_found.\n" );

    exit ( 1 );
  }

  cl_context context = clCreateContext ( NULL, 1, &device,
                             NULL, NULL, &err );
```

```
if ( err != CL_SUCCESS )
{
  printf ( "Error_creating_OpenCL_context.\n" );

  exit ( 1 );
}

cl_command_queue queue = clCreateCommandQueue ( context,
                                    device, NULL, &err );

if ( err != CL_SUCCESS )
{
  printf ( "Error_creating_OpenCL_command_queue.\n" );

  exit ( 1 );
}

float * a = new float [N*N];
float * b = new float [N*N];
float * c = new float [N*N];
int     n = N;
int     numBytes = N*N*sizeof(float);

for ( int i = 0; i < N; i++ )
  for ( int j = 0; j < N; j++ )
  {
    int k = i + j*N;

    a [k] = i == j ? 2 : 0;
    b [k] = i + j;
  }

cl_mem aBuf = clCreateBuffer ( context,
        CL_MEM_READ_ONLY | CL_MEM_COPY_HOST_PTR,
        numBytes, a, &err );
cl_mem bBuf = clCreateBuffer ( context,
        CL_MEM_READ_ONLY | CL_MEM_COPY_HOST_PTR,
        numBytes, b, &err );
cl_mem cBuf = clCreateBuffer ( context,
        CL_MEM_WRITE_ONLY, numBytes, NULL, &err );

const char * source = loadFile ( "matrixMul-2.cl" );

if ( source == NULL )
{
```

```
      printf ( "Error loading kernel source.\n" );

      exit ( 1 );
  }

  cl_program program = clCreateProgramWithSource( context , 1,
                       &source , NULL, &err );

  if ( err != CL_SUCCESS )
  {
     printf ( "Error creating OpenCL program.\n" );

     exit ( 1 );
  }

  if ( clBuildProgram ( program , 1, &device ,
             NULL, NULL, NULL ) != CL_SUCCESS )
  {
     size_t logSize ;

     clGetProgramBuildInfo( program , device ,
                 CL_PROGRAM_BUILD_LOG, 0, NULL,
                 &logSize );

     char * str = new char [logSize + 1];

     clGetProgramBuildInfo( program , device ,
                 CL_PROGRAM_BUILD_LOG,
                 logSize , str , NULL );

     printf ( "Error building program:\n%s\n", str );

     delete str ;

     exit ( 1 );
  }

  cl_kernel kernel = clCreateKernel ( program ,
                   "matrixMul" , &err );

  if ( err != CL_SUCCESS )
  {
     printf ( "Error creating OpenCL kernel.\n" );

     exit ( 1 );
```

```
}

clSetKernelArg( kernel, 0, sizeof(aBuf), &aBuf );
clSetKernelArg( kernel, 1, sizeof(bBuf), &bBuf );
clSetKernelArg( kernel, 2, sizeof(cBuf), &cBuf );
clSetKernelArg( kernel, 3, sizeof(float)*
                BLOCK_SIZE*BLOCK_SIZE, NULL );
clSetKernelArg( kernel, 4, sizeof(float)*
                BLOCK_SIZE*BLOCK_SIZE, NULL );
clSetKernelArg( kernel, 5, sizeof(n),       &n );

size_t localSize  [] = { 16, 16 }; // work-items per
                                   // work-group
size_t globalSize [] = { N, N };   // total work-items

err = clEnqueueNDRangeKernel( queue, kernel, 2, NULL,
                 globalSize, localSize, 0, NULL, NULL );

if ( err != CL_SUCCESS )
{
  printf ( "Error launcing OpenCL kernel.\n" );

  exit ( 1 );
}

err = clEnqueueReadBuffer( queue, cBuf, CL_TRUE, 0,
                 numBytes, c, 0, NULL, NULL );

if ( err != CL_SUCCESS )
{
  printf ( "Error getting array back.\n" );

  exit ( 1 );
}

for ( int i = 0; i < N; i++ )
  for ( int j = 0; j < N; j++ )
  {
    int   k = i + j*N;
    float r = (i+j) * 2.0f;

    if ( fabs ( c [k] - r ) > 0.001f )
       printf ( "Error\n" );
  }
```

```
delete a;
delete b;
delete c;

free ( (void *)source );

clReleaseKernel( kernel );
clReleaseCommandQueue( queue );
clReleaseContext( context );
clReleaseMemObject( aBuf );
clReleaseMemObject( bBuf );
clReleaseMemObject( cBuf );

return 0;
}
```

17.5 OpenCL – OpenGL interoperability

OpenCL memory objects can be created by the data from OpenGL objects. Here we will see how to create OpenCL memory buffer objects from OpenGL buffer objects. In order to do this we need to create an OpenCL context in a special way so it can access OpenGL data.

There are small differences between initializing the OpenCL context for Microsoft Windows and Linux.

In both cases we add context properties to a call of **clCreateContext**. In Microsoft Windows we add the following properties – a handle to OpenGL rendering context and a handle to the device context for the window used for rendering.

```
cl_context_properties props [] =
{
  CL_GL_CONTEXT_KHR,
    (cl_context_properties) wglGetCurrentContext(),
  CL_WGL_HDC_KHR,
    (cl_context_properties) wglGetCurentDC(),
  CL_CONTEXT_PLATFORM,
    (cl_context_properties) platform,
  0      // terminator
};
```

For Linux we add to properties current context and display.

```
cl_context_properties props [] =
{
  CL_GL_CONTEXT_KHR,
    (cl_context_properties) glXGetCurrentContext(),
  CL_GLX_DISPLAY_KHR,
    (cl_context_properties) glXGetCurrentDisplay(),
  CL_CONTEXT_PLATFORM,
    (cl_context_properties) platform,
  0       // terminator
};
```

When an array with context properties is ready, we can create a context using these properties.

```
cl_context context = clCreateContext( props, 1, &device,
                                      NULL, NULL, &err );
```

After we have created a context for interoperability with OpenGL, we can create an OpenCL memory buffer object for an existing OpenGL buffer object with a given identifier using the **clCreateFromGLBuffer** command.

```
cl_enum clCreateFromGLBuffer (
            cl_context context,
            cl_mem_flags flags,
            GLuint vbo, cl_int * errCode );
```

Here the *context* parameter specifies the OpenCL context created for OpenGL interoperability. Parameter *flags* can take only the following values – CL_MEM_READ_ONLY, CL_MEM_WRITE_ONLY and CL_MEM_READ_WRITE. The parameter *vbo* specifies an identifier of existing OpenGL buffer objects.

Thus, OpenCL and OpenGL can share data, but they cannot access this data at the same time. So there should be some synchronization which can lock data for OpenCL access and unlock data so OpenGL can use them.

To provide locking there are two OpenCL commands – **clEnqueueAcquireGLObjects** and **clEnqueueReleaseGLObjects**.

```
int clEnqueuAcquireGLObjects (
            cl_command_queue queue,
            cl_uint numObjects,
            const cl_mem * memObjects,
            cl_uint numWaitEvents,
            cl_event * waitEvents,
            cl_event * event );

int clEnqueueReleaseGLObjects (
            cl_command_queue command_queue,
            cl_uint numObjects,
```

```
                const cl_mem *memObjects,
                cl_uint numWaitEvents,
                const cl_event * waitEvents,
                cl_event * event );
```

Note that before acquiring (locking) shared memory objects we need to flush the corresponding queue by calling **glFinish** (before calling **clEnqueueAcquireGLObjects**) or **clFinish** (before calling **clEnqueueReleaseGLObjects**).

Now we will make the same particle animation as in Chapter 14, but this time we will use OpenCL instead of the transform feedback. The shaders are not shown here as they are trivial – just the transforming of particle coordinates with a model-view matrix. All animation will be moved into the OpenCL kernel which is shown below.

```
__kernel void animate ( __global float * pos,
                        __global float * vel,
                        float dt, int n )
{
  int idx = get_global_id ( 0 );

  if ( idx >= n )
    return;

  idx *= 3;

  float3 boxSize = (float3)( 0.7f, 0.7f, 0.7f );
  float3 acc    = (float3) ( 0, -0.07, 0 );
  float   damp = 0.7;
  bool    refl = false;

  float3 newPos = (float3)(pos[idx], pos[idx+1], pos[idx+2]);
  float3 newVel = (float3)(vel[idx], vel[idx+1], vel[idx+2]);
  float3 delta  = (float3)( dt, dt, dt );

  newPos += delta * newVel;
  newVel += delta * acc;

  if ( fabs ( newPos.x ) >= boxSize.x )
  {
        // return to state before collision
    newPos    = (float3)(pos[idx], pos[idx+1], pos[idx+2]);
    newVel.x = -newVel.x;
    refl     = true;
  }
```

```
if ( fabs ( newPos.y ) >= boxSize.y )
{
        // return to state before collision
    newPos    = (float3)(pos[idx], pos[idx+1], pos[idx+2]);
    newVel.y = -newVel.y;
    refl      = true;
}

if ( fabs ( newPos.z ) >= boxSize.z )
{
        // return to state before collision
    newPos    = (float3)(pos[idx], pos[idx+1], pos[idx+2]);
    newVel.z = -newVel.z;
    refl      = true;
}

if ( refl )
    newVel *= damp;

pos[idx   ] = newPos.x;
pos[idx+1] = newPos.y;
pos[idx+2] = newPos.z;
vel[idx   ] = newVel.x;
vel[idx+1] = newVel.y;
vel[idx+2] = newVel.z;
}
```

As you can easily see, the animation is the same as in the transform feedback examples – particles are moving under constant acceleration inside the box. When a particle hits the box it is reflected and its velocity is damped.

Our window class should contain buffers and various buffer objects, but it also should contain various OpenCL data as shown below.

```
class MeshWindow : public GlutRotateWindow
{
    vec3           eye;
    vec3           p [NUM_PARTICLES];
    vec3           v [NUM_PARTICLES];

                   // OpenGL part
    Program        program;
    VertexArray    vao;
    VertexBuffer   posBuf, velBuf;

                   // OpenCL part
    cl_platform_id    platform;
```

```
    cl_device_id        device;
    cl_context          context;
    cl_command_queue    queue;
    cl_mem              pBuf, vBuf;
    cl_program          prog;
    cl_kernel           kernel;

public:
    MeshWindow () : GlutRotateWindow ( 200, 200, 400, 400,
                                        "OpenCL_particles" )
    {
        eye = vec3  ( 3, 3, 3 );

        if ( !program.loadProgram ( "opencl-particles.glsl" ) )
        {
            printf ( "Error_loading_shader:_%s\n",
                        program.getLog ().c_str () );
                exit    ( 1 );
        }

        initParticles ();

        posBuf.create   ();
        posBuf.bind     ( GL_ARRAY_BUFFER );
        posBuf.setData  ( NUM_PARTICLES * sizeof ( vec3 ), p,
                            GL_DYNAMIC_DRAW );
        posBuf.unbind   ();
        velBuf.create   ();
        velBuf.bind     ( GL_ARRAY_BUFFER );
        velBuf.setData  ( NUM_PARTICLES * sizeof ( vec3 ), v,
                            GL_DYNAMIC_DRAW );
        velBuf.unbind   ();

        initOpenCL ();

        cl_int err;

        pBuf = clCreateFromGLBuffer ( context, CL_MEM_READ_WRITE,
                                        posBuf.getId (), &err );

        if ( err != CL_SUCCESS )
                printf ( "Error\n" );

        vBuf = clCreateFromGLBuffer ( context, CL_MEM_READ_WRITE,
                                        velBuf.getId (), &err );
```

```
  if ( err != CL_SUCCESS )
    printf ( "Error\n" );

  vao.create ();
  vao.bind   ();
  posBuf.bind             ( GL_ARRAY_BUFFER );
  posBuf.setAttrPtr ( 0, 3, sizeof ( vec3 ), (void *) 0 );
  velBuf.bind             ( GL_ARRAY_BUFFER );
  velBuf.setAttrPtr ( 1, 3, sizeof ( vec3 ), (void *) 0 );
  vao.unbind      ();
}
```

We will not present here already shown methods *initParticles* and *loadFile*. Method *initOpenCL* performs all necessary OpenCL initialization including creation of required OpenCL objects. Note that we use conditional compilation in this method so the code will work under both Microsoft Windows and Linux.

```
void initOpenCL ()
{
  cl_int err = clGetPlatformIDs( 1, &platform, NULL );

  if ( err != CL_SUCCESS )
  {
    printf ( "No_OpenCL_platform_found.\n" );
      exit   ( 1 );
  }

  err = clGetDeviceIDs( platform, CL_DEVICE_TYPE_GPU,
                        1, &device, NULL );

  if ( err != CL_SUCCESS )
  {
    printf ( "No_OpenCL_device_found.\n" );
      exit   ( 1 );
  }


#ifdef _WIN32
  cl_context_properties props [] =
  {
    CL_GL_CONTEXT_KHR,
    (cl_context_properties) wglGetCurrentContext(),
    CL_WGL_HDC_KHR,
    (cl_context_properties) wglGetCurrentDC(),
    CL_CONTEXT_PLATFORM,
```

```
    (cl_context_properties) platform,
    0        // terminator
  };
#else
  cl_context_properties props [] =
  {
    CL_GL_CONTEXT_KHR,
    (cl_context_properties) glXGetCurrentContext (),
    CL_GLX_DISPLAY_KHR,
    (cl_context_properties) glXGetCurrentDisplay (),
    CL_CONTEXT_PLATFORM,
    (cl_context_properties) platform,
    0        // terminator
#endif

  context = clCreateContext ( props, 1, &device,
                              NULL, NULL, &err );

  if ( err != CL_SUCCESS )
  {
    printf ( "Error_creating_OpenCL_context.\n" );
    exit    ( 1 );
  }

  queue = clCreateCommandQueue ( context, device,
                                 NULL, &err );

  if ( err != CL_SUCCESS )
  {
    printf ( "Error_creating_OpenCL_command_queue.\n" );
    exit    ( 1 );
  }

  const char * source = loadFile ( "particles.cl" );

  if ( source == NULL )
  {
    printf ( "Error_loading_kernel_source.\n" );
    exit    ( 1 );
  }

  prog = clCreateProgramWithSource( context, 1, &source,
                                    NULL, &err );

  if ( err != CL_SUCCESS )
```

```
{
    printf ( "Error_creating_OpenCL_program.\n" );
    exit    ( 1 );
}

if ( clBuildProgram ( prog, 1, &device, NULL,
                        NULL, NULL ) != CL_SUCCESS )
{
    size_t logSize;

    clGetProgramBuildInfo ( prog, device,
            CL_PROGRAM_BUILD_LOG, 0, NULL, &logSize );

    char * str = new char [logSize + 1];

    clGetProgramBuildInfo ( prog, device,
            CL_PROGRAM_BUILD_LOG, logSize, str, NULL );

    printf ( "Error_building_program:\n%s\n", str );

    delete str;

    exit ( 1 );
}

kernel = clCreateKernel ( prog, "animate", &err );

if ( err != CL_SUCCESS )
{
    printf ( "Error_creating_OpenCL_kernel.\n" );
    exit    ( 1 );
}
}
```

All animation is performed by the *doOpenCL* method, which performs locking of memory buffers and running the animation kernel.

```
void doOpenCL ( float dt )
{
    int    n             = NUM_PARTICLES;
    size_t localSize  = 512;   // work-items per work-group
    size_t globalSize = n;     // total work-items
    cl_int err;

    glFinish ();
```

```
clEnqueueAcquireGLObjects( queue, 1, &pBuf,
                            0, NULL, NULL );
clEnqueueAcquireGLObjects( queue, 1, &vBuf,
                            0, NULL, NULL );

clSetKernelArg( kernel, 0, sizeof (pBuf), &pBuf );
clSetKernelArg( kernel, 1, sizeof (vBuf), &vBuf );
clSetKernelArg( kernel, 2, sizeof (dt),   &dt   );
clSetKernelArg( kernel, 3, sizeof (n),    &n    );

err = clEnqueueNDRangeKernel ( queue, kernel, 1, NULL,
           &globalSize, &localSize, 0, NULL, NULL );

if ( err != CL_SUCCESS )
{
  printf ( "Error launcing OpenCL kernel (%d - %s).\n",
              err, oclErrorString (err) );
  exit    ( 1 );
}

clEnqueueReleaseGLObjects( queue, 1, &pBuf, 0, NULL, NULL );
clEnqueueReleaseGLObjects( queue, 1, &vBuf, 0, NULL, NULL );
clFinish ( queue );
}
```

The *redisplay* method calls *doOpenCL* to perform animation and then renders the particles.

```
void redisplay ()
{
  static float lastTime = 0;

  float t  = 0.001f * glutGet ( GLUT_ELAPSED_TIME );

  doOpenCL ( lastTime - t );

  glClear ( GL_COLOR_BUFFER_BIT | GL_DEPTH_BUFFER_BIT );

  mat4 mv = getRotation ();

  program.bind ();
  program.setUniformMatrix ( "mv", mv );
  vao.bind ();

  glDrawArrays ( GL_POINTS, 0, NUM_PARTICLES );
```

```
vao.unbind ();
program.unbind ();

lastTime = t;
}
```

Chapter 18

Elements of procedural texturing and modeling

Many objects in our life have very fine detailization and it would be costly to directly model such levels of the detailization. And here mathematics comes to our aid.

The whole domain of procedural methods can create highly detailed objects using rather simple mathematical ideas. There are procedural methods which can produce highly detailed textures, models of trees, landscapes and so on.

Usually such methods are parameterized, so if you have a method producing a tree model you can easily obtain hundreds and thousands of similar yet different trees.

18.1   Fractals, Mandelbrot and Julia sets

Many procedural methods are based on *fractals* with their most important property of *self-similarity*.

Self-similarity means that if we will take a small part of the fractal then it will be like the whole fractal. We can zoom into a fractal and we will always see the same or nearly the same patterns.

One example of fractals is the Peano curve, which is produced by applying the same steps to a curve. In Figure 18.1 you can see several iterations of the Peano curve and in Figure 18.2 – several iterations of the Hilbert curve.

Even from these first iterations, the self-similarity of the curves is clearly seen.

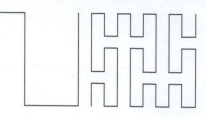

FIGURE 18.1: Two iterations of the Peano curve.

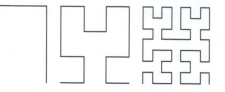

FIGURE 18.2: Three iterations of the Hilbert curve.

Another example of a fractal is the Sierpinski carpet; some first iterations of it are shown in Figure 18.3.

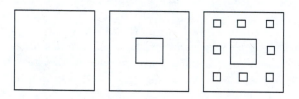

FIGURE 18.3: First iterations of the Sierpinski carpet.

One of the most well-known fractals is the *Mandelbrot set*. It is defined by a very simple recursive equation.

For every complex number c we can define the following sequence

$$\begin{cases} z_0 = 0, \\ z_{n+1} = z_n^2 + c. \end{cases} \tag{18.1}$$

The Mandelbrot set is defined as a set of all complex numbers c such that sequence $\{z_n\}$ is bounded, i.e., there exists such real number M that for all n the following inequality holds true $- |z_n| \leq M$. It was shown that it is always sufficient to take M equal to 2.

The Mandelbrot set is shown in Figures 18.4 and 18.5 (by the white color).

Quite often it is colored. Black color corresponds to the points of the Mandelbrot set itself and for all other points (which do not belong to the Mandelbrot set) we select color based on the first number n such that $|z_n| > M$.

We can implement computing of the Mandlbrot set in the fragment shader

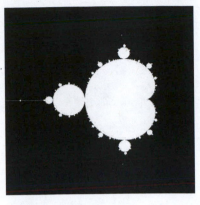

FIGURE 18.4: Mandlebrot set.

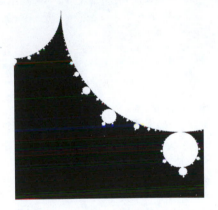

FIGURE 18.5: Part of the Mandlebrot set.

– it will receive c as its input and then perform computations. The resulting color is taken from the 1D-texture.

```
#version 330 core

in   vec2 c;
out vec4 color;

uniform sampler1D paletteMap;

void main()
{
   vec2 z = vec2( 0.0 );

   for ( int i = 0; i < 100; i++ )
   {
```

```
z = vec2( z.x*z.x - z.y*z.y+c.x,
          2.0*z.x*z.y + c.y );

    if( z.x*z.x + z.y*z.y >= 4.0 )
    {
        color = texture( paletteMap, float(i)/100.0 );

        return;
    }
}

color = vec3( 0.0 );
}
```

Another type of fractal is the *Julia set*. In order to plot a Julia set we fix some parameter c and we build a sequence for every complex number z defined by the following equations

$$\begin{cases} z_0 = z, \\ z_{n+1} = z_n^2 + c. \end{cases} \qquad (18.2)$$

If all elements of this sequence are bounded by 2 ($|z_n| \leq 2$), then point z belongs to the Julia set. Taking different parameters c we get different fractals.

These fractals can be computed in the fragment shader in much the same way as the Mandelbrot fractal and the way of coloring the image is the same too.

```
#version 330 core

in    vec2 z;
out vec4 color;

uniform sampler1D paletteMap;
uniform vec2      c;

void main ()
{
    vec2 p = z;

    for ( int i = 0; i < 100; i++ )
    {
        p = vec2( p.x*p.x - p.y*p.y+c.x,
                  2.0*p.x*p.y + c.y );

        if( p.x*p.x + p.y*p.y >= 4.0 )
        {
```

```
color = texture( paletteMap , float(i)/100.0 );

    return;
  }
}

color = vec3( 0.0 );
}
```

In the following figure (Figure 18.6) you can see the Julia set.

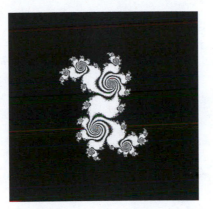

FIGURE 18.6: Julia set.

18.2 Fractal mountains

A very simple subdivision scheme can be used to generate various landscapes and mountains. We will start with a very simple midpoint algorithm.

Initially, we have a triangle. Then we split all of its edges in the middle and move up or down every split point by some random value (see Figure 18.7).

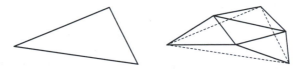

FIGURE 18.7: First iteration of triangle subdivision.

After this we have four triangles. Then we again split every edge and move every split point up or down by some random value. Note that for edges shared by two triangles we must ensure that the split point is moved the same value for both triangles or we will get a crack.

This procedure is repeated again and again. Usually the amount of displacement of the split points depends on the iteration number. A typical variant is to use for displacement $a^n \cdot rand()$, where $rand$ gives a random variable in the $[-1, 1]$ segment and a is some value $0 < a < 1$. This will ensure that with every new iteration the average displacement will be smaller.

After a sufficient number of iterations we will get a fractal mountain. It is clear that we can get any detailization we want by just performing a suitable number of subdivisions.

Another variant of procedural terrain generation is called the *diamond-square* algorithm. It starts not with a triangle but a rectangle instead. Each iteration of this algorithm consists of two steps – diamond and square.

In the first step we take four corner points, find the average of their heights, add some random value to the averaged height and create a new point with this height in the middle of the rectangles.

In our next step we subdivide the edges of the rectangle, for every subdivision point averages heights of vertices directly connected to the subdivision point and again adds some random displacement (see Figure 18.8).

FIGURE 18.8: First iterations of the diamond-square algorithm.

After the first two steps we will have four rectangles. We apply the algorithm to them and we get 16 rectangles and so on until we get a landscape with the required detailization.

Both of these algorithms can be used to generate a fractal terrain with any detailization level we want. Note that the shape of the terrain depends on the random number generator and its seed. So if we know what random generator is used and know its seed at the start, then we can reconstruct the landscape to any level we want, so the landscape depends on this seed number.

18.3   L-systems

An elegant and simple tool which can generate very complex fractals is called L-systems. They were initially proposed by biologist Aristid Lindenmayer for modeling the plant's growth when a simple element is repeatedly replaced by some pattern.

TABLE 18.1: Turtle commands

Symbol	Action
F	move forward drawing a line
f	move forward without drawing
+	turn left
-	turn right

Every L-system is described by

- *alphabet* – a set of valid symbols (or characters);

- *axiom* – an initial string composed of alphabet characters;

- *rules* – substitution rules for replacing symbols.

The state of the L-system is described by a string of symbols (characters). The initial string is called an *axiom*. The rules define how one symbol from the string should be substituted by a string of symbols. Note that for every iteration all substitutions are performed independently of each other.

We will start with a simple example where an alphabet consists of only two symbols – a and b and the axiom (initial string) is a.

For this system we will use the following rules

$$\begin{cases} a \mapsto ab, \\ b \mapsto a. \end{cases}$$

The initial state of the system is string a. In the first iteration the character a is replaced according to the first rule by the string ab. In the second iteration both symbols of the string will be simultaneously replaced using corresponding rules and the system will have the string aba. In the next iteration the string will become $abaab$.

This process can continue infinitely producing a new string for each iteration. So in fact the L-system is just a grammar. To make the L-system have some geometric meaning we need to define rules for interpreting the string.

For a 2D-case the so-called *turtle graphics* is used. Imagine a turtle with a pen. It can move some distance forward drawing a line or without drawing it. Also it can turn left or right by a given angle.

Table 18.1 lists symbols which will be interpreted as commands for a virtual turtle; all other symbols are simply ignored.

The string "$F+F+F+F+$" will draw a square if the turtle turns 90 degrees.

We will build an L-system which starts with this string. An alphabet for this system will contain only characters from Table 18.1. An axiom is $F+F+F+F+$. The rules are shown below.

$$\begin{cases} F \mapsto F + F - F - FF + F + F - F \end{cases}$$

Several first iterations of this systems are shown in Figure 18.9.

FIGURE 18.9: First iterations of Koch island.

You can see that the more iterations we perform the more complex curve we get. The resulting curve is a fractal called "Koch Island".

If we add to our alphabet symbols X and Y then we can build another L-system with the axiom FX and the following substitution rules

$$\begin{cases} X \mapsto X + YF \\ Y \mapsto FX - Y. \end{cases}$$

For this system the string will contain symbols that our turtle does not understand but we will assume that the turtle simply ignores all unknown symbols.

The resulting curve after several iterations is shown in Figure 18.10 and the corresponding fractal is called a *dragon curve*.

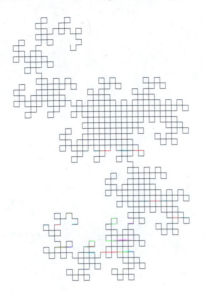

FIGURE 18.10: Dragon curve.

As you can see, we can build various fractal curves using L-systems but what we build does not have a tree structure. We need to modify a set of symbols for our turtle to draw tree-like structures. For that we need two additional symbols *[* and *]*.

The first symbol (*[*) will push the current state of our turtle (position and direction) onto the stack. The symbol (*]*) will pop the turtle state from this stack.

Now we can easily build L-systems resulting in tree-like structures. Our first system will have the F symbol as an axiom and use the following substitution rule

$$\left\{ F \mapsto F[-F]F[+F][F]. \right.$$

In Figure 18.11 you can see the first iterations of this system.

Another system generates a tree-like structure using an additional symbol X. The axiom for this system is X and rules for it are shown below. In Figure 18.12 you can see one of the iterations of this system

$$\begin{cases} X \mapsto F - [[X] + X] + F[+FX] - X \\ F \mapsto FF. \end{cases}$$

Below you can see different rules for the L-systems producing different tree-like curves

FIGURE 18.11: First four iterations of a tree-like system.

$$\begin{cases} X \mapsto F[+X][-X]FX \\ F \mapsto FF, \end{cases}$$

FIGURE 18.12: First four iterations of another tree-like system.

$$\begin{cases} X \mapsto F[+X]F[-X] + X \\ F \mapsto FF, \end{cases}$$

$$\begin{cases} X \mapsto F[++X] - F[--X]X, \end{cases}$$

$$\begin{cases} X \mapsto F - [[X] + X] + F[+FX] - X \\ F \mapsto FF. \end{cases}$$

TABLE 18.2: Turtle commands in 3D

Symbol	Action
F	move forward drawing a line
f	move forward without drawing
+	turn left (yaw)
-	turn right (yaw)
\\	increase roll
/	decrease roll
&	increase pitch
^	decrease pitch
|	turn around

We can add some randomness to the resulting curves by adding a small random value to the distance for F and f symbols.

It is easy to generalize the L-system to generate curves in 3D. We need only add more rotations for our turtle – now it will able to fly and have three basic angles – *yaw*, *pitch* and *roll*.

For every such angle we need two commands for turning. Also we add a new command for turning around. The resulting set of symbols our new turtle understands is shown in Table 18.2.

A simple L-system generating a 3D tree-like structure can be defined by an axiom F and the following substitution rule

$$F \mapsto F[-F]\backslash[F]/[+F][F].$$

Another system uses three additional symbols – A, B and C. The axiom for this system is AB and the rules are shown below

$$\begin{cases} A \mapsto [F[+FCA][-FCA]], \\ B \mapsto [F[\backslash FCB]][/FCB]. \end{cases}$$

All systems shown above are deterministic – the axiom and the rules completely define the resulting curve. But there are *stochastic* L-systems – in these systems it is possible to provide several rules for substituting the same symbol, each such rule has its probability.

Stochastic L-systems can provide more complex curves than the deterministic L-systems.

18.4 Perlin noise, turbulence, fBm

Practically all real-world objects have some elements of randomness in them. An ideal object without any randomness would look very unnatural.

So if we want to generate convincing images, we need ways to introduce some randomness in them. In many cases we need this randomness per point.

But in this case we cannot use the random number generator, because if we ask for a value at the same point several times we will get different results. And one more important issue – if due to some numerical inaccuracies we have passed a slightly different point, we can easily get a completely different result which is usually unacceptable.

Just to introduce some randomness into computer graphics which will not have those problems, Ken Perlin had introduced his *noise* function. In Figure 18.13 you can see values of a 2D-version of this function shown as gray tones.

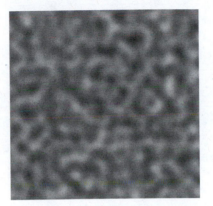

FIGURE 18.13: Noise function.

The noise function (to be safely used) must satisfy several properties:

- it is defined for every point;

- it is C^1 continuous;

- it takes values in the $[-1, 1]$ range;

- it has zero average;

- it is statistically invariant with respect to translations and rotations;

- it is *band-limited*.

If you look at Figure 18.13 you will notice that it really looks like noise; however, it is a smooth function. Also you can see that characteristic details in this image are of nearly the same size.

If we apply the Fourier transform to this function, then we will find that all frequencies outside some segment are very small – it means that this function is band-limited.

It is possible to create a noise function for any dimension, but typically 2D- and 3D-noise functions are used.

The listing below shows the noise function implemented as a C++ class.

```cpp
class    Noise
{
private:
  enum
  {
    n = 256
  };

  int    * p;
  vec3   * g;

  int fold ( int i , int j , int k ) const
  {
    return p[(p[(p[i&(n-1)]+j)&(n-1)]+k)&(n-1)];
  }

  float drop ( float t ) const
  {
    float ta = (float) fabs ( t );

    if ( t <= 1 )
      return 1 + ta*ta*(2*ta - 3);

    return 0;
  }

  float omega ( long i , long j , long k,
                const vec3& pt ) const
  {
    return (g [fold ( i , j , k )] & pt)*
            drop ( pt.x )*drop ( pt.y )*
            drop ( pt.z );
  }

  static vec3 large;

public:
  Noise   ( int seed = -1 );
  ~Noise ();

  float noise ( const vec3& pt ) const
  {
    long   ip  = (long) floor( pt.x );
    long   jp  = (long) floor( pt.y );
    long   kp  = (long) floor( pt.z );
```

```
float sum = 0;

for ( register long i = ip; i <= ip + 1; i++ )
    for ( register long j = jp; j <= jp + 1; j++ )
        for ( register long k = kp; k <= kp + 1; k++ )
            sum += omega( i, j, k,
                          vec3 ( pt.x-i, pt.y-j, pt.z-k ) );

    return sum;
}

vec3 noise3D ( const vec3& pt ) const
{
    return vec3 ( noise ( pt - large ),
                  noise ( pt ), noise ( pt + large ) );
}

float  turbulence       ( const vec3& pt,
                          int octaves ) const;
float  turbulence       ( const vec3& pt,
                          float minFreq,
                          float maxFreq ) const;
float  signedTurbulence ( const vec3& pt,
                          float minFreq,
                          float maxFreq ) const;
float  fBm              ( const vec3& pt, float h,
                          float lacunarity,
                          float octaves ) const;
};
```

It is possible to compute the noise function in the shader but we will be using a simpler approach – reading noise from a 3D-periodic noise texture.

Due to band-limitedness of the noise function, the direct application of this function can create only one level of details. So if we want to have several levels of details we can sum the noise function with different scale factors. Usually the following two noise-based functions are used – *turbulence* and *fBm* (the fractal Brownian motion function)

$$fBm(p) = \sum_{i=0}^{k} \frac{1}{2^i} noise(2^i \cdot p), \tag{18.3}$$

$$turbulence(p) = \sum_{i=0}^{k} \frac{1}{2^i} |noise(2^i \cdot p)|. \tag{18.4}$$

The *fBm* and *turbulence* functions are shown in Figures 18.14 and 18.15.

FIGURE 18.14: fBm function.

FIGURE 18.15: Turbulence function.

The main difference between these function is that turbulence due to taking absolute values has many points where the first-order derivatives are undefined.

18.5   Modeling marble, water, clouds with Perlin noise

One of the simplest effects we can get using *turbulence* (or *fBm*) functions is rendering an eroded object. The turbulence will give us the *rustFactor* for every fragment. Then we compare it with some threshold. If it is below the threshold, we assume that in this place the object was destroyed by rust and therefore discard the fragment.

Otherwise we modulate k_s and diffuse color by this factor using the *smooth-*

step function. The used threshold is passed as a uniform variable so we can control how eroded our object is.

The corresponding fragment shader is shown below.

```glsl
#version 330 core

in vec3 pos;
in vec2 tex;
in vec3 l;
in vec3 v;
in vec3 n;
in vec3 h;

out vec4 color;

uniform sampler3D noiseMap;
uniform float threshold;

vec4 turbulence ( in vec3 t )
{
    return 2.0*abs( texture(noiseMap, t)-vec4(0.5))+
           1.0*abs( texture(noiseMap, 2.0*t)-vec4(0.5))+
           0.5*abs( texture(noiseMap, 4.0*t)-vec4(0.5));
}

void main()
{
    const vec4  diffColor = vec4 ( 0.5, 0.0, 0.0, 1.0 );
    const vec4  specColor = vec4 ( 0.7, 0.7, 0.0, 1.0 );
    const float specPower = 30.0;
    const float delta     = 0.3;

    vec4  turb   = turbulence ( pos );
    float factor = turb.x+turb.y+turb.z+turb.w;

    if ( turb < threshold )
       discard;

    vec3  n2   = normalize ( n );
    vec3  l2   = normalize ( l );
    vec3  h2   = normalize ( h );
    vec4  diff = vec4( max( dot( n2, l2 ), 0.0 ) + 0.3 );
    vec4  spec = specColor * pow( max( dot( n2, h2 ), 0.0 ),
                 specPower );
    float f    = smoothstep( offs, offs + delta, factor );
```

```
     color = f * ( diff * diffColor + spec );
}
```

These functions can be successfully used for animating a water surface (as we did in Chapter 16) – we use the *turbulence* function to modify the height of the water surface in the vertex shader and also use its gradient to compute normal to the surface for every fragment.

It is also possible to use the *turbulence* function for modeling materials like marble, wood and many others.

A standard way for the modeling of marble is based on lerping between two basic colors c_1 and c_2 using the following function

$$t(p) = 0.5(1 + sin(p.x + scale \cdot turbulence(p).x)). \qquad (18.5)$$

This function takes values in the $[0, 1]$ range and parameter *scale* can be used to control the amount of turbulence. Then we mix two colors using its value. We also can use it to modify the specular factor k_s. The corresponding fragment shader is shown below.

```
#version 330 core

uniform float       scale;
uniform sampler3D noiseMap;

in vec3 n;
in vec3 v;
in vec3 l;
in vec3 h;
in vec3 pp;

out vec4 color;

vec4 turbulence ( in vec3 t )
{
   return 2.0*abs( texture(noiseMap, t)−vec4(0.5))+
          1.0*abs( texture(noiseMap, 2.0*t)−vec4(0.5))+
          0.5*abs( texture(noiseMap, 4.0*t)−vec4(0.5));
}


void main (void)
{
    const vec4  c1 = vec4 ( 0.7, 0.7, 0.7, 1.0 );
    const vec4  c2 = vec4 ( 0.0, 0.1, 1.0, 1.0 );
    const vec4  specColor = vec4 ( 0.7, 0.7, 0.0, 1.0 );
    const float specPower = 70.0;
```

```
vec4    ns    = turbulence ( 0.1*pp );
float   f     = 0.5*(1.0+sin(pp.x + scale*ns.x));
vec4    c     = mix( c1, c2, f*f*f );
vec3    n2    = normalize( n );
vec3    12    = normalize( l );
vec3    h2    = normalize( h );
vec4    diff  = vec4( max( dot( n2, 12 ), 0.0 ) + 0.3 );
vec4    spec  = pow( max( dot( n2, h2 ), 0.0 ), specPower ) *
               (1.0-f) * specColor;

color = diff * c + spec;
}
```

We can change the appearance of material by using powers of $t(p)$ to mix the colors. So we can get thin veins of one color inside the other color.

To model a wood surface we take the basic ring structure of the wood and modify it with a turbulence

$$t(p) = 0.5(1 + sin(\sqrt{p.x^2 + p.y^2} + scale \cdot turbulence(p).x)). \qquad (18.6)$$

To enhance the ring structure we use some power of this function to mix two basic colors and the k_s coefficient.

```
#version 330 core

uniform float      scale;
uniform sampler3D  noiseMap;

in vec3 n;
in vec3 v;
in vec3 l;
in vec3 h;
in vec3 pp;

out vec4 color;

vec4 turbulence ( in vec3 t )
{
    return 2.0*abs( texture(noiseMap, t)-vec4(0.5))+
           1.0*abs( texture(noiseMap, 2.0*t)-vec4(0.5))+
           0.5*abs( texture(noiseMap, 4.0*t)-vec4(0.5));
}


void main (void)
{
```

```
const  vec4   c1 = vec4 ( 0.7, 0.6, 0.1, 1.0 );
const  vec4   c2 = vec4 ( 0.21, 0.19, 0.0, 1.0 );
const  vec4   specColor = vec4 ( 0.7, 0.7, 0.0, 1.0 );
const  float  specPower = 70.0;

vec4   ns   = turbulence ( 0.1*pp );
float  f    = 0.5*(1.0+sin(12.0*sqrt(pp.x*pp.x+pp.z*pp.z) +
             scale*ns.x));
vec4   c    = mix( c1, c2, f*f );
vec3   n2   = normalize( n );
vec3   l2   = normalize( l );
vec3   h2   = normalize( h );
vec4   diff = vec4( max( dot( n2, l2 ), 0.0 ) + 0.3 );
vec4   spec = pow( max( dot( n2, h2 ), 0.0 ), specPower ) *
             (1.0-f) * specColor;

color = diff * c + spec;
}
```

Instead of mixing two colors with functions (18.5) and (18.6) we can use lookup into the 1D-texture. Thus, we can get more colors and more control over the resulting look.

Another application of *turbulence* and *fBm* functions is to create the appearance of the clouds. We can use the *fBm* function and two threshold values $v_1 < v_2$ for this case.

When the *fBm* value is less than v_1, we treat the current fragment as completely covered by a cloud and when the value it greater than v_2, we treat this fragment as the sky. When *fBm* takes values between v_1 and v_2, we interpolate between the cloud's color and sky color.

We can use values of one of the *fBm* components to change the appearance of the clouds adding dark regions.

18.6 Cellular textures

The noise function has been successfully used for adding irregularities and detailization. But there are other functions which also have been used in procedural texturing and modeling – *Worley cellular functions*.

An algorithm to create a 2D-cellular function is very simple. First, we need to uniformly distribute a group of points p_i on an area we want to build a cellular function. After that, we can define the first cellular function $F_1(p)$ as the minimal distance from p to points p_i

$$F_1(p) = min_i \|p - p_i\|. \tag{18.7}$$

We can generate the next function $F_2(p)$ as the second closest distance from p to p_i and so on. The process of building cellular functions is the following – we compute distances from p to all points p_i and sort them in ascending order. The function $F_k(p)$ is the k-th element in this sorted array of distances. For the cellular functions the following inequalities are always true

$$0 \le F_1(p) \le F_2(p) \le F_3(p) \le \cdots \tag{18.8}$$

We can adjust the calculation of distance so that for every cellular function the values on the opposite sides of the area coincide, so we can tile these functions.

All we need to do is to modify the function for computing distance to check not only the direct distance, but also the distance across the border as if all points were distributed not in a rectangle but on a surface of the torus. It will guarantee that all resulting functions will be tileable.

Also we can use different ways to measure the distance – the simplest is Euclidean distance, but we can use the sum of absolute values or the following function

$$d_s(p, q) = \left(|p.x - q.x|^s + |p.y - q.y|^s \right)^{1/s}, s \ge 1. \tag{18.9}$$

On the CRC website you will find python script which generates random points and builds a texture of a given size containing values of $F_1(p)$, $F_2(p)$ and $F_3(p)$ in RGB channels.

Here we won't be computing cellular functions in real-time – instead we will be taking them from the tileable texture.

Usually effects are created by combining several of the basis cellular functions; for example, the function from Equation (18.10) will create the texture looking like broken tiles

$$F(p) = clamp(scale \cdot (F_2(p) - F_1(p) - bias), 0, 1). \tag{18.10}$$

In Figures 18.16–18.19 you can see several images which were computed using functions F_1, F_2 and F_3.

The fragment shader, which creates an organic-looking object using cellular functions, is shown below.

```
#version 330 core

uniform sampler2D cellMap;

in   vec3  vt;
in   vec3  lt;
in   vec3  ht;
in   vec2  tex;
```

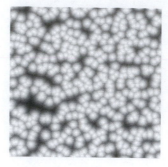

FIGURE 18.16: Function $(1 - F_1^2)^5$.

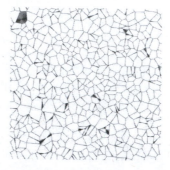

FIGURE 18.17: Function $scale \cdot (F_2 - F_1)$.

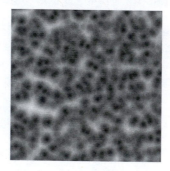

FIGURE 18.18: Function $F_1 + F_2 - F_1 F_2$.

```
in   vec3 n;
out vec4 color;

vec2     dcell ( in vec2 tex )
{
   float vx1 = texture( cellMap, tex + vec2 ( 0.01, 0.0 ) ).x;
   float vx2 = texture( cellMap, tex - vec2 ( 0.01, 0.0 ) ).x;
```

FIGURE 18.19: Function $2F_1F_2$.

```
float  vy1 = texture( cellMap, tex + vec2 ( 0.0, 0.01 ) ).x;
float  vy2 = texture( cellMap, tex - vec2 ( 0.0, 0.01 ) ).x;
vec2   res = 4.0*vec2( vx1*vx1 - vx2*vx2, vy1*vy1 - vy2*vy2 );

return res;
}

void main(void)
{
    vec2  tx        = vec2( 1.0, 3.0 )*tex;
    vec3  cel       = texture( cellMap, tx ).xyz +
                        0.5*texture( cellMap, 2.0*tx ).xyz;
    vec2  dn        = dcell ( tx );
    vec3  n         = vec3 ( 0, 0, 1 );
    vec3  t         = vec3 ( 1, 0, 0 );
    vec3  b         = vec3 ( 0, 1, 0 );
    vec3  nn        = normalize( n + dn.x * t + dn.y * b );
    vec3  l2        = normalize( lt );
    vec3  h2        = normalize( ht );
    float diffuse = 0.4 + max( 0.0, dot( nn, l2 ) );
    float spec    = pow( max( 0.0, dot( nn, h2 ) ), 30.0 );

    color = pow(1.0-cel.x,2.0)*diffuse*vec4( 1.0, 0.0, 0.0, 1.0 )+
            vec4( 1.0 ) * spec;
}
```

The next example combines both the noise function and the cellular function and adds time for animation to render another organic-looking object.

```
#version 330 core

uniform sampler3D noiseMap;
uniform sampler2D cellMap;
uniform float     time;

in   vec3 vt;
```

FIGURE 18.20 (See color insert.): Organic-looking object.

FIGURE 18.21 (See color insert.): One more organic-looking object.

```
in   vec3  lt ;
in   vec3  ht ;
in   vec3  pp ;
in   vec2  tex ;
in   vec3  n ;
out vec4  color ;

float f ( const in vec2 tex )
{
   float  t = texture( cellMap , tex ).x;

   return t*t;
}
```

```
vec3 df ( const in vec2 p )
{
  const float dx = 0.01;

  float fx = f(p+vec2( dx, 0 )) - f(p-vec2( dx, 0 )) / (2.0*dx);
  float fy = f(p+vec2( 0, dx )) - f(p-vec2( 0, dx )) / (2.0*dx);

  return vec3( fx, fy, 0 );
}

void main (void)
{
  vec3  ns1     = texture( noiseMap, pp +
                  4.0*time*vec3( 0.1, 0.0831, 0.119 )).xyz;
  vec2  t       = vec2( 1.0, 3.0 )*tex + 0.015*ns1.xy;
  float d1      = abs( f( t + vec2 ( 0.01, 0 ) ) - f ( t ) );
  float d2      = abs( f( t + vec2 ( 0, 0.01 ) ) - f ( t ) );
  vec3  n       = vec3( 0.0, 0.0, 1.0 );
  vec3  nn      = normalize( n - 7.0*vec3 ( d1, d2, 0 ) );
  vec3  ln      = normalize( lt );
  vec3  hn      = normalize( ht );
  float diffuse = 0.4 + max( 0.0, dot( nn, ln ) );
  float spec    = 0.5*pow( max( 0.0, dot( nn, hn ) ), 30.0 );

  color = vec4 ( f(t)+f(2.0*t), 0.0, 0.0, 1.0 )*diffuse +
          spec*vec4 ( 1.0, 1.0, 0.0, 1.0 );
}
```

Chapter 19

Non-Photorealistic Rendering (NPR)

Traditionally the goal of computer graphics is to generate realistic images, the more realistic the better. But there is an area in computer graphics whose goal is just the opposite – creating images which look like they were drawn by an artist.

This area is called *Non-Photorealistic Rendering* (NPR) and it aims to model or mimic various drawing and painting styles and create images and movies in these styles.

There are areas where photorealism is not wanted. Such areas include disciplines like engineering and medicine, where the specific drawing styles were established many years before computers and applications for such disciplines should conform to these styles.

Also educational programs for kids and computer games may benefit from using non-photorealistic rendering. Just in the last few years several games using NPR were successfully published.

In this chapter we will cover several techniques which can be used to create NPR images.

19.1   Cartoon rendering

One of the simplest non-photorealistic styles is *cartoon* rendering. It is characterized by having several discrete levels of brightness with a clear border between them. This effect can be easily achieved by the following fragment shader which is just a modification of the shader for the Phong lighting model.

```
#version 330 core

in vec3 n;
in vec3 v;
```

```
in vec3 l;
in vec3 h;

out vec4 color;

void main (void)
{
    const vec4   diffColor = vec4 ( 1.0, 0.9, 0.0, 1.0 );
    const vec4   specColor = vec4 ( 1.0 );
    const float  specPower = 50.0;

    vec3   n2   = normalize ( n );
    vec3   l2   = normalize ( l );
    vec3   h2   = normalize ( h );
    float  diff = max ( dot ( n2, l2 ), 0.0 );
    float  spec = pow ( max ( dot ( n2, h2 ), 0.0 ),
                        specPower );

    if ( diff < 0.2 )
      diff = 0.2;
    else
    if ( diff < 0.5 )
      diff = 0.5;
    else
    if ( diff < 0.8 )
      diff = 0.8;
    else
      diff = 1;

    if ( spec < 0.5 )
      spec = 0.0;
    else
      spec = 1.0;

    color = diff * diffColor + spec * specColor;
}
```

Note that we can replace checking brightness with a lookup into a special 1D-texture.

Usually all objects in cartoon rendering have outlined contour lines. For this purpose we can use some of the edge-detect filters from Chapter 16. But these filters should be applied to the depth buffer and (if possible) to the normal buffer.

FIGURE 19.1 (See color insert.): Cartoon rendering.

19.2 Extended cartoon rendering

There is a modification of cartoon rendering which uses lookup texture, a 2D-lookup texture. To access such a texture we need a second texture coordinate which can be one of the following – depth, specular brightness, ring highlight and so on.

The shader for the variant with depth is shown below.

```
#version 330 core

uniform sampler2D toonMap;

in vec3 n;
in vec3 l;

out vec4 color;

void main (void)
{
    vec3  n2   = normalize ( n );
    vec3  l2   = normalize ( l );
    float diff = 0.2 + max ( dot ( n2, l2 ), 0.0 );

    color = texture( toonMap, vec2 ( diff, gl_FragCoord.z ) );
}
```

19.3   Gooch lighting model

The Gooch lighting model was created specially for technical illustrations. It is based on the observation that sometimes cool and warm colors are used to indicate a direction of the normal vector.

The Gooch model uses two special colors c_{cool} and c_{warm}, which are mixed using the n and l dot product

$$I = \frac{1+(n,l)}{2}c_{cool} + \frac{1-(n,l)}{2}c_{warm} + max((n,h),0)^p. \qquad (19.1)$$

Those two colors are produced by adding to surface color c a certain amount of blue (for a cool color) and yellow (for a warm color)

$$\begin{cases} c_{cool} = c + \alpha \cdot \begin{pmatrix} 0 \\ 0 \\ 1 \end{pmatrix}, \\[4em] c_{warm} = c + \beta \cdot \begin{pmatrix} 1 \\ 1 \\ 0 \end{pmatrix}. \end{cases} \qquad (19.2)$$

Parameters α and β control the temperature shift in surface color. Corresponding vertex and fragment shaders are shown below.

—— vertex

```
#version 330 core

uniform mat4 proj;
uniform mat4 mv;
uniform mat3 nm;
uniform vec3 eye;
uniform vec3 light;

layout(location = 0) in vec3 pos;
layout(location = 1) in vec2 tex;
layout(location = 2) in vec3 normal;

out vec3 n;
out vec3 v;
out vec3 l;
out       vec3 h;

void main(void)
```

```
{
  vec4  p = mv * vec4 ( pos, 1.0 );

  v             = normalize( eye − p.xyz );
  n             = normalize( nm * normal );
  l             = normalize( light − p.xyz );
  h             = normalize( l + v );
  gl_Position = proj * p;
}
```

— fragment

```
#version 330 core

in vec3 n;
in vec3 v;
in vec3 l;
in vec3 h;

out vec4 color;

void main (void)
{
  const vec4   diffColor = vec4( 0.6, 0.6, 0.6, 1.0 );
  const vec4   specColor = vec4( 1.0 );
  const float alpha      = 0.45;
  const float beta       = 0.45;

  vec4  cool = diffColor + vec4( 0.0, 0.0, alpha, 0.0 );
  vec4  warm = diffColor + vec4( beta, beta, 0.0, 0.0 );

  vec3  n2 = normalize( n );
  vec3  l2 = normalize( l );
  vec3  h2 = normalize( h );
  float nl = dot( n2, l2 );
  float spec = pow( max( dot( n2, h2 ), 0.0 ), 70.0 );
  vec4  diff = 0.5*(1.0+nl)*cool + 0.5*(1.0−nl)*warm;

  color = diff + spec * specColor;
}
```

The separate pass can be used to highlight the contour lines just as in cartoon rendering.

19.4   Watercolor rendering

Watercolor drawing (see Figure 19.2) is a simple drawing style which can be implemented using shaders. It is based on modeling different layers which are later mixed together.

For every layer its thickness is computed and used for mixing the layers.

The first layer models diffuse lighting, its thickness is given by the following equation

$$t_{diff} = k_d(1 - (n, h)^p \cdot k_s). \tag{19.3}$$

The next layer corresponds to the unlit parts and its thickness is given by the equation

$$t_{unlit} = k_{diff} \cdot (1 - (n, l)). \tag{19.4}$$

The last layer uses the stretched noise values from the noise texture to model brush strokes. All these layers can be combined as shown in Equation (19.5), where c_{diff} is a diffuse color

$$c = 1 - c_{diff} \cdot t_{diff} \cdot t_{unlit}. \tag{19.5}$$

We can compute thicknesses of all layers in the vertex shader and in the fragment shader we just combine the layers and apply noise, stretched in one direction.

```
--- vertex

#version 330 core

uniform mat4 proj;
uniform mat4 mv;
uniform mat3 nm;
uniform vec3 eye;
uniform vec3 light;

layout (location = 0) in vec3 pos;
layout (location = 1) in vec2 texCoord;
layout (location = 2) in vec3 normal;

out vec3 diffuseThickness;
out vec3 unlitThickness;
out vec2 tex;

void main (void)
```

```
{
    const vec3   ambient    = vec3 ( 0.4, 0.4, 0.4 );
    const vec3   diffuse    = vec3 ( 0.0, 0.0, 1.0 );
    const float  specPower = 50.0;

    vec4 p = mv * vec4 ( pos, 1.0 );
    vec3 l = normalize ( light − p.xyz );
    vec3 v = normalize ( eye − p.xyz );
    vec3 h = normalize ( l + v );
    vec3 n = normalize ( nm * normal );

    diffuseThickness = (1.0−pow(max(dot(n, h), 0.0), specPower))*
                       (vec3(1.0)−diffuse);
    unlitThickness   = (1.0−max(dot(n, l), 0.0))*
                                (vec3(1.0)−ambient);
    tex              = texCoord;
    gl_Position      = proj * p;
}
```

— fragment

```
#version 330 core

uniform sampler2D noiseMap;

in vec3 diffuseThickness;
in vec3 unlitThickness;
in vec2 tex;

out vec4 color;

void main (void)
{
    vec3 c     = diffuseThickness;
    vec3 noise = texture(noiseMap, tex*vec2(6.3, 2.0)).xyz;

    color = vec4(vec3(1.0)−c*unlitThickness*noise.x, 1.0);
}
```

We can modify this algorithm by multiplying the diffuse thickness by $max((n, v), 0)$ to make contour lines softer.

```
#version 330 core

uniform mat4 proj;
uniform mat4 mv;
```

FIGURE 19.2 (See color insert.): Watercolor rendering.

```
uniform mat3 nm;
uniform vec3 eye;
uniform vec3 light;

layout(location = 0) in vec3 pos;
layout(location = 1) in vec2 texCoord;
layout(location = 2) in vec3 normal;

out vec3 diffuseThickness;
out vec3 unlitThickness;
out vec2 tex;

void main(void)
{
    const vec3   ambient   = vec3 ( 0.4, 0.4, 0.4 );
    const vec3   diffuse   = vec3 ( 0.0, 0.0, 1.0 );
    const float  specPower = 50.0;

    vec4 p = mv * vec4 ( pos, 1.0 );
    vec3 l = normalize ( light - p.xyz );
    vec3 v = normalize ( eye - p.xyz );
    vec3 h = normalize ( l + v );
    vec3 n = normalize ( nm * normal );

    diffuseThickness = (1.0-pow(max(dot(n, h), 0.0), specPower))*
                       (vec3(1.0)-diffuse)*max(dot(n, v), 0.0);
    unlitThickness   = (1.0-max(dot(n, l), 0.0))*(vec3(1.0)
                          -ambient);
    tex              = texCoord;
    gl_Position      = proj * p;
}
```

Index